ENCYCLOPEDIA OF SPORTS IN AMERICA

ENCYCLOPEDIA OF SPORTS IN AMERICA

A History from Foot Races to Extreme Sports

VOLUME TWO

1940 to Present

EDITED BY
MURRY R. NELSON

GREENWOOD PRESS
Westport, Connecticut • London

Library of Congress Cataloging-in-Publication Data

Encyclopedia of sports in America, two volumes : a history from foot
races to extreme sports / edited by Murry R. Nelson.
    p. cm.
  Includes bibliographical references and index.
  ISBN 978-0-313-34790-0 ((set) : alk. paper) — ISBN 978-0-313-34792-4
((vol.1) : alk. paper) — ISBN 978-0-313-34794-8 ((vol.2) : alk. paper)
  1. Sports—United States—History. 2. Sports—Social aspects—
United States—History. I. Nelson, Murry R.
  GV583.E64   2009
  796.0973—dc22   2008034749

British Library Cataloguing in Publication Data is available.

Library of Congress Catalog Card Number: 2008034749
ISBN: 978-0-313-34790-0 (set)
     978-0-313-34792-4 (Vol. 1)
     978-0-313-34794-8 (Vol. 2)

First published in 2009

Greenwood Press, 88 Post Road West, Westport, CT 06881
An imprint of Greenwood Publishing Group, Inc.
www.greenwood.com

Printed in the United States of America

The paper used in this book complies with the
Permanent Paper Standard issued by the National
Information Standards Organization (Z39.48–1984).

10 9 8 7 6 5 4 3 2 1

CONTENTS

CONTENTS

Volume Two, 1940 to Present

CHAPTER 8

AMERICAN SPORTS, 1940–1949

Ronald Briley

OVERVIEW

By the late 1930s, spectator sports and participation in sporting activities expanded as the nation recovered from the nadir of the Depression reached during the early years of the decade. Expanding employment in defense industries provided an economic foundation for greater amusement and recreation for the American people. For example, consumer expenditures on spectator sports in 1941 exceeded those of 1929 by more than 60 percent. This growing prosperity and American sport were threatened by the specter of war as Japan expanded into China, while in Europe the rise of fascist dictatorships in Italy and Germany, coupled with a Soviet regime under the control of Joseph Stalin, contributed to instability. The invasion of Poland on September 1, 1939, brought World War II to the European continent, and the Olympic Games scheduled for 1940 and 1944 were canceled.

Hopes that the United States might in some way escape the international conflict were dashed on December 7, 1941, when the American fleet in Pearl Harbor was attacked by the Japanese Navy. Responding to what President Franklin Roosevelt called "a date that will live in infamy," the U.S. Congress declared war on Japan. In support of their Axis ally, Germany and Italy joined the war against the United States.

An era of total war from 1941 to 1945 altered the face of American sport. Concerns about the rationing of gasoline and rubber tires led to the cancellation of automobile races such as the Indianapolis 500. Baseball commissioner Kenesaw Mountain Landis feared that it would be necessary to suspend America's number one spectator sport for the war's duration, but President Roosevelt asserted that the national pastime was essential for American morale during the international conflict. Nevertheless, the quality of play declined as major league players were drafted or volunteered for military service. Dependent upon players ineligible for conscription, the talent pool for major league baseball included the St. Louis Browns' one-armed outfielder, Pete Gray, and fifteen-year-old pitcher Joe Nuxhall of the Cincinnati Reds.

Major league franchises also emphasized their patriotism through promotions that raised over a billion dollars in war bond purchases. Continuing concerns that the major-league game might be terminated also led Phil Wrigley, owner of the Chicago Cubs, to organize the All-American Girls Professional Baseball League (AAGPBL) with franchises in small midwestern cities. The women's league paralleled the expanding role of women in the workplace during the war years.

Although lacking the popularity of baseball; professional hockey, football, and basketball persevered by curtailing traveling expenses during the wartime shortages. For example, during the 1943 season, the National Football League (NFL) franchises of the Pittsburgh Steelers and Philadelphia Eagles merged to form what fans called the "Steagles." Manpower shortages severely limited college football programs. In addition to nearly 200 smaller schools that discontinued football during the war, major university programs such as Alabama, Auburn, Florida, Michigan State, Mississippi, and Syracuse limited their scheduled games for the 1943 season. With smaller squads, freshman eligibility was allowed along with unlimited substitution. College basketball, on the other hand, was less impacted by the wartime manpower shortage as individuals over six feet, six inches were not eligible for military service.

Less reliant upon manpower, horse racing remained popular during the war years, with Whirlaway capturing racing's Triple Crown in 1941, surpassing Seabiscuit as the top money-winning racehorse. Major international golf and tennis championships, however, were discontinued during the war. In fact, the Augusta, Georgia, course, on which the Masters Golf Tournament was played, remained closed due to cattle grazing to support the war effort. Boxing events continued to be popular, but fewer championship bouts were scheduled, with prominent fighters such as heavyweight champion Joe Louis in the military.

American sports quickly rebounded following the war, taking advantage of pent-up demand fostered by wartime restrictions. College football programs expanded to ten-game schedules, with Army, Navy, and Notre Dame enjoying national followings. College basketball trailed football in popularity, but Madison Square Garden promoter Ned Irish drew huge crowds to the National Invitation Tournament (NIT) with games featuring such premiere New York City area teams as Manhattan, Long Island University, St. John's, LaSalle, and City College of New York. Major-league baseball attendance mushroomed with over 20 million fans attending games in 1948, more than doubling the prewar attendance of 1941. Attendance increased as well for horse racing, prize fighting, the NFL, and even such "minor" sports as professional basketball. Automobile racing returned after the war along with golf and tennis. With wartime restrictions on the production of golf clubs and balls lifted, there was a tremendous expansion of public golf courses and tennis facilities. Private golf and tennis clubs also grew, and many fees became affordable for the growing middle class. Meanwhile, working-class American families were flocking to bowling alleys. Consumption of sporting goods grew rapidly as Americans enjoyed more leisure time.

The postwar boom was fueled by the GI Bill, which made low-interest housing loans available for veterans, providing the foundation for the rise of suburbia. By the mid-1950s, approximately 60 percent of Americans had joined the middle class. But the affluent society and consumer culture also ushered in insecurities for Americans that were reflected in the world of sport.

The suburbs were bastions of white privilege, contrasting sharply with the American crusade against racist Nazi ideology during World War II. Proud of their contributions to the war effort and with an improved economic foundation bolstered by defense jobs (although a considerable racial gap continued to exist between white and black wages), black Americans were no longer willing to accept second-class citizenship, and the civil rights movement was launched. In the realm of sport, racial integration was already a major factor in boxing, while professional football integrated in the mid-1940s with Marion Motley and Bill Willis of the Cleveland Browns. Racial discrimination was apparent, nevertheless, in the reluctance of southern schools to play football games against northern universities with black athletes.

The focal point for racial integration, however, was the national pastime of baseball, which instituted a color barrier in the 1880s Jim Crow era. With the 1944 death of Commissioner Landis, who adamantly upheld the color line, and growing pressure from African American sportswriters, the postwar period appeared to be the moment to challenge baseball's policy of racial segregation. In 1945 Brooklyn Dodgers general manager (GM) Branch Rickey signed Jackie Robinson of the Kansas City Monarchs to play for Brooklyn's Montreal farm club. After a successful 1946 season with the Montreal Royals, Robinson was promoted to the Dodgers the following year. Robinson's debut in a major-league uniform was protested by abusive fans and opponents, while some members of the Dodgers were less than thrilled with a black teammate. Robinson paved the way for other black players by accepting these slings and arrows, while earning Rookie of the Year honors in 1947. Roy Campanella and Don Newcombe soon joined Robinson as key members of the Brooklyn club, while in the late summer of 1947 Bill Veeck of the Cleveland Indians made Larry Doby the first African American player in the American League (AL). But the pace of baseball integration was slow. When Robinson retired in 1956, the Detroit Tigers and Boston Red Sox had yet to add a black athlete to their rosters. Nevertheless, racial progress achieved by major-league baseball paradoxically led to the termination of a black business institution with the collapse of the Negro Leagues as black players and fans focused on the integrated game.

The paradoxical nature of the postwar society was also evident in changing gender roles and attitudes. Following the war's conclusion, there was considerable fear of another depression if working women did not leave the workforce. Unions, business, and the government were concerned that there would not be enough jobs for returning veterans. Accordingly, women were forced out of the factory jobs they had assumed during the war emergency. But this retreat by working women to the domestic sphere was not as monolithic as it is sometimes portrayed. In reality, by 1947, more women were working outside the home than during the war years, but much of this labor force was engaged with less than full-time jobs in secretarial or retail positions designed to supplement expanding patterns of consumption. Thus, women received conflicting messages regarding domesticity during the postwar period. In sport, these ambiguities were demonstrated by the growing sporting establishment acceptance of Mildred "Babe" Didrikson. The accomplishments of Didrikson during the 1932 Summer Olympic Games, as well as barnstorming baseball and basketball promotions, provided the female athlete with a "tomboy" image. This persona was softened or domesticated by her marriage in 1938 and

Jackie Robinson, the first African American in major-league
baseball, debuting in 1947, in the modern era. (Courtesy
of Photofest)

emergence in the late 1940s as one of the founders of the Ladies Professional Golf
Association (LPGA). The All-American Girls Professional Baseball League also
persevered during the post war period, although the league disbanded in 1954.

The busy work schedules of both women and men in the postwar years supporting the consumer economy, along with an increasing divorce rate, led to concerns
that children of working parents were the source of a growing juvenile delinquency
problem. Coaches began to assume the role of parent as youth sports were champ-
ioned as the antidote for delinquency by officials such as FBI director J. Edgar Hoo-
ver. By 1949 over 867 teams in twelve states were competing for a national
championship in the Little League World Series. The expansion of youth sport and
high school athletics also placed considerable pressure upon young players. For
example, in the steel community of Massillon, Ohio, high school football coach
Paul Brown (who would later move on to coaching success with the Ohio State
Buckeyes and Cleveland Browns) established a community football pipeline that
allowed him to appoint the football coaches for the town's three junior high
schools. The Massillon High Tigers drew over 187,000 fans to their home games in
1945, a figure only exceeded within the state by Ohio State University.

The nation's post–World War II obsession with sport was evident in the increasing revenues from radio and the emerging television media. Although baseball
owners in the 1930s were initially concerned that radio would negatively impact

attendance, by 1947 all clubs, with the exception of the Pittsburgh Pirates, negoti-ated local television contracts to accompany their radio broadcasts. And in 1949, major-league baseball established a seven-year World Series radio deal with the Gillette Razor Company for approximately $200,000 annually, some of which was earmarked for the sport's pension fund. A year later, baseball reached a six-year World Series television deal with Gillette for $1 million annually. The razor com-pany also enhanced the appeal of professional boxing through its radio and televi-sion sponsorship, but television was one of many factors contributing to an attendance decline for baseball beginning in 1949.

After reaching a peak of 20.9 million fans attending major-league games in 1948, attendance fell 3 percent the following year, bottoming out at 14 million in 1953. Between 1948 and 1953, minor-league attendance dropped over 70 percent, while the number of clubs contracted from 488 to 155. As the film industry in Hol-lywood was finding, it was imperative that baseball adjust to the challenges of tele-vision and suburbia. With white population departing northern inner cities for the suburbs, many ballparks suffered from a lack of parking as well as the racial perspective that facilities were located in less desirable areas. In the immediate postwar years, the All-American Football Conference (AAFC) challenged the NFL by establishing franchises in San Francisco and Los Angeles, and in 1946 the Cleveland Rams of the NFL relocated to Los Angeles.

The growing economic pie for sport, evident with an expanding population and increasing radio and television broadcast revenues, also drew the attention of gam-bling interests. While efforts to fix horse races and boxing matches provided exam-ples of corruption within postwar sport, the most publicized scandal involved point shaving in college basketball. With the emergence of the point-spread system of betting, in which the favorite team had to win by more than the number of points established by the bookmaker, it was possible for young athletes to convince them-selves that they could accept payments from gamblers for simply reducing their team's margins of victory. The scandal that erupted in 1951 revealed that in 1948 and 1949 the National Collegiate Athletic Association (NCAA) national cham-pion University of Kentucky Wildcats included three players who admitted to accepting bribes.

In addition to concerns with corruption as well as changing gender and racial roles, American insecurity in the postwar era was reflected by the emerging Cold War, manifest in sports with the 1948 London Summer Olympic Games. The 1936 Berlin Games were used by the Nazi regime for political purposes, and it proved impossible for the first post–World War II Olympics to escape the shadow of the looming Cold War. Seeking to contain what the administration of President Harry Truman termed Soviet expansionism, the United States implemented the Truman Doctrine and Marshall Plan, to which the Soviet Union responded with the Berlin Blockade. In the arena of sport, questions regarding the independence of the Soviet Olympic Committee and amateur status of Soviet athletes culminated in the deci-sion by the International Olympic Committee to not invite the Soviet Union and its Eastern European allies to the 1948 Games. With the exclusion of the Soviet bloc, the United States dominated the London Olympics, amassing 662 points to Sweden's distant second of 353 in an unofficial point system established by the press. The American values of hard work and individual achievement were her-alded by the victory of seventeen-year-old Bob Mathias in the grueling decathlon.

Tested by world war and conversion to a postwar era in which traditional racial and gender attitudes were in flux, the American people and their sporting culture demonstrated perseverance and resilience during the turbulent 1940s.

TEAM SPORTS

Baseball

Major League Baseball During World War II

As war raged on the continents of Europe, Africa, and Asia in 1940, major-league baseball remained largely unaffected, but the passage of the nation's first peacetime military draft on September 16, 1940, indicated that this would not likely remain the case. The Cincinnati Reds, behind the pitching of Bucky Walters and Paul Derringer, ran away with the National League (NL) pennant, while the Detroit Tigers narrowly defeated the New York Yankees and Cleveland Indians in the American League, ending the Yankee streak of four world championships. In the World Series, Cincinnati prevailed in seven games, achieving its first championship since the 1919 Black Sox scandal.

For baseball and for the nation, 1941 proved to be a most unusual year. Detroit was in no position to repeat in the American League, as slugger Hank Greenberg became the first major-league player to be drafted by the Army in May 1941. The Yankees were able to regain their dominance, and the nation was captivated by

JOE DI MAGGIO
Salutes His Bat

© 1941..The Sporting News Pub. Co.

Joe DiMaggio, Yankee great, salutes his bat during his record fifty-six-game hitting streak in 1941. (Courtesy of the Library of Congress)

Yankee centerfielder Joe DiMaggio's fifty-six-game hitting streak. DiMaggio's amazing feat tended to overshadow the exploits of Boston Red Sox outfielder Ted Williams, who won the 1941 All-Star Game with a three-run home run and batted .406 for the season; the first .400 hitter since Bill Terry in 1930 (In fact, no batter has achieved the .400 mark since Williams.). The Brooklyn Dodgers, meanwhile, garnered their first NL flag since 1920, narrowly edging out the St. Louis Cardinals in an exciting pennant race. The Yankees won two of the first three games in the 1941 World Series, but with two outs in the top of the ninth in game 4, the Dodgers were on the verge of evening the Series. When Dodger catcher Mickey Owen was unable to handle a third strike and Tommy Henrich reached first base, the Yankees rallied to win the game. The demoralized Dodgers were no match for the Yankees in game 5, and the New York Yankees had another world championship.

But baseball and America would confront far greater challenges following the Japanese attack on Pearl Harbor and entrance into

World War II. Many baseball officials thought that the sport might be curtailed as it was during World War I when Secretary of War Newton Baker issued a "work or fight" order in May 1918. To complete the season, baseball officials convinced Baker to extend the deadline until September.

During World War II, the baseball establishment was quick to assert its patriotism and deflect suggestions that the sport was nonessential to the war effort. The *Sporting News*, the so-called Bible of baseball, through articles in late 1941 and early 1942, maintained that the continuation of baseball would encourage morale. Baseball, editorialized the paper, "has a responsibility to fans and the nation heightened by war. It must go on fighting, buoyed by the fact that it is the fun, the entertainment, the joy, the sports interest of the common people." These sentiments were echoed by Detroit's Hank Greenberg who was discharged from military service two days before the attack on Pearl Harbor. "We are in trouble," explained Greenberg, "and there is only one thing for me to do—return to the service." The colorful Fiorello LaGuardia, mayor of New York City and director of National Civil Defense, maintained in February 1942 that baseball was the "fun" of the common people and would be his only source of entertainment for the coming summer. Referring to the rumors of Nazi air attacks on New York City, LaGuardia proclaimed, "If we are to be hit, I'd just as soon get hit in Yankee Stadium, the Polo Grounds, or Ebbets Field, as I would in my apartment. It seems to me; under the stands in the Stadium is as safe a place as any in the city. I am for baseball now, more than ever."

President Franklin Roosevelt agreed. In a letter to Baseball Commissioner Landis, Roosevelt wrote, "There will be fewer people unemployed and everybody will work longer hours and harder than ever before, and that means that they ought to have a chance for recreation and taking their minds off their work even more than ever." Although Roosevelt did not believe that major-league baseball constituted an essential occupation for draft-deferment purposes, he argued that the professional game should continue even if rosters had to be filled with non-draft-age players.

Officials of major-league baseball attempted to justify the faith expressed in the sport. At their annual meeting in 1942, major-league club owners made plans to aid the war effort and curtail expenses. They agreed to reduce team traveling, to increase night games so that baseball could be viewed by more working people, to set aside receipts from the All-Star Game for an armed services bat and ball fund, and to allocate 10 percent of all employees' salary toward the war effort. Organized baseball proved to be successful in its fundraising endeavors, contributing approximately $2 million to the United Service Organization (USO), American Red Cross, and other service organizations. In addition, major-league baseball promotions accounted for $1 billion of war bond purchases. Thus, baseball fulfilled the morale function perceived by Roosevelt.

Meanwhile, major-league baseball soldiered along on the field of play during the war years. Although rosters were depleted by draft quotas, the talent pool of the St. Louis Cardinals' farm system, established by GM Branch Rickey, allowed the Cardinals to prevail over Brooklyn in a tight 1942 pennant race, with both ball clubs winning over 100 games. The Yankees again triumphed in the American League, but the perennial champions were dethroned by the Cardinals in the 1942 World Series, the first loss for the Yankees in the fall classic since they were defeated by the St. Louis club in 1926. Key changes in baseball's executive suites

Pete Gray

One-armed outfielder Pete Gray, who played for the St. Louis Browns in 1945, is often perceived as a prime example of how desperate major-league baseball was for players to fill rosters during wartime manpower shortages. But Gray was more than a novelty. He was an athlete who worked hard to compensate for his disability, and the example he set by playing major-league baseball was an inspiration for many service personnel who lost limbs during the war.

Gray was born March 6, 1915, in the mining town of Nanticoke, Pennsylvania. When he was only six years of age, Gray slipped while riding in a wagon, and his right arm was caught in a spoke; leading to an amputation above the elbow. The accident, however, failed to damper the young boy's enthusiasm for baseball. Although he was naturally right-handed, Gray learned to bat and throw from the left side. He batted with one hand, choking up on the bat handle and hitting for average rather than power. Playing in the outfield, Gray wore his glove on his left hand. When he caught the ball, he would flip the ball in the air, drop his glove, and then catch the ball again before making his throw into the infield.

The young outfielder also possessed outstanding speed and displayed daring on the base paths. A semiprofessional baseball star in the coal towns of Pennsylvania, Gray signed a professional contract in 1942 with Three Rivers of the Canadian-American League, hitting .381 in forty-two games. The following year he batted .289 in a full season for Memphis of the Southern Association. Gray enjoyed a fine season in 1944 with Memphis, hitting .333 with five home runs and sixty-eight stolen bases. He was named the league's Most Valuable Player and earned a shot in 1945 with the Browns.

The St. Louis Browns were the perennial doormat of the American League, but with the war-depleted rosters of 1944 they attained their only AL pennant. Gray opened the 1945 season in the outfield for the Browns. On May 19 Gray collected five hits and two runs batted in during a doubleheader sweep of the Yankees in New York City. Despite a good start to the season, Gray, who played left and center field, struggled with hitting the curve ball. Without his right hand to check his swing, it was difficult for Gray to change his timing. With the return of major-league players after the defeat of Germany and Japan, Gray was sent back to the minor leagues. In seventy-seven games for the Browns, he was only able to hit for a .218 average. From 1946 to 1949, Gray struggled as a journeyman outfielder with such minor-league franchises as the Toledo Mud Hens, Elmira Pioneers, and Dallas Stars. In the early 1950s, Gray returned to his hometown of Nanticoke, where he lived as a recluse until his death on June 30, 2002.

While some dismissed Gray's career as a World War II novelty, the outfielder was an inspiration for many disabled veterans and amputees. During his brief major-league career, Gray visited hospitals and rehabilitation centers, reassuring injured veterans that they could find a niche in the postwar economy. Gray, nevertheless, remained somewhat bitter that his career was often dismissed as a wartime aberration.

---

occurred after the Series. Lee MacPhail resigned as president of the Dodgers to enlist for military service and was replaced by Rickey who had quarreled with Cardinals' owner Sam Breadon. These changes were destined to have considerable impact on postwar baseball when MacPhail returned from war to run the Yankees.

As the quality of play deteriorated in 1943 with lower batting averages and fewer runs scored, the Yankees and Cardinals again met in the World Series with the New York club triumphant. With over 90 percent of prewar rosters now in the military (although most former major-league players were seeing more action performing for military teams than in actual combat), baseball's offensive numbers continued to decline. Nick Etten of the Yankees led the American League in home runs with twenty-two, the lowest total for a home-run leader since 1918 and the dead ball era. The wartime shortage of talent also afforded an opportunity for perennial AL doormat, the St. Louis Browns, to win their first pennant in franchise history by edging the Yankees on the last day of the season. The 1944 baseball campaign concluded in a trolley series won by the Cardinals in six games.

The 1944 off-season was a significant one for the future of the game. On November 25, 1944, Baseball Commissioner Landis died at age seventy-eight. The former judge played a pivotal role in restoring the integrity of the game following the Black Sox scandal and "fixed" 1919 World Series, but Landis was also a fervent supporter of baseball's color barrier. His death offered an opportunity to alter the sport's racial profile, although this goal was not uppermost for baseball executives in selecting Landis's successor. Lee MacPhail of the Yankees submitted the name of Kentucky Democratic senator Albert B. "Happy" Chandler to his fellow owners, assuming that a politician might help the sport fend off challenges to the reserve system and baseball's antitrust exemption. Chandler accepted the position, resigned from the Senate, and took office as Baseball Commissioner on July 12, 1945. Although MacPhail advocated maintaining baseball's color line, Chandler did not share the racial views of Landis and MacPhail, allowing the sport to assume a leading role in the post–World War II civil rights movement.

With the unconditional surrender of Germany in May 1945, some major-league players began returning to their clubs. Nevertheless, continuing wartime travel restrictions did lead to the cancellation of the 1945 All-Star Game. Behind the pitching of Hal Newhouser and the hitting of Hank Greenberg, back in a Tiger uniform after military service, Detroit squeezed past the Washington Senators for the AL pennant. In the senior circuit, the Chicago Cubs toppled the Cardinals from their wartime pedestal. With the surrender of Japan on August 15, 1945, Americans were able to give their full attention to the first postwar World Series, won by the Tigers in seven games.

World War II and the Negro Leagues

Segregation in major-league baseball encouraged Andrew "Rube" Foster to form the Negro National League (NNL) in 1920. Although the NNL struggled financially, especially during the Depression years, with eighteen different franchises between 1933 and 1948, there was never any doubt as to the quality of play. In barnstorming games between Negro League players and white major leaguers, the black teams more than held their own. Two of the most prominent franchises in the NNL were located in Pittsburgh. The Homestead Grays were owned and managed by business and civic leader Cumberland "Cum" Posey, while the Pittsburgh Crawfords were operated by Gus Greenlee, a notorious figure in the city's numbers racket. The Grays featured players such as base stealer and centerfielder James "Cool Papa" Bell, first baseman Buck Leonard, and the "black Babe Ruth," catcher Josh Gibson. The star attraction in the NNL was Leroy "Satchel" Paige, who pitched for at least eight clubs. In 1938 the NNL was challenged by the formation of the Negro American League (NAL) with franchises in the South and Midwest.

All-American Girls Professional Baseball League (AAGPBL)

Fearing that major-league attendance might collapse with so many players in military service during World War II, chewing gum mogul and owner of the Chicago Cubs Phillip Wrigley assumed the lead in forming a girls' softball league to move into the big-league parks in case of an emergency. While the women's league never replaced major-league baseball, over 600 women were given an opportunity to display their athletic skills in a baseball organization that extended beyond the war years.

Initially called the All-American Girls Softball League, the new women's league began play in the spring of 1943. The game included elements of both baseball and softball, allowing for stolen bases and establishing base and pitching distances beyond traditional softball dimensions, but the pitching remained underhanded with a conventional softball. Wrigley's scouts believed they could find quality players in the softball leagues of cities such as Chicago, as well as in Canada where the sport of softball was popular. Nearly 300 women were invited to Chicago for final tryouts, and sixty were selected for the league's initial season. Salaries ranged from $45 to $85 a week, a decent salary for the era. In addition to athletic abilities, feminine qualities and appearance were high priorities for the women who were required to attend Helena Rubenstein's charm school. For uniforms, the women donned a one-piece short-skirted flared tunic fashioned after figure-skating uniforms of the time period.

Wrigley approached major-league owners to have the women play in vacant parks while the men were on the road. The proposal was not well received by his fellow owners, and instead Wrigley contacted business leaders in smaller midwestern cities, and the league opened with teams in Racine and Kenosha, Wisconsin; Rockford, Illinois; and South Bend, Indiana. To attain a degree of competitive balance, the rosters were assigned by the league office. The initial 1943 season was a success. Racine was the first champion of the All-American Girls Ball League (the name change was made near the end of the 1943 season, but the league became better known as the AAGPBL in the late 1940s when a smaller baseball and overhand pitching were incorporated into the game). With a 108-game schedule, the four-team league drew 176,612 fans. The games were well promoted by the local small-market media, and the women athletes were well accepted during the war years when women successfully performed traditional male roles in many professions.

For the second season of the AAGPBL, franchises were added in the larger minor-league cities of Minneapolis and Milwaukee, but these franchises failed to attract the local business and media support garnered by the smaller market clubs; although the Milwaukee Chicks did capture the 1944 championship.

Acknowledging that major-league baseball would persevere during the war, Wrigley sold the league to his Chicago advertising executive, Arthur Meyerhoff. Under Meyerhoff's leadership, the Milwaukee Chicks were moved to Grand Rapids, Michigan, while the Minneapolis Millerettes were transferred to Fort Wayne, Indiana. The charm schools were discontinued, but the quality of play remained strong and continued to attract crowds. League attendance in 1945 exceeded over 450,000 spectators. Accordingly, Meyerhoff saw no reason to disband the women's league when World War II ended, and the AAGPBL experienced the same postwar boom as the major leagues and other spectator sports.

The AAGPBL expanded to ten teams, formed a minor-league circuit, and toured Latin America. Attendance peaked in 1948 with ten clubs attracting 910,000 fans. But like its male counterpart, the AAGPBL experienced a downturn in attendance beginning in 1949. One reason for the league's economic problems was that team directors voted to purchase the AAGPBL from Meyerhoff and operate each team independently. The league also suffered from the growing leisure opportunities in the suburbs and the emergence of television. Similar to minor-league baseball, the AAGPBL responded to the crisis by contracting. Down to only five teams by the conclusion of the 1954 season, the league disbanded. During the AAGPBL's existence from 1943 to 1954, the Rockford Peaches earned four championships, and the Milwaukee/Grand Rapids Chicks claimed three titles. Over 600 outstanding female athletes performed in the AAGPBL; including Mary "Bonne" Baker, Jaynne Bittner, and Helen Callaghan. The AAGPBL was forgotten by many Americans during the 1960s and 1970s. However, the 1992 film *A League of Their Own* and the 1988 efforts of former players to gain recognition by the Baseball Hall of Fame recaptured the glory of women's baseball in the 1940s.

The two Negro leagues enjoyed their greatest success during the war years as defense jobs provided black Americans with greater income and the stability for a real Negro League World Series. In 1942 the Kansas City Monarchs, behind the pitching of the irrepressible Paige, defeated the Homestead Grays, while during the following two seasons the Grays prevailed over the Birmingham Black Barons. The 1944 East-West All-Star Game for the Negro Leagues drew 46,000 fans, many of them white, to Comiskey Park in Chicago. Following the postwar integration of the major leagues, the Negro Leagues rapidly declined in support as black fans opted for the racially mixed game. The NNL failed in 1948, while NAL clubs such as the Kansas City Monarchs continued to barnstorm during the early 1950s. Despite their collapse, Negro League clubs provided a sense of community and racial pride for black Americans during the Jim Crow era.

Post–World War II Baseball (1946–1949)

As World War II ended, increasing pressure was brought to bear upon major-league executives to integrate the game. Black baseball writers such as Wendell Smith of the *Pittsburgh Courier*, Frank Young of the *Chicago Defender*, and Sam Lacy of the *Baltimore Afro-American*, joined by white press allies such as Lester Rodney with the communist *Daily Worker*, editorialized that segregation was inconsistent with the democratic values pursued by the United States in World War II and the emerging Cold War. The publication of Swedish sociologist Gunnar Myrdal's *An American Dilemma* (1944) also made a strong case that segregation conflicted with American values.

Accordingly, political pressure was employed in such northern cities as Boston and New York. Because of political intervention by city councilman H. Y. Muchnick, the Boston Red Sox invited Jackie Robinson, Marvin Williams, and Sam Jethroe of the Negro Leagues to a Fenway Park tryout in April 1945. Although Robinson rattled line drives off Fenway's "Green Monster" in left field, the Red Sox were not interested in signing a black player. Commissioner Chandler also created a Committee on Baseball Integration in the spring of 1945, but Yankee owner and general manger Lee MacPhail blocked the commissioner's initiative.

Meanwhile, Branch Rickey was quietly paving the way for the signing of a black player in Brooklyn. After assuming the posts of president and general manager with the Dodgers in 1942, Rickey secretly informed club stockholders that he was

Branch Rickey

Wesley Branch Rickey served as an executive for the St. Louis Browns and Cardinals, Brooklyn Dodgers, and Pittsburgh Pirates. He pioneered the farm system for developing talent and played an instrumental role in shattering baseball's color line when he signed Jackie Robinson in 1945.

Rickey was born December 20, 1881, near Lucasville, Ohio. He was raised with a strong work ethic and religious faith. He played and coached baseball as well as football at Ohio Wesleyan from which he graduated in 1906. While coaching at Ohio Wesleyan, Rickey became incensed when African American first baseman Charles Thomas was refused accommodations with the rest of the team. According to biographers, this experience convinced Rickey to address racial injustice if he were in position to do so later in life.

Rickey played major-league baseball as a catcher with the Cincinnati Reds, St. Louis Browns, and New York Highlanders between 1904 and 1907. He retired after injuring his throwing shoulder and batting only .182 with the New York club. After a bout with tuberculosis, Rickey enrolled in law school at the University of Michigan, where he also coached baseball. After graduation, Rickey briefly practiced law in Boise, Idaho.

But Rickey's future was in baseball, not the legal profession. In 1913 St. Louis Browns owner Robert Hedges hired Rickey as field manager and general manager. Hedges selected Rickey because he was impressed that as a young player, Rickey followed his religious principles and refused to play on the Sabbath. Nevertheless, Rickey's lectures on baseball and temperance failed to turn things around for the Browns, and in 1917 Rickey moved across town to the Cardinals, serving as manager and president of the club. The patriotic Rickey, however, missed the 1918 season when he volunteered for military duty during World War I.

Rickey was relieved from his managing duties in 1925, but continued as vice-president and general manager of the Cardinals, who won the World Series in 1926, 1934, and 1942. Talent for the Cardinals was developed through Rickey's network of minor-league or farm clubs. Rickey also earned a percentage on sales of surplus players in the farm system, and the executive was perceived by St. Louis players as excessively frugal in his contract negotiations. Although St. Louis won the world championship in 1942, Rickey quarreled with Cardinals owner Sam Breadon, and his contract was not renewed.

The temperamental executive quickly landed a position with the Brooklyn Dodgers, serving as president, general manager, and co-owner of the club. To compete with the Cardinals, Rickey began to pursue mining a new market for talent with African Americans and the Negro Leagues, a business decision that coincided with his belief in equal opportunity. In October 1945 Rickey signed Jackie Robinson of the Kansas City Monarchs of the Negro Leagues to a contract with the Montreal Royals, the top farm club of the Dodgers. Rickey, however, failed to compensate the Kansas City club for Robinson's services, asserting that Robinson did not have a valid contract with the Negro League team.

After a successful season at Montreal, Robinson, with Rickey's support, broke major-league baseball's color line in 1947. With the addition of Robinson, as well as other black athletes such as Roy Campanella and Don Newcombe, the Dodgers won the NL pennant in 1947 and 1949. Rickey, nevertheless, was maneuvered out of Brooklyn by his rival Walter O'Malley in 1950. The following year, the seventy-year-old Rickey signed a contract to serve as general manager of the Pittsburgh Pirates. The Rickey magic failed to work with the lowly Pirates, and after five seasons he was eased out of his position. Some of the players developed by Rickey, however, contributed to the 1960 world championship in Pittsburgh.

Rickey refused to slow down, and in 1959 he accepted the presidency of the Continental League, a proposed third major league, which convinced the American and National Leagues to expand. He returned to the Cardinals in 1963 as special assistant to owner Gussie Busch, but Rickey's presence led to tension in the Cardinal front office. Rickey was asked to resign after the Cardinals won the 1964 World Series.

Rickey suffered a heart attack while delivering a speech upon his induction into the Missouri Sports Hall of Fame and died on December 9, 1965. Two years later he was elected to the Baseball Hall of Fame. The politically conservative Republican was perhaps a strange choice to lead baseball's civil rights movement, but Rickey was a sincere believer in the concept of equal opportunity, maintaining a life-long friendship with Jackie Robinson.

---

seriously scouting black players. Rickey's search was certainly motivated in part by his shrewd desire to be the first baseball executive to tap a rich talent pool in the Negro Leagues. But the conservative Republican also had a strong aversion to racism that could be traced to his pious Methodist roots and experience with racial prejudice against one of his black players when he coached at Ohio Wesleyan University in the early 1900s.

In 1945 Rickey announced that he was scouting black players in order to form a new Negro League team, the Brooklyn Brown Dodgers. This explanation was a subterfuge, and on August 15, 1945, Jackie Robinson of the Kansas City Monarchs was invited to Rickey's Brooklyn offices. It was immediately apparent to Robinson that Rickey was interested in a great deal more than the Brown Dodgers. The Brooklyn executive was intent upon breaking baseball's color line, but he wanted a black athlete who would succeed on and off the playing field. Thus, Rickey was impressed with Robinson's military service and athletic record at UCLA where Robinson played football, basketball, and baseball, in addition to running track. Robinson was not the best player in the Negro Leagues, but Rickey believed that Robinson at age twenty-six possessed the maturity to withstand the animosity he would be subjected to by racist fans, opponents, and even teammates. Rickey was also pleased to learn that Robinson was contemplating marriage, as the executive believed any athlete breaking the color barrier would need a supportive spouse. Finally, Rickey told Robinson that he was looking for a man who had the courage not to fight back against insults. As a racial pioneer, if Robinson failed, it might set baseball integration back for decades. Robinson assured the Brooklyn president that he indeed had the right player, and on August 25, 1945, Rickey signed Robinson to a minor-league contract. Rickey, however, failed to compensate the Kansas City Monarchs, asserting that Robinson did not have a valid contract with the Negro League franchise.

In October 1945 Rickey announced that Robinson would be assigned to the Montreal Royals, the Dodgers' top farm club in the International League, for the 1946 season. Robinson led the league in hitting with a .349 average and was embraced by Montreal fans. Even though the Dodgers were involved in a tight pennant race with the Cardinals, Rickey refused to call up Robinson to the parent club. The Cardinals and Dodgers finished the season in a tie, but St. Louis prevailed by winning the first two contests in the best-two-out-of-three-game playoff format. The 1946 AL season was dominated by the return of superstars such as Bob Feller and Ted Williams from the military. Feller recorded twenty-six victories for the Cleveland Indians while striking out 348 batters. Williams led the Red Sox to the pennant with 38 home runs, 123 runs batted in, and a batting average of .342. The 1946 World Series was won by the Cardinals in game 7 when Enos Slaughter scored from first base on a double by Harry Walker.

While baseball attendance boomed after the war and NL fans were treated to a thrilling pennant race, the major-league baseball establishment was confronted with significant challenges on the labor front. Jorge Pascual and his brothers, heirs to a Mexico City brewing fortune, attempted to lure major-league players to Mexico with lucrative bonuses and contracts up to $50,000 for three years. Cardinal stars such as Stan Musial were targeted by the Pascual brothers who did succeed in signing pitchers Hal Lanier and Fred Martin from the St. Louis franchise. In all, twenty-seven players from the major leagues journeyed to Mexico in 1946. Among the more significant players inking contracts with the Mexican League were Mickey Owen of the Dodgers, Vern Stephens of the Browns, and Danny Gardella of the New York Giants. Dissatisfied with living conditions in Mexico and the Pascual brothers' failure to meet their financial obligations, most of the American players returned to the United States by 1948. Commissioner Chandler labeled those who jumped to the Mexican League as "disloyal" to organized baseball and banned them from the game for violating the sport's reserve clause, which bound the player to the exclusive service of one club. In response to Chandler's decision, former Giants outfielder Gardella challenged the reserve clause in the courts as a violation of anti-trust law. Most jumpers disassociated themselves from the Gardella case and petitioned the commissioner for reinstatement. Mickey Owen asserted, "I think Danny is wrong. I would never sue baseball. Baseball didn't make us go to Mexico. I want to play baseball, not destroy it. Baseball must have the reserve clause" (*Sporting News*, February 23, 1949). Perhaps because of Owens's appeal or, more likely, due to the threat of Gardella's lawsuit, Chandler reinstated the delinquent players in June 1950. Gardella dropped his legal case against the reserve clause after a cash settlement with organized baseball.

In addition to the 1946 labor threat posed by the Pascual brothers and Mexican League, discontent with the working conditions in major-league baseball was evident in the efforts of labor leader Robert Murphy to form the American Baseball Guild. While the Guild's organizing endeavors ultimately proved unsuccessful, the threat posed by players' unionization convinced baseball ownership to increase the minimum salary to $5,000 annually, provide medical coverage for game-related injuries, and pursue the creation of a pension plan. Ownership, however, refused to consider changes to the sport's reserve clause.

Hoping that baseball labor unrest was tamed by these minor reforms, the baseball establishment confronted the issue of racial integration in 1947—a time in which Dodger announcer Red Barber later proclaimed "all hell broke loose" in baseball. The Dodgers announced that Jackie Robinson would open the season at first base for the Brooklyn franchise. Initial efforts by some southern players on the Dodgers, led by Dixie Walker, to form a team revolt against Robinson were squashed by manager Leo Durocher, upon whom Rickey depended to guide

Robinson through his difficult first season. Rickey's plans, however, were disrupted when, shortly before the season opened, Commissioner Chandler suspended Durocher for the season. Responding to complaints lodged by Yankee owner Lee MacPhail, Chandler launched an investigation into Durocher's association with gamblers, such as film star George Raft, and the circumstances surrounding the manager's marriage to recently divorced actress Laraine Day. A disappointed Rickey tapped his old friend Burt Shotton to manage the Dodgers and preside over Robinson's shattering of baseball's color line.

On April 15, 1947, Robinson made his major-league debut with the Dodgers at Ebbets Field in Brooklyn, becoming the first African American player since the inception of segregation in the sport during the 1880s. Warmly received by Brooklyn fans, Robinson faced his first major test on April 22 in Philadelphia, where Phillies manager Ben Chapman fostered a racial tirade aimed at the lone black player on the field. Chapman's language was so offensive that it led many Dodger players, especially second baseman Eddie Stanky and southern-born shortstop Harold "Pee Wee" Reese, to rally around their teammate. Opposition to Robinson also surfaced with reports that members of the St. Louis Cardinals, many of whom were from the South, were prepared to strike rather than play against Robinson. National League President Ford Frick made it clear that any striking players would be violating their contracts and face suspensions. The proposed boycott quickly fizzled.

Robinson, nevertheless, continued to suffer verbal and physical abuse throughout the 1947 season, replying to his critics with timely hitting and dazzling displays of daring and speed on the base paths. Robinson batted .297 and stole twenty-nine bases, while scoring 125 runs and leading the Dodgers to the NL pennant. He was named NL Rookie of the Year by the *Sporting News*; a paper that originally questioned the wisdom of Rickey's "great experiment."

In the American League, the New York Yankees were establishing a new dynasty that not even a triple-crown season by Ted Williams could overcome. The Yankees were led by the hitting of DiMaggio and the pitching of Allie Reynolds and reliever Joe Page. The 1947 World Series between the Yankees and Dodgers marked a rivalry that dominated baseball through the 1950s. The Yankees won in a seven-game series highlighted by game 3 in which Bill Bevens carried a no-hitter into the ninth inning, only to lose the game 3–2 on a double by Dodger pinch-hitter Cookie Lavagetto. The Yankee victory party after game 7 was marred by the heavy drinking of Lee MacPhail who resigned his position with the club.

The pace of baseball integration was slow; during the 1948 season, only the Dodgers, Indians, and Browns fielded black players. Robinson's numbers declined somewhat during his second season with the Dodgers, but he was joined in the Brooklyn starting lineup by African American catcher Roy Campanella. Durocher returned as Brooklyn manager, but he failed to motivate the team, moved to the Giants, and was again replaced at the helm of the Dodgers by Shotton. The Dodgers finished behind the Boston Braves who won the National League on the pitching of Johnny Sain and Warren Spahn. In the American League, the Cleveland Indians defeated the Red Sox in a one-game playoff. Indian owner Bill Veeck had integrated the American League in 1947 with Larry Doby, who hit .301 with fourteen home runs and sixty-six runs batted in during the 1948 campaign. While the

Cleveland pitching staff was led by nineteen-game-winner Feller, Veeck signed Satchel Paige, who as a rookie in his late forties contributed six wins and a save to the pennant drive. The Indians defeated the Braves in six games, earning their first world championship since 1920.

The decade concluded in 1949 with a World Series again featuring the Yankees and Dodgers, two franchises that would dominate the sport during the 1950s. Brooklyn clinched the NL flag over St. Louis on the last day of the season. The Dodgers were paced by a Most Valuable Player performance from Robinson who hit .342 with 124 runs batted in and thirty-seven stolen bases. Black players were crucial in the Dodger pennant drive as rookie Don Newcombe won seventeen games and catcher Roy Campanella slammed twenty-two home runs and drove in eighty-two runs. The Yankees, on the other hand, under the direction of George Weiss failed to sign black ballplayers. But Weiss did select Casey Stengel to manage the club and under his leadership the Yankees achieved a dynasty in the 1950s.

Major-league baseball weathered a world war and played an important role in sparking the civil rights movement. But the pace of racial integration in the sport was slow, and players were growing restive under the restrictions of the reserve clause. Attendance at major-league games began to decline in 1949, and the sport was confronted with new challenges to its status as the national pastime. Suburbia and increased leisure time presented new alternatives for the middle class, and baseball attempted to respond to these changing population patterns in the 1950s with the first franchise shifts since 1903.

Basketball

College Basketball

Similar to the situation in football, college basketball overshadowed the professional game during the 1940s. The popularity of college basketball was fostered through the efforts of Madison Square Garden officials in New York City and Ned Irish of the *New York World Telegram* to generate revenues during the Depression era by sponsoring doubleheaders between city teams and top schools from around the country. In 1935 Irish left the newspaper business and became director of basketball operations for Madison Square Garden, inviting sixteen teams to participate in a new tournament which he called the National Invitation Tournament (NIT). The success of the NIT encouraged the NCAA to establish its own championship tournament the following season, but the NIT remained the more prestigious event into the 1950s.

Overall, World War II impacted college basketball less than most sports. With only ten players on a squad, it was easier for basketball teams to gain permission for travel. The sport also benefited from the military's draft regulations. Because of standard sizes for beds and uniforms, the military exempted anyone over six feet, six inches from service. Accordingly, some of college basketball's best athletes, such as DePaul's 6′10″ star George Mikan, were ineligible for conscription. One of the strongest teams in the country during the early 1940s was Long Island University (LIU) coached by Clair Bee, author of the Chip Hilton book series crediting amateur sport for shaping character. In the 1941 NIT, Bee's club defeated the powerful Seton Hall Pirates, coached by "Honey" Russell, who entered the tournament with a forty-two-game winning streak. The primacy of New York City basketball was also upheld by St. John's University, which gained NIT titles in 1943 and 1944.

In the mid-1940s, big men from the Midwest challenged the New York City game based on ball control and precision passing by shorter players. In 1945 DePaul, behind center George Mikan, claimed the NIT title, while the NCAA championship was awarded to Oklahoma A&M, who defeated New York University by a 49–45 margin. The Oklahoma A&M (later Oklahoma State University) squad was led by seven-foot center Bob Kurland and coached by Hank Iba. Iba's club, which also won the 1946 NCAA tournament, was known for its deliberate style of play and tenacious man-to-man defense.

During the late 1940s another coaching legend emerged at the University of Kentucky. Adolph Rupp arrived at the university in 1930, making basketball respectable and popular among southern football fans. Rupp endeared himself to residents of the Blue Grass state by recruiting at home and winning, employing a lively fast-break style of play. The University of Kentucky Wildcats between 1946 and 1949 won 130 games, earning NCAA championships in 1948 and 1949. But the luster of these championships was tarnished when investigations into point shaving in college basketball revealed that star players Ralph Beard and Alex Groza accepted bribes from gamblers during their college careers.

This investigation into cheating at Kentucky was an outgrowth of a broader scandal in which New York City district attorney Frank Hogan discovered that gamblers had infiltrated the basketball programs of LIU and City College of New York (which won both the NCAA and NIT tournaments in 1950), as well as other clubs participating in the NIT. The point-shaving scandal cast a shadow over college basketball for the next decade.

But college basketball in the 1940s also reflected racial discrimination in the United States. Most of the major college teams in the decade were composed exclusively of white athletes. A notable exception to this picture of racial segregation in college basketball was Jackie Robinson at UCLA. During his tenure as a UCLA Bruin (1939–41), Robinson led the Pacific Coast Conference in scoring for two seasons before leaving the university for financial reasons. After military service during World War II, Robinson made his mark in baseball rather than basketball. William Garrett became the first black to play basketball in the prestigious Big Ten Conference during the 1947 season. Garrett earned All-American honors at the University of Indiana and was drafted by the National Basketball Association (NBA) in 1951. The state of Indiana, which was a stronghold of the Ku Klux Klan during the 1920s, was not an easy place for Garrett to play. Much like Jackie Robinson with the Brooklyn Dodgers, Garrett endured taunts from fans and opponents, while dealing with segregated facilities on the road. But Garrett paved the way for other black players, and by the time he left Indiana in 1951 Big Ten basketball rosters included a half-dozen black athletes. The civil rights movement confronted racial segregation in college basketball during the 1950s and 1960s, but during the 1940s most black college basketball players performed at black institutions such as Xavier University of Louisiana, Alabama State, Morgan State, Lincoln University, and Wiley College in Marshall, Texas.

Hank Iba and Bob Kurland

Hank Iba was basketball coach at Oklahoma A&M College (which became Oklahoma State in 1957) from 1934 to 1970, gaining a reputation for instilling discipline in his players. Iba's teams were characterized by tenacious defense and a patterned motion offense. With seven-foot center Bob Kurland, the Oklahoma A&M Cowboys were NCAA basketball champions in 1945 and 1946, providing fuel for the post–World War II interest in college basketball but avoiding the scandals that plagued the sport during the late 1940s and early 1950s.

Iba was born August 6, 1904, in Easton, Missouri. After graduating from Easton High School in 1923, he played basketball at Westminster College in Fulton, Missouri. Iba completed his education in 1928 at Marysville State Teachers College in Missouri, where he obtained a degree in physical education. Coaching at Classen High School in Oklahoma City, Iba's team won the state basketball championship in 1928. He then coached at Marysville State from 1929 to 1933 and the University of Colorado for the 1933–34 season before accepting the position at Oklahoma A&M.

Iba's teams were respected for their patient passing game, which spread out the opposing defense. When the Cowboys were on defense, Iba employed a physical half-court, man-to-man defense dependent upon teamwork and discipline, which Iba insisted upon in his players. In 1943 he offered a scholarship to a gangly and somewhat uncoordinated Bob Kurland, whom Iba helped develop into one of college basketball's outstanding players in the late 1940s.

Kurland was born December 23, 1924, in St. Louis. Kurland, 6'6" at age thirteen, led Jennings High School in suburban St. Louis to two berths in the Missouri state basketball tournament. Although Kurland was 6'9" during his senior year in high school, his awkwardness kept him from gaining much attention from college coaches. Iba, however, invited Kurland to a tryout in Stillwater, Oklahoma. Sensing the young player's potential, Iba offered Kurland a college scholarship in 1942, promising to teach him the game of basketball.

Because his height exceeded 6'6", Kurland was ineligible for military conscription. After learning a hook shot and getting his weight up to 225 pounds, Kurland was a starter for the 1943–44 season, averaging thirteen points per game while earning All-American honors. The defensive strategy Iba employed with Kurland caused a major controversy in college basketball. The coach stationed his center under the basket where Kurland was able to deflect shots on their downward arc. In response to this tactic, also allegedly employed by George Mikan at DePaul University, the NCAA adopted the goal-tending rule before the 1944–45 season.

This rule change, however, failed to slow down Kurland and the Cowboys, who finished the season with a 26–4 record. Kurland topped the 1944–45 season off by scoring twenty-two of his team's forty-nine points in the NCAA championship game victory over New York University at Madison Square Garden. Following the championship, the Cowboys played a Red Cross charity game against NIT champion DePaul and their big man, 6'10" George Mikan. With Mikan in early foul trouble, Kurland and the Cowboys prevailed 52–44.

The following year was another banner season for Iba and Kurland as the Cowboys successfully defended their national championship, becoming the first team to win repeat titles. In the championship 43–40 victory over North Carolina, Kurland was again dominant; scoring twenty-three points and earning Most Valuable Player honors.

Kurland turned down professional basketball offers following his senior year at Oklahoma A&M, accepting a job with Phillips Petroleum and playing for the company's AAU team. In addition to three AAU titles with the Phillip 66ers, Kurland played on the 1948 and 1952 gold medal–winning U.S. Olympic teams.

After the 1946 championship, Iba continued his winning ways in Oklahoma. His 1949 club lost the NCAA championship game to Kentucky, and Iba coached the U.S. Olympic basketball team to gold medals in 1964 and 1968. Iba believed that the United States should have been awarded another gold medal in 1972, but a controversial last-second basket gave the victory to the Soviet Union.

By the late 1960s, many critics asserted that the game was evolving beyond the legendary coach. Iba cared little for recruiting and fast-break basketball. He retired in 1970 with a record of 767 collegiate victories against only 338 losses. Iba died from heart failure on January 15, 1993, in Stillwater, Oklahoma, where he continued to live near his beloved Oklahoma State University.

Professional Basketball

During the 1940s, professional basketball was often considered a minor sport, but during the last years of the decade a foundation was established which allowed the sport to assume its major status during the 1950s and 1960s. For the 1949–50 basketball season, the National Basketball League (NBL) and Basketball Association of America (BAA) merged to form the NBA. This realignment provided stability for professional basketball as the sport penetrated national markets during the post–World War II period.

The NBL was formed in the Midwest in 1937. Playing a pivotal role in its formation were corporations such as Goodyear and Firestone in Akron, Ohio, and General Electric in Fort Wayne, Indiana. The corporate teams were powers in the Midwest Industrial League and joined with ten predominantly Midwestern independent clubs to establish the NBL. In 1940–41 and 1941–42, the Oshkosh (Wisconsin) All-Stars won the NBL title behind the shooting and rebounding of center Leroy Edwards. World War II and the military, however, deprived Oshkosh of some key players, and the 1942–43 league title was claimed by the Sheboygan (Wisconsin) Redskins. The 1943–44 and 1944–45 titles belonged to the Fort Wayne Pistons led by the backcourt duo of Buddy Jeannette and Bobby McDermott.

The racial integration of the NBL during the war years, however, is often a neglected story. The motivation for the signing of black players was primarily the shortage of white athletes due to military service. During the 1942–43 season, the Toledo Jim White Chevrolets and Chicago Studebakers were struggling franchises and signed ten black players to complete their rosters. But the infusion of black talent was unable to save the franchises, which folded. By the 1943–44 season, Willie Smith, who played for the all-black barnstorming New York Renaissance during the 1930s, was the only black athlete in the NBL, playing for the Cleveland Chase Brass. Nevertheless, during the postwar period several franchises signed black players, and in the 1948–49 season the New York Renaissance team was recruited to replace the league's Detroit franchise. The Renaissance became the Dayton Rens and compiled a 14–26 record during the last year of the NBL.

The black athletes of the NBL, however, failed to attract the attention garnered by George Mikan, the league's top recruit who, after leaving DePaul University, secured a $60,000 five-year contract with the Chicago Gears. Mikan led the Gears to the 1946–47 NBL championship, but the following year the Gears joined the new Professional Basketball League of America (PBLA). The PBLA, however, folded after only a few weeks, resulting in Mikan and his former teammates being parceled out to other NBL franchises. Mikan ended up with the Minneapolis Lakers. With Mikan as the unanimous choice for the NBL's Most Valuable Player, the Lakers defeated the Rochester Royals for the 1947–48 NBL crown. The following season the Minneapolis club, along with NBL franchises in Rochester, Fort Wayne, and Indianapolis, joined the rival BAA. These defections paved the way for the NBL merger with the BAA before the 1949–50 season.

To take advantage of the continuing popularity of college basketball as well as the boom in spectator sports after the war, the BAA was formed in 1946 with businessmen Walter Brown of Boston and Al Sutphin of Cleveland, along with Ned Irish and Madison Square Garden, assuming leading roles. The league opened with eleven clubs located primarily in eastern cities. Although crowds were initially small and few teams enjoyed radio contracts, the BAA survived its first season, with the Chicago Stags defeating the Philadelphia Warriors for the championship. The 1947–48 campaign indicated that the new league was struggling to survive. Four of the organized franchises collapsed, and, to provide a balanced schedule, the Baltimore Bullets of the American Basketball League were brought into the BAA. The general low caliber of play in the BAA was evident when the new Baltimore franchise won the 1947–48 championship.

The BAA, however, scored a coup before the 1948–49 season by getting four of the best NBL teams—Minneapolis, Fort Wayne, Rochester, and Indianapolis—to defect to the new league. With the addition of this new talent, attendance soared with much attention focused upon the league's new star, Mikan, who led the Lakers to the 1948–49 championship while averaging 30.3 points per game in the playoffs. The NBL played out the 1948–49 campaign with eight teams before a merger with the BAA, which resulted in the establishment of the NBA. The new, somewhat unwieldy, league included seventeen teams in three divisions, but the final results were the same, as Mikan and the Lakers garnered the 1949–50 NBA championship. A solid foundation was in place for the sport's growth during the 1950s.

But African Americans were excluded from the professional basketball league in the late 1940s. Thus, outstanding black players were recruited by the Harlem Globetrotters, who replaced the New York Renaissance as the nation's dominant black basketball team. The Globetrotters were formed by Chicago promoter Abe Saperstein. When he struggled to gain bookings for the barnstorming club, Saperstein turned to caricature, featuring the dribbling antics of Marques Haynes and the comedy routines of Goose Tatum. While the Globetrotters were drawing huge crowds, critics of the team asserted that their clowning reinforced racial stereotypes. With the integration of the NBA in the early 1950s, the Globetrotters were no longer able to secure the services of basketball's best black athletes. The team, nevertheless, remains a staple of American entertainment into the twenty-first century.

Women's Basketball

Although women were denied a professional league, their enthusiasm for basketball was apparent in the Amateur Athletic Union's (AAU) national basketball tournament beginning in 1928. During the early 1940s, AAU women's basketball was dominated by the American Institute of Commerce (AIC) of Davenport, Iowa. The AIC Stenos were AAU champions in 1942 and 1943, demonstrating the legacy of women's basketball in Iowa as all of the young players, with an average age of seventeen and one-half years old, were graduates of state schools. In the mid-1940s, the focus of AAU women's basketball shifted to the southeastern United States. Consolidated Vultee Aircraft was the largest manufacturing employer of women during World War II; 30 percent of the firm's workers at its Nashville plant were female. The women's factory team representing Vultee Aircraft, usually known as the Bomberettes, which was led by Alline Banks and Margaret Sexton, achieved its first AAU title in the 1944–45 season. With the reduction of employment for women in manufacturing following the war, the Bomberettes found new sponsorship with a beer distributor, Cook's Goldblum. As the Bloomers, the former aviation workers won AAU titles in the 1945–46 and 1946–47 seasons. Leaving a disappointing marriage, Alline Banks Pate was lured to Atlanta where she played for the Atlanta Sports Arena's Blues, leading the squad to the 1947–48 AAU championship. Alline Banks retired from basketball after her second marriage, but she returned for the 1949–50 season, securing a national AAU title for Nashville Business College and assuring her status as the predominant female player of the 1940s.

Women's basketball during the 1940s also featured its own barnstorming team with the All-American Red Heads, a team formed in 1936 in Cassville, Missouri, by Connie Mack Olson to promote his beauty parlors. Featuring their trademark red hair, the women, many of whom were former AAU stars, exhibited outstanding talent and flamboyance throughout the 1940s, barnstorming the country while winning approximately 70 percent of their games against mostly male teams. The All-American Red Heads' novelty wore off in the 1970s as opportunities for young women in college basketball expanded with congressional passage of Title IX mandating equality in educational funding for both women's and men's athletic programs. The 1940s demonstrated the widening popularity of basketball in American society for both men and women.

Football

College Football

Challenging baseball's national popularity was college football, which enjoyed a greater following than the professional game. The college game gained a wide audience during the 1920s with the emergence of the Notre Dame Fighting Irish under the direction of Knute Rockne and the exploits of the "Galloping Ghost," Red Grange, at the University of Illinois, but by the end of the decade there were clear indications of overzealous recruiting on the part of big football schools. At its December 1939 Chicago national convention, the NCAA voted to promote amateurism through a policy in which athletic scholarships would be based on need and administered through the university administrations rather than athletic departments. To enforce this new regulation, the NCAA could expel offenders through a two-thirds vote of the membership. The NCAA, nevertheless, lacked funding for investigating violations of its amateur code, and on the eve of American entrance into a global conflict, the organization's 1940 convention focused upon how athletic programs might encourage military preparedness.

Although there was considerable concern about the international situation and the emergence of a peacetime draft in 1940, college football programs faced few restrictions in the last year before America's entrance into the war. The University of Minnesota, based upon press association polling of sportswriters and coaches, was named the NCAA national football champions, while Michigan running back Tom Harmon was selected as winner of the Heisman Trophy. In 1941 the Minnesota Golden Gophers repeated as national champs, while their stellar running back, Bruce Smith, won the Heisman before volunteering for military service in the Navy.

World War II brought considerable change to college football. Following the bombing of Pearl Harbor, fears of a possible Japanese attack on the West Coast led to the Rose Bowl being played on January 1, 1942, in Durham, North Carolina, where Oregon State defeated Duke 20–16. Due to wartime shortages and travel restrictions, as well as manpower shortages, many smaller colleges shelved their football programs during the war, while larger schools curtailed schedules and travel. Manpower shortages were also responsible for the introduction of female cheerleaders to colleges and universities beyond the South. In addition to relaxing freshman eligibility during the war, the NCAA also allowed unrestricted substitution.

While some NCAA officials expressed optimism that the wartime idealism would reduce incidents of recruiting violations, manpower shortages and concerns about draft deferments produced the opposite effect. Disturbing to many fans was the fact that athletes switched schools to enter military training programs at rival schools. These players often joined the football teams of their new universities. For example, eight members from the 1942 University of Minnesota squad were playing with Northwestern University against the Golden Gophers the following season.

Also, military training schools and bases formed teams that rivaled intercollegiate athletics. Paul Brown, who coached the Ohio State Buckeyes to a national championship in 1942, was placed in charge of the football program for the Great Lakes Naval Station outside of Chicago. Brown actively recruited both college and professional football players. The squads assembled by Brown were challenged by former University of Missouri coach Don Faruot's Iowa Pre-Flight teams located on the campus of the University of Iowa.

The base teams defeated major university programs during the war years, but Notre Dame under the guidance of Frank Leahy continued to vie for national honors. Behind quarterback Angelo Bertelli, Notre Dame was undefeated in 1943 before playing Army. A week before the game, Bertelli, who won the 1943 Heisman Trophy, was ordered to report for military training. Leahy believed that Army coach Earl Blaik instigated the timing of Bertelli's call to duty, but reserve quarterback Johnny Lujack led the Fighting Irish to a 26–0 victory.

In 1941 West Point grad and Dartmouth football coach Earl Blaik was tapped to end the losing ways of Army's football program. Military officials allowed the new coach to begin open recruiting of high school players and outstanding athletes at other universities, believing that a strong West Point squad would be a morale booster for the nation during a period of crisis. The Naval Academy at Annapolis followed a similar pattern of recruiting but lacked the success, or perhaps the ruthlessness, of Blaik's Black Knights. College football historian Murray Sperber asserted, "The Army football teams assembled and coached by Blaik during the war exemplified the total-victory mentality of World War II and also foreshadowed future attitudes in intercollegiate athletics, not only in the Black Knights'

Frank Leahy

During the 1940s Frank Leahy returned the University of Notre Dame Fighting Irish to the level of success achieved by Knute Rockne during the 1920s. The rivalry between Notre Dame and Army in the 1940s helped revitalize interest in college football following World War II.

Leahy was born August 27, 1908, in O'Neill, Nebraska. After playing high school football in Winner, South Dakota, and Omaha (NE) High School, Leahy entered Notre Dame in 1927. He started at tackle on the 1929 undefeated national championship team. Leahy, however, missed the 1930 season with a severe knee injury. Rockne praised Leahy for his knowledge of the game, urging him to pursue a career in football coaching.

After he earned his degree in physical education in 1931, Leahy served as an assistant coach at Georgetown University, Michigan State College, and Fordham University. In 1939 he was named as head coach of the Boston College Eagles. After winning nine games in 1939, Leahy's Eagles were undefeated in 1940 with an upset victory over Tennessee in the Sugar Bowl.

The following season Leahy accepted the head-coaching position at Notre Dame. Although college rosters were depleted with players in military service, Leahy's Fighting Irish lost only three games between 1941 and 1943, and the 1943 squad was selected as national champions. The coach entered the Navy from 1944 to 1945, serving as a lieutenant commander in charge of recreation programs for submarine crews in the Pacific.

Returning to Notre Dame after the war, Leahy made the Fighting Irish college football's dominant power in the late 1940s. Led by All-Americans Johnny Lujack and Leon Hart, Notre Dame enjoyed four undefeated seasons (1946–49) and three national championships. Leahy was admired for his keen football mind and relentless work ethic, but critics complained that he was obsessed with winning. In a 1953 game against Iowa, for example, Leahy was widely censured for encouraging one of his players to fake an injury in order to stop the clock late in the game. After a severe pancreatic attack brought on by overwork, Leahy resigned from Notre Dame in 1954. During his tenure at the university, Leahy's teams captured five national championships, and his overall winning percentage of .864 ranks just behind his mentor Rockne. Following his retirement from coaching, Leahy was a prominent businessman and football analyst. He died on June 21, 1973, in Portland, Oregon, where he was in business with his son. Leahy helped restore the popularity of Notre Dame and college football following the difficult days of World War II.

---

annihilation of opponents but also in their coach's and their school's ability to wrap an obsession with sports victory in idealistic and patriotic language" (Sperber 1998, 138).

Blaik's most important recruits were running backs "Mr. Inside," Felix Anthony "Doc" Blanchard and "Mr. Outside," Glenn Davis, who were selected for the Heisman Trophy in 1945 and 1946, respectively. After Blanchard's freshman year at the University of North Carolina, the athlete was drafted and assigned to a regular Army unit. Blaik then intervened to secure Blanchard an appointment to West Point, a tactic that Blaik's critics referred to as "draft board recruiting." But Blaik's approach paid off on the gridiron, as between 1944 and 1947 the Black Knights enjoyed a thirty-two-game unbeaten streak. The Black Knights were national college football champions in both 1944 and 1945, but a 0–0 tie with Notre Dame in 1946, after Leahy returned from military service, denied Army its third straight national title. The 1946 game between Notre Dame and Army drew almost 80,000 fans, but the two institutions decided to discontinue the lucrative series, ostensibly because Army wanted a more national schedule and both programs were concerned that gambling interests might seek to become involved with the game.

And, indeed, college football was attracting a great deal of attention during the postwar sports boom. Average attendance for major college football games in 1939 and 1940 was hovering around 23,000, but in 1946 that number rose to approximately 27,000 spectators per contest. The total attendance for all college football games in 1947 rose to 11,715,370, a 5 percent increase over the previous year. The growing economic impact of football for universities was apparent in an increasing number of recruiting scandals. For example, Buddy Young, who starred at the University of Illinois before the war, allegedly received twenty-five lucrative financial college offers while he was still in the Navy, before finally deciding on his return to Illinois. Also, it was reported eight players from Tulsa's 1945 Orange Bowl team were lured to the University of Oklahoma the following season.

In response to such allegations, the NCAA sought to clarify its position on amateurism and scholarships. In 1948, the so-called Purity or Sanity Code adopted by the organization allowed for schools to pay for an athlete's tuition, incidental fees, and a meal per day in season, but direct aid would be awarded on the basis of need. Any jobs performed by athletes would "have to be commensurate with the services rendered." Schools in the South perceived these regulations as favoring established football programs in the East and Midwest, where jobs were more plentiful and affluent alumni could provide players with money and employment. In July 1949 the University of Virginia announced that it would not comply with the Sanity Code as between thirty and forty players on the football team were receiving scholarships. Virginia's defiance was supported by seven other southern institutions, which became known as "The Sinful Seven." In January 1950 a majority of schools within the NCAA voted to expel Virginia, but the total was short of the necessary two-thirds. This action, in effect, did away with the reform efforts of the Sanity Code. The postwar efforts of the NCAA to limit the growth of big-time college football failed, and the commercialization of the college game continued unabated.

On the gridiron, Leahy's Fighting Irish dominated play in the late 1940s, winning national championships in 1947 and 1949 and returning Notre Dame to the glory days of Knute Rockne. From 1946 to 1949, the Irish were 38–0–1 with two Heisman Trophy winners in quarterback Johnny Lujack (1947) and end Leon Hart (1949). Notre Dame's domination was interrupted in 1948 by the undefeated University of Michigan Wolverines who outscored the opposition 252–44, while the Heisman that year was awarded to Southern Methodist running back Doak Walker.

College football's growing popularity in the postwar era was marred, however, by continuing racial discrimination, especially in the American South. Many northern universities integrated their football programs in the early twentieth century with such outstanding players as Paul Robeson of Rutgers and Fritz Pollard of Brown. By the 1930s black college football players could be found in every section of the county except the South. To maintain Jim Crow, southern institutions insisted that visiting integrated college squads not play their black athletes. But

World War II fostered the integration of college football due to the shortage of athletes during the war years. Also, many northern institutions after the war found it increasingly difficult to discriminate against returning black veterans who wanted to play football. The lead in recruiting in black athletes was taken by the Pacific Coast Conference and Big Ten, and by the mid-1950s there were over sixty African American players in the Big Ten. Racial progress was celebrated on October 11, 1947, when Harvard played the University of Virginia at Charlottesville. The Harvard Crimson squad included lineman Chester Pierce, who became the first black athlete to play on the home turf of a white college in the former Confederacy. Harvard won the game 47–0, which was played without major incident. But such was not always the case. For example, black running back Johnny Bright of Drake University was one of college football's leading offensive stars in 1949 and 1950, but his 1951 season was cut short in Stillwater, Oklahoma, when a member of the Oklahoma A&M squad broke Bright's jaw with an unprovoked blow that many observers perceived as racially motivated. And the three major southern football conferences, the Southeastern (SEC), Southwest (SWC), and Atlantic Coast (ACC), remained segregated until 1963, reflecting white southern resistance to the civil rights movement. Meanwhile, black players in the South matriculated to the North or played for all-black colleges. Demonstrating the fundamental inequality of the "separate but equal" doctrine of Jim Crow, most black college football programs operated on meager budgets with poor equipment and facilities; performing before smaller crowds and away from the media spotlight. But as professional football began to expand during the post–World War II period, the talent in black college football was evident in the number of players coming from Grambling and other southern black colleges.

Professional Football

Formed in the early 1920s in predominantly medium-sized midwestern cities such as Green Bay, Wisconsin, and Canton, Ohio, the National Football League (NFL) lacked the national exposure of college football. The professional league struggled through the difficult Depression years and almost ceased operations because of World War II, but during the postwar economic expansion professional football would begin to find its place as a popular spectator sport. The NFL expanded to the West Coast and was challenged by a new league—the All-American Football Conference (AAFC). A merger of the two leagues solidified the appeal of professional football in the 1950s and 1960s, presenting a challenge to baseball's claim as the nation's premiere sport.

In 1940 the ten teams in the NFL consisted of the Washington Redskins, Brooklyn Dodgers, New York Giants, Pittsburgh Steelers, and Philadelphia Eagles in the Eastern Division; and Chicago Bears, Green Bay Packers, Detroit Lions, Cleveland Rams, and Chicago Cardinals in the West. The Chicago Bears of George Halas were the dominant team during the 1940 season, but they were defeated 7–3 by the Washington Redskins in a late-season game. Washington owner George Preston Marshall antagonized the Bears by remarking that they were "quitters" and "cry babies." The Bears enjoyed their revenge during the league title game when they humiliated the Redskins 73–0; the greatest margin of victory ever in a NFL title game. The 1941 season was tested by American entrance into World

War II. The league's title game, played only two weeks after the attack on Pearl Harbor, attracted only 13,341 fans to watch the Bears defend their title with a 37–9 victory over the New York Giants.

With players leaving for military service and wartime restrictions on travel, the NFL struggled to survive between 1942 and 1945. Chicago Bears owner and coach George Halas left the club midway through the 1942 season to join the Navy, but the Bears remained the league's dominant team, recording an undefeated regular season. In the 1942 title game, however, the Redskins, behind the passing and punting of Sammy Baugh, gained a degree of revenge for their humiliating 1940 loss in the championship contest. To survive the 1943 season, the NFL contracted. With owners Daniel F. Reeves and Fred Levy Jr. in military service, the Cleveland Rams were given permission by Commissioner Elmer Layden to suspend operations for a year, while Philadelphia and Pittsburgh combined franchises with the cities rotating home games. Bemused fans referred to the merged team as the "Steagles." The manpower shortage also led the NFL to allow free substitution, but rule changes failed to alter the teams playing for the league championship in which the Bears defeated the Redskins by a score of 41–21. Baugh was the league's best player, leading the NFL during 1943 in passing, punting, and interceptions.

The NFL continued its policy of consolidation during the 1944 and 1945 campaigns. The struggling Pittsburgh franchise was granted permission to merge with the Chicago Cardinals for the 1944 season. Cleveland rejoined the NFL, and a new franchise was awarded to Boston, but the club was forced to merge with the Brooklyn Tigers for the 1945 football campaign. The final years of the war also broke the stranglehold of the Bears and Redskins on the NFL championship. In 1944 the Green Bay Packers defeated the New York Giants 14–7, while the following season Bob Waterfield of the Cleveland Rams led his team to a 15–14 victory over the Redskins. While the NFL's very existence was brought into doubt by the war, the football league demonstrated its patriotism in numerous ways. Over 600 current and former NFL players saw military action in World War II, while the league also took a leading role in raising money for the war effort. In 1942 the NFL contributed $4,000,000 to the war bond drive, and fifteen exhibition contests provided nearly $700,000 for service charities.

After passing through the crucible of war, professional football was poised to assert its role in the postwar economic boom. The NFL faced competition from the AAFC, which was formed in 1944 under the auspices of *Chicago Tribune* sports editor Arch Ward. The AAFC launched play in 1946 with franchises in eight cities, including San Francisco and Los Angeles. Salaries for professional football players skyrocketed as returning veterans with professional and college experience were recruited by both leagues. The threat posed by the AAFC to the NFL was evident when 1946 AAFC rosters included over 100 players with NFL experience and over half of the 1945 College All-Stars. The NFL responded to this threat by replacing Commissioner Layden, who initially dismissed the activity of the millionaires backing the AAFC, with Bert Bell, co-owner of the Philadelphia Eagles. Under Bell's leadership, the AAFC's tapping of the lucrative California market was countered by the transfer of the Cleveland Rams to Los Angeles for the 1946 season. In addition, the Rams integrated the NFL by signing former UCLA stars Woody Strode and Kenny Washington to contracts. Black athletes played in the NFL during the 1920s, but from 1934 to 1946 league rosters contained no black athletes. This state

Kenny Washington of UCLA, one of the first African American players in the Pacific Coast Conference and, later, one of the first in the National Football League. (Courtesy of the Library of Congress)

of affairs is usually attributed to the influence of Boston Braves/Washington Redskins owner George Preston Marshall who opposed integration of his club and pressured other owners to follow suit.

The vacancy in Cleveland was filled by the AAFC, which named the franchise after its coach, the legendary Paul Brown, whose coaching résumé included Massillon High School, Ohio State University, and Great Lakes Naval Station. Brown integrated the AAFC by signing African American defensive tackle Bill Willis, who played for the coach at Ohio State, and former University of Nevada running back Marion Motley. Willis and Motley, along with quarterback Otto Graham and place-kicker Lou "the Toe" Groza, provided the talent that allowed the Browns to dominate the new league. The Browns won the AAFC's championship every season during the four-year existence of the league. But the dominance of one club may have hurt the league as even the rabid Cleveland fans became complacent. After averaging crowds of over 50,000 for their initial campaign, attendance at home games for the Browns fell to approximately 20,000 per contest by 1949. In fact, the crowd for the last AAFC championship game, in which the Browns defeated the San Francisco 49ers 21–7, attracted only 22,500 spectators to Cleveland's massive Municipal Stadium.

Marion Motley

The second African American elected to the National Football Hall of Fame, Marion Motley was an outstanding running back for the Cleveland Browns who played an important role in the integration of professional football.

Motley was born June 5, 1920, in Leesburg, Georgia, and played high school football at Canton McKinley High School in the football-obsessed state of Ohio. Although not a great student during his high school days, Motley was recruited for the University of Nevada Wolf Pack by coach Jim Aiken, an Ohio native, in 1940. Motley was an immediate star for the Wolf Pack at fullback and linebacker, but his college career was almost cut short in 1940 when he was convicted of involuntary manslaughter in an automobile accident. With the support of the school community and administration, Motley was able to pay a fine and avoid prison time, returning to Nevada as a star player from 1940 to 1942. He left college for military service in 1943, but he made little progress toward his degree, suggesting that the university was perhaps more interested in Motley as a football player than student.

He spent most of his Navy tour of duty at the Great Lakes Naval Station near Chicago, where Motley played football for Paul Brown. Following the war, Brown was signed to coach the new Cleveland franchise in the AAFC. To compete with the NFL for talent, Brown was prepared to break the color line in professional football by signing Motley and tackle Bill Willis. Cleveland dominated the AAFC, winning the championship each season during the league's four-year existence (1946–49). In 1950 the Cleveland Browns were incorporated into the NFL, shocking many football analysts by winning the NFL championship during their first season in the league. Suffering from a knee injury, Motley retired from the Browns in 1954, although he did attempt a brief comeback with the Pittsburgh Steelers the following season. During his eight-year tenure in Cleveland, Motley gained 4,721 rushing yards and scored thirty-one touchdowns.

Despite his accomplishments as a player, Motley's pay never exceeded more than $15,000 in a season. With little education, Motley worked as a postman and parking lot attendant after leaving professional football. But his desire to serve as a coach was thwarted by the racist hiring practices of the NFL. Although honored by his 1968 selection to the Pro Football Hall of Fame in Canton, Motley remained somewhat disillusioned with his treatment by the NFL following a spectacular playing career. Motley died June 27, 1999, at seventy-nine years of age.

Under the leadership of Commissioner Bell, the NFL weathered the challenge of the AAFC. While NFL turnstile counts also increased after the war, the higher salaries produced by the competition for talent reduced league profits. A gambling scandal also struck the league on the eve of the 1946 title game between the Chicago Bears and New York Giants. Gamblers approached Giants running back Merle Hapes to throw the game. Hapes turned the gamblers down and told teammate Frankie Filchock about the incident. Neither player reported the bribe offer, but when the press leaked the story, Commissioner Bell suspended Hapes. Filchock, however, was allowed to participate in the title game. Although Filchock turned in an outstanding performance in the Giants' 24–14 loss to the Bears, he was also suspended after the game for failing to share with league officials his knowledge of the bribe offer.

The NFL survived the crisis, but attendance figures indicated that the AAFC posed a real challenge. In 1946 the NFL outdrew the new league by 1.7 to 1.4 million spectators, while the AAFC attendance for the 1947 and 1948 seasons exceeded that of the more established league. But there were serious problems for some AAFC franchises. The Chicago Hornets found it difficult to compete with their NFL rivals, the Bears and Cardinals. A perennial loser, the Chicago Cardinals, behind the running of Charlie Trippi, defeated the Philadelphia Eagles 28–21 for the 1947 NFL title. The same two clubs played in the championship game the following season, but the Eagles prevailed 7–0 in a blinding snowstorm. The strong performance boosted the attendance of the Cardinals over their AAFC rival Hornets, while in Los Angeles the Rams won the 1949 Western title before losing to the Eagles in the championship game. The division victory, however, allowed the Rams to outdraw the AAFC Los Angeles Dons by a margin of 309,327 to 132,574. By the end of the 1949 season, both leagues were prepared to stop their bidding war. Despite its overall strong attendance figures, the AAFC reportedly lost $5 million in its four-year existence; while the NFL lost $3 million during the 1946–49 period. The merger favored the established league. Under the agreement, the Cleveland Browns, San Francisco 49ers, and Baltimore Colts were absorbed into the NFL, while the remaining five AAFC franchises were disbanded. With the merger complete, the NFL established a new attendance mark of 1,977,556 spectators in 1950, and professional football was on the road to challenging the popularity of baseball during the 1950s and 1960s.

SPORTS FOR INDIVIDUAL COMPETITORS

Boxing

Prizefighting in the 1940s remained a male preserve dominated by the African American heavyweight champion of the world, Joe Louis. Born into an Alabama sharecropping family, Louis gained the heavyweight title in 1937 and reigned as champion for thirteen years. Louis and his mother left Alabama in the mid-1920s and moved to Detroit, where he compiled an impressive amateur boxing record. Louis turned professional in 1934 with Detroit political operative and numbers racketeer John Roxborough as his manager. Roxborough and Louis's trainer, Julian Black, emphasized establishing a positive reputation that would appeal to white fight fans. Seeking to avoid the white backlash that plagued Jack Johnson, the first black heavyweight champion, Louis was urged by his handlers to cooperate with the white press and avoid being seen in public with white women. White Americans generally responded in a positive fashion, describing Louis as "a credit to his race." The press, however, never allowed Louis to forget his racial identity, referring to the boxer as the "Brown Bomber." Racial identity was also important to African Americans in the 1940s, and they perceived Louis as their champion. Louis defended his title against twenty-four white challengers, and every Louis victory was celebrated in the African American community.

Louis gained the championship on June 22, 1937, after knocking out James Braddock in round seven. At age twenty-three, Louis was the youngest man to win the heavyweight title. Between his defeat of Braddock and enlisting in the Army in early 1942, Louis defended his championship twenty times, but perhaps his most famous fight was a nontitle bout.

Portrait of Joe Louis (Joe Louis Barrow), seated on bleacher in
Greenwood Lake, NJ, in 1941. (Courtesy of the Library of Congress)

On June 12, 1936, Louis fought former champion Max Schmeling in New York
City. As a German citizen, Schmeling was touted by the Nazi regime as an example of Aryan racial superiority, and Adolf Hitler gloated when Louis was knocked
out by Schmeling in round twelve of their fight. On June 22, 1938, at Yankee Stadium, Louis defended his crown in a rematch against the German fighter. Seeking
to avoid the humiliation of their first bout, Louis scored a first-round knockout victory over the pride of the German Reich. The fight made Louis a national hero.

With the nation poised on the edge of war in 1941, Louis struggled in two title
defenses. On May 23, 1941, Louis won with a seventh-round disqualification over
challenger Buddy Baer. Baer's camp believed that Louis dropped their fighter with
a punch delivered several seconds after the bell to end round six. When the referee
refused to disqualify Louis for the blow, Baer failed to answer the bell for round
seven and was disqualified, giving the victory to Louis. The following month, Louis
was losing on points to former light heavyweight champion Billy Conn after twelve
rounds, but Louis rallied to knock out the popular Irish-American fighter from
Connecticut.

His status as a national hero was assured when Louis enlisted in the Army a
month after Pearl Harbor. Louis became an important symbol of national unity
during the conflict, and the War Department used photographs of the fighter in
uniform to promote war bond drives and defuse wartime racial tensions. His primary military duties consisted of public relations appearances and exhibition bouts
to entertain the troops.

Louis fought sparingly during the war, easily defeating Buddy Baer in a 1942
rematch. Nevertheless, there was considerable national interest in his 1946 postwar
rematch with Billy Conn, who had last fought on February 13, 1942, when he
defeated middleweight champion Tony Zale in a nontitle bout. Similar to Louis,
Conn spent the war years in the military. The skills of both fighters deteriorated

during their war inactivity, and Louis retained his title with an eighth-round knockout. Louis's declining abilities were evident as he struggled to defeat his former sparring partner Jersey Joe Walcott in two title defenses. Louis retired as undefeated heavyweight champion of the world in 1949, but financial considerations led him to make an ill-conceived comeback in the early 1950s, losing bouts to Ezzard Charles and Rocky Marciano.

The popularity of boxing in the 1940s, however, was hardly limited to the heavyweight division. Many Italian Americans, African Americans, and Latinos continued to perceive the ring as an avenue for social mobility as the nation emerged from depression and war into the more affluent postwar society. Notable fighters from these ethnic groups excelled in a classic boxing era during the 1940s. Among these pugilistic champions was Willie Pep. Born Guglielmo Papaleo in Middletown, Connecticut, featherweight Pep won sixty-two fights in a row before he was beaten by lightweight Sammy Angott, then won seventy-one more contests before his title was taken by Sandy Sandler on October 28, 1948. But in the rematch, Pep regained his title and ended the decade as champion. The bantamweight division was dominated by Manuel Ortiz, who was born in Mexico and raised in California, reflecting the growing Latino presence in prizefighting. Ortiz won the bantamweight title in 1942. He defended the title fifteen times before losing to Harold Dale in 1947, but he regained the championship later that year in a rematch.

Boxing legend and African American champion Sugar Ray Robinson also launched his professional fighting career in 1940. Robinson suffered his first defeat in his fortieth bout, losing to middleweight Jake LaMotta, whom Robinson had bested four months earlier. Robinson did not lose another fight in the decade, including two additional rematches with LaMotta, and in December 1946 he defeated Tommy Bell for the welterweight championship.

The most contested arena in boxing during the 1940s was the middleweight division. In 1946, Tony Zale and Rocky Graziano began a fierce rivalry when Zale defended his middleweight title by knocking out the challenger in the sixth round. The following year, Graziano returned the favor, knocking out Zale in the sixth round to claim the championship. The final chapter in the Zale-Graziano saga was played out on June 10, 1948, when Zale regained his crown, finishing off Graziano in three rounds. Zale, however, did not retain the championship for long as later that year he was defeated by French fighter Marcel Cerdan. On June 16, 1949, Jake LaMotta claimed the middleweight crown, knocking out the French champion in round ten of their bout. The anticipated rematch between Cerdan and LaMotta was canceled when the Frenchman perished in a plane crash.

Boxing retained its popularity even when the sport was shrouded with controversy during the late 1940s. On February 21, 1948, Sam Baroudi died after a bout with Ezzard Charles, who claimed the vacant heavyweight title in 1949 after Louis retired. Even more disturbing to many fight fans were allegations of fixed fights and the influence of underworld figures such as the notorious Frankie Carbo. Both LaMotta and Graziano were accused of being involved with gamblers and "fixing" bouts, but with the Gillette Corporation sponsorship of both radio and television bouts, along with large arena crowds, prizefighting maintained its hold upon the American public in the postwar world. The individualism of the sport was also a respite from a society in which the corporate values of amity and cooperation were stressed within the national conformity of suburban culture.

Tennis

World War II and its aftermath furthered the democratization of tennis and golf, sports originally associated with country clubs and white privilege. During the war both sports were curtailed as tennis and golf balls were rationed along with golf clubs. In addition, the major tournaments for these two sports were suspended during the war. In the postwar period, as most Americans gained greater income and leisure time, both tennis and golf expanded beyond the confines of the country club and white America.

Major tennis events such as the U.S. Open and Wimbledon were canceled during World War II. Another casualty of the war was the strict distinction between amateurs and professionals which the U.S. Lawn Tennis Association (USLTA) attempted to impose upon the sport. The elitist attitudes of the USLTA were challenged in the late 1940s by Jack Kramer. The son of working-class parents, Kramer won the U.S. Outdoor Championship along with Wimbledon singles and doubles titles in 1947; all of which were amateur championships. Following this success, tennis promoters offered Kramer $50,000 a year as well as a percentage of gate receipts to turn professional. On tour with Bobby Riggs, a Wimbledon champion in 1939, Kramer demonstrated that a market existed for professional tennis as the 1948 tour grossed nearly $400,000.

The democratic possibilities of tennis in the late 1940s were also apparent in the budding careers of "Pancho" Gonzales and Althea Gibson, who would make their marks in the tennis world during the 1950s and 1960s. Growing up in Los Angeles in the 1940s, Richard Alonzo "Pancho" Gonzales was banned from local tennis tournaments by Perry Jones, president of the Southern California Tennis Association; because the young Latino was too often truant from school. Gonzales spent 1945–46 in the Navy, and after he turned eighteen, the talented tennis player returned to California, entering local tournaments. By the end of 1947 Gonzales was ranked as the seventh-best player in the United States. Gonzales stunned the tennis world the following year by winning the U.S. Championship at Forest Hills, New York. He successfully defended his title in 1949 before turning professional.

In her rise to prominence in the world of tennis, Althea Gibson confronted both gender and racial bias. Gibson was born in South Carolina to a family of sharecroppers, but she grew up in Harlem. She learned to play tennis at the Harlem River Tennis Courts. Her training was promoted by Dr. Walter Johnson, a Lynchburg, Virginia, physician active in the black tennis community. In 1947 she participated in the segregated American Tennis Association (ATA). After dominating the ATA, Gibson was allowed to participate in the 1950 U.S. Championships. In 1957 Gibson was the first African American to win a title at Wimbledon, and after winning the U.S. Championship she was named the Associated Press Female Athlete of the Year.

Golf

After weathering the crisis of World War II, the country club sport of golf also widened its appeal. From 1942 to 1945, all major U.S. Golf Association (USGA) events were suspended. The U.S. Open in 1942 was temporarily replaced by the

Hale American Open, played as a war benefit and raising $20,000 for the cause. Although the majors were canceled and many members of the Professional Golfers Association were in military service, there was still plenty of golf in the United States during the war years. The accomplishments of Byron Nelson during World War II encouraged comparisons with golfing legend Bobby Jones. In 1944 and 1945 Nelson won twenty-six of fifty-one tournaments. After winning eighteen consecutive events in 1945, Nelson retired at age thirty-four in 1946.

Babe Didrikson Zaharias, 1911–56. (Courtesy of the Library of Congress)

The women's tour in the late 1940s was dominated by Babe Didrikson. In 1946–47, Didrikson won seventeen tournaments. Earning as much as $100,000 annually in endorsements, Didrikson decided to abandon her amateur status as a golfer and played a pivotal role in the formation of the Ladies Professional Golf Association (LPGA). Although the purses for the LPGA failed to match the prize money for the men's tour, Didrikson established the LPGA as a force in the golf world, and she dominated women's golf until experiencing failing health in 1953. Didrikson was criticized for being too masculine earlier in her athletic career as a basketball player and track star, but in the postwar period she presented a more feminine look with stylish clothes and hair, fitting into the consensus image of the suburban housewife. But like many of the women in suburbia, Didrikson was certainly working outside of the home and participating in the postwar economy.

Greater leisure time and affluence contributed to the expansion of golf and tennis beyond the country club set. City governments constructed public golf courses and tennis complexes to meet growing demand. And even the fees of new private golf and tennis clubs were within the reach of an expanding middle class. Sporting goods companies also contributed to the growing commercialization of sport by promoting sales of Jack Kramer tennis rackets and Byron Nelson golf clubs for the increasingly active middle class with leisure time on their hands.

OTHER SIGNIFICANT SPORTS

In addition to the expansion of golf and tennis facilities, bowling was a popular leisure activity in the postwar period. Often associated with the lower class and competing with pool halls for their clientele, bowling corporations such as AMF and Brunswick expanded their facilities with automatic pin-setters and air conditioning in order to enhance their appeal with a more affluent working class in the late 1940s and early 1950s. Bowling leagues were established for companies, churches, and housewives. The number of regular bowlers exceeded 20 million by the mid-1950s.

Horse racing, which continued during the war years, also attracted its share of the postwar sporting market. The 1940s were a golden age for thoroughbred horse racing with four horses winning the sport's Triple Crown (Kentucky Derby, Preakness, and Belmont Stakes); Whirlaway in 1941, Count Fleet in 1943, Assault in 1946, and Citation in 1948. Of these fine horses, perhaps Citation was the greatest champion. Including his Triple Crown victories, Citation won nineteen of twenty races in 1948, earning over $700,000 in prize money. Citation was ridden by legendary jockey Eddie Arcaro who won over 4,000 races in his career, including Whirlaway's 1941 Triple Crown. Due to a problem with his left fore ankle, Citation did not run in 1949. It was difficult for Citation to regain his top form, and the horse's last race was in July 1951. Citation was the first colt to garner more than a million dollars in total earnings, offering further evidence of the lucrative postwar sporting market.

While horse racing remained a staple of American sporting amusement during World War II, auto racing was heavily impacted by wartime rationing of gasoline and tires. In 1939 and 1940, Wilbur Shaw won the Indianapolis 500, and he was leading in 1941 with only sixty-two laps remaining. An accident, however, removed Shaw from the race, which was won by Mauri Rose. The drama of the 1941 race, however, was not repeated during the war years as the Indianapolis race was suspended from 1942 to 1945. The speedway was in need of considerable repairs after the war, and Indiana businessman Tony Husman tapped Shaw to manage the track. Under Shaw's leadership, the Indianapolis 500 assumed its position as the most significant automobile race in American with the Blue Crown Special team of Mauri Rose and Bill Holland dominating the competition during the late 1940s.

Indianapolis race cars were expensive, costing approximately $30,000 each. Seeking a less costly alternative, many southerners began to purchase cars from junkyards and modify them into race cars for several thousand dollars per automobile. Termed "stock-car races," these popular events were initially staged on farm pastures before the construction of compacted clay tracks. Many of the early drivers, such as Bob Flock, were former runners of illegal "moonshine" liquor. To provide greater respectability for stock car racing, entrepreneur Bill France organized the National Association for Stock Car Auto Racing (NASCAR). By modifying traditional passenger cars, NASCAR provided its fans with the illusion that their automobiles were capable of being race cars. Picking up on the growing popularity of the sport, sponsors such as the Ford Motor Company began to promote NASCAR. On June 19, 1949, the first of the Grand Nationals stock-car races was staged at the Charlotte (NC) Speedway, with Jim Roper declared the winner when Glen Dunway was disqualified. During the second half of the twentieth century, NASCAR would move beyond its southern roots to become a national obsession.

SUMMARY

After wartime sacrifices, Americans turned out in record numbers for sporting events in the late 1940s. But the postwar economic boom was full of paradox. The consensus vision of America from suburbia assumed that an expanding capitalist economy would place all Americans within reach of the middle class. The rise of mass spectator sports seemingly supported this ideal of a unified, classless society. For example, historian Benjamin G. Rader suggests that in post–World War II America, "To some degree spectator sports replaced or supplemented the church, the family, the local community, subcommunities based upon status or ethnicity, and the older system of mutual class obligations as one of the sinews which held modern society together" (Rader 1983, 360).

The image of consensus offered by suburbia, however, often proved to be a façade. The suburbs, as well as most of the nation's professional and collegiate teams were white, and it would take a mass movement composed of such courageous individuals as Jackie Robinson and Martin Luther King Jr. to shatter the walls of segregation in sport and society. The image of the contented suburban housewife also often masked a more competitive drive such as that displayed by Alline Banks during her AAU basketball career or a discontent later outlined by Betty Friedan in *The Feminine Mystique*.

Developing alongside the move to the suburbs was the growth of television. Although early television sets were expensive and reception poor, the demand for the new source of home entertainment proved almost insatiable. In 1950 only 20 percent of American households owned television sets, but by the mid-1950s this number jumped to over 70 percent. Along with increased leisure options in the suburbs, television played an important role in the decline of attendance for such sports as baseball by 1949. The new entertainment vehicle also fostered such programming as roller derby and professional wrestling which blurred the distinction between sport and entertainment. On the other hand, the challenge of television also spurred expansion and franchise transfers in professional sports in order to tap new markets. In the long run, the revenues garnered from television provided an economic bonanza for the growth of American sport during the second half of the twentieth century. The large profits generated by the expansion of professional franchises and television revenues produced labor unrest by athletes who were no longer willing to accept the restrictions imposed by ownership and such practices as baseball's reserve clause.

In addition to the paradoxes of suburbia, the Cold War loomed over post–World War II America. As diplomatic relations deteriorated between the Soviet Union and United States, Americans perceived the 1948 Summer Olympics as an opportunity to celebrate capitalistic achievement. The victories of American athletes during the London Games were somewhat tarnished by the exclusion of the Soviet Union and its Eastern European allies from the competition. American and capitalistic superiority, however, seemed assured following the athletic successes of the U.S. Olympic team at the 1952 Helsinki Games in which Bob Mathias defended his decathlon title. National insecurity regarding the Cold War, however, only increased following the 1949 explosion of an atomic bomb by the Soviet Union. Fears of the Soviet Union encouraged political conformity and a monolithic anticommunism apparent when Jackie Robinson testified before the House Un-American Activities Committee (HUAC) on July 18, 1949, to refute allegations by Paul Robeson that African Americans would not support the United States in a conflict with the Soviet Union. While acknowledging that racism was a major problem for American democracy, Robinson emphasized the patriotism of black Americans. Robinson later expressed regret over his testimony, but his appearance before HUAC demonstrated the shadow cast by the Cold War over American sport and society as the nation moved into the 1950s. The resiliency demonstrated by Americans and their sporting culture in dealing with World War II and its aftermath indicated that the nation would be ready to meet these new challenges.

RECOMMENDED SOURCES

Print Sources

Berlage, Gia Ingham. 1994. *Women in baseball: The forgotten history.* Westport, CT: Praeger.

Betts, John Richard. 1974. *America's sporting heritage: 1850–1950.* Reading, MA: Addison-Wesley.

Bullock, Steven R. 2004. *Playing for their nation: Baseball and the American military during World War II.* Lincoln: University of Nebraska Press.

Cahn, Susan K. 1994. *Coming on Strong: Gender and Sexuality in Twentieth-Century Women's Sport.* New York: Free Press, 1994.

Cayleff, Susan. 1995. *Babe: The life and legend of Babe Didrikson Zaharias.* Urbana: University of Illinois Press.

Davies, Richard O. 1994. *America's obsession: Sports and society since 1945.* Fort Worth, TX: Harcourt Brace College.

———. 2007. *Sports in American life: A History.* New York: Blackwell.

Dickey, Glenn. 1982. *The history of professional basketball since 1896.* New York: Stein and Day.

Gorn, Elliott J., and Warren Goldstein. 1993. *A brief history of American sports.* New York: Hill and Wang.

Ikard, Robert W. 2005. *Just for fun: The story of AAU Women's Basketball.* Fayetteville: University of Arkansas Press.

Isaacs, Neil D. 1984. *A history of college basketball.* New York: Harper and Row.

Koppett, Leonard. 2003. *Koppett's concise history of Major League Baseball.* Philadelphia: Temple University Press.

Lanctot, Neil. 2004. *Negro League baseball: The rise and ruin of a black institution.* Philadelphia: Temple University Press.

Lowenfish, Lee. 2007. *Branch Rickey: Baseball's ferocious gentleman.* Lincoln: University of Nebraska Press.

Mead, Chris. 1985. *Champion—Joe Louis: Black hero in white America.* New York: Scribner's Sons.

Peterson, Robert W. 1997. *Pigskin: The early years of pro football.* New York Oxford University Press.

Quirk, James P., and Rodney D. Fort. 1992. *Pay dirt: The business of professional team sports.* Princeton, NJ: Princeton University Press.

Rader, Benjamin G. 1983. *American sports: From the age of folk games to the age of spectators.* Englewood Cliffs, NJ: Prentice-Hall.

Roberts, Randy, and James Olson. 1989. *Winning is the only thing: Sports in America since 1945.* Baltimore: Johns Hopkins University Press.

Sammons, Jeffrey T. 1988. *Beyond the ring: The role of boxing in American society.* Urbana: University of Illinois Press.

Sperber, Murray. 1998. *Onward to victory: The crises that shaped college sports.* New York: Henry Holt.

Tygiel, Jules. 1983. *Baseball's great experiment: Jackie Robinson and his legacy.* New York: Oxford University Press

Watterson, John Sayle. 2000. *College football: History, spectacle, controversy.* Baltimore: Johns Hopkins University Press.

Wiggins, David K., and Patrick B. Miller, eds. 2001. *The unlevel playing field: A documentary history of the African-American experience in sport.* Urbana: University of Illinois Press.

Films

Baseball: Inning Six, The National Pastime, 1940–1950. 1994. Dir. Ken Burns. PBS.
The Jackie Robinson Story. 1950. Dir. Alfred E. Green. Legend Films.
Joe Louis: America's Hero … Betrayed. 2008. HBO Films.
A League of Their Own. 1992. Dir. Penny Marshall. Columbia Pictures.
75 Seasons: The Story of the National Football League. 1994. NFL Films.

CHAPTER 9

AMERICAN SPORTS, 1950–1959

Murry R. Nelson

OVERVIEW

The 1950s were a period of great political adjustment in the United States and the world, characterized by cautious, moderate legislation and policies. The ravages of World War II had deeply affected the entire European continent as well as Japan, and the United States was now the clear giant of economic power in the world. Though the United States had suffered nearly 500,000 casualties, this paled in comparison to the Soviet Union's 23 million or Germany's 7.5 million and Poland's 5 million. Of the latter, 3 million were part of the nearly 6 million Holocaust victims. Even countries that lost "only" a few hundred thousand lost mostly young men, upon which a country builds its economy. Most of Europe was also devastated by bombings and fighting on the continent.

The United States was able to absorb most of the approximately 15 million members of the American armed forces who fought in World War II back into a rapidly expanding economy. The Serviceman's Adjustment Act of 1944 (and its successor in 1952), known as the GI Bill, provided full college benefits for all returning veterans, and this kept the economy from falling into depression, as more than 50 percent of the veterans took advantage of the bill and attended or returned to college. This also led colleges and universities to expand their enrollments greatly, creating larger institutions of higher education and a greatly improved educational populace.

Many of the GIs were professional athletes. Major-league baseball had continued during the war, but with a number of players who would have been unable to be in the big leagues if not for the absence of so many top players fighting in the war. In pro football a few teams were forced to merge because of a lack of able-bodied players. The return of the servicemen allowed for both the NFL and a newly formed league, the All-American Football Conference (AAFC), to have enough top players to make for entertaining football. Professional basketball had been in desperate straits during the war, but now seemed poised to grow nicely after the merger of the NBL and the BAA to form the NBA.

Another great effect of the returning GIs was the enormous increase in the birth rate, which had been stagnant for the war years, as so many young men and women were fighting on the European and Pacific fronts. The great Depression of the 1930s also gave many families pause as to whether they could afford more (or any) children in the perilous economic times. The 1930s saw 24 million births in the United States. With the boom that began in 1946, 32 million American births were recorded in the 1940s and in 1954 the United States had more than 4 million births, the first year that had occurred. That number was met or exceeded every year until 1965, increasing the population of the United States from 132 million in 1940 to 152 million in 1950 and 181 million in 1960. This boom in population was replicated in the United Kingdom, Canada, Australia, and much of Western Europe. The effect was more than simply increased population; the influence that these "baby boomers" would have on social, cultural, and economic trends in the United States and worldwide has been profound. Trends in housing, fashion, music, education, transportation, and career choices have been largely led by the baby boom generation from the 1950s through the early years of the twenty-first century.

In housing, the trend of the 1950s was the continued expansion of the cities through large suburban movement. In many cases this was limited to the white middle class as many suburban areas were either segregated by law (de jure) or practice (de facto) and this movement to the suburbs was termed, in some cases, as "white flight." Large population movement to the suburbs led to a need for greater transportation access and superhighways and expressways were built throughout the nation to more easily connect the suburbs to the cities. This also led many families to purchase second automobiles, further increasing the need for more improved roads. President Eisenhower also made the interstate highway system a priority as part of national defense.

Most sports stadiums were in the city and attendance at some venues declined as more fans moved to the suburbs and the neighborhoods around old stadiums declined. Some professional teams used these changing demographics as one reason to move their franchises. In baseball, teams left some cities of the Northeast like Boston, New York, and Philadelphia to move westward.

One of the most significant cultural trends of the 1950s was the development of rock and roll music, which consisted of a fusion of two types of music: rhythm and blues (r&b), played mainly by African American entertainers, and country and western swing, played by white musicians. At first record companies had white artists cover r&b songs to make them more acceptable to a larger market, but as the popularity of black artists grew, radio stations began to adapt their playlists and play more rock and roll. Great black artists like Fats Domino, Ivory Joe Hunter, Chuck Berry, and Ray Charles, and great white artists like Bill Haley and the Comets, Jerry Lee Lewis, and Buddy Holly became stars, seemingly overnight. Radio airplay was enhanced by the invention of $33^{1}/_{3}$- and 45-rpm vinyl records, replacing the heavy and easily breakable 78-rpm records made of vulcanite. Rock and roll music was seen, by some, as dangerous, and laws were passed to restrict concerts in various locales because of fears of race mixing and rioting. It was referred to in some bigoted quarters as "jungle music."

There was a similar change in professional sports as more African Americans became prominent stars in baseball, football, and basketball. Following Jackie Robinson's integration of baseball in 1947, the Brooklyn Dodgers, Cleveland Indians, and New York Giants led the way in signing more and more top African American ball players.

In 1956 the most influential white rock and roll musician, Elvis Presley, made his mark nationally with the song "Heartbreak Hotel," and by the end of 1956, he had recorded five number 1 hits. Rock music was now the most popular musical form in the nation and it grew more so through the rest of the decade, aided greatly by the first nationwide teen music show, Dick Clark's *American Bandstand*. The music industry was tainted by the "payola" scandals of the late 1950s, but the music continued to play to larger and larger audiences. The scandals involved record companies paying disc jockeys for airtime for the companies' records, hoping to have hits created by constant play.

Surely, the greatest influence on all levels of culture and information in the 1950s was the widespread growth and accessibility of television. Invented in the 1920s in a mechanical form, television was not perfected in any electronic form until about 1935. Further development was hampered by the onset of World War II, but following the war, research and development began in earnest. Broadcasters became more prevalent, the cost of production was reduced, and by 1947 about 40,000 television sets were in use in the United States, as opposed to 40 million radios. When 1950 began, there were 5 million television sets in use; that figure doubled by the end of the year. By the end of the decade, 42 million American homes had televisions. The phenomenal growth was related to the fact that television productions were viewed as "essential" to one's basic awareness as an American at that time. Many television productions were live and some of the most popular things to telecast were local sporting events, most specifically professional baseball.

Television series that were most popular during the 1950s were westerns, variety shows, situation comedies, and quiz shows. In 1955 the *Mickey Mouse Club* was first aired on afternoon network television, following the success of the *Disneyland* television show that premiered in 1954. Walt Disney himself served as the host of his show, later called *Walt Disney Presents*, for thirteen years.

Television network news became more and more popular with fifteen-minute broadcasts each evening. The political conventions of the two major parties were covered from gavel to gavel each evening on all three major networks in 1952, 1956, and 1960. Television became the major source of news and entertainment in the 1950s and retained that title through the next forty years.

Television also became the preferred medium for sports in the 1950s as more and more fans purchased sets. Most baseball broadcasting was local, other than the World Series. Football broadcasting was limited, but by the end of the decade it was clear that television and football would be a match "made in heaven." The Kentucky Derby was regularly telecast beginning in the 1950s.

The United States and the world were deeply affected by the rise of Communism and the Soviet Union immediately following World War II. The destruction of much of Eastern Europe and the political instability of the region allowed the Soviets to swiftly establish Communist regimes under the influence of the Kremlin. In an effort to take over all of Eastern Germany, the Soviets blockaded entry into the western part of Berlin, which was controlled by the French, British, and Americans. The blockade, begun in June of 1948, prevented West Berlin from receiving food and supplies to keep the city's population alive and well. The Allied response was to organize a massive airlift of goods and supplies, with planes taking off and landing at Templehof Airport. Flights continued for almost twelve months until the blockade was lifted.

This action by the Soviets made the West even more fearful of expansionist desires on the part of Russia and its allies, the Chinese Communists, who now controlled the Chinese mainland. In 1950 civil war broke out in Korea, which had also been divided into a Communist-controlled North and a democratically supported South. The United States entered the Korean conflict (termed a "police action") in 1950, as part of the United Nations forces that repelled the North Korean and, later, Chinese troops. Hostilities ended in July of 1953 with a ceasefire, but no peace treaty was signed. More than 33,000 American troops were killed with more than 92,000 wounded in this undeclared war. The political result was a stalemate as the lines of separation between the two parts of Korea were essentially the same at the end of fighting as they had been at the beginning. Many American athletes, amateur and professional, served in Korea.

The war reinforced the Communist threat to many Americans, known as the "Red Scare," and made the United States ripe for fears and accusations of Communist sympathizers within the U.S. government and military. Senator Joseph McCarthy of Wisconsin used this issue as a platform for his election. A series of hearings followed in 1954, where McCarthy openly lied about lists of Communists in the government and accused others of being Communists. He was finally exposed, and, six months later, he was censured by the U.S. Senate. McCarthy died in 1957 of what was termed acute hepatitis, most likely caused by alcoholism. One of the most bizarre effects of McCarthyism was the decision by the Cincinnati Reds to change their name to "Redlegs" for much of the 1950s, finally reverting to the Reds name in 1959.

In 1957 the Soviet Union launched *Sputnik*, the first unmanned satellite, which put the Soviets in space. This increased fear of the growing Communist threat for many Americans, worrying that the Soviet entrance into space would be the first step in an attack on the United States. The Sputnik program spurred a "space race" between the United States and the Soviet Union, both striving to put the first man in orbit. Russian Yuri Gagarin became the first in April 1961, followed a month later by Alan B. Shepard of the United States.

The fear of Communism, combined with fears of atomic-bomb attacks during the 1950s, made air-raid drills a common occurrence in most American schools. Despite the 1950s' reputation as a seemingly carefree time, there was always the ever-present threat of war or Communism.

The most important social impact of the 1950s came from a U.S. Supreme Court ruling in May 1954, *Brown v. Board of Education of Topeka, Kansas*. The *Brown* case established that the notion of "separate but equal" public facilities for blacks and whites was inherently unequal, overturning a Supreme Court decision from 1896, *Plessy v. Ferguson*. The *Brown* ruling affected not just schools, but lunchrooms, train stations, water fountains, movie theatres, public bathroom facilities, and a host of other areas. Since most southern states had passed state laws that mimicked the *Plessy* decision, the federal decision in 1954 was at odds with many state laws. Some southern states fought the implementation of the *Brown* decision on the basis of "states' rights."

The decisions in *Brown* in 1954 and *Brown II* in 1955 were the impetus for the civil rights movement, which grew in the 1950s and extended into the 1960s. What might have seemed like a small incident actually sparked the first a major battle in the civil rights movement. City buses in Montgomery, Alabama, in 1955 required that African Americans sit in the back of the bus while whites sat in the front. The definition of where the "middle" was depended on how many whites were on the bus. Rosa Parks was in the "colored" section of a city bus and as more whites boarded, she was told to give up her seat to a white person. She refused to move and was subsequently arrested. African American civil rights activists called for a boycott of the city buses until the rules on seating were altered.

The local civil rights leaders asked for assistance from the Congress on Racial Equality (CORE) and Martin Luther King Jr., a twenty-six-year-old minister came to Montgomery to lead the boycott. The boycott lasted 382 days until the Supreme Court affirmed that segregation on public buses was, indeed, illegal. These events propelled King to national prominence as a civil rights leader.

In August 1957 nine African American students attempted to enroll at segregated Central High School, the best high school in Little Rock, Arkansas, but were stopped by order of Governor Orville Faubus. President Eisenhower called in the 82nd Airborne Unit to escort the teens to the high school and to ensure their safety. Amid a screaming crowd of whites, the nine students began school at Central, each of them accompanied by a paratrooper for the first days of school. At the same time, the Myers family in Levittown, Pennsylvania, faced hundreds of white protesters outside their new home as they became the first African American family to move into a previously all-white neighborhood.

For many white Americans in the 1950s, these events brought the first real awareness of segregation and racial inequality, and the civil rights movement gained more and more sympathizers. There were also backlashes, such as lynchings and Ku Klux Klan activity. The civil rights movement would continue throughout the 1950s with lunch-counter sit-ins and protest marches, but advance rapidly in the next decade.

When President Franklin D. Roosevelt died in April of 1945, Vice President Harry S Truman became president. He was elected for a full term in 1948, but chose not to run again in 1952. The election, held in the midst of the Korean War, was won by Dwight D. Eisenhower, a moderate Republican who had been the Supreme Allied Commander of the Armed Forces in World War II. Eisenhower, known as "Ike," promised that he would go to Korea and seek a solution to ending the war, an action he took shortly after taking office in 1953. Eisenhower was greatly respected by most Americans and was re-elected in 1956.

Eisenhower initiated an interest in golf among Americans because of his love of the game and the many rounds of golf that he played while president. He also was an avid football fan, having been an All America player at the U.S. Military Academy (West Point) during the early part of the twentieth century. Eisenhower and his vice president, Richard Nixon, were devoted college football fans. Their abiding interest made football watching (and interest in sports in general) almost a "patriotic duty."

TEAM SPORTS

Baseball

Baseball in the 1950s—Race and Ethnicity

The 1950s is seen as a golden age of baseball with almost limitless numbers of stars. It equates with the previous "golden age," the 1920s, with one significant difference—the inclusion of great young African American baseball stars, a group kept out of baseball until 1947, when Jack Roosevelt Robinson took the field for the Brooklyn Dodgers. The appearance of Robinson was the most significant action in organized baseball in the postwar period. Later that year, Larry Doby took the field for the Cleveland Indians. The Dodgers and the Indians were the most aggressive teams in the National and American leagues, respectively, in signing top African American talent. The Dodgers were the top team in the National League in the 1950s and their great African American players like Robinson, Don Newcombe, Roy Campanella, Jim Gilliam, and Joe Black were instrumental in that success. The Indians signed Doby, Luke Easter, and the ageless Satchel Paige and won the pennant in 1948, as well as 1954. Overcoming the Yankees, however, was simply too great a task as New York won pennants in 1949–53, 1955–58, and 1960–64.

Some teams were slower at signing African American players. The Boston Red Sox was the last team to do so in 1959 when Elijah "Pumpsie" Green took the field for Boston. The opening of opportunities in the major leagues for African Americans ultimately meant the decline and death of the Negro Leagues. The Negro National League disbanded in 1949, while the Negro American League continued through the 1950s, a shadow of its former greatness. That league ended in 1962.

The great African American players in the 1950s included Willie Mays, Frank Robinson, Henry "Hank" Aaron, Monte Irvin, Ernie Banks, and Elston Howard. Mays, Duke Snider of the Dodgers, and Mickey Mantle of the Yankees were often the topic of conversation among baseball fans who couldn't decide who was the best centerfielder in New York and baseball. Mays had played in the Negro Leagues since the age of sixteen and first appeared for the Giants in 1951 when he was twenty. By the time he retired in 1973, he and the Giants had won three pennants and one world championship; Mays had been voted Most Valuable Player (MVP) in the National League twice and appeared in twenty-four All-Star games. Robinson debuted with the Cincinnati Reds in 1956, was the Rookie of the Year, won Most Valuable Player Awards in both leagues, and led his teams (the Reds and the Baltimore Orioles) to five pennants and two world championships. Robinson played in twelve All-Star games and hit 586 home runs. Aaron played for the Braves in two cities (Milwaukee and Atlanta) and was the all-time leader in home runs with 755 until 2007. He also holds career records for extra base hits, runs batted in, and total bases. He was Most Valuable Player in 1957, led his team to two pennants and a world championship, and played in twenty-four All-Star games. Because of segregation and serving in World War II, Irvin did not play in the major leagues until he was thirty and his career ended seven years later. He played on one world-championship and two pennant-winning Giants teams. Ernie Banks, known as "Mr. Cub," hit 512 homers for the Cubs and was league MVP twice, but his team never won a pennant. Elston Howard was the first African American to play for the Yankees and he was on ten pennant-winning and four World Championship teams. Howard, a catcher, was a nine-time All-Star and league MVP in 1963. All of these players were voted into the Baseball Hall of Fame.

The 1950s were also a time when Latin Americans began to make noted contributions in the major leagues. Throughout the twentieth century Latinos were allowed to play in the major leagues unless they were "too black," in which case they were barred like African Americans. This was perplexing to most Latinos since most Caribbean countries had little overt discrimination on the basis of color. The postwar period saw some top Latinos take the field in the major leagues.

Milwaukee Braves' Hank Aaron. (Courtesy of Photofest)

Roberto (Bobby) Avila (from Mexico) was a three-time All-Star, playing for the pennant-winning Cleveland Indians. Both Alfonso (Chico) Carrasquel and Luis Aparicio were slick fielding shortstops from Venezuela, playing in the American League for the Chicago White Sox. Aparicio later starred for Baltimore and Carrasquel for Cleveland. Saturnino "Minnie" Minoso was a dark-skinned Cuban who played for the White Sox, Indians, Cardinals, and Senators. He debuted in the majors at the late age of twenty-eight, because of segregation, and was voted Rookie of the Year in 1951. He was one of only two players to play in five different decades and had a lifetime average of just under .300 (.298). Vic Power (born Victor Pellot Pove in Puerto Rico) had his name "Americanized" early in his career and made his major-league debut in 1954 at the age of twenty-six. He was renowned for his flashy, but expert fielding at first base. He also was known for his quick wit. Once, while in a restaurant in the South, the waitress told him that they did not serve Negroes. He replied, "That's okay. I don't eat Negroes." Camilo Pasqual was born in Havana, Cuba, where the Washington Senators had their top minor-league team from 1954 to 1960. Pasqual was a top pitcher for the Senators and the Minnesota Twins, winning 174 games in his career. In 1955 Roberto Clemente made his debut with the Pittsburgh Pirates at the age of twenty. He was Most Valuable Player in the National League in 1966 and led the Pirates to World Championships in 1960 and 1971. He had 3,000 hits before dying in a plane crash in 1972 while trying to bring provisions to the victims of an earthquake in Nicaragua. He and Aparicio were elected to the Baseball Hall of Fame.

The New Transience of Baseball

For the first half of the twentieth century, each league had eight baseball teams, each located in the same city for all those years. In 1953 the Boston Braves relocated to Milwaukee, Wisconsin, where they had their top minor-league team. The

Braves played in an old ballpark and were limited in their parking and other facility growth by their closeness to Boston University. In addition, the Red Sox seemed to be far more popular, so the Braves moved to Wisconsin, where they were welcomed with open arms.

In 1954 the St. Louis Browns of the American League moved their franchise to Baltimore and became the Orioles. The Browns were consistent losers in the 1950s and drew few fans. They were "second-class citizens" compared to their NL rivals, the St. Louis Cardinals. The Browns' move was the impetus for the Philadelphia Athletics, who relocated in 1955 to Kansas City (later moving to Oakland in 1968). These moves all reflected economics, in that the teams that moved were not doing well financially in their present locations. Two of the three were in cities with two teams and the changing demographics of the United States indicated that northeastern cities would continue to grow far more slowly than cities in the South and the West, the so-called Sun Belt.

In 1957 the migration of baseball teams took a very unexpected turn. Both the New York Giants and the Brooklyn Dodgers announced that they were leaving New York and moving to the West Coast, to San Francisco and Los Angeles, respectively. Both teams were highly popular and in the largest metropolitan region in the United States so this was not like the prior moves of the 1950s. Dodgers owner Walter O'Malley wanted to build a larger, new stadium in Brooklyn, but was thwarted by the city. After much negotiation, he decided that moving to Los Angeles was more attractive and he convinced his fellow owner, Horace Stoneham of the Giants, to also move. That way there could be two teams on the West Coast and road trips by other teams would not be so economically inefficient.

The movement of the two teams paralleled the enormous growth and movement of the American population since World War II. Los Angeles had grown from just under 2 million in 1950 to what would become 2.5 million by 1960, nearly a 25 percent increase. Though San Francisco had not grown much, since it is a relatively small city in area, the Bay area would jump from 2 million to over 2.5 million by 1960. Both areas continued to grow as more Americans migrated west and large numbers of immigrants chose to come to these areas, often from Mexico or other Latin American nations.

The abandonment of New York was not accepted well in the New York area, as one might expect, and Major League Baseball promised that a new NL franchise would be established there as soon as baseball chose to expand. That happened in 1962 when the Houston Colt .45s and the New York Mets were added to the National League. In their first year in Los Angeles the Dodgers nearly doubled their attendance from 1957 and the Giants did the same in San Francisco.

Media and Baseball

Baseball was widely covered in U.S. newspapers, although in the 1950s the number of daily newspapers began a slow but steady decline that continues to this day. Readership dropped precipitously. Many newspapers combined with other dailies. New York City, which had as many as ten daily papers in 1950, had only three (or four if one counts the New York edition of the *Wall Street Journal*) by the end of the decade. One of the biggest reasons for this decline was the rise of television and television news, brief though were the news broadcasts. Many busy Americans seemed to allot less time for reading about the news and were satisfied to get the summaries that television provided. Pictures took precedence over in-depth reading. Radio listening had not seemed to affect newspaper readership nearly as much.

Radio, however, was an important component to the continued popularity of baseball. Every team had at least one radio station that covered all or many of the team's games and many teams had "networks" of radio stations to allow listeners outside of the metropolitan area to hear game coverage. Some stations even provided simulcasts of games, a holdover from the earlier days of radio. In a simulcast, a radio engineer at a station would use the ticker-tape wire service like the Associated Press. Specific game information would be given to an announcer who would pretend to be at the game, giving "play by play" coverage. The announcer would be aided by people in the studio, who would provide sound effects to replicate the sound of a bat hitting a ball, or play an audiotape of crowd noises. It was quaint and harmless and seemed to bring the game into people's homes.

By the end of the decade such make-believe coverage was unnecessary as technology provided easier switching and hook-ups to get even distant games broadcast live. One of the great inventions of the time that brought baseball to people wherever they were was the transistor radio. People on the move could now follow the action of their favorite teams, no matter where they might be. By far the most popular games to listen to were the annual World Series contests, played in October, which pitted the NL champions against the AL champions. With only eight teams in each league and no playoffs, there was just the World Series, which took less than two weeks to complete in early October.

The Transistor Radio

Nothing made the World Series as accessible to baseball-crazed youngsters in the 1950s as the invention and development of the transistor radio. In 1953 the first transistorized portable radio was displayed in Dusseldorf, Germany, at an electronics fair. The radio operated with a flashlight battery and a transistor-based radio receiver, as opposed to the standard vacuum-tube radio that required large, heavy batteries. Transistor radios were first made commercially available in 1954, but were expensive ($50, over $350 in today's dollar equivalent). At that same time the largest Japanese electronics firms, like Sony and Mitsubishi, were developing their own transistor radios, which were cheaper to make and sell, because of cheaper labor costs and materials. In 1957 these models became available in the United States for about $30; prices fell to under $20 by the early 1960s. The radios came with earphones and were pocket-sized. In other words, they were ideal for listening to the World Series secretly while in school. Because of the radios' newness, most teachers were unfamiliar with them and their capacities and the most electronically savvy youngsters could hear the big games while seeming to be concentrating on their schoolwork.

The transistor radio remained popular throughout the rest of the twentieth century, although teachers became more aware of them. Some teachers even allowed them if students stayed on task in the classroom. Their in-school use for listening to the World Series became moot when the games were moved from day to night games beginning in 1971. One estimate suggests that at least 7 billion transistor radios are in existence today. The radios began to decline in popularity with the rise of portable digital audio players, though they remain popular for listening to news, weather, and emergency alerts.

Beginning in 1947, the World Series was televised, although there were only a few hundred thousand television sets in American homes. Since then, the series has continued to be televised on various networks over the years. In the 1950s, the Gillette Razor Company was the primary sponsor of this, and many other top sporting events. World Series games were played during the day so viewership was not as high as it might have been in evenings, but that was not a primary consideration. It was not until 1971 that some World Series games would be played at night at television sponsors' request.

The Seasons of the 1950s

The 1950s were dominated by one team, the American League's New York Yankees. From 1949 to 1964, they won fourteen pennants and nine world championships. The Yankees were led by the legends, Joe DiMaggio and Mickey Mantle, and Hall of Fame players Yogi Berra, Whitey Ford, Johnny Mize, Phil Rizzuto, Elston Howard, and Enos Slaughter. Casey Stengel, their manager from 1949 to 1960, also was elected to the Hall of Fame. The Yankees had the best players, but they also had a great psychological advantage, that is, they were sure that they would win the pennant and other teams were not. And the Yankees were usually right, as evidenced by their record. Some players acquired in the twilight of their careers somehow were rejuvenated by becoming Yankees and they became stars once again. Stengel platooned his players and went with hunches on who should be in his lineup on any given day. More often than not, he was correct. In 1954, when the Yankees did not win the league title, they still won 103 games, which would almost always be enough to ensure a pennant. The Cleveland Indians had a remarkable year, winning 111 games, the AL record for a 154-game season and the best winning percentage ever in the league.

In 1950 the Korean War had not yet begun to siphon players from the leagues as would gradually happen over the next three years. One of the most prominent was Ted Williams, a veteran of World War II who was recalled to active duty as a fighter pilot at the age of thirty-three in 1952 and flew thirty-eight combat missions in Korea over the next two years. When Williams returned, he never hit below .328 and won two batting titles over the next five years. Many other players volunteered or were drafted into the service and fought in Korea.

The Yankees won the AL pennant in 1950 in a close battle with the Detroit Tigers. It was Joe DiMaggio's last full year as a player. DiMaggio, known as the "Yankee Clipper," had starred for the team since joining the Yankees as a twenty-one-year-old in 1936. He was the Most Valuable Player in the league three times and hit in fifty-six straight games in 1941. DiMaggio had 32 home runs and 122 runs batted in for 1950 and led the Yankees to the pennant. He was slowed at times by heel injuries, but played in 137 games. The Yankees met the Philadelphia Phillies in the World Series. It was the first Phillies' pennant since 1915 and only their second ever, a huge surprise keyed by the "Whiz Kids," namely, Robin Roberts, Richie Ashburn, Curt Simmons, Granny Hamner, and Del Ennis. The Phillies' elation was short-lived, as the Yankees swept them in four games.

The next year saw one of the most dramatic pennant races in history as the New York Giants came from 13$\frac{1}{2}$ games back in August to defeat the Brooklyn

Dodgers in a playoff for the pennant. The Most Valuable Players were two New York catchers, Yogi Berra of the Yankees and Roy Campanella of the Dodgers. After the dramatic playoff victory, the Giants seemed ready to topple the champion Yankees. Both teams had exciting rookies who would fashion Hall of Fame careers, Willie Mays for the Giants and Mickey Mantle for the Yankees. The series would also be the last games of Joe DiMaggio's career; he retired at age thirty-six. The Giants took a two-games-to-one lead, but the Yankees won three straight to repeat as World Series champion for the third year in a row.

The 1952 season saw the Yankees victorious once again, in a tight contest with Cleveland. The Dodgers (who lost Don Newcombe to the military) surprised the Giants (without Willie Mays, also drafted into the service) and topped the Giants and Cardinals for the pennant. Stan Musial of the Cardinals won his sixth batting

"The Shot Heard Round the World"

No baseball game in the 1950s is more renowned than game 3 of the National League playoffs, October 3, 1951. The Brooklyn Dodgers held a 13$\frac{1}{2}$-game lead over the New York Giants in mid-August. Besides the rivalry of teams from two New York boroughs, there was the additional intensity created by Giants' manager Leo Durocher. He had been the Dodgers' manager from 1939 until the middle of 1948, when he clashed with the Dodgers' general manager, Branch Rickey. Rickey and the Giants worked out a deal that let Durocher out of his contract and allowed him to sign with the Giants. Beating the Dodgers became of great importance to Durocher.

The Giants won thirty-seven of the final forty-four games to catch the Dodgers, who went 26–22. At that time playoffs only occurred when two teams tied for the pennant, and the playoffs were considered an extension of the regular season. The playoffs were a best-of-three series and the Giants took game 1, 3–1 as Bobby Thomson hit a two-run home run.

Thomson was one of the few European-born players of the time, coming from Glasgow, Scotland. His family immigrated to Staten Island, New York, when he was a child. Thomson began his career in 1946 at the age of twenty-two and hit twenty-four or more homers for the Giants in six of his seven full seasons with them. The losing pitcher in game 1 was Ralph Branca, the Dodgers' starting pitcher.

The Dodgers triumphed easily in game 2, 10–0 behind rookie pitcher Clem Labine. In game 3, played in the Polo Grounds, the Giants' home field, Brooklyn took an early lead of 1–0. The Giants tied it in the seventh, but the Dodgers got three runs in the eighth to lead 4–1. Don Newcombe, the Dodgers' ace pitcher, tired in the ninth, since he was pitching on only two days rest. The Giants scored one run and had one out with two men on when the Dodgers manager Charlie Dressen finally pulled Newcombe. Surprisingly, he inserted Branca, the game 1 loser, who had had trouble with Bobby Thomson, the next batter, all year. Thomson had hit several home runs off Branca, but Dressen's pitching staff was tired and there were few other choices.

Thomson took the first pitch for a strike. The second pitch was intended to push Thomson off the plate, but the ball drifted a bit and Thomson yanked it down the short left-field line. As the ball carried into the stands, the Giants' local radio announcer immortalized the blow with his excited shouts of "There's a long drive, it's gonna be, I believe … The Giants win the pennant! The Giants win the pennant! The Giants win the pennant! The Giants win the pennant!"

title, but the MVP award went to Hank Sauer of the Chicago Cubs. Bobby Shantz, who won twenty-four games for the fourth-place Philadelphia Athletics, was the MVP in the American League. The Yankees topped the Dodgers in seven games in the World Series to win their fourth straight championship, only the second team in history to do so.

One of the unusual events of 1953 was the decision by the Cincinnati Reds to alter their name, in response to the McCarthy-era fears of Communists. The Reds officially became the Redlegs, retaining that name until 1959, when they reverted to their former name. No matter what they were called, the Reds were still a bad team; they finished in sixth place, thirty-seven games behind the Dodgers, who won the pennant by thirteen games. Once again they would meet the Yankees, who had also won easily, by $8^{1}/_{2}$ games over the Indians. The Indians, however, had the league's Most Valuable Player. He was Al Rosen, one of the few Jewish American major leaguers. Rosen received all twenty-four of the first-place votes after leading the league in home runs, runs batted in, total bases, runs, and slugging average.

Rosen's counterpart in the National League was Roy Campanella, the Dodgers' catcher, who won his second MVP award after leading the league in runs batted in with 142 and finishing third in home runs and slugging. He also played the most difficult position, catcher. Campanella and his teammates wanted to end their run of losses to the Yankees in the World Series. The Yankees took the first two games in Yankee Stadium, but the Dodgers came back to win the next two before the Yankees closed out the series with two more victories. The Yankees became the first and only team to win five consecutive world championships and the Dodger fans uttered their famous cry, "Wait 'til next year!"

The Cleveland Indians broke the Yankees' streak in 1954, setting a new record for victories, and were favored to top the New York Giants in the World Series. The Giants were led by Willie Mays, best in the league with a .345 batting average and MVP winner. He also made the greatest catch in World Series history in game 1. With the score tied at 2–2 and two Indian runners on base with nobody out, Vic Wertz hit a smash to the deepest part of the Polo Grounds, which was 483 feet to dead center. Mays caught the ball at full speed, his back to the infield, about 450 feet from home. He turned, fired the ball in, and neither runner could even advance. The Indians failed to score in the inning; the Giants won the game in the tenth. The game 1 loss deflated the Indians and they were swept by the Giants in four games.

The next two years saw a return to Dodger-Yankee battles in the World Series. For the Dodgers, 1955 was "next year" as they finally defeated the Yankees in seven games for the championship. Campanella and Berra, the opposing catchers, were again the league MVPs, the third time for both. The Yankees reversed the outcome in 1956, which was the year Mickey Mantle won the triple crown (leading the league in batting average, home runs, and runs batted in) and the MVP award, his first. The highlight of the series was game 5, when Don Larsen of the Yankees pitched a perfect game. The win gave the Yankees a three-games-to-two lead, but the Dodgers tied the series with a ten-inning 1–0 victory. New York came back to crush the Dodgers, 9–0, to win the championship.

For the next two years, the Milwaukee Braves were NL champions, playing against the Yankees both times in the World Series. Milwaukee had a pennant winner just five years after the Braves arrived in town, and the city was ecstatic. The

The Perfect Game

There have been only seventeen perfect games in major-league baseball history and only one in the postseason, game 5 of the 1956 World Series, played on October 8, 1956. A perfect game is one where no player on a team reaches first base. The hero of that game was Don Larsen, a player with a lifetime record of thirty wins and forty losses in four regular seasons. On that October day, however, everything he threw went where he intended. There were only two close plays and a questionable third strike on the twenty-seventh and last batter, Dale Mitchell. Larsen was opposed by Dodger pitcher Sal Maglie, who gave up only five hits in the game.

Larsen's control was so good that he had a three-balls count on only one batter, Dodger shortstop Pee Wee Reese. In the second inning, Jackie Robinson, playing in his final game, hit a smash off the third baseman's glove that ricocheted directly to the shortstop, who threw out Robinson. In the fifth inning, Gil Hodges hit a long drive to left center that Mickey Mantle managed to snare with a one-handed running catch.

Baseball superstition says that teammates don't mention a no-hitter in the dugout, but Larsen talked about it. His teammates, however, either responded with silence or told him to "shut up." Larsen said that he even ducked into the tunnel connecting the dugout to the clubhouse for a cigarette between the seventh and eight innings. In the ninth Larsen got the first two batters easily, then had a one-ball, two-strike count on Dale Mitchell before throwing a ball that the umpire called a strike (though most observers thought that it was high) and ending the game. Catcher Yogi Berra ran to the mound and leaped into Larsen's arms, a shot often reproduced in baseball anthologies.

Larsen received the MVP award for the series, which the Yankees took, four games to three. He retired twelve years later with a lifetime mark of eighty-one wins and ninety-one losses. As one sportswriter called it, "The imperfect man pitched the perfect game."

1957 Braves were led by veteran pitcher Warren Spahn, who would retire as the all-time leading left-handed pitcher in baseball with 363 wins; Ed Mathews, who was the game's top third baseman and would hit 512 home runs in his career; and Henry "Hank" Aaron, who led the league in home runs and won the MVP award. Aaron would go on to be baseball's all-time home-run king, until his record was broken in 2007 by Barry Bonds.

The Yankees were led by Mickey Mantle, who won his second consecutive MVP award, edging Ted Williams who had hit .388, the closest anyone had come to hitting .400 since Williams himself had done so in 1941. Both teams had won their league races by eight games, but the Yankees' experience made them the Series favorites. Nevertheless the Braves edged the Yankees four games to three, as pitcher Lou Burdette tied a World Series record with three victories in one World Series.

Near the end of the season the Giants and Dodgers announced their moves to the West Coast and it was a sad end of the season for New York City baseball fans. The next year the Dodgers debuted in the Los Angeles Coliseum, a building made for the Olympics of 1932 and used for football. It seated over 90,000, but the baseball dimensions were unusual, and the Dodgers commenced building a new stadium that was ready in the Chavez Ravine area for the opening day of 1962. The Dodgers finished in seventh in 1958. The Giants moved to Seals Stadium in San

Francisco where the Pacific Coast League Seals had played. The stadium only seated 22,500, but a new ballpark, Candlestick Park, was ready for occupancy in 1960.

For the first time in many years, neither MVP was from the pennant-winning team. Jackie Jensen of the Red Sox won in the American League, and Ernie Banks of the Chicago Cubs, who finished tied for fifth, won the NL award. The World Series again went to seven games, with the Yankees regaining the championship from the Braves.

The last year of the 1950s produced some unusual events. For the first time in five years, the Yankees did not win the pennant. Instead, the Chicago White Sox with speed and pitching edged the Cleveland Indians for the AL title. The double-play combination of Luis Aparicio and Nelson Fox was the heart of the White Sox and Fox won the MVP award. Ernie Banks won the MVP award for the second straight year after hitting forty-seven home runs. The Dodgers rebounded from seventh to win the pennant. The Dodgers tied the Milwaukee Braves and the Dodgers won the pennant in a two-game playoff. The Dodgers had no big stars, but their team play was excellent.

San Francisco Giants' centerfielder Willie Mays shows his batting form in the eighth inning of the game with American League during the All-Star game in Pittsburgh, July 7, 1959. Mays walloped a triple to the right center that won the game. Baltimore Orioles' catcher Gus Triandos is seen at left. (AP / Wide World Photos)

In the World Series, the White Sox pounded the Dodgers 11–0 in game 1, but the Dodgers won the championship in six games. The Dodgers were still playing in the Los Angeles Memorial Coliseum and the contests there set records each day for major-league attendance with more than 92,000 fans attending, records that will never be broken.

The next year (1960), the Pittsburgh Pirates won their first pennant since 1927 and went on to defeat the Yankees in seven games on a dramatic ninth-inning home run by Bill Mazeroski. Dick Groat of the Pirates and Roger Maris of the Yankees were voted league MVPs.

By the end of the 1950s baseball was ready to consider expansion, confident that the path followed by the Dodgers and Giants, that is, moving west, was the direction for major-league baseball. There was also the matter of fulfilling the promise to New York City to have a new NL team in the nation's largest city. These actions would all be taken in the early 1960s.

Basketball

College Basketball

College basketball had grown tremendously in popularity in the 1940s, but the revelation of point shaving at top universities in 1951 disgusted many people. It took until the end of the decade to recapture lost fans and to return college basketball to a position of trust among the fans and the media. Of the two postseason tournaments, the National Invitation Tournament (NIT) and the National Collegiate Athletic Association (NCAA) tournament, the former was both larger and more prestigious. It was possible for a squad to play in both tournaments, which both Bradley and City College of New York (CCNY) did. By 1959 the NCAA tournament was up to twenty-three teams and viewed as the better tournament than the NIT with its twelve teams, most of which were conference runners-up rather than champions. College basketball drew millions of fans, but most coverage was regional. Unlike football, there were intersectional rivalries, many of which played out in tournaments held between semesters, as well as before league seasons began in January. Thus, there were greater opportunities for fans and media people to see teams from around the country, even though television coverage was not national in scope.

The biggest story of 1950 was CCNY's victories in both the NCAA and the NIT tournaments, but this was quickly overwhelmed by the revelations of point shaving. Point shaving is not throwing a game as such. Rather, it involves players from a team trying to keep a game closer than the point spread. So, if a team is favored by ten points and they only win by six, people who bet on the underdog team win money because the winning team did not beat the point spread. The point-shaving scandals were a direct result of big gamblers paying off certain players to keep games closer. With that done, the gamblers could bet either for or against the spread (depending on who was paid off) and win thousands of dollars.

The scandals involved some of the top programs and players in the country in 1950, including Long Island University (LIU), coached by Hall of Famer Clair Bee; CCNY, coached by Hall of Famer Nat Holman; Bradley University, coached by Forrest "Fordy" Anderson; the University of Kentucky, coached by Hall of Famer Adolph Rupp; University of Toledo, coached by Gerard Bush; New York

CCNY Does a Double

In March of 1950 both Bradley University and CCNY entered the NIT and the NCAA tournaments. This was possible because the NIT ended on March 18 and the NCAA ran from March 23 to March 28. The previous year the University of Kentucky had entered both tournaments, won the NCAA, but lost in the quarterfinals of the NIT. CCNY was not even ranked in the Top 20 in the basketball polls, but they were able to get into the NIT when some teams chose not to enter. The Beavers were 17–5 and a local favorite.

CCNY was coached by Nat Holman, one of the Original Celtics of the 1920s. That team was voted into the Hall of Fame as a unit in 1959. Holman's players were all from the New York area, most directly from the city itself. CCNY had two African American starters, Ed Warner and Floyd Lane, with Ed Warner and Irwin Dambrot the top scorers and rebounders. There were twelve teams in the tournament, staged at the most famous venue in basketball, Madison Square Garden. CCNY was not seeded so they needed to play in the first round, where they beat the defending NIT champion University of San Francisco easily. Then they played 1949 NCAA champion Kentucky and won by thirty-nine, one of the worst defeats ever for an Adolph Rupp–coached team. In the semifinals, CCNY topped number 6–ranked Duquesne by ten, then defeated number 1–ranked Bradley in the finals, 69–61. Ed Warner of CCNY was MVP.

The NCAA tournament consisted of only eight teams and they were divided into two regions. In the Eastern Region, which was played in Madison Square Garden that year, CCNY edged Ohio State, 56–55, and then topped North Carolina State, 78 to 73. In the Western Regional, Bradley had beaten BYU and Baylor in Kansas City to win the right to play CCNY. For the only time in the decade the NCAA finals were played in New York City, a decided advantage for the CCNY Beavers. In a tense contest, CCNY topped Bradley for the second time in ten days, 71–68, to claim the NCAA championship, the only time that this was ever accomplished. Irwin Dambrot was voted Most Outstanding Player and coach Nat Holman was carried off the court in triumph.

A year later a number of CCNY players were found guilty of point shaving and the school reassigned Holman, and moved to de-emphasize basketball. The Beavers would never be a top basketball program ever again, but in March, 1950 they did the seemingly impossible.

University, coached by Hall of Famer Howard Cann; and Manhattan College, coached by Ken Norton. Top players involved in the point shaving were fined and/or prohibited from playing professional basketball, and a few served prison time. The effects were felt throughout the sports world. Some of the schools moved to de-emphasize their big-time basketball programs, such as LIU, CCNY, and Manhattan. Some coaches, though not implicated, were removed from their positions since they were seen as somewhat complicit by not having control of their teams. College basketball struggled to clear its institutional reputation, which took most of the next ten years. Gambling, however, on these and other sporting events did not go away; it merely became more hidden.

Media and College Basketball

Most college basketball interest was regional. Beginning in the mid-1950s regional television packages provided coverage of the top leagues like the Big Ten, the Pacific Coast Conference, the Big Eight, and the Atlantic Coast Conference. There was also selected coverage of various teams in the Northeast, but there were no major leagues at that time. Most eastern teams were independents and it was not until the 1970s that the Atlantic 10 and Big East conferences came into existence. Radio coverage was extensive but, again, there was no national radio network coverage. Most colleges had their own announcers and some, like the University of Kentucky, had a large regional network throughout Kentucky, southern Indiana, and southern Illinois. The two major tournaments, the NIT, held at Madison Square Garden in New York, and the NCAA, held at various sites (five of the years the finals were in Kansas City) were not televised until the mid-1950s and then only the championship contests. The NIT was only televised in selected regions through the 1950s. Newspaper coverage was intense throughout the period in both large and small daily papers.

Ethnicity and College Basketball

Many of the top college basketball conferences were either barred by law, or custom, from admitting African Americans, into the middle of the 1950s. The Southeastern Conference (SEC) remained segregated until the late1960s and the Atlantic Coast Conference (ACC) nearly as long. The Big Ten and the various Pacific Coast leagues had African American players in the 1940s and many of the Big Eight (later the Big 12) schools played African Americans starting in the 1950s.

Until 1955 no NCAA champion had more than one African American starter and most had none. The concerted efforts at recruiting African Americans changed that. In 1955 the University of San Francisco Dons, led by Bill Russell and K.C. Jones, won all but one game and swept to the NCAA title. Russell and Jones were joined by Hal Perry in the starting lineup, the first time a major college power had started three African Americans. Their disciplined play belied the inaccurate stereotypes that some prejudiced observers had about how African Americans played basketball. The next year, USF went undefeated and won the NCAA tournament again. This was a big boost for exploding those aforementioned stereotypes, and for the recruitment of top African American players at major college powers. In 1957 Wilt Chamberlain, the most highly recruited schoolboy in history, took his University of Kansas team to the NCAA finals, but they were defeated in triple overtime by the University of North Carolina. Chamberlain, a 7'2" African American center, was constantly triple-teamed by the smaller UNC players. This was Chamberlain's sophomore year and, at that time, players were required to play on a freshmen team their first year in college. Chamberlain left the University of Kansas after his junior year, but he and Bill Russell would impact professional basketball from the late 1950s through the 1960s.

Chamberlain was named Most Outstanding Player of the NCAA tournament in 1957, just as Russell had been in 1955. Hal Lear, a guard from Temple, won the honor in 1956 and Elgin Baylor of Seattle University received the award in 1958. All are African Americans. The NIT champions in the 1950s were mostly lacking in African American starters with a few exceptions like Ed Warner of CCNY in 1950, Walter Dukes of Seton Hall in 1953, Sihugo Green of Duquesne in 1955, Tony Jackson of St. Johns in 1959, all of whom were selected as the Most Valuable Player in the NIT.

In the 1960s there would be a great rush to recruit African Americans as a result of the foundation that these black pioneers had laid in the 1950s. In 1963 a team with four African American starters (Loyola of Chicago) won the NCAA title, and in 1966 Texas Western won the NCAA tournament with five African American starters.

Women were not represented on NCAA basketball teams until the 1970s, their inclusion coming largely as a result of Title IX of the Education Amendments Act of 1972. Some National Association of Intercollegiate Athletics (NAIA) teams like Nashville Business College and Wayland Baptist University had top women's basketball teams in the decade.

Professional Basketball

In 1949 the National Basketball League (NBL), begun in 1937, and the Basketball Association of America (BAA), founded in 1946, merged into one new league, the National Basketball Association (NBA). The newly created league had seventeen teams, which was more teams than could be supported economically at that time. Within a year, the league had lost six teams and was a manageable eleven teams located within the Northeast and Upper Midwest of the United States. This was where the largest number of people resided and where basketball was the most popular. The league had one franchise move and another fold the next year so it was at ten teams in 1951–52. In 1953 another franchise folded and another followed in 1954. Beginning in 1955 the NBA remained at eight teams for the rest of the decade, but there were franchise shifts during this period. At the beginning of the 1959–60 season, the Eastern Division had teams in Boston, New York, Philadelphia, and Syracuse, all of which had been in those cities since the NBL-BAA merger. The Western Division consisted of four teams, three of which had relocated since 1950. These were the St. Louis Hawks, the Minneapolis Lakers, the Detroit Pistons, and the Cincinnati Royals. By 1972 three of these had relocated, with Detroit the only stable franchise.

Geography and the NBA

As just noted, the NBA was quite "fluid" during the 1950s. Team moves reflected economics, that is, movement was needed to improve team profit margins. That might mean moving to a city that had never embraced pro basketball, but was growing (a kind of westward expansion that paralleled the changing demographic of the United States), or it might mean moving to a city that was simply bigger and could attract a larger fan base.

In 1950 although both Baltimore and Washington had teams, the local population was not growing as fast as other areas. There was growth in suburban areas, but there was reluctance to return to the city center to view basketball at night, and the cities' populations were shrinking. The owners could not find buyers and there was no assurance of profit from moving to an unknown city, so both franchises folded, Washington after a year, Baltimore after four years.

The West had greater geographical volatility. The team in Moline, Illinois, drew well, but felt that the escalating costs of maintaining the team required a bigger venue in a bigger city. Thus, in 1951 the franchise relocated to Milwaukee, Wisconsin, as the Milwaukee Hawks. Four years later, owner Ben Kerner decided that more money could be made at in an even larger city and moved his franchise to St. Louis, where they would remain for the next thirteen years. The NBA remained, basically, a northeastern and upper midwestern league through the 1950s.

Ethnicity and Pro Basketball

The NBL had integrated as early as 1942, but the BAA was never integrated. The NBL had had an all African American squad in the league in 1948–49, but the Dayton Rens (actually the New York Renaissance squad playing out of Dayton) had disbanded after the 1948–49 season. So the new NBA, with nine former NBL clubs and eight former BAA clubs, had no African Americans in 1949–50. The next season, however, New York Knicks owner Ned Irish signed Nate "Sweetwater" Clifton; the Boston Celtics drafted and signed Chuck Cooper from Duquesne University; the Washington Capitols signed Earl Lloyd from West Virginia State to a contract and Hank DeZonie, the former Ren who had played for Dayton in 1948–49, was signed by the Tri-Cities Blackhawks and played in five games near the end of the season.

Though there were difficulties in integrating the league, the problems were less than Jackie Robinson had faced in 1947 in major-league baseball, for a number of reasons. First, three years had passed since baseball had integrated. Second, many of the white players in the NBA had gone to college and had had some contact with African Americans. Third, black and white basketball teams had been playing against each other since at least the 1920s. There was a greater respect for their respective abilities as basketball players.

This is not to pretend that there were not problems for these first four pioneers and the African Americans that followed them into the NBA. Many of the cities where they played still practiced aspects of Jim Crow laws, with Baltimore, Indianapolis, and Washington the most pronounced. This would affect hotels and restaurants. Fans made racial slurs in almost every NBA city. Finally, many NBA teams played exhibitions in various other cities, and those below the Mason-Dixon line sometimes prohibited blacks and whites from taking the court together. These practices continued even after the *Brown* decision of 1954 and made some African American players feel that they needed to speak out regarding these kinds of discriminatory practices, which were the basis for the civil rights movement in the 1950s and 1960s.

In 1951 Don Barksdale from UCLA joined the Baltimore Bullets, but Earl Lloyd was out of the league in the military. New players were Davage Minor and Bob Wilson. Lloyd returned in 1952, but only Blaine Denning, who played one game that year, was a new African American in the NBA. The next year, 1953, Ray Felix from LIU became the starting center for Baltimore and was named Rookie of the Year and two other players, Rollen Hans and Isaac Walthour, appeared briefly in the NBA. There were no African Americans on any of the Western Division teams other than Walthour's four games for Milwaukee. Ken McBride, Jim Tucker, Bob Knight, and Jackie Moore entered the NBA in 1954, but all were out within two years. African American players were added in 1955 to both the Knicks (who had three of the twelve African Americans in the league) the Pistons, the Lakers, and the Royals. The Knicks had selected Walter Dukes from Seton Hall and the Royals drafted Maurice Stokes from St. Francis of Pennsylvania. Stokes was terrific, averaging more than sixteen points and sixteen rebounds per game and being named Rookie of the Year for 1955–56. He became one of the top players in the league and set a league rebounding record, but was stricken by posttraumatic encephalopathy after hitting his head in a fall in a game in Minneapolis, late in his third year in the NBA. Stokes went into a coma three days later and recovered enough to live a life as an invalid, cared for by a former teammate, Jack Twyman. Stokes died in 1970 at age thirty-six.

In 1956 the NBA had fifteen African Americans and the most important was Bill Russell, the former star of the USF NCAA championship team, who entered the league in December after competing in the Olympics in Australia. Russell changed the NBA dramatically and became the greatest winner in the NBA. An unbelievable defender, he specialized in blocking shots and tipping them to his teammates to start fast breaks. He also was a rebounding demon, who broke Stokes's year-old record for rebounds in a year in 1957–58. That year Russell also led the Celtics to the NBA finals for the second straight year.

The number of African Americans in the NBA remained at fifteen in 1957–58, but the players had changed. Philadelphia added Woody Sauldsberry, who became the Rookie of the Year and the first of five African Americans in a row to win the award. At this point, seven of the eight NBA clubs had at least one African American; the St. Louis Hawks were the only one without one. (They did have Worthy Patterson on their roster for four games.) Ben Kerner, the Hawks' owner, was not sure that St. Louis, a border city, would be very receptive to this "social change." The next year (1958–59) the Hawks obtained Si Green in a trade with the Royals and a number of other African Americans entered the league, most notably, future Hall of Famers Hal Greer with Syracuse, Elgin Baylor with Minneapolis (named Rookie of the Year), and K.C. Jones for Boston. Green's trade and Stokes' loss left the Royals with only rookie Wayne Embry.

In the last year of the decade (1959–60), the NBA had twenty-four African Americans on the rosters of the eight teams with three or four on at least six of the teams. Over the next decade the ratio would continue to grow. In 1959, the most famous of these players was Wilt Chamberlain, who came into the NBA after playing a year for the Harlem Globetrotters. His impact was immediate as he shattered the league scoring record (37.6 points per game) as well as the league rebounding record (27 rebounds per game).

The NBA Seasons of the 1950s

The NBA's first league champion in the seventeen-team league was the Minneapolis Lakers, led by George Mikan. The next year the Rochester Royals beat the Lakers in the NBA Finals to win their only NBA title. For the next three years (1952, 1953, 1954) Mikan and his Lakers won the NBA title. Then Mikan retired at age twenty-nine. He did return two years later for thirty-one games, but then retired permanently. The Syracuse Nationals, led by Dolph Schayes, won the title in 1956.

The championship situation was considerably altered by Bill Russell's entrance to the league in December of 1956. He and the Celtics won the title eleven of the next thirteen years, beginning with 1956–57. The following year Russell was injured in the NBA finals and the St. Louis Hawks and Bob Pettit were able to claim the NBA championship. The Celtics closed the decade with a title in 1959 and won the next eight years in a row.

The Best Basketball Player of the Early Twentieth Century

In the 1950s, basketball writers and coaches voted on the top player of the first half of the twentieth century and George Mikan won easily. This would have been hard to fathom when Mikan graduated from high school in 1942. He had played sparingly in high school at Quigley Prep in Chicago and Joliet Central, from which he graduated. His only asset was height, but he was clumsy and had little shooting skill. What he did have was indomitable determination and intelligence.

Mikan wanted to go to Notre Dame, but was rebuffed by their coach, who suggested that he enroll and play at DePaul University in Chicago. Mikan did and his coach there, a twenty-eight-year-old named Ray Meyer, saw that Mikan had great potential if he would agree to work hard. Hard work was never George Mikan's problem. Long hours in the gym on specially designed drills turned Mikan into a star and he in turn turned DePaul into a champion. Behind Mikan, DePaul won the NIT in 1945, at that time the most prestigious tournament in college basketball. He was college player of the year in both 1945 and 1946 and he led the nation in scoring both of those years.

Mikan's superior height (6'10") and agility allowed him to block balls before they went into the basket and led to the creation of the goal-tending rule. His dominance in the center lane also led to a rule that widened it from six to twelve feet.

At the conclusion of his senior season, Mikan signed with the Chicago Gears of the National Basketball League and led them to the 1946–47 NBL playoffs, which they won, defeating Rochester in the Finals. The next year, however, the Chicago Gears' owner decided to start his own league, which collapsed within a month. The Gears players were then put into a special draft and Mikan became a Minneapolis Laker. It was a great union.

Starting in 1947–48, Mikan led the Lakers to titles in the NBL (1947–48), the BAA (1948–49), and four titles in the NBA (1949–50, 1951–52, 1952–53, 1953–54). Because the NBA did not institute a Most Valuable Player award until Mikan had retired, he only won such an award in the NBL. When he retired he was the all-time leading scorer in the NBA in both points and points per game.

Mikan briefly coached the Lakers, but spent the majority of his career after the NBA as a lawyer and running a travel agency. He had attended law school while playing for the Chicago Gears and did very well in real estate investments. In 1967 he was instrumental in the formation of the American Basketball Association and became its first commissioner, remaining in that office until 1969.

In 1959 Mikan was elected to the Basketball Hall of Fame and was also named one of the NBA's Greatest Fifty Players ever in 1996. Mikan battled diabetes and other ailments at the end of his life and died at his home in Arizona in 2005 at the age of eighty.

The teams in the league were gaining financial stability, but there were not the enormous profits that would characterize professional sports beginning in the late 1970s. Most of the players held second jobs in the off-season and the top salary was probably that of Bob Cousy of the Celtics, at less than $50,000 per year.

Teams traveled for the most part by train, but by the end of the decade air travel would predominate for the western trips to Minneapolis and St. Louis. Fort Wayne remained a difficult city to get to, even by train, and in 1957 Fort Wayne and Rochester relocated to Detroit and Cincinnati, respectively. Les Harrison, the Royals' owner, had been having troubles making ends meet, and he moved the

Royals in the hope of improving that. Things did get better in Cincinnati, but not enough for him to keep the team, and he sold it in 1959.

Through the 1950s the level of play continued to improve as the players entering the league were bigger, stronger, and faster than their predecessors. Besides the emerging stars like Cousy, Russell, Baylor, Greer, Chamberlain, Pettit, and Schayes, other new talents joined the league. These included Paul Arizin, Tom Heinsohn, Bill Sharman, Cliff Hagan, Jack Twyman, George Yardley, and Tom Gola.

College Football

Bowl Games

Though not nearly as popular as baseball, college football was probably the second most popular sport in the United States in the 1950s. Some of the teams that were most dominant in the decade were Oklahoma, Notre Dame, Texas, Michigan State, Ohio State, and UCLA. Most teams played regionally, and intersectional games were rare. Only in the bowl games was there often assurance that intersectional games would be able to indicate real superiority at the college ranks. Even these games were subject to a number of restrictions. During most of the 1950s many southern or border schools neither allowed African Americans to play on their squads nor would they play teams with African Americans. Until the *Brown v. Board of Education* case of 1954, many of these same schools simply did not allow blacks to enroll, and, even after *Brown*, the "foot dragging" was enormous. Thus, it is difficult in retrospect to truly gauge how good some of these teams were, since they carefully limited with whom they would compete.

Another restriction was self-imposed; some schools simply would not play postseason games. Faculty felt that the season was already long enough or that postseason games were time-consuming and meaningless. The expenses also outweighed any economic or reputational rewards. In addition, some leagues only allowed one team to play in a bowl game, most often the league champion. Thus, the number of bowls played was quite small and the eagerness of some teams to compete in those games was problematic.

The Rose Bowl, the oldest bowl game (started in 1902), pitted the Big Ten champion against the Pacific 8 (or 10) champion beginning in 1947. The Big Ten had one wrinkle, however, not allowing its members to participate two years in a row. Thus, the top team was not always represented. During the 1950s, Ohio State won three Rose Bowls, Michigan State two, Iowa two, Michigan one, and Illinois one. The Big Ten had only one loss in the decade, 1953, when Southern Cal edged Wisconsin.

The Orange Bowl, played in Miami (first year 1933), beginning in 1954, established a relationship with the Big Eight (later the Big 12) that tied the league champion to the Orange Bowl contest, against a highly ranked opponent. Before that, teams were selected at large and were usually highly ranked. (The Associated Press started a college football poll in 1936.) The 1954 Orange Bowl pitted number 1 Maryland against number 4 Oklahoma with the latter winning 7–0. This was in the first year of what would become an amazing forty-seven-game winning streak on the part of Oklahoma that stretched into the 1957 season. The next year Duke beat Nebraska, but for the rest of the decade the Big Eight teams were victorious as Oklahoma won in 1956, 1958, and 1959, and Colorado in 1957. From 1954 to 1958 an ACC team played against the Big Eight team.

The Sugar Bowl, played in New Orleans (begun in 1935), during the 1950s featured the Southeastern Conference (SEC) champion against a top-ranked opponent. In the 1950s, the SEC team won six of the ten games played. In the 1951 Sugar Bowl, Kentucky upset number 1 Oklahoma 13–7. The next year, number 1 Tennessee was upset by Maryland, 28–13.

The Cotton Bowl began in Dallas in 1937 and, beginning in 1942, matched a Southwest Conference (SWC) team against an at-large opponent. For the 1950s, the SWC teams went 5–5 over the decade. The most meaningful Cotton Bowl of the decade may have been the one in 1960, which followed the 1959 season. Number 1 Syracuse played fourth-ranked Texas, and Syracuse defended the poll voters by winning 23–14. The 1950s marked the last decade in which smaller universities would still be ranked in the Top 20 in the college football polls. Major universities and their programs would be overwhelmingly dominant by the end of the decade, a pattern that would continue over the next fifty years and beyond. Schools such as Princeton, Cornell, San Francisco, Yale, and the service academies would largely disappear from these rankings.

Media and College Football

Until the late 1950s the bowl games were not televised; in fact, very few college football games were televised on anything but a regional basis. There was no network package and games on Saturday were shown on various stations recruited by a regional company. Thus, most people in the Southwest saw SWC games and those in the Midwest would generally get Big Ten games, but even those shown were not necessarily the top game, since most conferences had agreements to provide coverage of all of their teams on a somewhat equal basis. Television showed national games only two times a year in this era. One was during Thanksgiving Weekend when a few traditional games were shown such as Texas–Texas A&M or Army-Navy, which sometimes was televised the next weekend. The other televised date was New Year's Day and the bowl games. College football had a huge following, but it was very fractionalized; most people in a region would not have seen teams from other regions play, either in person or on television. There were some notable exceptions like Southern Cal and Notre Dame, a rivalry that began when Knute Rockne was coaching at Notre Dame in the 1920s. Every region had its "big game" and these were well covered by the regional media, both newspapers and radio, but television was problematic until the end of the decade. Thus, Harvard-Yale, Alabama-Auburn, Michigan–Ohio State, Texas–Texas A&M, USC-UCLA, Stanford-California, and Oklahoma-Nebraska, just to name a few, were all well covered by the local print and radio media.

Ethnicity and College Football

Up until World War II, most of the top football conferences had little, if any, access, for African American players. The Big Ten had no rules about segregation, but few African Americans played football there until after World War II. Part of the reason for this was that the percentage of students who went on to college was less than 30 percent until that time and the percentage of blacks going on to college was half of that. Of those, many went to traditionally black colleges or universities. The Pacific Coast Conference (Pac 8) had a slightly better record on recruiting of African

Americans. Also, there were far fewer schools in the West so the likelihood of an African American going to a PCC school was simply greater if the student was from that state.

The Jim Crow laws in the South meant that African Americans were barred from most schools in the SWC, SEC, and ACC. It also meant that schools not bound by such law or practices became more successful as they recruited more and more African Americans, enlarging their pool of potential players.

One indication of these changes was the fact that no Heisman Trophy winners were African Americans until 1961. Beginning a decade later, in 1972, the next eleven Heisman Trophy winners in a row were African Americans. The Outland Trophy, awarded to the nation's best college lineman, was first awarded to an African American in the mid-1950s. These awards, however, were as much based on public relations as abilities, since few people (coaches, fans, players, media) ever got to see players out of their own region until television began carrying more games at the end of the decade.

The coaches of college football had more longevity than the players who left school within four or five years. Thus, the big "stars" were Bud Wilkinson of Oklahoma; Paul "Bear" Bryant of Kentucky, Texas A&M, and Alabama; Woody Hayes of Ohio State; Chalmers "Bump" Elliott of Michigan; Frank Leahy of Notre Dame; Forest Evashevski of Iowa; Lynn "Pappy" Waldorf of California; and Darrell Royal of Texas.

Professional Football

At the beginning of the 1950s, professional football had a limited audience. There was local radio coverage and fans attended games with occasional sellouts, but the overall appeal of the game was limited. By the end of the decade, pro football had surpassed college football in interest and popularity and was nearing the formerly unchallenged popularity of baseball. The biggest reason for this was television, specifically national television. During the early 1950s, the Dumont Television Network carried Saturday night NFL games, but in 1955 the network folded and the games were no longer carried. That same year NBC began broadcasting the NFL championship game, paying $100,000 to the league for the game's television rights. At that time the league was limited in number of teams and real fans of the game.

In 1950 the NFL had absorbed its only rival, the All-American Football Conference (AAFC), which had begun in 1946 with eight teams. By 1949 the league was down to seven teams and some franchises were in financial trouble. The NFL took three of the franchises, the Cleveland Browns, San Francisco 49ers and the Baltimore Colts, making the NFL a thirteen-team league. The league also adopted the "free substitution" rule, which meant that there were no limits on how many players could be substituted and how often. This made the game much faster since players could be fresher and increased interest and popularity of the sport. Only the Los Angeles Rams and the Washington Redskins had local television contracts to televise all of their games, home and away.

The league made two divisions, no longer just based on geography, and each team played twelve games. At the end of the season, the Los Angeles Rams and the Chicago Bears tied for the National Conference title with records of nine wins and three losses. In the American Conference, the Cleveland Browns, late of the AAFC, tied the New York Giants with records of ten wins and two losses each.

Bud Wilkinson and the Streaks of the 1950s

Charles (Bud) Wilkinson (1916–94) was an all-around athlete in high school in Minnesota and went on to star on national championship teams in football at the University of Minnesota, graduating in 1937. After receiving an English degree and working for a time in banking, Wilkinson joined the U.S. Navy in 1943. There he assisted with football coaching and served on an aircraft carrier, When he was discharged he was recruited to be an assistant coach at Oklahoma in 1946 and when the head coach left for Maryland, Wilkinson was appointed head coach and athletic director at the university. He was thirty-one.

In Wilkinson's first year as head coach, the squad went 7–2–1, winning their last five in a row and tying Kansas for their second league title in a row. The Sooners of Oklahoma won the next thirteen titles in a row under Wilkinson. After a loss to Notre Dame in September 1953, the Sooners went on to win every game that they played until November of 1957, when they were upset by Notre Dame once again, 7–0. Their streak of forty-seven straight victories is still the record in college football. Amazingly, the Sooners under Wilkinson had a thirty-one-game winning streak from 1948 to 1950. From 1948 to 1958, Wilkinson's record at Oklahoma was 107–8 with two ties, 91 percent wins. His teams went twelve seasons without losing a conference game and Oklahoma was voted the national champion in football in 1950, 1955, and 1956. In 1954 they defeated number 1 Maryland in the Orange Bowl, but the polls were conducted before bowl games so Oklahoma was only ranked number 4.

In 1956 Wilkinson recruited Prentice Gault, the first African American to be recruited and play football at a major university in the Southwest. The University had waged a long legal battle into the 1950s to remain segregated, so Gault was not universally well received by Wilkinson's players. Wilkinson held firm and Gault became an All-American running back.

President John F. Kennedy appointed Wilkinson as the first director of the President's Council on Physical Fitness. Wilkinson retired as football coach after the 1963 season at the age of forty-seven and a record of 145–29–4, a winning percentage of .815. He ran for the U.S. Senate in 1964, but was defeated and became a football analyst for ABC in 1965. In 1969 he was elected to the College Football Hall of Fame.

Wilkinson was persuaded to return to coaching in 1978 with the St. Louis Cardinals of the NFL, but went only 9–20 in two seasons and was fired. He returned to broadcasting and died in 1994 at the age of seventy-seven.

The Browns had lost to the Giants twice during the regular season, but upset them 8–3 in the playoffs. The Rams topped the Bears, 24–14, to win their division.

This set up a championship game pitting the Browns of Cleveland (and the supposed weaker former AAFC) against the Rams, who had moved to Los Angeles from Cleveland after the 1945 season because of financial losses. This made pro football the first major sport to expand to the West Coast. The AAFC had teams in both Los Angeles and San Francisco that year.

The championship game matched great quarterbacks Bob Waterfield from the Rams against Otto Graham of the Browns. Both played well, but the Browns managed to intercept five of Waterfield's passes and this proved to be the difference. A field goal by Lou Groza with twenty-eight seconds remaining gave the Browns the title.

Ethnicity and the NFL

The NFL and professional football had a number of African Americans playing in the 1920s, but in 1933 the NFL owners made an unwritten agreement to not continue signing black players, a policy that continued until after World War II. The creation of the AAFC in 1946 set off a bidding war for NFL players and, amidst this frenzy, both leagues found it necessary and useful to sign some African Americans. The Los Angeles Rams signed Woody Strode and Kenny Washington, both of whom had starred at UCLA. The local connection and their talents made these acquisitions a smart business choice for the Rams. In the AAFC, the Cleveland Browns signed fullback Marion Motley and guard Bill Willis, who were the best at their positions in the league. Both played with the Browns until 1953. Their presence paved the way for a number of other African Americans at Cleveland. Len Ford, a veteran of World War II, who then played at Michigan, signed with the Los Angels Dons of the AAFC in 1948, right out of college. He was a great player, but the Dons folded after the 1949 season and Paul Brown was able to draft Ford for the Browns, where he played until 1957. He then played one year with Green Bay before retiring. Motley, Willis, and Ford were all inducted into the Pro Football Hall of Fame in Canton, Ohio,

In 1948 the San Francisco 49ers signed Joe Perry as a running back. He had only played in junior college and in the military, so some thought signing him was a mistake, plus some opposed any black players. Perry scored a touchdown on his first rushing play, led the AAFC in rushing in 1949, and played for fourteen seasons. He, too, was inducted into the Pro Football Hall of Fame.

Buddy Young was only 5'5", but a dazzling runner from the University of Illinois who was signed by the New York Yankees of the AAFC in 1947 as a back. He remained with them for three years, then went to the new Yankee franchise, which had been the New York Bulldogs, of the NFL in 1950. In 1952 the franchise moved to Dallas, then to Baltimore as the Colts the next year. Young was a fixture on this team until he retired after the 1954 season and later became the NFL's Director of Player Relations.

Paul "Tank" Younger was the first African American from a historically black university (Grambling) to play in the NFL when he was signed by the Rams in 1949. He played in the Rams' backfield with Dan Towler, whose nickname was "Deacon" because he was a graduate student in religion. Towler retired in 1955 to become a minister. Younger was later an NFL executive with the Rams and the San Diego Chargers.

In 1948 Emlen Tunnell became the first African American to play for the New York Giants and he remained with them through the 1958 season, starring as a defensive back. He finished his career with three years in Green Bay. Tunnell returned to New York in 1963 as an assistant coach, one of the first African Americans to coach in the NFL. He was also the first African American elected to the Pro Football Hall of Fame in 1967.

The 1950s saw more and more African Americans signed to play pro football including stars like Dick "Night Train" Lane, Ollie Matson, Roosevelt Brown, Roosevelt Grier, and Lenny Moore. In 1957 Jim Brown was signed by the Browns and was the leading rusher in the NFL eight of the next nine seasons. Brown never missed a game, despite the pounding that he took. He was voted the league's MVP three times and retired to pursue an acting career after the 1965 season. He returned to New York in 1967 as an assistant coach.

By the end of the decade every NFL team had at least one African American, except for the Washington Redskins. Their owner, George Preston Marshall, had been one of the three owners to propose the "gentlemen's agreement" in 1933 that kept Africans Americans out of the league. Art Rooney of the Pittsburgh Steelers and George Halas of the Chicago Bears had broken that agreement as early as 1953, but Marshall persisted, claiming that Washington was a southern city and his fans wouldn't accept integrating the team. It took until 1962 for that to change.

Media and Pro Football

Football got good local coverage in the daily newspapers and every team had local radio broadcasts. As noted earlier, television coverage was uneven, depending on the market. The lack of a league package for the NFL, other than for the championship game, kept salaries relatively low and some top college players even refused to go to professional careers, feeling that it was safer and more lucrative to end their football careers and pursue some line of business. Unlike baseball, which signed players out of high school, almost all football players in the 1950s attended college, with most graduating, so football was not their only avenue for professional advancement. The league needed to attract more fans, generate more income, and raise salaries in order to capture all of the best players. During most of the decade, college football outdrew pro football and had higher ratings on television.

The big 'break" for pro football came in 1958 when the Baltimore Colts played the New York Giants for the NFL championship. After stumbling along with local television coverage in the 1950s, the NFL and, later, the AFL got large national television contracts in the 1960s. Pro football turned out to be the sport made *for* television, as well as the sport made *by* television.

The 1950s Pro Football Seasons

After the Browns topped the Rams in the first NFL season following the collapse of the AAFC, Los Angeles reversed the results in the 1951 championship game, winning 24–17. The Rams were led by quarterbacks Bob Waterfield and Norm Van Brocklin, who threw to Tom Fears and Elroy "Crazy Legs" Hirsch for over 200 yards. The Browns had topped the American Conference with a record of 11–1, while the Rams had barely won their conference with an 8–4 record, only a half-game better than Detroit and San Francisco's 7–4–1 records.

In 1952 the New York Yankees moved to Dallas as the Texans, where they failed to draw fans. (Having a record of 1–11 can do that.) The Browns won their conference with an 8–4 mark, while Detroit and Los Angeles tied for their title at 9–3. In a playoff, the Lions, behind quarterback Bobby Layne, defeated the Rams 31–21. The Lions then defeated the Browns for the championship, 17–7. The Detroit Lions made it two in a row the next year, topping the Browns once again, this time 17–16. The Browns got their revenge in 1954 as they humiliated the Lions in the title game, 56–10. Otto Graham threw three touchdown passes and scored three himself to lead the Browns in the romp. The last game of Graham's career was the 1955 championship contest, and he ended his professional career

The Greatest Game Ever Played

December 28, 1958, was the date of what most sport historians call the best NFL championship game ever. The weather was cold and blustery and the field at Yankee Stadium still had dirt areas left from the baseball diamond. NBC broadcast the game and as the game got better, the audience increased. One of the combatants was the Baltimore Colts with six future Hall of Fame players (and a future Hall coach, Weeb Ewbank.) The Colts also had four African American starters. The opponents were the New York Giants with six future Hall of Fame players and two future Hall coaches. The Giants had had to beat the Browns on the last day of the season to tie for the Eastern title, then had to beat them again to get into the championship game. They had won the title in 1956. The Colts had been a "wandering" franchise for a number of years earlier in the league's history, but had settled successfully in Baltimore in 1953. They had never been in a championship game.

The Colts were led by Johnny Unitas, a young quarterback who had been cut by the Pittsburgh Steelers, then played semiprofessional football while working construction to support his family. In 1956 Unitas had a tryout with the Colts and made the team. He became the starting quarterback in the fourth game of 1956 when George Shaw, the starter, was injured. In 1957 Unitas made the Pro Bowl after throwing twenty-four touchdown passes in twelve games. He went on to throw touchdowns in forty-seven consecutive games, a record.

The New York Giants were led by quarterback Charlie Connerly and a trio of top running backs—Frank Gifford, Mel Triplett, and Alex Webster. The Giants' defense, anchored by linebacker Sam Huff, was deemed almost impregnable. The Giants scored a field goal in the first quarter, but two Gifford fumbles led to Alan Ameche scoring two touchdowns, and the Colts led at halftime, 14–3.

The Giants scored a touchdown in the third quarter and another in the fourth to take a 17–14 lead. Unitas and the Colts got the ball at their own fourteen-yard line with two minutes to go. Unitas then marched the Colts down the field, throwing precision passes to his receivers, Raymond Berry and Lenny Moore. Unitas completed four of six passes, using all but thirteen seconds before Steve Myhra kicked the field goal that tied the game.

The gun sounded and the players were surprised to find that the game would go on, into a sudden-death overtime period, the first time that this had occurred. The Giants won the toss and received, but failed to gain a first down. They punted and the Colts took over at their own twenty-yard line. Unitas then led the Colts eighty yards, mixing his passes (he completed four of five) with handoffs to Ameche and Moore. The Colts drove to the one-yard line where Ameche took a handoff and plunged through the right side of the line for the game-ending score.

The game electrified not just the more than 64,000 fans in attendance, but millions who watched on television that Sunday evening. Before this game the NFL had never averaged more than 40,000 in attendance for its games. From this point on, the league never averaged less than 40,000 per game. Two years later the NFL and NBC signed a $4.65-million deal, enormous for the time. A new league began in 1960, confident that pro football was a growth enterprise, all as a result of this stimulating contest. Each of the winning Colts got $4719 as their share for winning the championship. Each player in the 2007 Super Bowl received $68,000.

with a 38–14 victory over the Rams. Grahams threw two touchdown passes and ran for two others.

With Graham's retirement, the Browns dropped below .500, and the New York Giants won what was now called the Eastern Conference. The Western title went to the Chicago Bears, who edged Detroit by a half game. The Rams were rebuilding and they fell to 4–8. The Giants destroyed the Bears, 47–7, in the championship game. The Browns came back in 1957 with their great rookie running back, Jim Brown of Syracuse, who led the league in rushing. Cleveland went 9–2–1 and then met the Lions for the championship in Detroit. Detroit had edged San Francisco in a playoff for the Western Conference crown, but easily topped the Browns, 59–14, in the championship game. In 1959 the Colts repeated their victory over the New York Giants of the previous year. The game was not nearly as close, as Unitas threw a touchdown and scored another in a 24-point fourth quarter and Baltimore won, 31–16. In 1960, the Philadelphia Eagles, led by quarterback Norm Van Brocklin, defeated the Green Bay Packers, 17–13, Coach Vince Lombardi's only playoff loss.

Professional Hockey

In the 1950s there were six teams in the National Hockey League (NHL) and they represented two Canadian (Montreal and Toronto) and four American cities (Boston, New York, Chicago, and Detroit). The geographic appeal was limited to the Northeast, though hockey was very popular in the upper Midwest. Still, it would take until the 1967–68 season for the NHL to expand beyond the six franchises.

Hockey was popular in Canada throughout the twentieth century, but its appeal was limited in the United States. "Hockey Night in Canada" began on radio on the Canadian Broadcast Commission (CBC) in 1931 and began airing on television in 1952 on Saturday nights. The television transmission could be picked up by Americans close to the northern border, but for the rest of the United States, television coverage of the NHL was limited to telecasts by local stations until 1956–57, when CBS began telecasting games on Saturday afternoons to the four American cities.

The players were almost entirely Canadian; about 10 percent or fewer were Americans. The top stars, however, were embraced by the local fans, and the 1950s had plenty of top stars. These included Maurice "the Rocket" Richard and Bernie "Boom Boom" Geoffrion of the Montreal Canadiens, Bobby Hull ("the Golden Jet") of the Chicago Blackhawks, Gordie Howe and Alex Delvecchio of the Detroit Red Wings, Andy Bathgate of the New York Rangers, Tim Horton of the Toronto Maple Leafs, and Johnny Bucyk of the Boston Bruins. The Bruins also signed Willie O'Ree as the first black player in the NHL.

Two teams dominated the 1950s in the NHL. The Detroit Red Wings won the league championship in 1950, 1951, 1952, 1953, 1954, 1955, and 1957. The Montreal Canadiens won in 1956, 1958, 1959, as well as the next three years.

The Olympic Games of the 1950s

The Olympics of the 1950s had increased numbers of teams and participants. The 1948 Games in London had been put together at relatively short notice and the 1952 Summer Games in Helsinki, Finland, allowed for more time for planning. The additional years allowed a number of countries to recover from World War II and enter the Games of 1952, and the most prominent was the Soviet Union, which had not competed since it was Russia in the 1912 Games. The Soviets were excellent and pressed the United States to such a degree that it took the United States nearly the entire Games to win the unofficial medals race even though it far outdistanced the Soviets in gold medals won. Sixty-nine nations competed in 149 events, the largest total ever.

Emil Zapotek of Czechoslovakia won three gold medals in the 5,000-meter, 10,000-meter, and marathon races. Bob Mathias of the United States won his second decathlon title in a row. In 1948 he had been a surprise victor in London as a seventeen-year-old. As a twenty-one-year-old he set a new world record for the event in winning his gold medal. Most of the favorites won their events with some upsets. Floyd Patterson, the future heavyweight boxing champion of the world, won a gold medal at the middleweight division.

There was a new tension to the Games with the addition of the Soviets and the Soviet-bloc nations. The Soviets and their allies chose to not be housed in the Olympic Village; instead, they were housed in their own village, closer to the Soviet border, which allowed them to limit contact with the athletes of other nations. The desire to "beat the Russians" was quite strong among the athletes, and probably the same desire to top the Americans was prevalent among Soviet competitors.

Olympics coverage was generally limited to newspaper reports and some movie newsreel highlights shown in theaters for a few weeks. The technology and time differences made the Olympics a source of interest to Americans, but a very distant interest. This remoteness was even more pronounced for the Winter Games held in Oslo, Norway, in February 1952 where thirty nations competed. Almost all the medals won went to countries from Europe or North America. The United States, surprisingly, finished second in the medals' total to host Norway, but American interest was minimal, as was media coverage.

The 1956 Winter Games were held in Cortina d'Ampezzo, Italy, marking the Soviet Union's first appearance in the Winter Games. They surprised the rest of the world by taking home the most medals. The United States fell to fourth in total medals won, behind Austria and Sweden. Five of the seven medals won by Americans were in figure skating, with Hayes Jenkins and Tenley Albright winning gold medals. These Games were televised for the first time, though they were unable to be shown live in the United States. Instead, American television showed taped highlights later in the week after the competition was held. This helped increase American interest in figure-skating competition, since these events were highlighted after the American victories.

The 1956 Summer Games were the first held in the Southern Hemisphere (in Melbourne, Australia) and this necessitated having the Games in November and December, spring and early summer in that hemisphere. Political events also altered the inclusion of some nations. The Suez Canal crisis caused Lebanon, Egypt, and Iraq to pull out of the Games. The Soviet invasion of Hungary led to withdrawal from the Games by Netherlands, Switzerland, and Spain. Then the People's Republic of China withdrew, protesting the inclusion of the Republic of China (Taiwan). This would be the first of many protests on the Olympic stage over the next fifty years.

Overall the Soviets dominated, winning the most medals by far, and the most gold medals, five more than the United States. The Soviet mastery of gymnastics was instrumental in their large victory margin, leading one noted American paper to call gymnastics a "minor sport." American Bobby Morrow won three gold medals by winning the 100-meter and 200-meter and being part of the 400-meter relay team. Bob Richards of Illinois won his second straight Olympic pole vault. He was then pictured on the front of a Wheaties cereal box in 1958, a tradition begun with athletes in 1934. American men won fifteen of the twenty-four track events, but Australia was the leading nation in swim medals. Because of the great difference in time zones, taped highlights again were shown on American television on weekends.

The American dominance in basketball continued unabated. From the inception of the sport at the 1936 Olympics, the Americans had not lost a game. The 1956 team, led by Bill Russell, continued that tradition, winning games by over fifty points regularly and winning the gold medal game by thirty-four points over the Soviet Union. Coverage of the basketball team in the Olympics was better than American coverage of any other sport in the Games.

In 1960 the Winter Olympics were in Squaw Valley, California, near Lake Tahoe in the Sierra Nevada Mountains. This was the first Winter Olympic Games to be held in North America since the Lake Placid Games in 1932. Many of the events, particularly skiing and skating, were televised live in the United States, which brought more recognition to the athletes and more popular interest in their sports. The Soviets were dominant in the number of medals won, but Carol Heiss and David Jenkins of the United States won gold medals in figure skating, as did the U.S. ice hockey team, defeating the heavily favored Soviet Union in the semi-finals and the Czech team in the finals.

The 1960 Summer Games were held in Rome in July and a number of American performances were memorable, though the Soviets dominated in terms of total medals. Rafer Johnson set a new record in the decathlon, Wilma Rudolph won three gold medals in track, Chris von Saltza won three golds in swimming and Cassius Clay (later Muhammad Ali) won the gold in the light-heavyweight boxing division. In addition, the greatest amateur basketball team ever assembled, led by Jerry West, Oscar Robertson, Walt Bellamy, and Terry Dischinger, annihilated opponents by an average of more than forty points with the closest victory being by twenty-four points. Abebe Bikila of Ethiopia won the marathon running barefooted, becoming the first black African to win an Olympic medal.

INDIVIDUAL SPORTS

Boxing

Boxing in the 1950s was at its zenith because of great fighters at many weight classes, and because television took to boxing early in the decade, where it was a popular sport through that medium. Conversely, boxing in the 1950s was mired in gambling and fight-fixing scandals and a number of boxers or promoters were connected to organized crime figures. The federal government became involved with investigating boxing, beginning in 1960 when Senator Estes Kefauver's Subcommittee on Antitrust and Monopoly investigated the hold that crime figures had on boxers, most often through being managers or promoters of the top boxers. The results were fixed fights, top fights only shown on closed-circuit theater broadcasts, and unhappy fight fans.

Law and Gambling in Boxing

Various legal issues plagued boxing in the decade, most revolving around known gamblers or people with gambling connections being associated with or controlling fighters or scheduling of top bouts. An additional problem was the unevenness of enforcement in each of the states, which governed boxing through the individual state athletic or boxing commissions. Tough rulings in one state had no weight, necessarily, in other states, so if a boxer or manager lost his license or had it suspended in New York, for example, it had little effect on the fighter's ability to box in Nevada. Many of the fighters and/or managers were associated in some manner with the International Boxing Club (IBC), which seemed to have intertwined relationships with some figures connected to organized crime.

The U.S. Department of Justice brought suit against the IBC under the Sherman Antitrust Act, which prohibited monopolies. A district court ruled for the IBC, citing a 1922 Supreme Court decision that had allowed baseball to be exempt from the Sherman act. After the Supreme Court and Congress each tried to get the other entity to make a definitive decision on the issue, there was a ruling in 1955 that boxing fell under the Sherman Antitrust Act, and in 1959 the Supreme Court essentially demanded the disbanding of the IBC. There was resistance and subterfuge, but the IBC did finally have its control (and that of organized crime) on boxing loosened by the end of the decade.

Media and Boxing

Since the 1920s, top boxing matches had been carried on the radio and been very popular. In the early 1950s, television was eager to produce and promote boxing matches on almost any evening of the week. With various weight classes, the opportunity to carry boxing seemed almost limitless. Then the promoters began showing lesser fights on some nights and charging for closed-circuit telecasts of some championship bouts. By the end of the decade, televised boxing was generally limited to one or two nights a week, and in the early 1960s the only regularly shown boxing matches were the *Friday Night Fights*, usually sponsored by Gillette. Just as television had embraced and furthered boxing popularity, the saturation of boxing coverage, coupled with the corruption in the industry, soured the public on boxing. In 1952 it was estimated that about one-third of the available audience watched boxing telecasts. By the end of the decade, that figure was about one-tenth. Sponsors were lost and the fight telecasts were dramatically reduced.

The top heavyweight fights were not being televised, rather shown in theaters, but were broadcast on the radio and this continued into the 1960s. A number of top bouts for other weight classes were shown on live television, however.

Ethnicity and Boxing in the 1950s

Boxing had seen discrimination against African Americans since at least the early part of the century and Jack Johnson's championship years had hardened racism in boxing. These racists wanted to make sure that another black champion would not emerge, particularly at the heavyweight division, but Joe Louis overcame that to become champion in 1937 and held the title until retiring in 1949. The title was then awarded to Ezzard Charles, who successfully defended it nine times before losing the title to Jersey Joe Walcott in 1952.

Possibly the greatest fighter, pound for pound, of that era was Sugar Ray Robinson. At various times, he held the world's middleweight and welterweight titles from 1946 to 1952, then, after a two-and-a-half-year retirement, 1955–57, after which he lost to Gene Fulmer. Robinson defeated Fulmer in a rematch for the middleweight crown. In 1958 Robinson lost to and then defeated Carmen Basilio for the title, Robinson's fifth time of regaining a title. He continued to fight until 1965, when he was forty-four. Robinson was named the greatest fighter of the century, by the Associated Press and the greatest fighter in history by ESPN.com in 2007.

Besides his boxing, Robinson was also an accomplished singer and dancer and very noticeable on the New York social scene. He owned a popular nightclub in New York. His smoothness as a fighter and an entertainer made him the idol of an entire generation of young African Americans in the 1950s. In homage to him, a number of other top fighters added "Sugar" in front of their first names, most notably boxing champion Sugar Ray Leonard in the 1970s.

Floyd Patterson won the heavyweight title in 1956, which had been vacated when Rocky Marciano retired as champion. Patterson had won a gold medal at the 1952 Olympics at the middleweight class at the age of seventeen. He became the youngest heavyweight champion ever at twenty-one. In 1959 Patterson lost his title to Ingemar Johannson, but won it back in 1960.

Noted Champions of the Era

The most-admired heavyweight of the era was Rocky Marciano, who won the title in September of 1952 and retired, undefeated, in April of 1956. Marciano had served in World War II for two years and became a professional boxer in 1947. Marciano won all of his fights, almost 90 percent of those by knockouts.

Archie Moore was another top African American fighter, who was light heavyweight champion from 1952 to 1960 and again from 1961 to 1962. He also fought for the heavyweight title twice, but lost to Marciano and Patterson. Moore's career began in 1936, when he was twenty-three, and lasted until 1963 when he was fifty. He is the only fighter to have faced both Rocky Marciano and Muhammad Ali and had 145 knockouts in his career.

Jake LaMotta, perhaps best known for a film biography of his life called *Raging Bull*, was middleweight champion from 1949 to 1951. LaMotta also testified before the U.S. Senate in 1960 that he had thrown a fight in 1947 in order to get an opportunity to fight for the title. This was necessary for him being allowed to fight because of the control that organized crime and the IBC had on boxing at the time.

Golf

Golf grew tremendously in popularity during the 1950s due to a number of factors. First, economic times improved greatly in the postwar period and more people had the time and money to spend on golf. The demographic shifting of the

Seated on bench, with golf clubs (*left to right*): Byron Nelson, Dwight D. Eisenhower, Ben Hogan, and Clifford Roberts. Photo by Morgan Fitz, Augusta, Georgia. (Courtesy of the Library of Congress)

population also led to more interest in the sport. The general movement toward warmer U.S. climates meant that more people lived in areas where golf could be played more months of the year.

The movement from city to suburbs, which continued apace during the 1950s and 1960s, put more people in reach of golf courses and this, in turn, stimulated the growth in the number of new public and private courses available to play. More public course access meant that golf could expand from being an exclusively upper- and upper-middle-class sport to being one that could include the middle class, as well as some members of the working class. About 6,000 new golf courses were built in the 1950s.

The president of the United States from 1953 to 1960, Dwight D. Eisenhower, was a dedicated golfer and he was often shown playing the game. (His scores were not revealed.) Thus, Americans might model themselves after their president and play golf, now seen as a real American pastime.

Finally, there was television, which began to televise more and more (almost exclusively male) golf tournaments, or parts of them, and the very telegenic golfers who were prominent in the 1950s. These included Sam Snead, Ben Hogan, and Arnold Palmer among men and Mickey Wright, Betsy Rawls, Louise Suggs, Patty Berg, and Babe Didrikson Zaharias among women.

Women and Golf in the 1950s

The struggle for women to play and be recognized for their golfing ability was pioneered by Mildred "Babe" Didrikson Zaharias. Born in Texas in 1911, she was a basketball and track star in her younger years, winning two Olympic gold medals in the 1932 Games in Los Angeles. She was also a softball star, but in about 1935, she began playing golf and was almost an immediate sensation at the game. Most tournaments at the time were for amateurs, which limited who might be successful at the game, since one needed to be independently wealthy to afford to play very much. Didrikson won all the national amateur titles before becoming a professional in 1947 and working to form and nurture the Women's Professional Golf Association (WPGA) and later the Ladies Professional Golf Association (LPGA). In the late 1940s she won seventeen straight amateur tournaments and by 1950 she had won the U.S. Women's Open (begun in 1946) twice. She was a vibrant, dynamic woman who drew large crowds and she was instrumental in the success of professional golf for women.

After winning the 1950 U.S. Open, Didrikson Zaharias was the leading LPGA money winner for 1951 and 1952. The next season she was diagnosed with cancer, but recovered enough to win the U.S. Open again in 1954. She also was president of the LPGA from 1952 to 1955. Her cancer returned in 1955 and she died in 1956 at the age of forty-five. She was voted Associated Press Female Athlete of the Year six times and was named the Female Athlete of the first half of the twentieth century.

Patty Berg, born in 1918, won the U.S. Women's Amateur in 1938 before turning pro in 1940. She served as a lieutenant in the Marines in World War II from 1942 to 1945, and turned professional in 1948. She joined with Didrikson in founding the LPGA and was its first president in 1948. She won the first U.S. Open in 1946 and was voted the Associated Press Woman Athlete of the Year in 1938, 1942, and 1955. Berg won a total of fifty-seven pro tournaments in her career. The LPGA established the annual Patty Berg award for sportsmanship and contributions to golf.

Louise Suggs, born in 1928, was one of Didrikson's top rivals. A top amateur before turning pro in 1948, Suggs won the U.S. Open in 1949 and 1952 as well as the LPGA championship in 1957. She won a total of fifty-eight pro tournaments before retiring.

Betsy Rawls, born in 1928, finished second in the U.S. Open to Babe Didrikson Zaharias in 1950, turned professional in 1951, and won the U.S. Open in 1951, 1953, 1957, and 1960. She won the LPGA championship in 1969. Rawls won a total of fifty-five pro tournaments.

Mary Kathyrn (Mickey) Wright, born in 1935, was a top amateur golfer and became a professional in 1955. She won the U.S. Open in 1958, 1959, 1961, and 1964, and the LPGA championship in 1958, 1960, 1961, and 1963, among her total of eighty-two pro tournament victories. She was named the Associated Press Female Athlete of the Year in 1963 and 1964. Many observers call her the best female golfer ever.

Despite these great players who popularized golf, there was almost no television coverage in the 1950s of women's tournaments, and the prize money was not very large. The top LPGA money winners in the 1950s never won more than $27,000 in any year, whereas the top men's winners regularly won $60,000–$75,000 in a year. In 1955, the average annual income for Americans was $5,000.

The Men of Golf in the 1950s

The 1950s were a transitional period for men's professional golf. The 1940s were dominated by three golfers, namely, Byron Nelson, Ben Hogan, and Sam Snead. Many tournaments were canceled during World War II, but all had resumed by 1946. Nelson chose to retire in 1946 and devote his time to ranching, leaving Snead and Hogan as the undisputed kings of the game. Other top players like Cary Middlecoff, Doug Ford, and Billy Casper challenged the two, but the dominance of Snead and Hogan is clearly seen by victories in the major tournaments in the period from 1949 to 1957. Either Hogan or Snead won the U.S. Open three times, the Masters five times, the PGA twice, and the British Open once. The latter tournament was not as commonly played by the top Americans at that time as it is now. In some years (1953 was a good example) the British Open and the PGA Championship overlapped.

Hogan was born in Texas (1912–97) and won nine major championships between 1946 and 1953. He won a total of sixty-four championships before retiring at age fifty-nine in 1971. His fame was enhanced by a 1951 film made of his life, *Follow the Sun*, starring Glenn Ford as Hogan. In 1953 Hogan won five of the six tournaments that he entered, including the Masters, the U.S. Open, and the British Open. He was unable to play in the PGA championship. Hogan was not a big man (5'7", 140 pounds) and many American golfers admired him because of how he could beat the "big boys" with his great swing and technique. His popularity was greatly enhanced after his amazing recovery from a near-fatal automobile accident in 1949. His golf instruction book was one of the best-selling golf books ever.

Sam Snead, a native of Virginia, was also not a big man (5'11", 190 pounds), but he was much bigger than Hogan. The two were born within three months of each other in 1912 (d. 2002). Snead turned pro in 1934 and won eighty-two PGA tournaments before retiring in 1979 at the age of sixty-seven. He continued to play in senior tournaments and won thirteen. Snead won seven major championships between 1942 and 1954. In 1979 he was the first PGA Tour player to shoot his age (67) in a round. Snead's folksiness made him popular with galleries and sportswriters.

As Snead and Hogan faded from golf dominance, a young golfer named Arnold Palmer was beginning an illustrious career. The son of a professional golfer, Palmer attended Wake Forest University before joining the Coast Guard for three years. Upon his discharge, he returned to serious golf playing and won the U.S. Amateur in 1954. He turned pro the next year and won the Canadian Open and throngs of admirers. Palmer was a risk taker on the course, and was known for his long drives, after which he often hitched up his pants and strode down the fairway. He was intense, but had a sense of humor and the galleries loved him. He was the biggest factor in making golf so popular in the late 1950s and convincing television network executives to carry more golf tournaments in the 1960s. Palmer won the Masters four times, the British Open twice, and the U.S. Open once, among his sixty-two tour victories.

The men's professional golf tour was segregated until 1960. Charlie Sifford was the first to break this color barrier. He had attempted to play in a PGA event in

1952, but was denied. He won the Long Beach Open in 1957, which was not a PGA Tour event, but was co-sponsored by the PGA. One of the problems for the PGA was that a number of the courses that were used for tournaments were private and segregated. The best example was the Masters in Augusta, Georgia, which remained segregated until 1974.

Tennis

Unlike golf, tennis maintained amateur demands for its top players and tournaments. Thus Wimbledon only allowed amateurs to compete until 1968, and most other top tournaments were barred to professionals. The result was that interest in tennis tournaments appealed more to those with more money than the average American. There was interest in playing tennis and the number of public courts grew during the 1950s, but there was not the connected interest in "big-time" tennis. In the 1960s, the development of the Hard Tru (composite) court surface also made tennis courts easier to build and maintain.

Australian men were the dominant players in the world in the 1950s, although there were some excellent American men playing, such as Tony Trabert, Alex Olmedo, and Vic Seixas Jr. Two American women were most prominent in the 1950s, Maureen Connolly and Althea Gibson.

Connolly was born in 1934 and was a star in tennis as a teenager, winning the Girls National 18-and-under championship when she was fifteen. In 1951, at the age of sixteen, she won the U.S. Open, the youngest woman to ever do so. She repeated that in 1952 and also won Wimbledon. In 1953 she won all four major tournaments, the Australian Open, the French Open, Wimbledon, and the U.S. Open, the first woman to ever do so. The next year she bypassed Australia, but won both Wimbledon and the French Open once again. In July she was in a horseback riding accident with a truck, which resulted in her right leg being crushed, ending her career at age nineteen. In 1966 she was diagnosed with cancer, to which she succumbed in 1969 at the age of thirty-four.

Althea Gibson was a rarity in competitive tennis in the 1950s, an African American. Gibson was born in South Carolina in 1927, but her family moved to Harlem in New York City in 1930. She began playing tennis as a young teen, but she was often unable to play in various locations or tournaments because of being African American. Denied membership in the U.S. Tennis Association (USTA), she played under the American Tennis

Althea Gibson. (Courtesy of the Library of Congress)

Association (ATA), an all-black organization. Starting in 1947 she won ten straight ATA tournaments. In 1950, thanks to the assistance of tennis great Alice Marble, she was allowed to enter her first USTA events and the next year played in the All England championships at Wimbledon.

Gibson graduated from Florida A&M University in 1953 and moved to Missouri to work as an athletic instructor. She also continued to hone her game, and in 1955 she won the Italian Championship. The next year she won both women's singles and doubles at the French Championships. Her doubles partner was an Englishwoman, Angela Buxton. Buxton was Jewish and had suffered discrimination similar to Gibson's.

The next year Gibson and Buxton captured the doubles title at Wimbledon, becoming the first Jew and the first black to win at that venue. In 1957 and 1958 Gibson won both the women's singles and doubles titles. She also won the U.S. Outdoor Championships those same two years.

In both 1957 and 1958, Gibson was named the Female Athlete of the Year by the Associated Press. She retired in 1959 from amateur tennis because it was too costly to continue playing without a steady income. In 1964 she tried to become a professional golfer, but her late start (she was 37) prevented her from ever becoming a golf star. Gibson served as New Jersey State Commissioner of Athletics for ten years until 1985 and died in 2003 at age seventy-six. She was inducted into the International Tennis Hall of Fame in 1971.

Horse Racing

During the decade, there were a number of great horses, but no horse won the Triple Crown of racing (Kentucky Derby, Preakness, Belmont Stakes). Three horses won two legs of the Triple Crown. Tim Tam in 1958 won the Derby and the Preakness, but fractured a bone in the Belmont Stakes and still finished second. Both Nashua (1955) and Native Dancer (1953) won the Preakness and the Belmont Stakes. Nashua was edged by Swaps in the Kentucky Derby and Native Dancer barely lost to Dark Star in the Derby. Both Nashua (1955) and Native Dancer (1953) were each named Horse of the Year.

Three jockeys were most prominent in the decade, Willie Shoemaker, Bill Hartack, and Eddie Arcaro. Arcaro was the most successful in the 1950s, winning two Kentucky Derbys, two Belmont Stakes races, and four Preaknesses. When he retired in 1962 he had ridden over 4,700 winners and amassed purse winnings of more than $30 million. Shoemaker won the Derby twice and the Belmont twice during the decade. In 1986 he was the oldest jockey to win a Kentucky Derby at the age of fifty-four.

OTHER SIGNIFICANT SPORTS
Bowling

During the 1950s, bowling became quite popular in the United States. It was carried regularly on television and at least two male bowlers became well known and highly emulated, Don Carter and Dick Weber. Bowling was something anyone could do, though not necessarily well, but size was not a factor in how well one bowled since balls were of various weights. The advent of automatic pinsetters at bowling lanes in the 1950s put pin boys out of business, but made the game faster and more "reliable." Chicago and St. Louis were the centers of bowling popularity in the 1950s, though there were increasing numbers of lanes throughout the United States.

Don Carter of St. Louis and Dick Weber of Indianapolis (who moved to St. Louis) were teammates on a top bowling team, the Budweisers, sponsored by the beer company. Carter was the bowler of the year in 1953, 1954, 1957, 1958, 1960, and 1962. In 1962 he was also named professional athlete of the year, the only bowler ever to win the Hickok Belt. Dick Weber was a founding member of the Professional Bowlers Association and won his first title in 1959. He would become the top male bowler of the 1960s.

Don Carter poses with his bowling ball at the American Bowling Congress Master's Tournament in St. Louis, April 20, 1959. (AP / Wide World Photo)

Auto Racing

The Indianapolis 500 race was highly popular during this decade, often drawing more than 100,000 people to the Indianapolis Speedway for the Memorial Day Race. The top racer during decade was Bill Vukovich, who took two Indy 500 races in 1953 and 1954. No one else won more than once, although Howard Keck, John Zink, and George Saith all finished second twice during the decade. In 1954 the average speed for a winning car exceeded 130 miles per hour for the first time.

SUMMARY

Team sports in the 1950s were characterized by dynasties. The Yankees won eight American League pennants and five championships during the period 1951–60 and were the dominant force in baseball. The Dodgers were the best of the National League, winning five pennants and two World Series titles. The Giants won pennants in 1951 and 1954. Most of the titles won by the Dodgers and the Giants were when the teams were located in Brooklyn and New York, respectively, and the relocation of both franchises to California after the 1957 season was as compelling a story as the pennants.

In basketball the Boston Celtics began their domination with the signing of Bill

Marshall Teague is shown after qualifying, May 26, 1957, for the Indianapolis 500. One of NASCAR's first stars and pioneers, Teague sits behind the wheel of a Sumar Special Indy Car. (AP / Wide World Photo)

Russell, who led them to eleven world titles in thirteen seasons. In college basketball, Kentucky and San Francisco were the only schools to win more than one NCAA title in the decade.

Oklahoma and Notre Dame were seen as the top college football programs and both enjoyed long winning streaks during the decade. The Cleveland Browns and the Detroit Lions each won three NFL titles during the decade, with Baltimore's Colts winning in 1958 and 1959. Hockey, too, was a league of little parity with Montreal and Detroit dominating the league.

The first postwar decade was one of great success for sports throughout the nation as teams and individual players became wealthier and more recognizable to sports fans throughout the country thanks to the growing influence of television. The growth would grow exponentially in the following decade.

RECOMMENDED RESOURCES

Print Sources

Bromberg, Lester. 1962. *Boxing's unforgettable fights*. New York: Ronald Press.

Grimsley, Will. 1971. *Tennis, its history, people and events*. Englewood Cliff, NJ: Prentice-Hall.

Halberstam, David. 1994. *The Fifties*. New York: Ballantine Books.

Koppett, Leonard. 1968. *24 seconds to shoot: An informal history of the National Basketball Association*. New York: Macmillan.

Mantle, Mickey, with Herb Gluck. 1985. *The Mick, an American hero*. New York: Doubleday.

McFarlane, Brian. 1967. *Fifty years of hockey, 1917–1967: An intimate history of the National Hockey League*. Toronto: Pagurian Press.

Nelson, Murry. 2005. *Bill Russell: A biography*. Westport, CT: Greenwood.

Rader, Benjamin G. 1983. *American sports: From the age of folk games to the age of spectators*. Englewood Cliffs, NJ: Prentice-Hall.

Sullivan, Neil. 1987. *The Dodgers move west*. New York: Oxford University Press.

Thomas, Ron. 2002. *They cleared the lane: The NBA's black pioneers*. Lincoln: University of Nebraska Press.

William, Juan, and Julian Bond. 1988. *Eyes on the prize: America's civil rights years, 1954–1965*. New York: Penguin.

Films

Follow the Sun: The Ben Hogan Story. 1951. Dir. Sidney Lanfield.

CHAPTER 10

AMERICAN SPORTS, 1960–1969

Maureen Smith

OVERVIEW

America in the 1960s was a decade marked by tremendous societal change. Changes in demographics, gender relations, technology, pop culture, the free speech movement, and civil rights had profound effects on the decades to follow. Moreover, the Vietnam War divided the nation.

At the start of the decade, Americans faced the Cuban Missile crisis. American troops were deployed to Vietnam and those left at home eventually protested the war. Women made slight gains, but most of these were to wait until the next decade. Betty Friedan wrote *The Feminine Mystique* in 1963, the same year the Presidential Commission on the Status of Women presented its report. During the decade, the number of Hispanics living in the United States tripled and Cesar Chavez and Dolores Huerta organized the United Farm Workers of America. The British band, The Beatles, invaded the United States and changed the rock and roll scene for millions of teenagers. Illegal drug use was popular and rock and roll ruled, with the Woodstock music festival attracting hundreds of thousands of young Americans in 1968. The hippie movement thrived, and neighborhoods like San Francisco's Haight-Ashbury became destinations for these free-loving folks. Technology led to an American being launched into space in 1961, with astronaut John Glenn orbiting the earth two years later, and in 1969 Neil Armstrong and Buzz Aldrin became the first men to walk on the moon. The civil rights movement was the decade's most important and significant shift in American society. These changes had a direct impact on sporting fields.

The civil rights movement began with sit-ins and marches and led to legislation that allowed African Americans to vote, as well as other rights owed to them as American citizens, such as the 1964 Civil Rights Act and the Voting Rights Act of 1965. The 1960s were a politically charged and turbulent time; newspaper headlines and television screens covered daily doses of student movements, free speech movements, urban riots, assassinations and killings, the Vietnam War, women's rights demonstrations, and the various factions within the civil rights struggle for black rights and citizenship. It was during the 1960s that larger numbers in the black community and the civil rights movement sought to enact changes in social, political, economic, and legal aspects for black American citizens. Moreover, the focused attention on integration efforts by the media informed white Americans to a greater extent. Led into the decade by Martin Luther King Jr. and his fight for integration, the struggle for freedom evolved into a more politically active and liberating movement with Malcolm X and the Nation of Islam, the black student movement, and in the second half of the decade, the Black Power movement.

There was an undeniably strong link between the sports world of the 1960s and politics, both nationally and globally. Still, few leaders of the decade made any mention of sports as being part of the larger political scene, except to state that it was not an appropriate arena for political discourse. Just as the civil rights movement gained momentum and progressed from gradualism to direct action, so, too, did the behaviors and efforts of black athletes. Previously silent and seemingly accepting of the status quo, most black athletes who had been integrated into the white sporting arena had maintained a low profile, staying away from controversy.

Sport, too, experienced great change during the 1960s. The increased popularity of television played a major role in the growth of sport. Professional leagues expanded across the country, claiming new territories in newly constructed stadiums paid for by cities desperate to have a professional team. By the end of the decade, some players began to recognize the financial boons reaped by the owners at their expense and began to address the labor issue. Colleges and universities faced great changes on the playing fields, with the process of integration causing coaches and players alike to shift their attitudes about race. These same issues played themselves out on professional playing fields and locker rooms. The Olympic Games provided an international stage for Cold War politics between the United States and the Soviet Union. Women struggled to gain respect, recognition, and opportunity in sports.

College football and basketball were the most popular college sports of the decade. Moreover, with the integration of colleges and athletic teams, both sports faced issues related to the integration process. With the integration of college campuses and college athletics, black college athletes emerged as central figures in increasing campus activism. College sport became a viable and visible platform for black college athletes to express their discontent at their treatment as black Americans and black athletes. Black college athletes employed similar tactics used in other protest activities of the civil rights movement, which eventually culminated in various boycott movements. The first half of decade was the actual integration of athletic teams, while the second half of the decade dealt with the impact and effects of the integration efforts, culminating when several black college athletes actively worked to change the athletic landscape for black athletes through protests and boycotts

Several factors contributed to the growth and success of the civil rights movement, as well as advances made by blacks in sport during the 1960s, including World War II and the Cold War, legal rulings such as *Brown vs. Board of Education* (1954), the Civil Rights Voting Act (1964), and the Voting Rights Act (1965), along with an economic boom that helped to propel blacks into the economic mainstream. The political climate allowed for the intersection of civil rights and the involvement of athletes within such movements. At a time when the civil rights movement was dominated by images of Dr. Martin Luther King Jr., Malcolm X, Freedom Riders, and news coverage of racial demonstrations, the protests by black male athletes during this decade merits attention as part of the larger discourse of race relations in the United States as they played out on athletic fields.

The image of black athletes in the 1950s and the gains they had seemingly made, along with the injustices they continued to face, laid the groundwork for the athletes that followed them in the next decade (Hutchinson 1977).[1] Baseball finally had at least one African American player on each roster when the Boston Red Sox signed Elijah "Pumpsie" Green in 1959. There were a greater number of black participants in professional sport, with several becoming national figures. With the integration of educational institutions came a significant rise in the number of black college athletes. While females, both black and white, were gaining some recognition, it was primarily every four years in Olympic competition, with few professional and college opportunities organized on the same scale as their male counterparts. Sport enjoyed a reputation for being an equal playing field, where talent was more important than someone's socioeconomic status or race, though this belief was certainly challenged throughout the decade. Some felt that sport was ahead of society in terms of race relations, noting that baseball had integrated before the military and schools. And yet within this sporting world emerged a number of black athletes whose race consciousness had been raised, and, unlike their predecessors, they acted upon this new consciousness. Black athletes began to notice inequities still apparent in sport, the discriminations still faced within athletics. Coupled with increasing pressure from the black community on U.S. race relations and cries to end discriminatory practices in country, black athletes began to see their positions in sport as a possible platform to propose change and to confront current thinking. These challenges to the democracy of sport were an expression of the black militancy and the general re-examination of American culture that peaked in the late 1960s.

In this transition, several black athletes risked their careers, their personal safety, their financial security, and their image and status as athletes for a meaning that many Americans could not comprehend, much less respect. In looking back at these athletes, one magazine wrote of the black athlete of the 1960s; "He understands that his ability to hit a 30-foot jump shot does not give him a better chance for equal housing. He now knows that running one hundred yards in record time won't help him get a better job. He realizes that while he may be a hero with a uniform on, after the game, he is just another Black face in the crowd" (Gumbel 1972).

Moreover, these players were viewed by their coaches as being unable to perform in certain "thinking" positions, such as quarterbacks in football. Black

---

[1] All-star teams were dominated by black players, who set records for the amount of money they were making and the increasing total number participating in professional sports. In 1954, 5 percent of the NBA was black, by 1970 56 percent was. In 1957 the NFL was 14 percent black, by 1971 34 percent (Hutchinson 1977, 16). Between 1947 and 1964, eleven of the eighteen National League MVPs were black. Between 1954 and 1964, the NL batting leader was black seven of the eleven years and the home-run leader eight of the eleven years (152). In 1967 the first college All-American teams was named for the 1966–67 year and the starting five were black (163). During the 1967–68 season, the NBA had 71 blacks out of 139 players, and in 1972 in the rival league ABA 63 of 110 athletes were black (164). In track and field, of the fifteen gold medals won by Americans at the 1968 Olympic Games, ten were won by black athletes, with eight world records being set (246). The years 1957–58 were the first time that more than two "Negroes" were named to first-team All-American teams, and five black players were predicted to be All-Americans the next season. For 1966–67, *Look* magazine named six African Americans in a list of ten All-Americans, and the next year named eight African Americans out of ten spots.

athletes were considered to be intellectually inferior to their white teammates. In the coverage of sport, few newspapers employed black journalists, with the exception of the black press, which was losing much of their coverage to mainstream newspapers, with the same exclusion occurring in television coverage. Blacks were generally excluded from front-office and managements positions. Still, as a result of the protests by a number of black athletes at the college and professional level, by the end of the 1960s some results were noticeable, such as the hiring of black coaches, creation of new organizations, and the support of white teammates.

By the early 1970s, the race issue in the sporting world, like the civil rights movement, had lost much of its momentum, and an attitude of grudging acceptance seemed to prevail, leaving the sporting nation with the "acceptable" belief that while African Americans were superior athletes and could help their team climb to the top of the standings, they were still inferior in every other way, politically, socially, economically, and legally.

TEAM SPORTS

Baseball

Major-league baseball in the 1960s experienced great changes with new teams added to the league, several teams relocating across the country, and a number of record performances, both good and bad. Two themes were prominent in baseball, expansion and integration.

The expansion of major-league baseball was prompted in 1960 by the creation of a proposed third major league, the Continental League, which hoped to operate an eight-league team in cities where major-league baseball did not have teams; the eight teams were proposed in New York, to replace the departed Dodgers and Giants, Houston, Toronto, Denver, Minneapolis–St. Paul, Dallas–Fort Worth, Atlanta, and Buffalo. Expansion in baseball came as a result of several factors, including population growth in the United States, postwar affluence, and the expansion of air travel, which made transportation much easier and more efficient. Another major factor was pressure from Congress to expand the business of baseball. Equally, if not more significant, was the relocation of the two New York teams to California, as well as the Milwaukee Braves' move to Atlanta, which established those previously uncharted territories of the United States, namely cities who did not have their own teams. Many cities sought a team to solidify their civic standing. Of course, when one team left for another city, the bereaved city was in need of a new team. Expansion and relocation worked together to create a bigger league with more teams spread across the country.

While the Continental League was unsuccessful in its challenge to major-league baseball, four teams were invited to join the league, beginning the expansion era in baseball. In 1961 the Washington Senators relocated to Minneapolis–St. Paul and became the Minnesota Twins. To replace the departed Senators, a new team with the same name, the Washington Senators, arrived in the nation's capital. Los Angeles was awarded a second team, the Angels, who changed their name to the California Angels by 1965 (and in later years, to the Anaheim Angels and, eventually, the Los Angeles Angels of Anaheim). In 1962 two more teams were added who had been part of the Continental League proposal, the New York Mets and the Houston Colt 45s, who became the Houston Astros in 1965. The Milwaukee

Braves moved to become the Atlanta Braves in 1966, leaving a vacancy in Milwaukee, which was filled by the Milwaukee Brewers, who arrived in 1970 after spending the previous season as an expansion team called the Seattle Pilots. The Pilots were joined that first season by the San Diego Padres, the Montreal Expos, and the Kansas City Royals. By the end of the decade, the American League (AL) and National League (NL) had two divisions, East and West, and held a playoff between the top team in each division before playing for the league championship, which determined the World Series representative.

New teams prompted the construction of new sport facilities, with a number of notable stadiums being built during this time. The San Francisco Giants, who had moved from New York to San Francisco prior to the 1958 season, moved into their new stadium, Candlestick Park, at the start of the 1960 season, with Vice President Richard Nixon attending the opening ceremonies. Their main rivals, the Los Angeles Dodgers, opened their new stadium at Chavez Ravine in 1962, the only privately financed stadium of the decade. The New York Mets, after playing at the Polo Grounds for two years, moved into Shea Stadium in 1964. In a remarkable advent of stadium construction, the Houston Astros moved into the Astrodome, a one-of-a-kind domed stadium, in 1965.

Integration was also a major theme in professional baseball during the 1960s. After Jackie Robinson had integrated major-league baseball in the 1947 season, it took another twelve years before every team had at least one African American player on their roster. After the introduction of African Americans into major-league baseball, Latin American players gradually increased their presence in the American game. During the 1960s, a greater number of players from the Dominican Republic, Puerto Rico, and Cuba earned spots on major-league rosters and their performances earned praise and awards. Still, they faced discrimination due to their skin color as well as the language barrier since the majority of them spoke Spanish.

Even after all professional teams had been fully integrated, black and Latin American athletes continued to face discrimination. Though the color line had been crossed over a decade earlier, owners failed to challenge the segregation that continued to exist in spring training sites in Florida. Though black players played a role in the attempts to end these practices, much of the protests came from the black communities within the cities where spring training occurred. St. Petersburg, for example, known as the center of spring training, had been the site of several lunch-counter sit-ins in 1960. Bill Veeck, owner of the Chicago White Sox, became the first owner to take action to end segregation when in 1961 he canceled reservations for his players to stay at a segregated hotel. After Veeck's initiative, other owners followed. Yet, even after the integration of facilities, southern practices of segregation seemed to prevail.

The San Francisco Giants in the early 1960s had the greatest number of African American and Latin American players on their roster, including the three Alou brothers in the outfield. A notable incident came when manager Alvin Dark instituted an English-only rule that created tensions with the Latin American players. Dark was quoted in a newspaper interview saying that he believed that African American and Latin American players were not as mentally alert as their white teammates. Dark named Willie Mays as the team captain, hoping to alleviate any concerns players had related to his comments. Dark finished the season, but did not return the next year.

The Houston Astrodome

The Houston Astrodome was the first domed sports stadium when it became the home of baseball's Houston Astros in 1965. Constructed at a cost of $35 million, the Astrodome was designed by a team of architects: Hermon Lloyd & W. B. Morgan and Wilson, Morris, Crain & Anderson. The Astrodome hosted a number of special events in the 1960s, such as the Houston Livestock Show and Rodeo beginning in 1966, as well as the Bluebonnet Bowl, a college football postseason game. Elvis Presley appeared in concert at the Astrodome. The Astrodome also hosted college basketball's "Game of the Century," when the number 1–ranked UCLA Bruins traveled to the Astrodome to face the number 2–ranked Houston Cougars. In an upset, the Cougars led by Elvin Hayes beat the Bruins 71–69, ending UCLA's forty-seven-game winning streak. Because of field configurations, seating capacity varied by sport. For baseball, the Astrodome held over 54,000 spectators. Football games had an increased capacity of over 62,000. When the Astrodome was built, it was nicknamed the Eighth Wonder of the World, in part because no other sport facility resembled it and it represented a new era of stadium construction.

A domed, air-conditioned stadium was especially suitable for Houston because of the unpredictable weather, which in most stadiums might cause delays or cancellations. A domed stadium avoided the inconvenience of rainouts and made for a new exciting sport facility. Houston's former mayor, Judge Roy Hofheinz, conceived the idea for the stadium and used it as a means of attracting a major-league team to Houston.

The Astrodome, completed in 1964, was designed to be eighty-one stories tall and covered over nine acres. Though the first season was played on a Bermuda grass surface, the grass died after the ceiling panes were painted to help reduce the glare, which players had complained about. The second season, the Astros played on a dirt field with green paint. By 1966, artificial grass was installed on part of the field with the rest of the field painted green. After the All-Star break, the remainder of the artificial grass was installed. The grass, called ChemGrass, came to become known as Astroturf. Another unique feature of the Astrodome was its four-story-tall scoreboard. The Astrodome inspired other cities to construct stadiums that allowed for play during inclement weather, as well as the multipurpose approach to stadium design.

Despite the racism faced by both groups on and off the field, a number of notable performances by blacks and Latin Americans were among the best of the decade, including Mays, Roberto Clemente, Juan Marichal, and Bob Gibson. Roberto Clemente was an all-star outfielder with the Pittsburgh Pirates. In 1961 Clemente led the National League in batting average, hitting .351. Clemente batted over .300 every season in the 1960s with the exception of 1968, when he hit .291, leading the National League four years (1961, 1964, 1965, 1967). Clemente enjoyed a MVP season in 1966 when he hit .317 with a career-high 29 home runs and 119 runs batted in. The next year, he hit a career-high .357. He was voted to every All-Star game of the 1960s and was awarded the Gold Glove Award beginning in 1961 until 1972. On June 28, 1970, the last season the Pirates played at Forbes Field, the team hosted Roberto Clemente Night, to honor the player and his accomplishments.

Willie Mays came to the San Francisco Giants when the team moved west from New York in 1958. In their 1962 pennant-winning season, Mays hit .304. Mays

Curt Flood

During the 1969 season, St. Louis Cardinals outfielder Curt Flood was a little more outspoken than usual and had a few rifts with management (Flood with Carter 1970, 1971; Herzog 1995, 182; Miller 1991, 190). After the team had a poor showing in 1969, Flood, who had batted .285 in the losing season, was traded in the off-season to the Philadelphia Phillies.

Flood refused to be traded to the Phillies and challenged baseball's antitrust exemption and the reserve clause. The reserve clause was an agreement binding a player to his current team. Essentially, the team owned the rights to the player for the following season and unless the player was traded or released, he was bound to his team for life. Flood decided to sue Commissioner Bowie Kuhn, the presidents of both leagues, and the twenty-four team owners for $3 million, triple damages, and free agency. Flood's goal was to create a ruling that allowed a player to "establish his value in an open market" (Koppett 1969, 42; Miller 1991, 190–92).

Curt Flood was represented by former U.S. Supreme Court Justice Arthur Goldberg, who was selected by Marvin Miller. In a motion heard by Judge Irving Ben Cooper, Flood was denied an injunction to make him a free agent for the 1970 season. His trial began in May 1970, and three months later, the federal district court ruled against Flood. Despite the backing of the players' association, no active player testified on Flood's behalf, though former players Jackie Robinson, Hank Greenberg, and Jim Brosnan and former owner Bill Veeck spoke out in support against the reserve clause. Judge Cooper ruled that the reserve clause did not violate civil rights statutes. After Flood and Miller appealed the decision, the Second Circuit Court of Appeals upheld the lower court's ruling in January 1971. Flood was anxious to have his case resolved. He said, "Let's put it in the open. Let the Supreme Court decide what's right" ("Flood tide" 1970). Surprisingly, the Supreme Court agreed to hear another appeal. In Flood's final appeal, the U.S. Supreme Court ruled 5–3 against the baseball player in the case of *Flood v. Kuhn*.

Flood's baseball career suffered as a direct result of his challenge to baseball. Sitting out the 1970 season and living overseas, Flood signed with the Washington Senators for the 1971 season at an increased salary. Flood's stint with the Senators lasted thirteen games, in which he hit seven singles and barely batted over .200. Flood was depressed at his poor performance. He retired from the game at the age of thirty-three. Moreover, Flood was plagued by legal, fiscal, and marital problems, eventually escaping to Europe.

was an offensive and defensive asset to the Giants. In 1963 and 1964 he combined for 85 home runs and had over 100 runs batted in (RBI) each season, along with scoring 100 runs both years. Mays won the MVP award in 1965 with a career-high fifty-two home runs. That same season, he hit home-run number 500 on September 13, 1965. He enjoyed his last 100-RBI season in 1966, becoming only the second NL player to hit over 100 RBIs eight seasons in a row. Mays hit his 600th career home run in September 1969. In 1970 *Sporting News* named Mays the "Player of the Decade" for the 1960s.

Notable performances in baseball begin with Roger Maris's single-season home-run record of sixty-one dingers in 1961, leading the New York Yankees to a World Series victory against the Cincinnati Reds. The Yankees made it three titles in a

Roger Maris

Roger Maris joined the New York Yankees in 1960. Previously, Maris had played on the Cleveland Indians and Kansas City Athletics. In his first season with the Yankees, Maris won the American League's MVP award. In 1961 Maris became a household name when he and his teammate, Mickey Mantle, began to hit home runs at a record pace challenging Babe Ruth's single-season record of sixty home runs. Maris was portrayed in the press as a grouchy outsider, while Mantle was much more popular with New Yorkers and playful with the media. As they battled head to head in the lineup trading home runs, the two teammates helped lead their team to a 109–53 record. During the home-run chase, Mantle injured his knee and it became clear that it would be a chase for Maris alone, with many baseball fans rooting against the Yankee, including Commissioner Ford Frick. Frick insisted that Ruth's record should stand because his achievement was accomplished in 154 games, while Maris would have the advantage of playing in an extended 162-game season. Frick insisted that if Maris hit more than sixty home runs and it occurred after the 154th game, an asterisk would accompany his achievement. After 154 games, Maris's home run tally was fifty-nine. Maris tied Ruth's record on September 26, 1961. On October 1, 1961, Maris hit his sixty-first home run, establishing a new single-season record. The home-run chase has been dramatized in the HBO film *61.

row when they defeated the San Francisco Giants in game 7 in 1962, ending a dramatic series between the two teams who had once been crosstown rivals. The Giants had ended the regular season tied with the Los Angeles Dodgers and had to play a three-game playoff to determine who would go to the World Series. The expansion team, the New York Mets, set a record for the most losses in a season with 120, while tallying a meager 40 wins. The next year, in the 1963 World Series, the Yankees faced another former crosstown rival, the Los Angeles Dodgers, losing in four games. Dodger pitcher Sandy Koufax capped off a stellar year on the mound, winning the Cy Young Award and the World Series MVP award.

For the fifth year in a row, the New York Yankees appeared in the Fall Classic, when they faced the St. Louis Cardinals in 1964. This marked the end of a dominating Yankees franchise and the end of their postseason appearances for several years. The team dissolved into one of the worst in the following years after losing to the Cardinals in seven games. In game 7 of the 1964 Series against the Yankees, Bob Gibson gave up two ninth-inning home runs but was able to pull out the victory and the World Series MVP award.

Koufax, enjoying another Cy Young Award season, led the Dodgers to the World Series in 1965. The Dodgers and Giants were battling for the pennant and in an incident that some feel aided the Dodgers met each other on August 22, 1965. During the game, Giants pitcher Juan Marichal was batting against Koufax and felt that Dodger catcher John Roseboro's throw back to the pitcher was too close to his ear. Marichal took his bat and hit Roseboro over the head with it, creating an on-the-field scuffle between the two rival teams. Marichal was suspended for over a week and missed two starts that ultimately helped contribute to his team's fading at the end of the season with the Dodgers winning the pennant by only two games. The incident marred Marichal's reputation and fueled the rivalry.

Pitcher Sandy Koufax (*left*) and catcher John Roseboro celebrate on the field in Los Angeles, October 6, 1963, after the Los Angeles Dodgers beat the New York Yankees 2–1 to take the 1963 World Series in four straight games. (AP / Wide World Photo)

Marichal had begun his major-league career with the San Francisco Giants in 1960. In his first game, he pitched a one-hit shutout to beat the Philadelphia Phillies. Marichal enjoyed his first twenty-game-win season in 1963, an accomplishment he repeated several times, leading the league with twenty-six games in 1963 and 1968. He maintained an earned run average (ERA) that never rose above 2.76. Marichal won the most games for any pitcher during the 1960s with 161 victories, but was never awarded the Cy Young Award.

Koufax was scheduled to pitch game 1 of the 1965 World Series for the Dodgers, but because the game fell on Yom Kippur, the Jewish Day of Atonement, the Jewish pitcher opted to sit out his start, creating a stir among baseball fans who debated the role of religion and sports. The Dodgers went on to defeat the Minnesota Twins in seven games with Koufax winning the Series MVP Award. Koufax won his third unanimous Cy Young Award in 1966, his final season, though his Dodgers lost in the World Series to the Baltimore Orioles in four games.

The Boston Red Sox made it to postseason play in 1967 led by their triple-crown, MVP-winning outfielder Carl Yastrzemski, who hit .326 with 44 home runs and 121 runs batted in. Facing the St. Louis Cardinals, the Red Sox lost in seven games. Bob Gibson of the Cardinals was the 1967 Series MVP, pitching three complete games in games 1, 4, and 7 and giving up only three earned runs. In 1968 Gibson's ERA was 1.12, a record low. He pitched forty-seven consecutive scoreless innings. In addition to winning the Cy Young Award that season, he also won the NL MVP award in what has since become known as "the Year of the Pitcher."

Some believe that the pitcher's mound was lowered five inches by the start of the next season to control for Gibson's dominance. It had little effect on him, with Gibson pitching to a 20–13 record and 2.18 ERA. He won the Cy Young Award in 1968 and 1970. Between 1963 and 1970, he won 156 games and lost 81, along with nine Gold Glove awards.

The Cardinals met the Detroit Tigers in the World Series. Gibson struck out seventeen Tigers in game 1. Pitching against Gibson's Cardinals in the 1968 Series was Denny McLain, the AL MVP and Cy Young Award winner who compiled a 31–6 record. In the Series, McLain met his match with Gibson, losing both games 1 and 4. He was able to win game 6 on two days rest and the Tigers won the Series in game 7. McLain won his second Cy Young Award the next season.

In one of the most improbable matchups of the decade, and perhaps baseball history, the young New York Mets, a team created to replace the Dodgers and Giants, found themselves in the World Series against the Baltimore Orioles. Because of the growth of the leagues, the 1969 postseason marked a change in the playoff structure. With the American and National Leagues each now having East and West Divisions, the division winners played each other to determine who would play in the World Series. Leading the Mets into the playoffs was pitcher Tom Seaver, who had won Rookie of the Year honors with the Mets in 1967, tallying sixteen victories for the last-place team. In his second season, Seaver again won sixteen games with over 200 strikeouts, but his team continued to find themselves in the bottom of the NL standings. In 1969 the Mets and Seaver enjoyed tremendous years. Seaver won twenty-five games and the Cy Young Award. In the playoffs, the Mets defeated the Atlanta Braves with the Orioles beating the Twins. In the Series, Seaver lost game 1, but won game 4 with a complete game, ten-inning victory. The "Miracle Mets" won the series in five games over the Orioles. At the end of the season, Seaver was awarded the Hickok Belt as the top professional athlete of the year and named "Sportsman of the Year" by *Sports Illustrated*. Following his World Series season, Seaver set a record on April 22, 1970, when he struck out the last ten batters, finishing with nineteen strikeouts, tying a record set by the Phillies' Steve Carlton. The Orioles bounced back from their World Series loss to the Mets to reach the postseason in 1970 and defeated the Cincinnati Reds in five games.

Basketball

Professional Basketball

The NBA underwent a number of changes during the 1960s, including the format of playoffs, expansion, and the challenge of the American Basketball Association. At the start of the decade, NBA seasons were seventy-nine games long with a seven-game championship playoff series. In 1961, the East Division had four teams (Boston Celtics, Philadelphia Warriors, Syracuse Nationals, and New York Knicks) and the West Division had five teams (Los Angeles Lakers, Cincinnati Royals, Detroit Pistons, St. Louis Hawks, and Chicago Packers). By the end of the decade, the professional basketball landscape had expanded across the country with five additional teams, an expanded playoff structure, and a young rival league.

Expansion and relocation in professional basketball, much like other professional sports, were prominent themes during the 1960s and one that forced fans to pay close attention to who was playing where and with what team name. Prior to the 1960–61 season, the Minneapolis Lakers moved to Los Angeles. The next year, a team was added to Chicago. Before the 1962–63 season, the Philadelphia Warriors moved to San Francisco and into the Western Division, with Cincinnati switching to the Eastern Division. That same season, the Chicago Packers changed their name to the Chicago Zephyrs, though not for long. A year later, the Zephyrs relocated to Baltimore and changed their name to the Bullets. The Syracuse Nationals moved to fill the void in Philadelphia, becoming the 76ers. To fill the void left by the Zephyrs, Chicago was awarded a new franchise, the Bulls in 1966–67. The Bulls made the NBA a league of ten teams, split into two divisions of five teams. Using a new playoff format that year, the division winners played the fourth-place teams in a first round, with a division championship round to follow, and then the league championship. In 1967–68, two more teams were added, the Seattle Supersonics and the San Diego Rockets, for a twelve-team league playing eighty-two games per season. It was in this same year, with the growing popularity of basketball and other cities wanting a team of their own, that the American Basketball Association began play in cities where NBA teams were not located, including Dallas, Denver, Houston, and Oakland.

The ABA started the 1967–68 season with eleven teams playing seventy-eight games per season. The ABA was able to attract some NBA talent, with the new Oakland franchise signing one of the NBA's leading scorers, Rick Barry, and hiring former NBA star George Mikan as the league's commissioner. The next season, the NBA responded by adding two more teams, the Milwaukee Bucks and the Phoenix Suns. Just as the NBA relocated franchises, the ABA suffered similar growth pangs. The Anaheim Amigos became the Los Angeles Stars in 1968 before becoming the Utah Stars in 1970. The Houston Mavericks became the Carolina Cougars in 1969. The Minnesota Muskies were the forerunners of the Miami Floridians (1968) and later, simply, Floridians (1970). Before the league even started, the New Jersey Firefighters changed their moniker to the Americans and the next year became the New York Nets in 1968. The Oakland Americans, who began as the Oaks, moved to become the Washington Capitals in the first season and two years later were the Pittsburgh Condors. The New Orleans Buccaneers relocated to become the Memphis Pros in 1970, leaving the Dallas Chaparrals, Denver Rockets, Indiana Pacers, San Diego Conquistadors, and Kentucky Colonels as the only teams to stay in one place for the first four years of the league. The National Basketball Association was dominated by the Boston Celtics' dynasty during the 1960s. The Boston Celtics won titles in 1961, 1962, 1963, 1964, 1965, 1966, 1968, and 1969, leaving two titles for other teams during the ten-year period. With a cast of terrific players, including Bill Russell, Bob Cousy, and K.C. Jones, along with their coach, Red Auerbach, the first championship of the decade came at the hands of the Minneapolis Lakers. Over the 1960s, the Celtics and Lakers would square off regularly in the postseason creating a rivalry that was unparalleled. With new players and a returning cast, such as John Havlicek, Sam Jones, Frank Ramsey, and Satch Sanders, the Celtics won eight consecutive titles, with six of those titles coming against the Lakers. Over the 1961–62 season, the Celtics won a record sixty games. They defeated the Lakers for their fourth consecutive title in game 7 overtime. The next season, Bill Russell won the season MVP award and led the Celtics to their fifth straight championship title, this time needing only six games to beat the Lakers.

Auerbach was a great coach who had the respect of his players. In 1964 he started five African Americans, the first time that had occurred in an NBA game. Auerbach retired in 1966 and became the general manager, handing the reins over to player Bill Russell, who served as player-coach. Russell was the first African American to coach a modern American professional sport team. Russell's first season as a player-coach resulted in the Celtics losing their first championship title in eight years, to the Philadelphia 76ers. The Celtics went on to win titles again in 1968 and 1969, beating the Lakers both times. When Russell retired after the 1969 season, his Celtics team had won eleven of the previous thirteen titles.

The other two teams to win an NBA title during the 1960s were the Philadelphia 76ers in 1967 over the Warriors, and the New York Knicks, who in 1970 won their first title. In the ABA, the Pittsburgh Pipers defeated the New Orleans Buccaneers for the inaugural title in 1968, with the Oakland Oaks defeating the Indiana Pacers the next year, and the Pacers returning in 1970 to defeat the Los Angeles Stars.

Oscar Robertson, Jerry West, Elvin Hayes, Wes Unseld, Willis Reed, Rick Barry, John Havlicek, Dave Bing, Billy Cunningham, Sam Jones, and Lenny Wilkens were some of the top stars of the 1960s. Elgin Baylor was a scoring machine for the Lakers in the first years of the 1960s. He averaged 34.8 points per game (ppg) in 1960–61, 38.3 in 1961–62, and 34.0 in 1962–63. Jerry West was drafted second by the Lakers in 1960 and was part of the Laker team that established the rivalry with the Celtics. West's Lakers lost to the Celtics in the 1969 finals, but he became the first player from the losing team to win the series MVP. Oscar Robertson, the Big "O," joined the Cincinnati Royals in 1960. As a rookie, Robertson averaged 30.5 ppg, 10.1 rebounds per game (rpg), and a league-leading 9.7 assists per game (apg). He earned Rookie of the Year honors and was selected to the All-NBA First Team, as well as playing in the All-Star Game. Robertson was selected to the All-NBA First Team nine seasons in a row. In his sophomore campaign, Robertson rewrote the history books when he averaged a triple-double, with 30.8 ppg, 12.5 rpg, and 11.4 apg. The Royals even made the playoffs after finishing at the bottom in the prior season. By the 1962–63 season, the Royals, led by Robertson, played their way into the NBA finals, losing to the Celtics dynasty. He won another MVP award in 1963–64 for his 31.4 ppg, 9.9 rpg, and 11.0 apg. The Royals traded Robertson to the Milwaukee Bucks before the 1970–71 season, a move that surprised many basketball experts.

One of Robertson's important contributions to the NBA is referred to as the Oscar Robertson suit, which he filed in 1970 as the president of the Players Association. The lawsuit contended that the NBA was in violation of antitrust laws when they restricted player movement. Eventually the suit was settled in 1976, after Robertson's retirement, and allowed free agency for the players, leading to higher salaries.

Jerry Lucas joined Robertson and the Cincinnati Royals in 1963–64 after enjoying a tremendous college and Olympic career. Winning Rookie of the Year honors, Lucas averaged 17.7 ppg and 17.4 rpg in his first NBA campaign. Rick Barry won the Rookie of the Year award in 1965–66 after averaging 25.7 ppg and 10.6 rpg. His Warriors team played in the 1967 NBA championships and lost to the 76ers in six games. Barry jumped from the NBA to the ABA prior to the 1967–68 season after a contract dispute with the Warriors and eventually played for the Oakland Oaks of the ABA, earning a championship in 1968–69. Barry relocated with the

Oaks when they moved to Washington, DC, and later Virginia, before returning to the NBA and the Warriors in 1972.

In the 1968–69 draft, Elvin Hayes was picked first by the San Diego Rockets and Wes Unseld was selected second. In his rookie year, Hayes led the league in scoring with 28.4 ppg. He averaged 17.1 rpg and was named to the All-Rookie Team. Unseld was voted Rookie of the Year and MVP in 1968–69 playing for the Baltimore Bullets. The year before he was drafted, the Bullets finished in sixth place, but with Unseld they won first place in their division. They lost in the division semifinals. Lew Alcindor was drafted first by the Milwaukee Bucks in 1969, after turning down a $1-million offer from the Harlem Globetrotters. Alcindor made an immediate impact on the league and his team, who jumped to second place in his rookie season. He won Rookie of the Year honors after finishing second in scoring with 28.8 ppg and third in rebounding with 14.5 rpg. In only his second season in the NBA, Alcindor won the MVP award, along with the scoring title with 31.7 ppg. He led the Bucks into the postseason, which included a championship over the Baltimore Bullets in a four-game sweep. After the finals, Alcindor announced that he had changed his name to Kareem Abdul Jabbar, Arabic for "noble, servant of the powerful one."

"Pistol" Pete Maravich graduated from Louisiana State University in 1970 and was the third pick of the NBA draft. He signed a record $1.6-million contract with the Atlanta Hawks, making him one of the league's highest-paid players. As a rookie he averaged 23.2 ppg and was named to the All-Rookie Team.

The two players who dominated the NBA during the 1960s were Wilt Chamberlain and Bill Russell, two centers who matched up time after time, big game after big game. Chamberlain was the more flamboyant performer, with statistics and record performances that amazed basketball fans and players alike. Russell, though he was a terrific athlete and accumulated plenty of impressive statistics of his own, was also a member of the Celtics' dynasty and the NBA titles he won far outmatched Chamberlain's various teams.

Chamberlain's historic accomplishments during the 1960s include becoming the first player to score 3,000 points in a season, as well as the first player to collect more than 2,000 rebounds in a single season. In one game, Chamberlain grabbed a record fifty-five rebounds. In 1961–62, Chamberlain set another scoring record when he tallied 4,029 points with an astounding 50.4 ppg and 25.7 rpg. On March 2, 1962, Chamberlain established an all-time single-game scoring record when he scored 100 points in a game against the New York Knicks, leading the Warriors to a high-scoring 169–147 victory. Chamberlain led the Warriors to the NBA finals in 1964 against the powerful Celtics, losing in five games.

During the 1964–65 season, the Warriors traded Chamberlain to the Philadelphia 76ers and renewed his Eastern Division rivalry with the Celtics and Bill Russell. Chamberlain and Bill Russell enjoyed an intense but friendly competition over the span of their careers with their team meeting in postseason play and often spoiling the hopes of the other. At the end of the 1964–65 campaign, the 76ers met the Celtics in the division championships. In game 7, the 76ers lost in the final seconds to the Celtics, marking the fifth time in seven years that the Celtics had beaten Chamberlain and whichever team he was playing for in postseason play. Chamberlain responded the next year by winning the NBA MVP award for his performance of 33.5 ppg and 24.6 rpg. After losing in the postseason to the Celtics again in 1966, Chamberlain and the 76ers retooled in their efforts to beat their

Wilt Chamberlain (November 1965), Philadelphia vs. San Fransico at Madison Square Garden. (Courtesy of Photofest)

nemesis. With a new coach who implemented an offense that spread the ball around, and Chamberlain's efforts to work with his teammates, the 76ers met the Celtics in the Eastern Conference finals in 1967. In a five-game series, the 76ers were finally able to defeat the Celtics, led by player-coach Russell, who had replaced Auerbach. Once past the Celtics, the 76ers faced the Warriors in the finals, and won the series in six games, giving Chamberlain his first title.

After enjoying their championship season, the 76ers continued to win, the next season (1967–68) owning the best record in the league. Chamberlain won his fourth MVP award for his performance of 24.3 ppg, and 23.8 rpg, as well leading the league in assists with 702, an amazing stat for a big man. He also became the first player to score 25,000 points over his career. The 76ers met the New York Knicks in the Eastern Division semifinals, winning in six games. Like clockwork, the 76ers then faced the familiar Russell and his Celtics. The 76ers led the series three games to one, but the Celtics rallied back to win game 5 and then game 6, causing a game 7 matchup for the NBA title. The Celtics beat the 76ers in Philadelphia, 100–96, winning back their title and marking the first time that a team had lost the series after leading by three games to one. Chamberlain's teams were now 1–6 against the Celtics in playoff series.

Prior to the 1968 season, Chamberlain was traded to the Los Angeles Lakers, the first time a MVP winner was traded the next season. Ticket sales for the Lakers went up over 10 percent, but Chamberlain's statistics were not as gaudy as past years, though still respectable at 20.5 ppg and 21.1 rpg. It seemed as if Chamberlain's teams were now a perpetual playoff contender and the Lakers beat the Warriors and then the Hawks in the Western Division playoffs before meeting up with the team Chamberlain had played the prior year, the Celtics. The series went to down to the deciding game 7 for the second year in a row between Chamberlain and Russell. This game 7 resulted in another title victory for the Celtics, who were able to pull out a win by a score of 108–106, with Chamberlain sitting out the last six minutes. For the fourth year in a row, Chamberlain's team made it into the NBA finals when the Lakers met the New York Knicks in 1970. For the third year in a row, Chamberlain's team was denied the NBA title in game 7.

College Basketball

College basketball generally provided the manpower for America's Olympic teams. Several teams were very successful over the decade, making regular appearances in postseason play. The NCAA Tournament typically included twenty-five teams over several rounds of play with single elimination. Ohio State won the NCAA title in 1960 and lost the next two years to Cincinnati. The Buckeyes were led by Olympic gold medalist Jerry Lucas and coach Fred Taylor. Lucas was an All-American and won Big Ten Player of the Year three years in a row (1960–62), and his team never lost a game on their home court during his tenure. His Buckeyes lost only one game in 1961, a year after winning their NCAA title, and he was named *Sports Illustrated*'s Sportsman of the Year, selected among college and professional athletes.

Cincinnati lost the title in 1963 to Loyola (Illinois), a team that started four black athletes, the first time for an NCAA championship contest. In 1963 Mississippi State did not compete in the NCAA Basketball Tournament because of an unwritten law that forbade interracial competition. In 1964 UCLA emerged to win their first of a record number of national championships. Led by coach John Wooden, UCLA won the NCAA title in 1964, beating Duke, after winning every game that season, capping off a perfect 30–0 campaign. UCLA became only the fifth school to repeat as champions in 1965, beating Michigan 91–80 and finishing the season at 28–2. The signing of the first African American basketball player at Texas Christian University in 1965 was significant enough to merit attention in *Sports Illustrated*. Texas–El Paso (UTEP) was the lone winner during UCLA's stretch defeating the University of Kentucky in 1966, in a game that has since been documented in a Hollywood film,

Rick Barry, future NBA Hall of Fame player, pictured as a collegian at the University of Miami, where he led the nation in scoring. (AP / Wide World Photo)

Glory Road. That UTEP squad had five black starters, the first time that had occurred in a championship game.

UCLA did not qualify for the postseason tournament that year, but returned the next season, with a new player, Lew Alcindor, and their second perfect 30–0 season, ending with their NCAA title victory over Dayton, 79–64. The number 1–ranked Bruins were matched against the number 2–ranked University of Houston Cougars in the first ever nationally televised college basketball game, played in the spacious Houston Astrodome in front of over 52,000 spectators. The Bruins' forty-seven-game winning streak was snapped by the Cougars by a score of 71–69 and the game was dubbed the "Game of the Century." Later that season, UCLA faced Houston in the semifinals of the NCAA tournament and avenged their earlier loss with a 101–69 win and a trip to the finals against the University of North Carolina, whom they defeated 78–55 for their second straight title. The Wooden-led Bruins finished Alcindor's senior season with a 29–1 record ending with their third consecutive NCAA title, beating Purdue 92–72. For their fourth straight title, the Bruins defeated Jacksonville 80–69 for the 1970 crown and finishing with a 28–2 record. UCLA basketball would roll into the 1970s with four straight titles and continue on for a total of seven straight titles and nine titles over eleven seasons. No other college basketball team would come close to John Wooden and the dynasty of the UCLA Bruins during the 1960s and 1970s.

Football

Professional Football

Professional football at the start of the 1960s offered football fans two options, the National Football League (NFL) and its new rival, the American Football League (AFL), a group of owners left out of the NFL who started the league in 1960. For several years these two leagues competed for fans, players, and television dollars before finally merging to become one league.

The National Football League heading into the 1961 season was comprised of fourteen teams and divided into two divisions, East (New York Giants, Philadelphia Eagles, Cleveland Browns, St. Louis Cardinals, Pittsburgh Steelers, Dallas Cowboys, Washington Redskins) and West (Green Bay Packers, Detroit Lions, Baltimore Colts, Chicago Bears, San Francisco 49ers, Los Angeles Rams, Minnesota Vikings). At the end of each season, a championship game was played between the winners of each division.

The American Football League began play in 1960 and at the start of the 1961 season was comprised of eight teams in two divisions, East (Houston Oilers, Boston Patriots, New York Titans, Buffalo Bills) and West (San Diego Chargers, Dallas Texans, Oakland Raiders, Denver Broncos), with a similar playoff format as their NFL counterparts.

Pete Rozelle was elected commissioner of the NFL in 1960, while Lamar Hunt served as the president of the AFL, with Joe Foss as commissioner. When the AFL arrived on the football scene in 1960, the two leagues made a "no tampering" verbal pact that helped define the boundaries between the two leagues as they scouted talent. The upstart AFL signed a five-year television deal with ABC.

Television and radio contracts were an additional source of revenue for both leagues, and over the decade each league made a number of deals that helped solidify its standing. Despite the NFL's tradition and efforts to proclaim its league as the "better" league, the AFL media deals were continued evidence of the league's legitimate standing as a challenger to the NFL. In 1961 the NFL signed a two-year deal with NBC for the rights to the championship games, at a cost of $615,000 each season. Almost half that money was earmarked for the player benefit package. That same season Congress passed a bill that legalized single network television contracts by each professional football league. In 1962 CBS poured its money into the NFL, agreeing to telecast regular-season games for $4.65 million a year. The AFL secured a television contract with NBC to air their championship game for $926,000 in 1963. Both leagues enjoyed paydays in 1964 when the NFL and CBS inked a $14.1 million a year deal for two years to air regular-season games with an additional $1.8 million for the championship games. The AFL and NBC agreed to a five-year, $36-million television contract, making it clear that the renegade league was going to be a permanent fixture in professional football. CBS and the NFL signed a new contract in 1965 for the 1966 and 1967 seasons for $18.8 million per year and the next year agreed to $2 million for each championship game. In an important agreement, CBS and NBC paid $9.5 million for the rights to air a proposed AFL-NFL championship game. In 1969 ABC signed a deal to televise *Monday Night Football*, thirteen games a season, with a contract that would run three years.

Each league culminated its season with a championship game. The Green Bay Packers and the New York Giants met in the NFL championship game for the first two titles of the 1960s, with the Packers winning both, blanking the Giants, 37–0 in 1961, and winning 16–7 in 1962. The Giants lost their third championship game in a row, falling to the Chicago Bears 14–10 in 1963. The Cleveland Browns defeated the Baltimore Colts 27–0 for the 1964 title. The next year, the Packers and Colts met in a Western conference playoff game to determine which team would meet the winner of the Eastern Conference. Green Bay won in overtime, 13–10, and went on to defeat the Browns 23–12 for their third title in five years. In the final NFL championship game before the merger of the two leagues, the Packers beat the Dallas Cowboys 34–27 in the 1966 title game.

The AFL's first championship game in 1960 was won by the Houston Oilers, who defeated the Los Angeles Chargers, 24–16. Houston won its second title in 1961 over the relocated San Diego Chargers, by a score of 10–3. The Oilers were led by 1961 MVP QB George Blanda, who threw for over 3,000 yards and 36 touchdowns. Blanda also kicked for the Oilers, making sixteen of twenty-six field goals. The Dallas Texans ended Houston's run in 1962, beating the Oilers in overtime, 20–17. The Texans were led by QB Len Dawson, who in 1962 threw for almost 2,800 yards and seventeen touchdowns. The Boston Patriots beat the Buffalo Bills 26–8 in an Eastern Division playoff, and were then trounced by the Chargers in the 1963 championship game, 51–10. The Chargers were led by two top players, flanker Lance Alworth and quarterback (QB) Tobin Rote. That season, Alworth caught sixty-one passes for 1,205 yards and eleven touchdowns from QB Rote, who threw for 2,510 yards and seventeen touchdowns. The Chargers made it to their fourth title game in five years in 1964, but lost to the Bills 20–7. Jack Kemp was the QB for the Bills and, after leading the Bills to the AFL title in 1964, he had an MVP season in 1965, throwing for 2,368 yards and ten touchdowns, while running in the end zone for four more, and leading the Bills to the 1965 title game where they beat the Chargers 23–0. Paul Lowe, playing for the Chargers, became the first AFL player to rush for more than 1,000 yards in two seasons. In his 1965 MVP season, Lowe rushed for 1,121 yards, following up a 1963 season with 1,010 yards. In 1966 the Kansas City Chiefs defeated the defending champion Bills, 31–7.

While relocation was not frequent, it did occur, and as each league grew in popularity, expansion became a trend in both leagues. The AFL's Los Angeles Chargers moved to San Diego after their first season of play. In 1963 the Dallas Texans relocated to become the Kansas City Chiefs. Atlanta was awarded an AFL franchise for the 1966 season, with a team awarded to Cincinnati the following season.

Certainly there was a great deal of friction between the two leagues. One league would secretly convince a player to sign with them, one league would pay more money than the other, and fans debated which league was stronger and had the better players. The AFL owners took their complaints through legal routes and filed an antitrust lawsuit against the NFL, which the AFL lost in 1962. The rivalry only intensified. The AFL stunned the football world by signing rookie quarterback Joe Namath out of the University of Alabama for $400,000, a record amount and an indication that the challenge league was legitimate. Namath's signing surely contributed to NFL owners considering the merger of the two leagues. The recruiting and signing of college players was one of the main disputes between the two leagues.

The integration of professional football was underway in both leagues, though each league had a different approach to the issue. The AFL was more proactive in recruiting and signing African American players and benefited from their level of play, making

Weeb Ewbank, head coach of the American Football League's New York Jets, takes a look at Joe Namath, the team's $400,000 quarterback from the University of Alabama during a light workout on Namath's surgically repaired knee in New York, on June 29, 1965. (AP / Wide World Photo)

the AFL more exciting and high-scoring than the NFL, which was slow in integrating its rosters. Several racial incidents in professional football merit discussion. In September 1964 the San Diego Chargers were in Atlanta for an exhibition game with the New York Jets. Several African American players were playing pool in a hotel and were asked to leave the facilities. In January 1965 the African American players selected for the AFL All-Star game decided to boycott the game hosted in New Orleans because of several incidents of discrimination in their first day in the southern city. Instead of playing the game without the players or canceling the game, the AFL owners and commissioner moved the game to Houston. Several players believed that NFL teams had quotas for the number of African Americans on each roster. At least one player had trouble finding housing in Dallas.

Finally, after years of competition between the two leagues off the field, the leagues decided to compete on the field. It was announced on June 8, 1966, that

1965 AFL All-Star Game Boycott

The 1965 American Football League All-Star Game boycott occurred as a result of African American players who, after arriving in New Orleans and facing a number of racial incidents, voted to leave the southern city and skip the game. The players presented their concerns to the leadership of the AFL, who instead of dismissing the concerns of the players decided to relocate the game from New Orleans to Houston in less than a week. The boycott stands as an example of a group of players standing together to fight against discrimination.

Several events during the week preceding the All-Star Game led to the protest. African American all-stars were refused service at nightclubs and confronted by nightclub doormen brandishing guns. Several players were stranded at the airport for up to three hours because no taxis would pick them up, while others were refused taxi service around the city. Other players recounted statements directed at them. The players were led to believe that they would not encounter such incidents and were quite surprised by the reception they received.

On January 10, 1965, the African American players from both teams met at the Roosevelt Hotel, the headquarters for the East All-Star team, and discussed their treatment and possible responses to the treatment. The players included at least one from each AFL team. After a long discussion about the treatment they had received, the twenty-one African American All-Star players from the American Football League decided to boycott the All-Star Game in New Orleans scheduled for January 16, 1965. Arguing that the city and its citizens discriminated against them, the African American players voted 18–3 to boycott the game and informed Commissioner Joe Foss of their decision.

Efforts to convince the players to stay by the New Orleans branch of the NAACP were unsuccessful. Commissioner Foss found the situation regrettable, but agreed the players had adequate reasons for the walkout. The players also had the support of the American Football League Players Association. The athletes' collective protest succeeded when Commissioner Foss decided to relocate the game to Jeppeson Stadium in Houston, a much smaller venue, which virtually guaranteed a financial loss. African American newspapers nationwide recognized the collective effort and compared the players' protest with other civil rights protests in their reports on the incidents and related editorials. The relocated game, won by the West, 38–14, drew only 15,446.

the two leagues would merge to form a twenty-four-team league. The two leagues continued to play separate schedules until 1969 but agreed to meet in a world championship game matching each league's top team against the other. Until then, the former NFL realigned themselves into the East (with Capital and Central divisions) and West (Central and Coastal divisions). The new merged league proposed to expand to twenty-six teams by 1968 and twenty-eight by 1970. Congress approved the merger. The structure of the new National Football League was divided into two conferences, the National Football Conference (NFC) and the American Football Conference (AFC), with two divisions in each. That year, the AFL and NFL spent a combined $7 million on their draft picks and AFL Commissioner Joe Foss resigned his position. The Oakland Raiders' owner Al Davis took over Foss's position until the merger was complete.

The 1967 Oakland Raiders were led by MVP QB Daryle Lamonica, who threw for 3,228 yards and thirty touchdowns, leading the team to the AFL title game against the Oilers. Lamonica continued to post impressive numbers, and the next season he passed for over 3,200 yards and twenty-five touchdowns. Lamonica and Namath shared MVP honors in 1969, the last year an AFL MVP award was given. Lamonica had his third straight season of over 3,000 yards with 3,302 yards and thirty-four touchdowns, and helped lead the Raiders to a playoff victory over the Oilers, before losing to the Jets. Namath, following his Super Bowl victory, passed for 2,734 yards and nineteen touchdowns.

On January 15, 1967, Los Angeles Coliseum hosted the first AFL-NFL World Championship Game, pitting the Green Bay Packers representing the NFL against the AFL's Kansas City Chiefs. The game was aired on both CBS and NBC, and was witnessed by 61,946 fans at the game. The Packers defeated the Chiefs 35–10, giving the NFL the first win in the merging of the two leagues in postseason play. The Packers were rewarded with $15,000 for each player and the losing Chiefs earned $7,500 each. In the second World Championship matchup between the NFL and AFL, played on January 14, 1968 in Miami, the Packers repeated their title with a 33–14 win over the Oakland Raiders. For the first time, a football game received over $3 million in gate receipts. Prior to the 1969 season, the postseason format was reconfigured. In the AFL, the winner of one division was scheduled to play the runner-up in the other division, providing a round of games before the big NFL-AFL game. Played in Miami on January 12, 1969, and now called the Super Bowl, the New York Jets faced the Baltimore Colts. Jets QB Joe Namath had thrown for a record-high 4,007 yards in 1967 and followed up his record-setting performance by winning the AFL MVP award, throwing for 3,147 yards and fifteen touchdowns, and leading the Jets to the Super Bowl game versus the heavily favored Colts and their MVP-winning QB Earl Morrall. Namath guaranteed a win for his underdog team and unexpectedly led his team to a 16–7 over the Colts, marking the first time the AFL emerged as the victors in the postseason clash. Namath's prediction and subsequent win cemented his legendary status in the game, some of it established with his commercial endorsements and luxurious New York lifestyle.

During the 1969 season, four NFL teams (Miami, Baltimore, Pittsburgh, Cleveland) were shifted to the new AFC for a total of thirteen AFC teams. The playoff format added a "wild card" team. In Super Bowl IV, on January 11, 1970, the AFC's Kansas City Chiefs defeated the NFC's Minnesota Vikings, 23–7, at the annual showdown hosted in New Orleans. Nine months later, Green Bay Packer coach Vince Lombardi died on September 3, 1970, and the NFL renamed the trophy awarded to the Super Bowl winner the Lombardi Trophy in honor of the legendary coach.

Gambling became a concern in 1963 when two NFL players were suspended for placing bets on football games, including ones in which their teams played. NFL commissioner Pete Rozelle suspended Green Bay Packer QB Paul Hornung and Detroit Lion Alex Karras for one year for gambling on the football games. Hornung had been the NFL MVP in 1961. Five of Karras's teammates were fined $2,000 for betting on games they did not play in. Both Karras and Hornung were reinstated for the 1964 season.

On September 7, 1963, the Pro Football Hall of Fame opened its doors in Canton, Ohio, and four years later inducted their first African American member, Emlen Tunnell. The Buffalo Bills guard Bob Kalsu, drafted by the team in 1968, had to fulfill his ROTC obligation and serve in Vietnam. Kalsu was killed in action on July 21, 1970, becoming the only active NFL player killed in duty. A major labor advance was reached in 1970, when the league consented to a four-year agreement with the Players Association that guaranteed $4,535,000 a year to the player pension and insurance benefits.

Notable players in professional football in the 1960s include a list of all-star performers. Quarterbacks and running backs dominated the MVP list in both the AFL and NFL. Notable QBs of the 1960s included New York Giants QB Y. A. Tittle, who won the NFL MVP award in 1962 and 1963, Colt QB Johnny Unitas, who won the NFL MVP in 1964 and 1967, and Bart Starr, Green Bay Packers QB, who won the award in 1966. In 1969 Los Angeles Rams QB Roman Gabriel won the NFL MVP with John Brodie, QB of the San Francisco 49ers, following in 1970.

Abner Hayes, a halfback for the Dallas Texans, won the AFL MVP award, along with the Rookie of the Year award, after leading the league in rushing yards (875 yards) and touchdowns. Cookie Gilchrist enjoyed a great career with several AFL teams beginning with the Buffalo Bills after playing in the Canadian Football League (CFL). In his first AFL season, 1962, Gilchrist rushed for over 1,000 yards, the first time in AFL history. He scored fifteen touchdowns as a rusher and receiver, along with kicking fourteen extra points and seven field goals. Packers RB Jim Taylor enjoyed a MVP season in 1962. Clem Daniels, a halfback on the Oakland Raiders, had a great season in 1963, gaining over 1,000 yards on the ground and close to 700 yards in receptions, scoring seven touchdowns. In the NFL, the dominant running back was Jim Brown of the Cleveland Browns, who won the NFL MVP in 1963 and 1965. Gino Cappelletti was another terrific receiver, catching seven touchdown passes in 1964, while gaining 865 yards in receptions. Cappelletti also served as the Patriots' field-goal kicker and made twenty-two of thirty-eight attempts in 1964, making him the highest-scoring kicker in AFL history. Jim Nance, a fullback for the Boston Patriots, was the AFL MVP in 1966, rushing for a record-high 1,458 yards and eleven touchdowns.

College Football

College football and basketball were the most popular college sports of the decade. Moreover, with the integration of colleges and athletic teams, both sports faced issues related to the integration process. With the integration of college campuses and college athletics, black college athletes emerged as central figures in increasing campus activism. College sport became a viable and visible platform for black college athletes to express their discontent at their treatment as black Americans and black athletes. Black college athletes employed similar tactics used in other protest activities of the civil rights movement, which eventually culminated in various boycott movements. In 1968 thirty-seven athletic protests, rebellions, and boycotts occurred in intercollegiate athletics.

In 1963 the University of Pittsburgh was invited to compete in the Sugar Bowl but had to turn down the invitation when bowl officials could not guarantee the integrated squad would find integrated facilities in the host city. That same year, Baylor University opened its athletic rosters to black athletes, and two years later, the lily-white Southeastern Conference (SEC) finally began to recruit black athletes. One football coach who held fast to segregated play was Gene Stallings of Texas A&M, who explained, "I've got nothing against the Negro athlete, but I don't believe he fits into our plans right now. What we need is a team that will work and pull and fight together and really get a feeling of oneness. We need to be a complete unit. I don't believe we could accomplish this with a Negro on the squad" (Scorecard 1965).

At San Jose State in 1967, the United Black Students for Action threatened to prevent the opening game of the football game from being played. Their protests were related to the treatment of black student-athletes. Eventually, the university president canceled the game. The success of the movement at San Jose State encouraged similar actions at other universities. African American football players protested their treatment at a number of universities, including Michigan State, University of Washington, University of Wyoming, Indiana University, and Syracuse University. Some were removed from their team for their protests, while some schools responded by hiring an African American coach, usually as an assistant.

College football crowned a number of champions throughout the decade, with no team dominating the top spot. While some years there was a consensus national champion, most years the top honor was shared by two teams, which was determined by reporter and coach voting. For example, in 1961, Ohio State and Alabama shared the national championship. The next year USC was named champion, a title they claimed again in 1967. Texas wore the title crown in 1963 and the next year three teams, Alabama, Arkansas, and Notre Dame, shared the top spot. Alabama repeated their winning ways, claiming the title in 1965, although this time sharing the top spot with Michigan State. Michigan State repeated in 1966, sharing the title with Notre Dame. Ohio State and Texas claimed sole ownership of the national championship in 1968 and 1969 respectively, with Texas and Nebraska sharing the honors in 1970. The most prestigious award given to college football during this era was the Heisman Trophy, with Ernie Davis of Syracuse winning in 1961. Other notable winners include Navy's Roger Staubach in 1962, Mike Garrett of USC in 1965, Steve Spurrier of Florida in 1966, and USC's O.J. Simpson in 1968. Stanford's Jim Plunkett won the award in 1970.

Hockey

Two teams dominated the National Hockey League during the 1960s, the Montreal Canadiens and the Toronto Maple Leafs. Montreal had been a power in the 1950s and they began to slide early in the 1960s. Despite the Canadiens' having the best record in the league in 1960–61, the Stanley Cup Playoffs were won by the Chicago Blackhawks and their young stars, Bobby Hull, Bill Hay, Murray Balfour, and Stan Mikita. Montreal's Doug Harvey, Bernie "Boom Boom" Geoffrion, and Jean Beliveau were beginning to age a bit. The Toronto team, led by Frank Mahovlich and Dave Keon, won the Stanley Cup three straight years from 1962 to 1964 and then in 1966. Montreal added young stars Yvan Cournoyer, Bobby Rousseau, John Ferguson, and Gilles Tremblay and won the Stanley Cup in 1965, 1967, 1968, and 1969. Bobby Orr entered the league in 1966 and became the top player in the game for the Boston Bruins, who would win the Cup in 1970 and 1972.

In 1967, the National Hockey League doubled in size from six to twelve teams, adding franchises in Philadelphia, Pittsburgh, Los Angeles, Oakland, Minnesota, and St. Louis. The rapid expansion put all the new squads in the Western Division, which was decidedly weaker than the older Eastern Division. It took until 1974 for an expansion team (the Philadelphia Flyers) to win a Stanley Cup.

Olympic Games

After the first televised Olympic Games in 1960, the next Olympiad occurred in 1964, with the Winter Games hosted in Innsbruck, Austria, and the Summer Games in Tokyo, Japan. Grenoble, France, hosted the 1968 Winter Games while Mexico City hosted the 1968 Summer Games. The Olympic Games during the 1960s exemplify the nexus of international politics and sport. Boycotts, student protests, apartheid, amateurism, and nationalism were the order of the day, with the IOC's President Avery Brundage standing at the helm of the growing sport

Gatorade

The famous sports drink Gatorade was invented in 1965 by a team of professors at the University of Florida and named for the team's mascot, the Gators. The coaching staff approached university physicians to identify why so many of the football players were affected by heat-related illnesses, common in the humid environs of Florida. The doctors, Robert Cade, Harry James Free, Dana Shires, and Alejandro de Quesada, determined that when the athletes sweat their bodies were not replacing the electrolytes excreted during exercise, and that the amount of carbohydrates the athletes utilized for energy expenditure were also not being replaced during exercise. The group of researchers worked to develop a beverage that would combat both problems. The result of the researchers' work was a carbohydrate-electrolyte drink that replaced what the body was excreting through sweat and exercise. They dubbed the cocktail "Gatorade." Dr. Cade patented the beverage and worked with Stokely-Van Camp, Inc., a fruit and vegetable canning company located in Indianapolis, to produce the beverage.

The football coaching staff supplied Gatorade to their players during practice and games, and the team performed successfully on the field, racking up a 7–4 season. The next season the Gators went 9–2 and won the Orange Bowl for the first time in school history. Other college football teams began to use Gatorade, and professional teams followed suit. In 1969 the Kansas City Chiefs began using Gatorade and ended up winning the Super Bowl. Players and coaches attributed their success to the sweet drink. Soon, recreational athletes were drinking Gatorade sold in stores across the country.

spectacle. Although the IOC required all participating athletes to be amateurs, there was a marked difference between the collegiate American athletes and their Eastern European competitors, who received support from their government. A number of record-setting performances and surprising victories also marked the era.

1964 Winter Olympic Games

Innsbruck, Austria, hosted thirty-six nations, including a combined East and West Germany team, and 1,091 athletes competing in thirty-four events at the 1964 Winter Olympic Games. One problem leading up to the Games was a lack of snow, which was solved by the Austrian army who delivered snow and ice bricks to the various venues. It was the first year luge events were held. The Olympic team from the United States won a total of six medals, finishing eighth among the countries and well behind the Soviet Union's 25 medals. The sole gold medal for the U.S. was won by speed skater Richard McDermott in the 500-meter. One woman won two medals for the U.S.; Jean Saubert won silver in the giant slalom and a bronze in the slalom. The other three medals came in men's slalom and men's figure skating.

1964 Summer Olympic Games

The Tokyo Olympic Games marked the first time the Olympic Games were hosted by an Asian nation. From ninety-three nations 5,051 athletes, including 678 women, participated in 163 events. Two sports, judo and volleyball, were included in the Games for the first time. It also marked the last time a cinder track was home to the track and field events. At the Toyko Games, American athletes battled the Soviet Union on the track, in the swimming pool, and on the courts. The United States won the unofficial medal count, collecting 36 golds, 26 silvers, and 28 bronze medals, for a total of 90 medals, a few medals short of the Soviet Union's 96 total medals, but outmatching their gold medals 36–30, thus putting them at the top. The host nation Japan finished third with 29 total medals, with the United Team of Germany coming in fourth with 50 total medals, but with only 10 gold medals compared to Japan's 16 first-place finishes.

Several Americans had stellar gold medal performances. In track and field, Billy Mills won a surprise victory in the 10,000-meter run, with Bob Hayes sprinting to victory in the 100-meter dash. The United States finished first and second in the men's 110-meter high hurdles and 200-meter dash. American male track and field athletes won medals in the 400- and 5000-meter run, and both relays (4×100- and 4×400-meter). Al Oerter won a gold medal in the discus with teammate David Weill claiming the bronze. High jumpers John Thomas and John Ranbo tied for second place. Ralph Boston won gold in the long jump, Fred Hansen won gold in the pole vault, and Dallas Long won gold in the shot put. Female tracksters won a number of medals, with Wyomia Tyus winning the 100-meter dash and Edith McGuire finishing second, but winning gold in the 200-meter race. The U.S. women won the 4×100-meter relay race.

American swimmers won twenty-nine of the medal count, with Don Schollander collecting four gold medals in the pool. Kathleen Ferguson won gold in the 100-meter backstroke, with teammate Virgina Duenkel claiming the bronze. Sharon Stouder won gold in the 100-meter butterfly and silver in the 100-meter freestyle. Kathleen Ellis collected two bronze medals, one in the 100-meter

Tennessee State Tigerbelles

The Tennessee State Tigerbelles were the most successful women's college athletic team prior to the passage of Title IX in 1972. Tennessee State dominated AAU competition, which was integrated, unlike several other sports. Tennessee State won indoor and outdoor national titles in the 1950s and 1960s. Led by Coach Ed Temple, the Tigerbelles represented the United States at Pan American Games, annual track meets between the Soviet Union and the United States, and U.S. Olympic teams. Temple ran a summer camp for his athletes, and included high school athletes as a means of introducing them to his training system and the Tennessee State campus. Many of the high school athletes attended Tennessee State for their college years.

One of the most famous Tigerbelles was three-time Olympic gold medalist Wilma Rudolph. Rudolph had been recruited to run for Temple when he saw her playing a high school basketball game. Rudolph ran as a sixteen-year-old in the 1956 Melbourne Olympic Games, winning a bronze medal as a member of the 4×100 meter relay (all four were part of Coach Temple's summer program). Four years later, Rudolph stunned the world watching the Rome Olympic Games in the first televised Games when she won three gold medals in the 100-meter dash, the 200-meter dash, and anchored the 4×100-meter relay with three teammates from Tennessee State. Upon returning from Rome, Rudolph finished her college education earning her degree in elementary education. She continued to compete in track meets, becoming the first woman to run at the Millrose Games in New York.

Other famous Tigerbelle Olympians include Mae Faggs, Lucinda Williams, Martha Hudson, Margaret Mathews, Barbara Jones, Willye White, and Isabelle Daniels. Faggs was an Olympian in 1948, 1952, and 1956. Eight Tigerbelles competed on the U.S. team at the American-Soviet Union meet hosted in Philadelphia in 1959. Later that year, ten Tigerbelles competed on the American team at the PanAm Games. In 1960 eighteen American women were on the track and field team, eleven of the women were African American and eight of those eleven were Tennessee State Tigerbelles. Tigerbelles continued to succeed on the international stage throughout the 1960s. Wyomia Tyus was the next great sprinter filling Rudolph's shoes. Tyus won the 100-meter dash in the 1964 Olympics and became the first track and field athlete to win the event in successive Olympic Games when she repeated her gold-medal performance in 1968, beating her Tigerbelle teammate Edith McGuire. McGuire won gold in the 200-meter dash.

---

butterfly and the other in the 100-meter freestyle. American men swept the top three spots in the 200-meter backstroke. American women swept the medals in the 400-meter freestyle and the 400-meter individual medley, including the remarkable gold medal performance by seventeen-year-old Donna De Varona, who also won gold in the 4×100-meter freestyle relay. De Varona had been the youngest member of the U.S. Olympic swim team at the 1960 Olympic Games. For her 1964 Olympic performances, De Varona won the Female Athlete of the Year Award from the Associated Press and United Press International. She became the first female sports broadcaster in 1965 with ABC and in 1968 worked as a commentator at the Mexico City Summer Olympic Games. American divers tallied eight medals, winning gold in the women's and men's 10-meter platform, and first in the men's and women's 3-meter springboard events.

Other medal performances at the 1964 Tokyo Games came in sailing, rowing, modern pentathlon, equestrian/eventing, weightlifting, shooting, judo, and wrestling. Boxer Joe Frazier won the gold medal in the heavyweight division and the U.S. men's basketball team won gold. Canoe/kayaker Marcia Jones-Smoke won a gold medal in the K-1 500-meter event

Prior to the Games, African American comedian and human-rights activist Dick Gregory tried to organize a boycott of the Tokyo Olympic Games, but failed. He was able to get people to protest and picket at the track and field trials. There were reports of incidents at the Tokyo Games which included unequal treatment of African American Olympians, including social activities, housing accommodations, and athletic assignments.

1968 Winter Olympic Games

The Winter Games of 1968 in Grenoble, France, had 1,158 athletes from thirty-seven nations compete in thirty-five events. The 1968 Games were the first Olympics that required female athletes (there were 211 at the event) to undergo sex testing. Norway claimed the unofficial medal count with a total of fourteen, with the Soviet Union in second with thirteen, and France in third with nine. The U.S. team tallied a total of seven medals, all coming on the ice. Two American figure skaters won medals. Tim Wood finished second in the men's event and Peggy Fleming won the prestigious gold medal on the women's side. The remaining five medals came in speed skating. Richard McDermott won silver in the 500-meter, while three American women, Jennifer Fish, Mary Meyers, and Dianne Holum, tied for the silver in the 500-meter women's event. Holum also won a bronze in the 1000-meter race.

1968 Summer Olympic Games

The Summer Games in Mexico City were the first ever hosted in Latin America and were rife with controversy even before the first competition occurred. University students protesting in a public plaza about the cost of the Games to the host country were shot and killed by government forces in the days leading up to the Games. The high altitude of the city was a major concern, with officials concerned that performances would be affected. These concerns proved to be real with world records being established in sports that required short bursts of power, such as sprinting and jumping events, and making endurance athletes, any event over two minutes, struggle in high-altitude environment. Consistent with what had occurred in Grenoble in the Winter Games, female athletes were sex tested. It was the first Games to include shooting as a women's event. At these Summer Games, 112 nations participated, bringing with them 5,516 athletes competing in 172 events. Noticeably absent was South Africa, suspended from the IOC as a result of other African nations threatening to boycott the Games if the apartheid nation was invited. Leading up to the Games, there had also been threats of a boycott by a contingent of African American athletes.

The Olympic trials for track and field were held during the summer of 1968. Many African American athletes, in all sports, had given thought to a boycott. Using the trials to promote the idea of a boycott, protesters held signs, one reading "WHY RUN IN MEXICO AND CRAWL AT HOME" (Underwood 1968). Talk of the boycott

Olympic Project for Human Rights

The Olympic Project for Human Rights (OPHR) was an organization started by Harry Edwards as a response to the inequities faced by black athletes in college and professional sports. The main focus of the Olympic Project for Human Rights during 1967 and 1968 was to promote a boycott of the Mexico City Olympic Games by America's black athletes. The OPHR also sponsored boycotts by college athletes of their own collegiate competitions prior to the October Games as a popular means of protest. Prior to the 1968 Olympic Games, the OPHR discussed the idea of African America athletes boycotting the games to help establish that the United States needed the athletic talent of African Americans to beat the best of other nations. Tired of being exploited for their athletic abilities, but being discriminated in sport and society, the athletes debated for months about what they should do.

The OPHR helped shape the debate and dialogue and created a list of six demands at the Black Youth Conference hosted in Los Angeles on November 22–23, 1967, attracting over 200 attendees. At a meeting held in New York City on December 15, 1967, at the Americana Hotel, the demands were presented. The first demand was the "restoration of Muhammad Ali's title" and Ali's right to box in the United States. The second demand was the removal of "Avery Brundage from his post as Chairman of the International Olympic Committee." Brundage was seen as both anti-Semitic and antiblack. The group's third demand was the "curtailment of participation of all-white and individuals from the Union of South Africa and Southern Rhodesia in all United States and Olympic Athletic events." The groups also demanded that there be the "addition of at least two black coaches to the men's track and field coaching staff appointed to coach the 1968 United States Olympic team; though Stan Wright was a Black coach, he was not considered acceptable because of his political leanings as a "devout Negro." The group's fifth demand was for the "appointment of at least two black people to policy making positions on the United States Olympic Committee; and their sixth and final demand was the "complete desegregation of the bigot dominated and racist New York Athletic Club" (Edwards 1969, 58–59).

OPHR organized a boycott of a track meet at the New York Athletic Club (NYAC). The committee wanted to attract international press coverage. There were mass withdrawals by teams and individual athletes, cancellation of the high school competition, and only nine black athletes registered for competition. Villanova's team withdrew as a result of a team vote. The boycott of the NYAC meet was successful in that attendance was down 50 percent, race times were mediocre, and the Russian National team withdrew from competition.

Despite the failure to inspire an all-out boycott of the 1968 Olympic Games, OPHR's presence was felt in a number of ways. Neither South Africa nor Rhodesia had teams competing at the Games as a result of pressure from other African nations, resulting in both countries being uninvited to participate. American athletes, white and black, wore OPHR buttons. The Harvard crew team members wore OPHR buttons. In photos of the famous victory stand gesture of Tommie Smith and John Carlos, all three medalists, including Australia's Peter Norman, are wearing OPHR buttons.

was mixed, with rumors spreading about threats on black athletes' lives if they did or did not boycott. African American track and field coach Stan Wright was shadowed by bodyguards after having his life threatened. Wright was not in support of the proposed boycott.

For some of the athletes, the proposed boycott had been a theme that resonated throughout the year, even if they were not planning on actually boycotting the Olympics. At the trials the black athletes who were certain to make the team had a meeting, with the group evenly divided about going ahead with the boycott. Many of the athletes felt their hard work and talent would go to waste if they were not able to compete at the Olympic Games. Others believed that their boycott would not send the desired message to the American people. It was decided that all the athletes would be released from their commitment to boycott the Games. For one, the boycotters could have been replaced by blacks who were not committed to a boycott; two, the sports establishment could point to black athletes who decided not to boycott and undermine the revolt that way; and perhaps most important, the unity among black athletes would have been strained. The plan accepted by fifty athletes at the trials meeting called for all the athletes to compete at Mexico City, but stated that no black athlete was to celebrate in any victory celebrations. There was talk of sitting during the national anthem and sewing emblems on their team uniforms. The athletes left the trials prepared to compete at the Olympics, but to make their displeasure with American racial practices known on the international stage.

In the medal count, the United States topped the unofficial medal count with 107 medals to the Soviet Union's 91, and well ahead of third-place finisher Japan's 25 medals. East and West Germany each had their own teams, with the German Democratic Republic finishing in fifth among nations and the Federal Republic of Germany close behind in eighth place, winning more medals than their former countrymen, but fewer golds. American track and field athletes, including many of the African American men who threatened to boycott earlier in the year, collected 28 medals of all three colors in a variety of events, with some world record–setting performances. Jimmy Hines and Charlie Greene finished first and third in the 100-meter race. On the women's side, Wyomia Tyus became the first athlete to repeat a gold-medal performance in the 100-meter race after her 1964 win in the same event. Tyus was trailed by teammate Barbara Ferrell for second place. The women's 4×100-meter relay put on a gold-medal performance. Madeline Manning-Jackson won a gold medal in the 800-meter run. Decathlete Bill Toomey earned a gold medal for his efforts, and American men swept the 400-meter race, with Lee Evans finishing first, followed by Larry James and Ron Freeman. Distance runner Jim Ryun won a silver in the 1500-meter run and Willie Davenport won a gold medal in the 110-meter high hurdles followed by his teammate Ervin Hall for the silver. James Matson repeated his 1964 gold-medal performance in the shot put, as did discus thrower Al Oerter, who won his fourth consecutive gold medal in the event.

In the high jump, American Dick Fosbury utilized a jumping style that had him use a curved approach and a takeoff over the bar which had his back clear the bar first in a move dubbed the "Fosbury Flop." Other jumpers used the traditional western roll approach, but Fosbury's innovative move changed the event and he won a gold medal at the Games. Long jumper Bob Beamon was one of the beneficiaries of the thin air in Mexico City. He long jumped to a world record distance of 29 feet, $2^1/_2$ inches, breaking the old record by more than 21 inches and establishing a new record that stood for twenty-three years.

After the 200-meter race, won by San Jose State's Tommie Smith with his teammate John Carlos finishing third, the reality of the pre-Olympic boycott and protest discussions became a reality. On the victory stand during the playing of the national

Extending gloved hands skyward in racial protest, U.S. athletes Tommie Smith (*center*) and John Carlos stare downward during the playing of the "Star-Spangled Banner" after Smith received the gold and Carlos the bronze for the 200-meter run at the Summer Olympic Games in Mexico City on October 16, 1968. Australian silver medalist Peter Norman is at left. (AP / Wide World Photo)

anthem, the two Americans stood in their bare stocking feet with each man holding a black gloved fist in the air, as a symbol of their stand against racial discrimination in America. The two athletes quickly left the Games returning to a mixed reception in the United States. The American press criticized the two African Americans for their inappropriate gesture and both men endured personal troubles following the event. The image of the two athletes, gloves in the air, became a renowned symbol of the Games and eventually gained respect from mainstream America, although after over thirty years and plenty of time to recognize the historic symbolism of the gesture and far removed from the tumultuous times of the late 1960s.

In response to the victory stand gesture, American heavyweight boxer George Foreman, also African American, proudly waved an American flag after his gold medal win, one of seven medals won by American boxers. The U.S. men's basketball team also won gold. Medals were won by American athletes in diving, equestrian/eventing, equestrian/jumping, sailing, weightlifting, wrestling, shooting, and swimming. American swimmers collected 52 medals, sweeping the men's 100-meter butterfly, the women's 100-meter freestyle and 200-meter freestyle, the men's and women's 200-meter individual medley, and sweeping all five relay events. Don Schollander returned from the 1964 Games to win silver in the 200-meter freestyle and a gold medal in a relay event. Mark Spitz won silver in the 100-meter butterfly, bronze in the 100-meter freestyle, and two gold medals in relay events. Debbie Meyer, a sixteen-year-old, became the first swimmer to win three gold medals in individual events in the same Olympic Games, setting Olympic records in the women's 200-meter, 400-meter, and 800-meter freestyle. Meyer had set world records in each of the events at the Olympic Trials.

The 1968 Olympic Games were best remembered for the image of Smith and Carlos on the victory stand, despite all efforts by the U.S. Olympic Committee and the IOC to shift the focus from the gesture. The events had been chronicled in books, articles, and documentaries, as well as popular culture, such as t-shirts, and the two athletes in the victory-stand gesture were embodied in statue form almost forty years later on the campus of San Jose State University.

SPORTS FOR INDIVIDUAL COMPETITORS

Boxing

The sport of boxing enjoyed great popularity in the 1960s, with a number of exciting championship bouts and the emergence of the "Greatest of All Time," Muhammad Ali. African American boxers dominated in the ring, holding the heavyweight title almost the entire decade. Ali's reign as titleholder ended only when the sport's organizing bodies suspended him for his refusal to be drafted into the U.S. Army, not as the result of another boxer's skill and strength.

Entering the 1960s, Sweden's Ingemar Johannson was the heavyweight champion of the world. Boxing enjoyed popularity in part because of the televised fights.

Benny Paret

Benny "The Kid" Paret (born March 14, 1937) won the welterweight title on March 27, 1960, beating Don Jordan. On April 1, 1961, Paret lost the title to Emile Griffith by a knockout, but was able to reclaim the title seven months later on September 30. A third match, the "rubber match," to determine which man would hold the title, was scheduled for March 24, 1962. Prior to the fight, Paret had taunted Griffith by calling him a "maricón" (homosexual). Griffith took out his anger on Paret in the ring. In the twelfth round, he hit Paret twenty-nine times in a row. Referee Ruby Goldstein was criticized for not stopping the fight sooner. After the fight, Paret went into a coma and died on April 3, 1962. Only 100 days before, Paret had lost to Gene Fullmer in a fight for the middleweight championship. In that fight, Fullmer punished Paret so badly that he suffered from headaches until his meeting with Griffith.

The fight was nationally televised on *Friday Night Fights*. The punishment from Griffith was the first time millions of fight fans witnessed a boxing match resulting in a boxer's death. After Paret's death, politicians worked to ban boxing and were successful in reducing the sport's popularity on mainstream television. The 2005 documentary, *Ring of Fire: The Emile Griffith Story*, focuses on Griffith's boxing career and his fight with Paret.

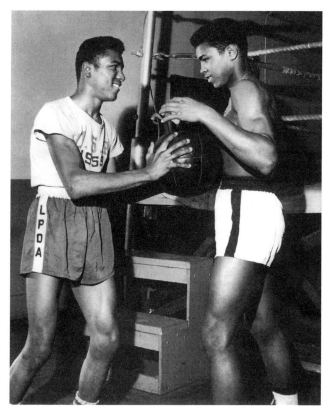

Muhammad Ali (a.k.a. Cassius Clay, right) (ca. 1960).
(Courtesy of Photofest)

Boxing was a suitable sport for television with the small confines of a ring easy for a camera to follow. Concerns over gamblers' involvement were frequent, as well as the occasional debate about the violence and morality of boxing. Johannson, who had won the title against Floyd Patterson in 1959, lost his title to Patterson in a rematch on June 20, 1960. With Patterson as the new titleholder, the boxing ring took on a new dimension during the 1960s, with African American boxers continuing the trend as the latest ethnic group to use the sport in their quest for success and upward mobility. Over the course of the next decade, several championship bouts gained the attention of people around the world.

Patterson was always trying to prove that he was a great fighter and was criticized for fighting inferior boxers, for not being able to last a full fight, and for being too nice to his opponents. Patterson's next challenge was Sonny Liston, who had been arrested over nineteen times, charges including assault, assault on a police officer and armed robbery, before he met Patterson in the ring. Once out of prison, Liston became connected to the underworld, specifically John Vitale, Frankie Carbo, and Frank "Blinkie" Palermo; Carbo and Palermo were both facing prison time for their illegal activities in boxing.

When the boxing commission denied Liston a license to fight Patterson, his failed efforts at redemption were cited. In preparation for the fight against Patterson, Liston lived for three months in a Denver rectory and worked with Father Edward Murphy, learning to read, write, and "become a law-abiding citizen" (Scorecard 1961).

To increase his chances at a shot at the title, Liston changed management twice before being granted a shot at Patterson. Patterson's clean image was put up against Liston's criminal record and they finally met in the ring on September 25, 1962, on the infield of Chicago's Comiskey Park. Liston knocked Patterson out in the first round in two minutes and six seconds. Liston immediately predicted, "You're next, Loudmouth," to onlooker Cassius Clay. Liston's victory did little to solve his problems in the press or his public image.

Liston and Patterson met for the second time in the ring on July 22, 1963, in Las Vegas in Liston's first defense of his title. Needing only four additional seconds, for a total fight time of two minutes and ten seconds, Liston held on to his title. Liston had outmatched Patterson in two fights and Patterson was out of contention for the heavyweight title. Now it was Liston who faced the challengers—up first was Cassius Clay.

Clay had won the Olympic gold medal at the 1960 Games in Rome. By the time he met Liston in the ring as a challenger, he had already earned $1 million with his fists, with a 19–0 record. Sponsored by the Louisville Group, a collective of white businessmen from Clay's hometown, the fighter's backers were a breath of fresh air to the dirty world of boxing. In opposition to the mobsters that surrounded Liston, the issue of Clay's "right" to fight for the title never came into question. The guidance of the Louisville Group provided the young fighter with "the benefit of all their experience and business acumen," and they surrounded him with a substantial moral and ethical environment, a rare commodity in professional boxing. Clay was predicted to be too inexperienced to face a man of Liston's size, strength, and experience. Despite the oddsmakers tagging him as a longshot, Cassius Clay signed a contract to fight Liston. Clay's lawyer attempted to delay the bout, confident that his client was unprepared for such a challenge, but Clay insisted. Ultimately, Clay got his way and the fight was on. Days after the ink was dry on the contract, Clay got a notice from his draft board for a preinduction physical. However, the military could be deferred on account of the scheduled fight. Still, the young fighter, with only nineteen professional fights under his belt, was viewed by many as the savior of the tainted and corrupt boxing world, though most thought he could not beat the champion. But Clay, who was his own best salesman, essentially made himself the official, though some thought illogical, challenger to Liston. Former champ Rocky Marciano saw the Liston-Clay bout as a "mismatch of the first magnitude" (Horn 1963). While many thought the prefight banter was publicity to build up the fight, it became a legitimate grudge match when Clay ribbed Liston about his prison record. Even Clay knew that his chatter did not endear him as a fan favorite: "It's easier to like an ugly old man than it is to like a loudmouth kid, and everybody wants him to teach me a lesson" (Clay 1964).

For all the prognosticating about the fight, Liston continued to be the favorite. His size and strength, along with his brutal left jab, made him an overwhelming pick. It was believed that Clay's best weapon against Liston could actually be "his very arrogance, his youthful, absurd confidence." When considering defeat, Clay was sure it would be no easy victory for the champ. He thought there might be a slim chance that he could lose to Liston, but for the champ to keep his title Clay predicted that Liston would have to "knock me down and then I'll get up and he'll have to knock me down again and I'll still get up.... I'm gonna have to be killed before I lose and I ain't going to die easy" (Clay 1964; Maule 1964).

When the two fighters finally met in the ring in Miami Beach, Clay had officially beaten Liston when the champ remained in his corner at the start of the seventh round. Liston, who had once seemed like Superman in the ring, had been beaten convincingly. First on America's agenda, though, was Clay's religious conversion, his membership in the Nation of Islam, and his subsequent name change to Cassius X and then to Muhammad Ali. Clay's rumored Nation of Islam Muslim membership was confirmed at a press conference in the days following the fight. After the fight, the press focused more on Ali's conversion than his surprise victory over Liston.

Ali's public image was shaped by the Muslim newspaper, *Muhammad Speaks*, and was in sharp contrast to the images that white writers were presenting of the fighter. *Muhammad Speaks* documented Ali's donations, his work with children, with his community, his black pride, and his politics regarding race and religion. Simultaneously, white mainstream newspapers referred to him as Cassius Clay, discredited him based on his religion and his call for the separation of the races, as well as his loud mouth.

Most fight fans had a difficult time with Ali's conversion. The World Boxing Association echoed the fans' sentiments when it debated taking Ali's title from him. The WBA stated, "Clay has set a poor example for the youth of the world" and they felt the same about Liston and his troubles with the law. Ali's assessment of the fight scene was this, "We both villains. So naturally, when we get in the ring, the people, they would prefer if it could happen for it to end in a double knockout, because they don't want either one of us to win" (Scorecard 1964; Maule 1965).

The two met in the ring over a year later, this time in Lewiston, Maine, on May 25, 1965. When Ali agreed to fight Liston for the second time, the WBA withdrew its title from Ali, but he maintained the World Boxing Council (WBC) title. After postponing the fight due to an Ali injury and relocating it from Boston to Maine in part due to the reactions about Ali's religious beliefs, Ali beat the favored Liston with a "phantom" punch in the first round. Many cried that the fight was fixed, though there was no proof of such a scandal.

Less than six months later, Ali and Floyd Patterson met in Las Vegas on November 22, 1965. The fight was not born out of Patterson's need to get back into the ring, but was rather an attempt on his part for redemption; his own personal redemption, and to redeem the sport that had made him into the man he had become. Patterson thought if he won, it would be his contribution to civil rights.

The ideologies and politics of the two fighters drew lots of media attention in the weeks prior to the fight. While some thought it was more of Ali's antics to build up the gate, it was really Patterson who contributed to the heightened tensions between the two men, citing Ali's religious choices as detrimental to boxing. Ali mocked Patterson's decision to integrate his family into a white neighborhood and questioned Patterson's blackness. Ali predicted that Patterson would not only lose, but would be so humiliated by the punishing blows that he would have to don a disguise to escape the shame, just as he did years earlier in his loss to Sonny Liston.

The fight lasted twelve long rounds for Patterson and many criticized Ali for not putting his challenger out of his misery. It was a mismatch and a letdown to many. Perhaps it was a letdown to some because the sentimental favorite lost, but to others it was a great symbolic victory. Ali talked to Patterson through the fight, bantering at his opponent, who finally had to listen to Ali's antics with little recourse. Ali yelled, "Come on American, come on white American." The white press was sure that Ali's in-the-ring antics were "part of his juvenile scheme to embarrass Patterson" (Rogin 1965). Patterson's shot at redemption left him embarrassed and ashamed, exactly what Ali had wanted.

Ali defended his title nine times, the first against Liston and the last against Zora Folley in March 1967. He was scheduled to fight Ernie Terrell, who held the WBA belt, in March 1966, but Terrell backed out and Ali instead faced George Chuvalo. Ali then fought two bouts in England against Henry Cooper and Brian London, and then traveled to Frankfurt, Germany, where he beat Karl Mildenberger. Ali's next fight in the U.S. was against Cleveland "Big Cat" Williams, in November 1966 in Houston's Astrodome. Finally, Terrell could not avoid Ali and they faced off in Houston on February 6, 1967. In the leadup to the match, Terrell had repeatedly called Ali "Clay," and as Ali landed punches he taunted Terrell saying "what's my name, Uncle Tom?" After fifteen rounds, Ali was declared the winner. In the final defense of his title, against Zora Folley on March 22, 1967, Ali knocked Folley out in the seventh round.

Though Ali failed the exam to be drafted into the Army in 1964, the military revised the exam and Ali was reclassified as 1-A, making him eligible for the draft. At his induction ceremony held on April 28, 1967, in Houston, Ali refused to be inducted, claiming conscientious objector status, as it was against the principles of Islam. He had said in 1966, "I ain't got no quarrel against them Viet Cong." For refusing to be inducted, Ali faced five years in prison and a $10,000 fine. The New York State Athletic Commission suspended his boxing license and stripped him of his title, as did other boxing commissions. In Ali's absence, Joe Frazier was able to win the title.

Two months later, a jury found Ali guilty and the judge sentenced Ali to the maximum penalty. Ali's conviction was upheld by a court of appeals and his case moved its way to the U.S. Supreme Court. As the popularity of the war dwindled and the protesters grew in numbers, there was also growing support for the suspended fighter, who resorted to giving lectures across the country at colleges. Finally, in 1970, Ali was granted a license to fight in Georgia. He met Jerry Quarry in the ring in Atlanta on October 26, 1970, and beat Quarry after only three rounds. Soon after the New York State Supreme Court ruled that Ali had been wrongly denied a license in New York and he was able to schedule a bout in Madison Square Garden on December 12, 1970. He beat Oscar Bonavena in fifteen rounds and won the North American Boxing Federation (NABF) title.

Golf

Golf during the 1960s was dominated by two American men, Arnold Palmer and Jack Nicklaus. Golf tournaments were very international, with men from all over the world competing for titles. Three of the four major tournaments, the Masters, the U.S. Open, and the PGA Championship, were hosted in the United States, with the other, the British Open, hosted in the United Kingdom. The Masters Tournament was held every year in Augusta, Georgia. Typically, CBS covered the final four holes of the tournament using six cameras. In between the four major tournaments, golfers played smaller tournaments all over the United States. A women's professional golf league, the Ladies Professional Golf Association (LPGA), also played tournaments, but received much less attention and money for their play.

Palmer and Nicklaus won a combined fourteen major titles. Palmer began the decade as the sport's top athlete, winning the Masters and U.S. Open titles in 1960 along with the Hickok Belt, given to the top professional athlete of the year, as well as being named Sportsman of the Year by *Sports Illustrated*. Palmer enjoyed a streak of victories between 1960 and 1963, winning twenty-nine titles and close to $400,000. He captained the U.S. Ryder Cup team in 1963. Other majors won include the Masters again in 1962 and 1964, and the British Open in 1961 and 1962. Prior to Palmer's success at the British Open, most American players did not compete in the annual tournament. However, Palmer's success at the tournament (televised in the United States) encouraged other golfers to make the trip across the ocean, a trip made much easier with the increased popularity of air travel. In 1968 Palmer became the first golfer to earn $1 million over his career. That same year, Billy Casper was the first golfer to break the $200,000 mark for annual earnings, pulling in $205,168. Palmer's success during the 1960s was so great he was named "Athlete of the Decade" by the Associated Press.

Jack Nicklaus attended Ohio State University and as a student won the U.S. Amateur title in 1959 and 1961, and the NCAA title in 1961. Nicknamed "the Golden Bear," Nicklaus became a professional in 1962 and won Rookie of the Year honors. In his first professional event, the Los Angeles Open, Nicklaus finished fiftieth. Nicklaus emerged as the of the game's hottest stars, winning the U.S. Open his rookie season and the Masters and PGA championships the next year. Other majors won during the decade include the Masters again in 1965 and 1966, the U.S. Open in 1967, and the British Open in 1966 and 1970. Other golfers who won major tournaments in the 1960s include Ken Venturi, Gary Player, Bobby Nichols, Billy Casper, Raymond Floyd, Lee Trevino, and Julius Boros.

In 1961 Gary Player became the first non-American to win the Masters. Four years later, Player became the first non-American to win a U.S. Open in forty-five years, and only the third player to win the career Grand Slam (Gene Sarazen and Ben Hogan). The next year Jack Nicklaus joined the exclusive club, when he won the British Open in 1966 at age twenty-six, becoming the youngest golfer to have won all four of the majors.

Other notable events in men's golf during this time period include Pete Brown becoming the first African American to win a PGA Tour event in 1964 at the St. Petersburg Open, only three years after the PGA had removed wording in their constitution that barred non-Caucasians from participating in PGA tournaments. In 1965 qualifying school was introduced and the format of the U.S. Open changed from three days of competition with thirty-six holes on the final day to four days of eighteen holes each. The next year, the British Open followed suit in changing their format to four days, eighteen holes per day and for the first time, the tournament was televised live in the United States. Titleist introduced the icosahedron dimple pattern, an aerodynamically superior design, on their golf balls in 1970.

The LPGA hosted a seventy-two-hole Championship tournament every year. Most tournaments held throughout the year were limited to fifty-four holes (for example, St. Petersburg Women's Open, Dallas Civitan Open, Babe Zaharias Open, Bluegrass Ladies Invitational, and Buckeye Savings Invitational). Between 1961 and 1966, the LPGA Championship was hosted at the Stardust Country Club in Las Vegas. It was then moved to Pleasant Valley Country Club in Sutton, Massachusetts. Other majors for women included the Western Open (which ceased play in 1967), the Titleholders, and the U.S. Women's Open. In 1965, the U.S. Women's Open Tournament final round was nationally televised for the first time. Mickey Wright (born February 14, 1935) won the LPGA Championship three times in the 1960s (1960, 1961, and 1963). Wright also won the U.S. Women's Open in 1961 and 1964, along with the Western Open title in 1962, 1963, and 1966, making her one of the decade's top female golfers. She topped the LPGA money list four years in a row beginning in 1961, as well as winning the Vare Trophy, awarded for the low scoring average, every year from 1960 to 1965. For four consecutive years, Wright won at least ten LPGA tournaments a year. She earned over $31,000 in 1963. That same year, Arnold Palmer became the first golfer to win more than $100,000 in a year, winning $128,230. Wright was named the Associate Press Athlete of the Year in 1963 and 1964. She retired from professional golf in 1970.

Other top women on the professional circuit during that time period include Louise Suggs, Kathy Whitworth, Sandra Haynie, Carol Mann, Marlene Hagge, Marilynn Smith, and Betsy Rawls. Winnings during the time period varied. In 1961 winnings for tournaments ranged between $475 and $1,300. The winner of the 1964 LPGA title won $2,400. When Mickey Wright won the Ladies World Series of Golf in 1966, she pocketed $9,500, the highest payday of the year. The average that season ranged between $1,500 and $3,000. In 1969 the winnings ranged between $2,500 and $4,500. In 1968 Kathy Whitworth topped the money list with $48,379, only to be bested the nest year by Carol Mann's $49,152 earnings. Both Whitworth and Mann won 10 LPGA events in 1968.

Tennis

Amateurism ruled the sport of tennis at the start of the 1960s. Tennis players could compete in the four Grand Slam tournaments only if they were amateurs, with professionals only able to compete in other tournaments for prize money. The four Grand Slam tournaments were the Australian Championships, the French Championships, Wimbledon, and the U.S. Championships. Victors at Wimbledon would raise their trophy in victory, but leave with empty pockets. While professional male tennis players could compete in other tournaments to earn money, opportunities for female tennis players to earn money were few and far between. During the amateur reign of tennis, American men and women competed against the world's best and often came up short on the court. Australians, both male and female, dominated the Australian Championships, which makes sense as many Americans did not compete in the tournament because of the travel expenses and no chance to earn money to pay for the tournament. Roy Emerson won on the men's side in 1961 and 1963–67, with fellow Australian Margaret Court dominating on the women's side winning the tournament from 1960 to 1966 and again for 1969–71. Court did well at the French Championships, winning in 1962, 1964, 1969, and 1970.

In 1967 many male players participated in tournaments that were part of the National Tennis League (NTL) or World Championship Tennis (WCT), organizations that granted their players permission to compete in certain tournaments. Billie Jean King worked as a playground instructor and earned $100 a week prior to the open era. She was vocal in her criticism of the U.S. Lawn Tennis Association's

(USLTA) amateurism rules which she called "shamateurism," in part because many of the sport's top players were given money under the table to encourage them to participate in certain tournaments. Prior to the open era, amateur tennis players, both male and female, relied on sponsors, or their own personal wealth, to help cover their travel expenses, which fostered the image of tennis as an elite sport.

Technology was another factor that began to alter the equipment used in tennis. Wilson developed the revolutionary racquet, the T2000, which was made of steel and not the regular wood, making the racquet lighter. Later, in 1968, Spalding introduced the Smasher, which was made of aluminum.

The open era in tennis started in 1968 and ushered in the age of professional tennis. The four Grand Slam tournaments changed their names from championships to Open (e.g., the French Open), and welcomed professional tennis players and those who remained amateurs. Commercial pressures and rumors of amateurs taking money under the table led to the "open era." Once the open era began, the opportunity to earn prize money increased, with the U.S. Open prize money totaling $100,000 in 1968. Again, Billie Jean King's efforts were significant as she fought for equal prize money for the women. As women's tennis became more popular, the prize money gradually improved between the two genders, and in 1971 King became the first female athlete to earn over $100,000 in prize money. She was also fundamental in the creation of the Virginia Slims tour, the first professional women's tennis tour.

American men were generally not the top winners on the tennis circuit in the 1960s. Stan Smith and his doubles partner Bob Lutz found some success, as did Donald Dell. Smith had been a three-time All-American tennis player at the University of Southern California and won three NCAA titles, the 1968 singles titles and the 1967 and 1968 doubles titles. Perhaps the most well-known American tennis player of the decade was Arthur Ashe.

Arthur Ashe attended UCLA on a tennis scholarship beginning in 1963, the same year he was selected as the first African American member of the U.S. Davis Cup team. Ashe won the NCAA singles title in 1965 and his team won the NCAA title the same year. In 1968 Ashe became the first African American male to win the U.S. Open and lent his support to the formation of the Association of Tennis Professionals, an organization of male tennis players, though he was still an amateur. Ashe was scheduled to compete in the South African Open in 1968, but was denied a visa to enter by the apartheid nation. As a result, Ashe believed that South Africa should be expelled from professional tennis. He turned professional in 1969 and in 1970 won the Australian Open, his second Grand Slam win.

American women found greater success on the international stage, but did not reap the same financial benefits as their male counterparts once the open era had begun. Darlene Hard began the decade as the best American women's player, winning the French Championships in 1960 and the U.S. Championships in 1960 and 1961. She was also an outstanding doubles player and won the last of her thirteen doubles titles in 1969 at the U.S. Open. Another American female tennis player of note was Karen Hantze Susman. In 1961 and 1962 Susman teamed with Billie Jean Moffitt to win the women's double title at Wimbledon. She also won the singles title at Wimbledon in 1962. Susman and King won the U.S. Championships doubles title in 1964. Nancy Richey was another top American female tennis player and ranked second in the world in 1969. Richey won the singles title at the 1967 Australian Championships and the 1968 French Open, as well as four doubles titles, including three of the four majors in 1966 (she did not win the French Championships that year). Between 1963 and 1968 Richey won six consecutive U.S. clay court singles titles.

The top American female tennis player during the 1960s was Billie Jean Moffitt, who married Larry King in 1965 and was thereafter Billie Jean King. At the age of fifteen she lost in her Grand Slam debut at the 1959 U.S. Championships. The next year, she won the Philadelphia and District Women's Grass Court Championships before losing again at the U.S. Championships for the second straight year. By the end of the year, she was ranked fourth among American women tennis players by the USLTA. King paired with Karen Hantze Susman to win the 1961 women's double crown at Wimbledon. She rose to number three in the rankings. In a major breakthrough on the international stage, the unseeded King played her way into the finals of Wimbledon where she lost to Margaret Court. That year, she finished second in the USLTA rankings behind Darlene Hard. In 1964, King decided to commit to tennis year round. She trained with a coach in Australia after a businessman offered to sponsor her tennis training. King finished ranked seventh in the world and second in the United States behind Nancy Richey.

In 1965, for the third year in a row, King lost in the semifinals of Wimbledon. Winning six tournaments that year, she finished ranked fourth in the world, and tied for first in the U.S. with Gunter. King's breakout year was 1966, when she ended her losing streak against Court and won her first Grand Slam singles title, beating Maria Bueno in the finals of Wimbledon. She finished ranked first in the world. In 1967, she played at the French Championships for the first time and lost in the quarterfinals, before winning her second straight singles title at Wimbledon, beating Virginia Wade. She swept Wimbledon, winning the singles title, but also the women's double and mixed doubles titles, a feat she repeated at the U.S. Championships. She competed in her first Australian Championships in 1968, beating Court in the finals. The French Championships had become the French Open, where King lost to Richey in the semifinals, before winning her third consecutive Wimbledon singles title. In the final of the inaugural U.S. Open in 1968, King lost in the finals to Wade. For the first time, King did not appear on the USTLA rankings list because she was considered a professional.

King continued to make regular appearances in the semifinals and finals of championships, losing in the semifinals of the 1969 French Open and being upset in the finals of Wimbledon a month later. At the U.S. Open, she lost in the quarterfinals and ended the year with no Grand Slam titles for the first time since 1965. Margaret Court won all four Grand Slam singles titles in 1970, leaving King second in the world rankings, though first in the United States. King would continue to leave her mark on women's tennis and women's sport in the 1970s.

Horse Racing

Thoroughbred racing had no Triple Crown winners in the decade, but seven times horses won two of the three races in a single year. Carry Back in 1961 took both the Kentucky Derby and the Preakness Stakes, but finished far back in the Belmont Stakes, the longest of the three races. Two years later, Chateaugay won both the Derby and the Belmont, but finished second in the Preakness. The next year, Northern Dancer won the first two legs of the Crown, but finished third in the Belmont. In 1966 Kauai King also won the first two races, but slipped to fourth in the Belmont. The following year Damascus, later named Horse of the Year, won the last two races, after finishing in third in the Derby.

Commission on Intercollegiate Athletics for Women (CIAW)

The CIAW was created in 1967 as the organizing body for the governance of women's intercollegiate athletics. In 1956 three organizations, the National Association for Physical Education for College Women, National Association for Girls and Women in Sports, and the American Federation of College Women, formed the Tripartite Committee. Out of this committee another group was formed, the National Joint Committee on Extramural Sports for College Women. The CIAW evolved out of the NJCESCW.

Basketball was one of the more popular sports for women to participate in at the college level, though the sport was not always organized in a way where the best teams were identified and competition was often local. Moreover, the AAU was still largely responsible for the organization of play. With the CIAW and other organizations, such as the Division of Girls and Women in Sports (DGWS, part of AAHPERD), there was an increasing effort being made for universities to have organized sport teams. AAU teams generally did not have age limits or require school affiliation.

During the 1960s numerous rule changes made the women's game more resemble the men's game. For instance, in 1961, a rule allowing two players to run the full court was made, as was a rule that allowed for three dribbles, creating more court movement. In 1964 it was ruled that a player could hold the ball indefinitely or five seconds if she was guarded. In 1966 a rule change allowed for continuous, unlimited dribbling. Overseeing the rule changes were the AAU and DGWS. Games were often played in small gyms where there was no room for bleachers and spectators, and where each team wore different colored singlets in the absence of uniforms.

Between 1964 and 1968, Wheaton College was one of the better teams in the country with a 41–3 record. Between 1962 and 1969 Nashville Business College won eight consecutive AAU national championships.

In 1969 CIAW organized an invitational women's basketball tournament with sixteen teams hosted by West Chester State College in Pennsylvania. In the final game, West Chester State defeated Western Carolina. A National Women's Invitational Tournament (NWIT) was also held that year with Wayland Baptist beating Ouachita Baptist in the final game. In 1970 Northeastern University of Boston hosted the CIAW Tournament. California State–Fullerton was the winner after beating West Chester State. AT the NWIT, Wayland Baptist beat Midwestern Oklahoma State for the title. CIAW expanded their organization of women's college sport and championships in other sports began, including badminton, golf, gymnastics, diving, swimming and diving, track and field, and volleyball. The CIAW developed into the Association for Intercollegiate Athletics for Women (AIAW).

In 1968 a first occurred as the winning horse, Dancer's Image, was disqualified after the race when an illegal substance was found in the after-race testing. Forward Pass, who had finished second, was declared the winner and then won the Preakness. Amidst fears of a "tainted" Triple Crown winner, Stage Door Johnny won the Belmont with Forward Pass second.

The next year Majestic Prince won the first two races, but injured a tendon in the Belmont. Trainer Johnny Longden wanted to hold the colt out of the Belmont, but was pressured to enter him because of the possible history-equaling win. The horse finished second to Arts and Letters, but was injured severely enough to never race again.

The leading jockeys of the decade were Bill Hartack with six Triple Crown victories (including four Kentucky Derby wins), Willie Shoemaker with five Triple Crown victories, and Braulio Baeza who won three Belmonts and a Derby.

SUMMARY

American sport during the 1960s was marked by tremendous change, such as expansion of professional sport leagues, technological advances, developing opportunities for women, and a shift in the roles and identities of African American athletes in college and professional sport. The 1960s established excellence in a number of sports—records set, championships won, and heroes crowned. Well into the twenty-first century, American sport fans still recall Palmer and Nicklaus in golf, the Bill Russell–led Boston Celtics dynasty, the bold predictions of Broadway Joe Namath in Super Bowl III, and the unrivaled dominance of the UCLA basketball team and their coach John Wooden.

Set against the backdrop of an America undergoing societal and cultural changes, such as the civil rights movement, the free speech movement, a growing women's movement, as well as protests of the Vietnam War, sport was not immune. Despite all the changes in American sport and society during the 1960s, some things remained the same. Women, though they were afforded opportunities to compete professionally in golf, were still limited in the sports offered to them at the Olympic Games, and by their educational institutions. For female athletes, their opportunities in American sport, and enjoying a similar status as their male counterparts was still decades away.

The increasing number of African Americans in college and professional sport, and their skillful use of sport as a platform for exposing racism in sport and American society, must be singled out as the most significant "event" of the era. Every sport was impacted by the issue of race and ethnicity; from golf, and the decision to integrate PGA tournament play; the influx of Latin American athletes into major league baseball; the integration of college teams; the decision of Muhammad Ali to refuse his induction into the military; to the image of Tommie Smith and John Carlos on the Olympic victory stand, and their black gloved fists in the air—sport became another American landscape shaped by the people who played the games.

RECOMMENDED RESOURCES
Books and Dissertations

Ashe, Arthur, Jr. 1988. *A hard road to glory: A history of the African-American athlete since 1946*. New York: Warner Books.
Ashe, Arthur, and Arnold Rampersad. 1993. *Days of grace: A memoir*. New York: Knopf.
Bass, Amy. 2002. *Not the triumph but the struggle: The 1968 Olympics and the making of the black athlete*. Minneapolis: University of Minnesota Press.
Burgos, Adrian, Jr. 2007. *Playing America's game: Baseball, Latinos, and the color line*. Berkeley: University of California Press.
Early, Gerald. 1989. *Tuxedo Junction: Essays on American culture*. Hopewell, NJ: Ecco Press.
———. 1994. *The culture of bruising: Essays on prizefighting, literature, and modern American culture*. Hopewell, NJ: Ecco Press.
Edwards, Harry. 1969. *The revolt of the black athlete*. New York: Free Press.

Flood, Curt, with Richard Carter. 1970. *The way it is*. New York: Trident Press.

Gorn, Elliott J., ed. 1995. *Muhammad Ali: The people's champ*. Urbana: University of Illinois Press.

Hartmann, Douglas. 2003. *Race, culture, and the revolt of the black athlete: The 1968 Olympic protests and their aftermath*. Chicago: University of Chicago Press.

Herzog, Brad. 1995. *The Sports 100*. New York: Macmillan.

Hult, Joan, and Marianna Trekell. 1991. *A century of women's basketball: From frailty to Final Four*. Reston, VA: National Association for Girls and Women in Sport.

Hutchinson, George. 1977. The black athletes' contribution towards social change in the United States. Ph.D. diss., U.S. International University, San Diego.

Jackson, George. 1985. *Soul brother superfighter*. Placerville, CA: Green Valley Graphics.

Korr, Charles P. 2002. *The end of baseball as we know it: The players union, 1960–81*. Urbana: University of Illinois Press.

Marqusee, Mike. 1999. *Redemption song: Muhammad Ali and the spirit of the sixties*. London: Verso.

Miller, Jeff. 2003. *Going long: The wild ten-year saga of the renegade American Football League in the words of those who lived it*. Chicago: Contemporary Books.

Miller, Marvin. 1991. *A whole different ballgame: The sport and business of baseball*. New York: Birch Lane Press.

Oriard, Michael. 2007. *Brand NFL: Making and selling America's favorite sport*. Chapel Hill: University of North Carolina Press.

Regalado, Samuel O. 1998. *Viva baseball! Latin major leaguers and their special hunger*. Urbana: University of Illinois Press.

Roberts, Randy, and James Olsen. 1989. *Winning is the only thing: Sports in America since 1945* Baltimore: Johns Hopkins University Press.

Sammons, Jeffrey T. 1988. *Beyond the ring: The role of boxing in American society*. Urbana: University of Illinois Press.

Scott, Jack. 1971. *The athletic revolution*. New York: Free Press.

Smith, Tommie, with David Steele. 2007. *Silent gesture: The autobiography of Tommie Smith*. Philadelphia: Temple University Press.

Wiley, Ralph. 1989. *Serenity: A boxing memoir*. New York: Henry Holt.

Wushanley, Ying. 2004. *Playing nice and losing: The struggle for control of women's intercollegiate athletics, 1960–2000*. Syracuse, NY: Syracuse University Press.

Zang, David W. 2001. *SportsWars: Athletes in the age of Aquarius*. Fayetteville: University of Arkansas Press.

Articles

Bout proceeds to go to starving: World champion offers to fight for Mississippi children. 1967. *Muhammad Speaks*, July 21, 7.

Champ Ali urges Blackstone Rangers to practice messenger's "black unity." 1966. *Muhammad Speaks*, September 2, 8.

Champ fights to save children from blighted lives—takes time out to work with children of the poor. 1966. *Muhammad Speaks*, July 15, 7.

Champ offers closed TV of fight to 6 colleges. 1966. *Muhammad Speaks*, October 28, 9.

Clay, Cassius. 1964. "I'm a little special." *Sports Illustrated* 20, no. 8 (February 24): 15.

Flood, Curt, with Richard Carter. 1971. My rebellion. *Sports Illustrated*, February 1, 25.

Flood tide. 1970. *Newsweek*, January 12, 45.

Gumbel, Bryant C. 1972. The black amateur athlete: Not just an athletic animal—Part 3. *Black Sports* 2, no. 1 (May/June): 63–66.

Horn, Huston. 1963. A rueful dream come true. *Sports Illustrated* 19, no. 21 (November 18): 26.

How days of a boy on borrowed time were extended by heavyweight champ. 1966. *Muhammad Speaks*, April 22, 9.

Koppett, Leonard. 1969. Flood backed by players, plans suit to challenge baseball reserve clause. *New York Times*, December 30, 42.

Maule, Tex. 1964. Liston's edge: A lethal left. *Sports Illustrated* 20, no. 9 (March 2): 21.

———. 1965. The baddest of all looks over the universe. *Sports Illustrated* 22, no. 7 (February 15): 21.

Muhammad Ali becomes single biggest black contributor to UNCF charities. 1967. *Muhammad Speaks*, March 3, 20.

Muhammad Ali chosen to head black Watts summer festival in California. 1967. *Muhammad Speaks*, August 8, 4.

Muslim champ spends day at Chicago school, molds concept of "black heroes." 1966. *Muhammad Speaks*, February 18, 9, 12.

Rogin, Gilbert. 1965. Champion as long as he waits. *Sports Illustrated* 23, no. 22 (November 29): 24.

Scorecard. 1961. A good decision. *Sports Illustrated*, 4, no. 15 (July 24): 10.

———. 1964. Boxing's silliest hour. *Sports Illustrated* 20, no. 13 (March 30): 9.

———. 1965. *Sports Illustrated* 23, no. 1 (July 5): 13.

Spiritual example displayed by champion overshadows strength, physical prowess. 1966. *Muhammad Speaks*, November 25.

Underwood, John. 1968. The non-trial trials. *Sports Illustrated*, July 8, 13.

Films

Fists of Freedom: The Story of the '68 Summer Games. 1999. Home Box Office.

Glory Road. 2006. Dir. James Gartner. Glory Road Productions LLC.

CHAPTER 11

AMERICAN SPORTS, 1970–1979

John Wong

OVERVIEW

In the 1970s, the construction of a national sporting culture in the United States was more or less complete. Modern sports, characterized by standardized rules, bureaucratic governing bodies, recordkeeping, and extensive media promotion, became more geographically widespread and more inclusive by extending participatory opportunities to women and minority groups. By no means, however, did women and minorities have equal access to organized modern sports. The advent of television technology and its importance as a medium of popular culture only helped to popularize modern sports and the concomitant ideology. On the other hand, those who were on the fringes of society and excluded challenged modern sports' underlying assumptions based on racial, gender, and class stereotypes. Begun in the mid 1960s, this "Athletic Revolution" continued through the early 1970s as more Americans began to question entrenched social and political relationships in sport. Activists from both inside and outside organized sports pushed to correct past injustices, discrimination, and denial of opportunities.

Political, economic, social, and environmental crises in this decade reflected some of the old concerns as well as awareness of new problems. Yet, the 1970s also witnessed opportunities and achievements in American politics and social awakenings. Social movements that divided America and at times led to ugly confrontations continued into the early 1970s but increasingly, many more Americans who once deemed these protests and demands for change as radical now accepted them as necessary, if not unavoidable. President Richard Nixon continued the previous administration's Vietnam policy although secretly the Southeast Asian conflict was extended from Vietnam into neighboring Laos and Cambodia. But in January of 1973, the United States agreed to withdraw U.S. forces by March of 1973, though the final withdrawal was not until 1975.

While President Nixon called the peace treaty ending the Vietnam War for the United States "Peace with Honor," many Americans understood that the might of the nation and its foreign policies had been questioned if not undermined. As the

Vietnam conflict was winding down, however, an opportunity for diplomatic triumph presented itself. After some clandestine negotiations, in February 1973 Nixon became the first sitting U.S. president ever to visit Communist China. Nixon, who made his political career as a staunch anticommunist, met with Chinese leaders Mao Zedong and Zhou En Lai, an unprecedented meeting between capitalism and communism.

It was sport, however, that paved the way for Nixon's visit, the first official exchange (also known as Ping-Pong Diplomacy) between the two countries since the Communists came to power in 1949. In April 1971 the Chinese invited the American Table Tennis team to visit China after the completion of the sport's World Championship in Japan. With American journalists accompanying the team, the public at home was captivated by reports of the American team in a country that had closed its doors to the outside world. The Americans played a series of exhibition matches against their hosts, toured historical landmarks, and were feted by their hosts.

China's emergence onto the world's political stage signaled both the growing power and importance of third world nations once relegated to the fringes of world affairs and their impact on American foreign and domestic policies. No development, however, demonstrated the emergence of a third power bloc in world politics more than the oil-producing nations in the Middle East, who carried much clout in the Organization of Petroleum Exporting Countries (OPEC). Originally organized as a cartel to regulate production output and, therefore, prices, OPEC had a heavy Arabian presence. These Arab countries had a long-standing conflict with Israel since that the establishment of an Israeli state in Palestine in 1948. Shortly after the Yom Kippur war in 1973, they convinced the cartel to impose an oil embargo to western nations, which lasted from October 1973 to March 1974. Drivers in the United States faced long lines at gas stations, and prices at the pumps jumped fourfold. Less observable, but just as damaging nevertheless, an economic recession ensued. The success of the embargo reversed the power relations between the formerly colonized, oil-producing countries and the industrial, affluent West, and forced western nations, including the United States, to pay attention to OPEC concerns.

With Israel and its Arab neighbors constantly at odds and the new power of OPEC, the United States took steps to stabilize the region. In 1979, as a first step, Egypt and Israel signed the Camp David Accord under the initiative of President Jimmy Carter. Yet, the importance of oil also emboldened nationalists in these countries who disdained western domination and influences. These anti-West and anti-American feelings materialized when the Shah of Iran fled his country in 1979. Seen as too westernized and corrupt, the shah and his government were overthrown by revolutionary forces under Ayatollah Khomeini, who then proceeded to establish an Islamic state. Angered by the United States' role in supporting the shah's regime, American support for Israel, and the deposed Shah's presence in the United States after the coup, Iranian students broke into the American embassy in Teheran and took American hostages in November of 1979. For the second time in the decade, the United States suffered humiliation at the hands of a so-called minor nation.

With American hostages held captive in Iran and the nation still trying to recover from the wounds of Vietnam, President Carter took a strong stance when the Soviet Union invaded Afghanistan in December of 1979. In January of 1980, Carter linked the Soviet invasion with threats to American security. To demonstrate his toughness against the Soviet Union further to an increasingly skeptical Congress and public, he chose a most visible event. In February, Carter urged a boycott of the 1980 Moscow Olympic Games and proceeded to pressure the U.S. Olympic Committee to withdraw its team from the Games. Even though the American team did not attend the games (as the president wished), many other nations did. Yet the boycott and his other initiatives (including a daring but failed attempt to save the hostages) did not help Carter in the subsequent presidential election. Ronald Reagan defeated Carter to become the fortieth president of the United States in 1980.

While international events impacted the American psyche, internal turmoil, leftover from the 1960s, and advancements in race and gender issues also made their marks in the 1970s. In the 1960s the civil rights and women's liberation movements encountered entrenched resistance; but both had gained wider acceptance by the 1970s. Federal involvement in affirming the rights of African Americans in the sixties had translated into some successes in the 1970s. In 1971 fifteen African American members of Congress formed the Congressional Black Caucus to address the interests of the African American population. In the same year, the Supreme Court ruled in favor of busing children to schools outside their neighborhoods in order to achieve the goal of racial desegregation. As the civil rights movement concerning African Americans and other minorities continued through the 1970s, gender equity gained similar federal protection during this decade.

One of the more important pieces of legislation that addressed equal opportunity for women in this decade was the Education Amendments Act, specifically its Title IX provisions, in 1972. Signed by President Nixon, the act prohibits discrimination based on sex in all federally funded education programs or activities. In the same year, Congress also passed the Equal Rights Amendment affirming equal treatment for both sexes. Under Article V of the Constitution, three-quarters of the states had to ratify the amendment within seven years in order for it to become law. By the March deadline in 1979, however, only thirty of the required minimum of thirty-eight states had ratified the amendment. Although the Equal Rights Amendment failed to become law, twenty-one states enacted similar statutes in their constitutions, which often had stricter sanctions against sex discrimination. As significant as Title IX and state Equal Rights Amendments were to affirm equal opportunity to women, so was the Supreme Court's decision in *Roe v. Wade* in 1973, which legally upheld a woman's right to control her own body concerning reproduction. These events gave legal and political backing to the women's rights movement in challenging the patriarchal power establishment.

As both African Americans and women gained legal protections, other minorities also pushed for a greater voice and sought to redress past discrimination. Continuing his struggles for better working conditions and pay for migrant farm workers, often of Latino heritage, César Chávez organized the National Farm Workers Association (later United Farm Workers) in the 1960s, but achieved success in forcing grape producers to recognize the union when the two parties signed a contract in 1970. Commemorating the Stonewall riots in which the New York City police battled with members of the gay community, the first Gay Pride Parade took place in the city in 1970. In 1975 Congress passed the Education for all

Handicapped Children Act, which required all public schools to provide equal accommodation to children with physical and mental disabilities. While prejudices and inequities still existed, these events signaled a willingness on the public's part to acknowledge and remedy past injustices.

Despite some successes for minorities to challenge the status quo, a number of domestic events confirmed the younger generation's general suspicion of those in power, especially the Nixon administration. A year after the Pentagon Papers were published, operatives from the Republican Party broke into the Democratic Party's headquarters at the Watergate Hotel in Washington, DC. Subsequent investigations revealed that the Watergate burglary was but one of many illegal activities that were linked to the inner circle of the presidency. During the course of the scandal, Vice President Spiro Agnew pleaded no contest to charges of corruption (unrelated to Watergate) and resigned from office in 1973. Seeing that his administration suffered an image problem, Nixon chose Gerald Ford, a former University of Michigan football player and House of Representatives leader, to succeed Agnew. Yet Nixon's effort to boost the credibility of his office failed, as more and more details of wrongdoings came to light, and his attempts to derail the Watergate investigation drew condemnation. Amidst calls for impeachment, Nixon resigned his post on August 9, 1974. Ford's presidency inherited the problems of recession and inflation, largely a result of the energy crisis, from his predecessor.

The 1970s witnessed a concern for the environment that, together with the civil and women's rights movements, dovetailed into a human rights movement–a more inclusive and global initiative. As early as April 1970, people across the country joined in the celebration of Earth Day. Modeled after the strategies of anti–Vietnam War protests, Earth Day was an educational and informational event that brought environmental issues to the American public consciousness. First prompted by a concern for the safety of automobiles, which led into activism against major corporations and government agencies, Ralph Nader in 1971 created Public Citizen, an organization that researched and published findings on a wide range of issues, one of which was the environment. In 1978 residents in a Niagara Falls (NY) neighborhood, Love Canal, were evacuated because of toxic waste in the area. This national spotlight on indiscriminate exploitation of the environment was followed by a March 1979 incident at the Three Mile Island Nuclear Generating Station, near Harrisburg, Pennsylvania, where the station's nuclear reactor core had a meltdown. When Mount St. Helens in Washington State erupted in 1980, the earth's full fury was evident for all to witness. Although not manmade, the volcano's destructive power demonstrated the fragility of human existence. The concern for the environment and, by implication, for fellow human beings would eventually evolve into a political force in the 1990s.

At the same time that Americans paid attention to global issues, some also turned inward for both spiritual and physical fulfillment and satisfaction. Others pursued physical well-being in the fitness movement. Still others immersed themselves in hedonistic pleasures, such as frequenting discotheques (dance clubs that played a genre of music blending black and Latino sounds), imbibing recreational drugs, and pursuing casual sexual encounters (pre-AIDS crisis). Indeed, author and journalist Tom Wolfe labeled the Seventies the "Me Decade" when many Americans turned from the political and social idealism of the 1960s to personal enrichment.

Although Americans looked for inner peace through different pursuits, the idea of "community" did not vanish. And sports benefited. Indeed, sport both reflected and created the social tensions in American society.

TEAM SPORTS

Baseball—The National Pastime

As the oldest professional team sport, Major League Baseball (MLB) experienced a shift in the power relationship between management and players that started in the late 1960s and continued throughout the 1970s. Legal challenges, fostered by a militant union leadership, eventually eroded the owners' almost totalitarian rule. Ever since 1968, when the owners reluctantly entered into the first collective bargaining agreement (CBA) with the union, they realized that the union had been chipping away at their control over baseball through successive renegotiations of the CBA. In the 1970s the owners decided to test the union's strength and tried to recapture their power over professional baseball, which led to the first strike by professional baseball players in 1972.

Through the union director, Marvin Miller, the players asked for adjustments to their health care benefits and pension plans. When the owners refused, the players walked out. The strike lasted thirteen days, including the first nine days of the season. Since neither side had established an emergency fund for such an occasion, both owners and players suffered financially from lost income because of the strike. The owners' losses, however, were much larger and led them to capitulate to the union's original demands. On April 15 the baseball season opened without making up for the games missed during the strike. This labor action, however, would not be the last and foretold many more disputes between the two sides in the coming decades.

Although the strike was a dramatic illustration of the players' growing power and assertiveness, many more gains came through negotiations and judicial and legislative means. In the 1970s, the players gained the right to settle disputes, including salaries, through a third-party arbitrator. Indeed, it was binding arbitration that brought down the century-old reserve clause. Negotiated into the agreement reached after the 1972 strike, binding arbitration on salary disputes allowed players with two or more years of service to argue their case before a three-person panel (with one member from management, one from union, and a third person agreed upon by both sides) who had to make a decision either in favor of management or the player. No splitting of the difference was allowed. Immediately many qualified players used this avenue. Although the outcomes did not always favor the players, enough decisions were and forced the owners to re-evaluate their salary offers from then on.

Binding arbitration also brought down the reserve clause that had bound a player to a club for his entire career until retirement or the team released him. Curt Flood had challenged the reserve clause under antitrust law in 1969. Through successive appeals that eventually reached the Supreme Court, MLB's antitrust exemption remained intact when the Supreme Court ruled against Flood in 1972 (see sidebar in previous chapter, p. 357). The reserve clause would disappear by the end of the decade as the union attacked it via binding arbitration. The first crack at the reserve clause came when James "Catfish" Hunter of the Oakland Athletics filed a grievance against owner Charlie Finley for breach of contract in 1974 and asked that he be declared a free agent. On December 13 arbitrator Peter Seitz stunned the sporting world by siding with Hunter. Finley then filed suit against the Seitz judgment, but failed to have it overturned. The New York Yankees finally signed Hunter away from the Athletics for an unheard-of sum, $3.75 million over five years. Hunter's case demonstrated to the players, owners, and public alike, the possibility of free agency, despite the existence of the reserve clause. Without free agency, a player's worth was always under market value.

For the union and the players, the main assault to the reserve clause came when Andy Messersmith of the Los Angeles Dodgers and Dave McNally of the Montreal Expos played without signing contracts in 1975. (McNally actually had retired from baseball early in the 1975 season.) On behalf of both players, the union filed a grievance at the end of the 1975 season claiming that both players were now free agents because, as stated in the contract, the reserve clause only reserved an unsigned player's service for one year. In December arbitrator Seitz ruled that both players were free agents, in effect dismissing the league and owners' argument that the one-year extension carried over from year to year. (On demand from management, Seitz was fired from the arbitration panel after this verdict.) Immediately, the owners filed suit against the judgment but again failed to win. The consequence of this verdict was significant because players could now shop around their services if they refused to renew their contract for the next season. Realizing, and grudgingly accepting, this new development, owners began signing players for longer terms and more generous offers in order to keep them from going on the market. Salaries in professional baseball rose. In 1970 the average player salary was about $29,000. In 1975 it was around $46,000. By 1980 the figure had jumped to $146,000. Moreover, since other professional leagues had similar if not exact language of the reserve clause in their contracts, the implication of the Seitz decision went beyond professional baseball.

In spite of the owners' cries of demise of the sport because free agency would bankrupt the teams, MLB did well in this decade. In 1971 MLB Commissioner Bowie Kuhn negotiated a $70-million, four-year television package with the National Broadcasting Company (NBC). In part on the strength of the exciting 1975 World Series between the Cincinnati Reds and the Boston Red Sox, MLB's 1976 newly negotiated television package paid each club $23.2 million per year. Especially for large-market teams, revenues from this new television deal and local television broadcast (which the team did not have to share with others in the league) added to their profits. Despite spiraling salaries, television revenues more than covered increased salary expenses. By 1980 player salaries, on average, only constituted about 39 percent of team expenses. Moreover, franchise value also jumped in this decade because of this prosperity. In 1970 a MLB franchise was valued approximately at just over $10 million. This figure had increased threefold by 1980.

Not all the action occurred at the negotiating table or in the courtrooms for baseball in the 1970s. To give offense a boost, the American League (but not the National League) adopted the designated hitter rule in 1973. Despite the addition of this rule, twelve starting pitchers recorded twenty or more victories even as batting averages increased that year. But arguably the most significant event on the

Hank Aaron

Born on February 5, 1934, in Mobile, Alabama, Henry Louis "Hank" Aaron was one of seven children of Herbert and Estella. His professional baseball career began with the Mobile Black Bears, a team in the Negro League, for $10 per game. Aaron then moved up the Negro League hierarchy when he signed with the Indianapolis Clowns in 1951 and, then, with the Boston Braves of MLB in 1952. Initially, Aaron played for the Braves' minor-league team, the Eau Claire Bears of Wisconsin, where he would be the only African American on the team. He was then promoted to Jacksonville (FL), at a time when segregation was still the rule in the South. He was one of the first African Americans in that league (the South Atlantic League) and had to endure racial taunts while playing. Aaron made his Braves' debut in 1954. The next year, Aaron was selected as an All-Star, the first of twenty-four such designations. As he neared Ruth's record near the end of the 1973 season, the national media began to follow his games closely and, at the same time, Aaron began receiving threats and hate mail. There was also immense public support for Aaron once these threats were revealed. When Aaron's playing career was over in 1976, his total home-run record stood at 755 and was only surpassed by Barry Bonds in 2007. Aaron retired with a career average of .305, 2,297 RBIs, 1,477 extra base hits, and 6,856 total bases; the latter three statistics are still MLB records as of 2008. Besides his athletic abilities, Aaron was an outspoken critic of the lack of managerial opportunities in professional baseball. After he finished his playing career, Aaron worked as an executive vice-president for the Atlanta Braves.

field occurred on April 8, 1974, in Atlanta when Hank Aaron broke Babe Ruth's lifetime home-run record. Ruth's record, set at a time of a segregated MLB, also stood as a last vestige of white superiority to some. To have the record broken by a black man seemed to indict the segregationist policy of the old MLB that excluded so many talented black athletes.

Aaron, of course, was not the only player who had distinguished himself on the diamond. Pitching for the California Angels, Nolan Ryan had two no-hitters in 1973 and added another two by 1975. Then there was Steve Carlton. After a salary dispute with the St. Louis Cardinals, he was traded to the Philadelphia Phillies, a team that had languished at the bottom of the Eastern Division of the National League in the previous season. In his first season, Carlton led the league in victories (27), complete games (30), strikeouts (310), and earned run average (ERA) (1.97), even as the Phillies remained last in the division. It was an especially impressive feat since the Phillies only won fifty-nine games for the season. His twenty-seven victories represented 46 percent of the team's success and earned him the 1972 Cy Young Award by unanimous vote. Carlton continued to help the Phillies as the team improved in the latter half of the decade, capturing the division title three times (1976, 1977, and 1978). In 1980 the Phillies won the World Series with Carlton pitching in the final game.

While the Phillies became a very successful team in the latter half of the 1970s, the Cincinnati Reds and the Oakland Athletics were two of the most dominant teams of the decade. The Reds appeared in three World Series, winning two (1975 and 1976) of them, the same record as the once dominant New York Yankees in

California Angels pitcher Nolan Ryan hurls the ball in the first inning, August 21, 1974, against the Detroit Tigers. Despite a stellar pitching performance, fanning nineteen Tigers, Ryan lost in the eleventh inning to Detroit's Mickey Lolich, 1–0. Ryan struck out nineteen batters for the second time in three starts and set a major-league record for most strikeouts in three consecutive games, a total of forty-seven. (AP / Wide World Photo)

the 1970s. On the other hand, the A's won three (1972–74) consecutive World Series.

Other than the outstanding achievements by teams and players, professional baseball also received some sad news in this decade. Approximately two years prior to Aaron's record-breaking game, Jackie Robinson, the first black player to break the color line in MLB, passed away at the relatively young age of fifty-three. Robinson, however, was not the only famous player whose time had come too soon. In 1972 Roberto Clemente of the Pittsburgh Pirates died at the age of thirty-eight in a plane crash. A Puerto Rican by birth and a humanitarian by temperament, Clemente was on his way to deliver relief supplies to earthquake victims in Nicaragua.

Robinson and Clemente were evidence of the gradual desegregation of professional baseball, and public admiration of the two perhaps indicated acceptance of minorities in sport. One year after Aaron set the home-run record, another Robinson, Frank (no relation to Jackie), made MLB history when the Cleveland Indians named him manager of the club, making him the first African American in a management position in professional baseball. Robinson had been an outstanding (and later Hall of Fame–elected) outfielder and he continued his career as manager with several more clubs in the coming decades. Yet, minorities in upper-management positions remained few and far between, even though over one-third of the players were African Americans and Latinos by the 1970s. The paucity of management opportunities continued after the decade was over.

Basketball

Professional Basketball

Similar to the other professional sports in the 1970s, professional basketball experienced a boom, with a rival league taking advantage of the demand for sport entertainment in the marketplace. For the established league, the National Basketball Association (NBA), franchises' values went from $200,000 in 1961 to $3.75 million in 1970. In the 1970s the NBA expanded from seventeen teams in 1970 to twenty-three teams in 1980, in part a reaction to the rival league, the American Basketball Association (ABA), created by Gary Davidson and Dennis Murphy (who would later create the World Hockey Association). Unlike the NHL teams, which often owned minor-league teams to maintain and develop talent, the NBA conscripted their young talent relatively cheaply as the NCAA became the major proving ground for aspiring basketball players. Hence, Davidson and Murphy created the ABA in 1967 with eleven teams spreading from coast to coast. While major metropolitan areas such as Anaheim, Oakland, Dallas, and New York hosted ABA franchises, ABA could also be found in smaller markets, such as Indianapolis and Louisville, but had a tradition of successful college basketball teams. The idea was, of course, to tap into existing basketball audiences in hope of transferring their enthusiasm for the college game to the professional teams.

By 1970 the bidding war between the two leagues led to discussions of a merger, which would not materialize until 1976 as the NBA faced two court challenges accusing it of being a monopoly and thus violating the federal antitrust law. Both

---

Spencer Haywood

Spencer Haywood was one of ten children born (1949) in a poor family in rural Mississippi. A member of the 1968 gold-medal Olympic basketball team, Haywood signed with the new American Basketball Association (ABA) in 1969 because the NBA prohibited signing any player until four years after he graduated from high school. The rule, in large part, was to placate the NCAA who feared competition on top recruits from the professional league. While the ABA had a similar rule, the league decided to exempt Haywood because he was such a high-profile prospect that signing him would bring credibility to the new league. After one year with the ABA's Denver Rockets, Haywood left the team and signed with the NBA's Seattle Supersonics. Unlike the ABA, NBA owners voted not to exempt Haywood, who then filed suit against the NBA. Haywood and his lawyer argued that the NBA's refusal to sign him amounted to a group boycott and violated the Sherman Antitrust Act. As to the four-year rule, Haywood countered that the rule created a hardship for him and his family since he was the sole wage earner. After the Supreme Court verdict, the NBA changed the four-year rule and included a "hardship" clause that allowed any underclassman to petition to be included in the draft if he could show evidence of hardship. In 1976 the NBA eliminated the four-year provision entirely and any college player could enter the draft if he notified the league at least forty-five days before the draft. That was subsequently modified in 2006. Haywood played for thirteen seasons, averaging just over 20 points per game in his pro career.

lawsuits came from NBA players. Oscar Robertson led one of the lawsuits and Spencer Haywood the other.

Robertson, generally known as "the Big O," had been in the NBA for ten seasons. A legitimate all-star, Robertson had had successes in college, the Olympic Games, and the NBA. Playing guard, not only was he a superb scorer and passer, Robertson was also a good rebounder. By 1970, Robertson had been the president of the National Basketball Players Association (NBPA) for four years. Knowing that the merger between NBA and ABA would eliminate opportunities for professional basketball players, Robertson, joined by a bevy of NBA stars, filed suit in New York against the NBA, the ABA, and their member franchises. Among the complaints were the reserve clause, college draft, and a list of league polices and practices that, they argued, constituted collusion among the owners to restrain trade.

In the 1970–71 season, Spencer Haywood also filed a lawsuit against the NBA in the Los Angeles federal court, alleging that the NBA policy of disallowing its member franchises from drafting any player until four years after his class had graduated from high school violated the Sherman Antitrust Act. Although Haywood's lawsuit was filed after the Robertson case, the court expedited the process because Haywood claimed a delay would seriously harm him from earning a livelihood as the NBA threatened to expel Haywood's club, the Seattle Supersonics. The case went all the way to the Supreme Court, and on March 22, 1971, Justice William O. Douglas wrote the opinion in favor of Haywood. Douglas's ruling would play an important part in the final ruling of the Robertson suit four year later. Citing the Haywood case as precedent, the Court found for the players in 1976 that a merger between the NBA and ABA would constitute a restraint of trade as it would eliminate competition for players' services. Yet, the merger did take place. In 1976 the NBA took four ABA teams, San Antonio, New York, Denver, and Indiana after negotiating a settlement with the NBPA. Known as the Robertson Agreement, the NBA, among other concessions, agreed to abolish the reserve clause and limit the rights of a team to retain its drafted players to one year after which time the players would go back to the draft if the team was unable to sign them.

To a certain extent, the 1976 merger in professional basketball came as a result of the ABA's ability to compete with the NBA. The ABA had positioned itself as a young, dynamic league that produced a flashy product and, it was hoped, would attract paying customers and a national television contract. In 1971 ABA's Virginia Squires acquired a player who would epitomize the exciting nature of all the changes the league had promoted in its brand positioning. Foregoing his senior year at the University of Massachusetts, Julius "Dr. J" Erving signed a four-year, $500,000 contract with the team. While the ABA had other star players such as Spencer Haywood, Connie Hawkins, and George Gervin, none of them came close in generating fan excitement as Julius Erving.

Despite the drawing power of Erving and other ABA star players, the inability to acquire a national television contract magnified the financial problems of some of the franchises. Erving's team, the Virginia Squires, was a good example. First entered into the league as the Oakland Oaks in 1967, the team moved to the nation's capital after only two years in the Bay Area. One year later, the franchise moved again to Virginia. Gambling on Erving's potential as a draw, it gave Erving a big contract. With his electrifying skills, Erving led the team to the ABA finals in his first two seasons with the team. Yet, financial problems forced the team to trade Erving to the New York Nets in 1973. With Erving in the lineup, the Nets went on to win two ABA titles (1974 and 1976), and Erving was chosen as the league's Most Valuable Player in three consecutive seasons. The Squires never reached the finals again.

While the ABA faced problems with weak franchises and its inability to acquire a network television contract, the NBA had its games broadcast on ABC (1972–72) and CBS (1973–82) during the 1970s. Moreover, the established league was also able to produce a new group of star players. In 1969 the Milwaukee Bucks signed UCLA's 7'2" sensational center, Lew Alcindor, to a $1.4-million contract. As a superb player with size, Alcindor followed the footsteps of dominant NBA centers Wilt Chamberlain and Bill Russell. Since Russell had retired in 1969 and Chamberlain was nearing the end of his career (he retired in 1974), Alcindor became the premier center of the decade and the result was immediate. The Bucks improved by winning twenty-nine more games than the previous season and reached the second round of the playoffs in Alcindor's rookie year. When the Bucks traded for Oscar Robertson in Alcindor's second season, the team won the NBA championship, often beating their playoff opponents by eleven points or more. A convert to Islam, Alcindor officially changed his name to Kareem Abdul-Jabbar the day after the Bucks won the championship. Unlike Muhammad Ali (see boxing section below), his name change did not elicit a public outcry and was a testament to the American public's changing attitude. As a devout Muslim and a private man, Abdul-Jabbar asked the team in October 1974 to trade him to a metropolitan center, either New York or Los Angeles, because he did not feel the Midwest could provide his cultural needs. In a six-player swap, the Los Angeles Lakers acquired Abdul-Jabbar and another Milwaukee player in 1975.

Although no one team dominated the NBA in the 1970s—eight different teams won the championship—the acquisition of Abdul-Jabbar would develop a dynasty battle between Los Angeles and Boston in the late 1970s and lasted well into the 1980s. Abdul-Jabbar did not immediately help the Lakers to a championship. But in the 1979 NBA draft, Los Angeles used its number one pick to select Michigan State University's Earvin "Magic" Johnson Jr. Johnson was a fantastic ball handler and passer. At 6'9", he was also a versatile player. Although he played guard, he could fill in as a forward on occasions and in the 1980 NBA championship series against Dr. J and the Philadelphia 76ers, Johnson even played center in game 6 after Abdul-Jabbar sustained an injury in game 5. Together with Abdul-Jabbar, Johnson constituted the core of the Lakers dynasty.

As strong as Los Angeles was with the duo, it was not without competition. In 1978, Boston picked Larry Joe Bird, a junior from Indiana State University, sixth overall but was unable to sign him until 1979 because Bird chose to remain in college for his senior year. Although still a good team, the Boston Celtics no longer dominated the NBA like they had in the previous decade. In his first year, Bird improved the Celtics to a 61–21 season, the best regular-season record up until that time. (The team posted a 29–53 record in the previous season). Despite Johnson's brilliance, Bird won the league's Rookie of Year award. The Celtics, however, did not reach the NBA championship, losing in the conference finals to the 76ers. In 1980 the Celtics added center Robert Parish and drafted Kevin McHale. Together with Bird, the trio would make the Celtics one of the dominant teams in the 1980s, rivaled only by the Lakers.

The infusion of Johnson, Bird, and McHale, among others, also helped to revive the NBA. Rumors of drug abuse by players, complaints against franchise movements, and legal troubles plagued the league throughout the decade. Thus, even before the arrival of this new crop of young talent, the league began tinkering with the product in hope of stimulating fan interests. In the 1978–79 season, it added a third court official and the next year saw the NBA adopting the ABA invention, the three-point line, which opened up the game by drawing the defense out to the perimeter. In 1979 Commissioner Larry O'Brien negotiated a three-year cable television deal with the USA Network in addition to the existing CBS contract. This experiment with cable television would eventually lead the NBA to a partnership with the newly formed ESPN in 1982. By the end of the 1970s, then, the NBA was well positioned to grow in the marketplace.

College Basketball

Men's college basketball also blossomed in the 1970s. Its popularity in part had to do with the relatively small financial requirements for any school to operate a team. Basketball needed only fifteen players (and scholarships), a miniscule number compared to college football. While its revenues were also smaller than football, the advantageous cost-benefit ratio made basketball a viable and important program with NCAA-member institutions. Although basketball was a team game—more so in the college than the professional ranks—it was entirely possible to be successful if a team had one or two dominant players. Thus, many more schools in the NCAA had a basketball program than had a football program.

Despite the easier path to institutional glory through a good basketball program, NCAA oversight of intercollegiate athletics favored schools that had established programs up until the early 1970s. From the mid-1960s to the mid-1970s, the most dominant school in college basketball was University of California at Los Angeles (UCLA). Coached by the legendary John Wooden, UCLA basketball teams won ten NCAA titles during that period, including an unprecedented run of seven consecutive championships from 1967 to 1973. The NCAA rule of banning freshmen student-athletes from the varsity squad for their first year in college helped programs such as UCLA's. Originally designed to help freshman student-athletes acclimatize to college life, the rule effectively channeled top talent to prestigious programs as high school seniors realized that their chances of developing into top-notch college players would be better there. When the rule was repealed in 1972, however, schools that had not been able to compete for the same high school talents as the top schools were now able to entice high school seniors with promises of immediate playing time; thus making many more schools

Earvin "Magic" Johnson, NBA Hall of Famer, while a collegian in 1979. (AP / Wide World Photo)

competitive. After Wooden retired following the 1974–75 season, no schools would have the dominance of UCLA of the 1960s and 1970s.

The success of Wooden's teams did not rest entirely on the program's ability to recruit talented players. It also speaks volume about the importance of coaching. Coaches such as Adolph Rupp of Kentucky, who would finish his career in 1972, Dean Smith of North Carolina, and a young Bobby Knight, who started his tenure as head coach at University of Indiana in 1971, became celebrities in their respective campuses. Yet, opportunities for African Americans to lead a major university's program remained scarce despite the abundance of African American players and programs in traditionally black colleges. Like Jackie Robinson, Will Robinson (no relation) broke the color line in 1970 and guided Illinois State University to a winning record before departing to take up a scouting position with the Detroit Pistons. Despite his success, college basketball did not immediately welcome black head coaches.

Although coaches increasingly developed their reputation based on the success (and failure) of a particular program, college basketball also trumpeted individual players. Aided by television's thirst for stars, athletic departments actively promoted their top talent through game broadcasts. With the passing of the UCLA dynasty era and the diffusion of talent, television increasingly focused on the use of marquee players as promotional draws for the college game. Nowhere was this tactic more important in 1979 when two lesser-known programs in college basketball, Michigan State University and Indiana State University, met in the NCAA finals. Led by Magic Johnson, Michigan State defeated Indiana State and its superstar, Larry Bird, 75–64, in what was at the time the most-watched game in both college and professional basketball. The 1979 NCAA final drew 38 percent of the television viewing audience. As Johnson and Bird extended their rivalry into the NBA, the connection of college basketball as a path to a professional career became even closer.

A professional career in basketball was not available to the women's game in the 1970s although the sport was also very popular in woman intercollegiate athletics. Not until 1969 did the first women's intercollegiate basketball tournament take place; however, it was an invitational organized and hosted by West Chester State, a small former teachers' college in Pennsylvania.

Title IX would change the direction of women's intercollegiate athletics, including women's college basketball. (See below). In 1972 the newly formed Association for Intercollegiate Athletics for Women (AIAW) hosted its first basketball championship. Since college athletic departments generally did not adequately fund women's sports, many basketball teams had to resort to other measures in order to participate. The eventual winner of the first AIAW championship, Immaculata College, for example, had to seek donations to defray travel expenses. Like UCLA in men's basketball, Immaculata College (the Mighty Macs) in Pennsylvania dominated AIAW championships in the first half of the 1970s, winning the first three. Its coach, Cathy Rush, ran two-hour practices and recruited players, a change from former practices.

Unlike men's college basketball, small colleges actually won most of the AIAW basketball championships for much of the decade. After the last Immaculata victory in 1974, Delta State (Mississippi) took the trophy in the next three years. Not until 1978 did a major university, UCLA, win the women's title. In 1973, however,

AIAW reversed its no-scholarship policy and the shadow of Title IX drove many smaller schools that did not have a football program (football being the largest scholarship recipient) to offer scholarships to women athletes, and basketball benefited.

For various reasons, the NCAA, university athletic departments, and the media had long left women athletics alone, content with the separate but not equal treatment. As the Mighty Macs continued winning national championships, the media began to take notice. Television covered the Mighty Macs' 1975 regular-season game against the University of Maryland, and the game against Queens College at Madison Square Garden drew 12,000 spectators. Perhaps most satisfying to women athletic administrators and AIAW officials was a $12,000 profit from the 1975 championship. They might not have expected a financial success but the profit demonstrated that women sports, at least basketball, did not have to drain the resources of any athletic department—a major argument for the opponents of Title IX. The positive outlook in women's college basketball attracted interests from the corporate world as well. In 1976 Eastman Kodak sponsored the Kodak All-American Award presented annually to the top female basketball player. With the increasing attention to AIAW basketball, the NCAA and some athletic departments began to notice women basketball. In 1974 Ann Myers became the first female basketball player to receive a four-year scholarship from a major school, UCLA.

While women's basketball had come a long way, it had nevertheless been under the shadow of the men's game. Critics argued that the women's game was inferior. They pointed to the fact that the ball was smaller than the men's, and women could not dunk the ball. In other words, the men's version was still a standard against which all was to be measured. Nancy Lieberman, for example, was an exceptional player who, at the age of seventeen, was selected to represent the United States in the 1976 Olympic Games. She then led Old Dominion University to two consecutive (1979 and 1980) AIAW titles and was a three-time all-American. Despite all her achievements, she was dubbed "Lady Magic," a title that on the surface put her at the same level as Magic Johnson in the men's game. Yet this nickname also privileged the men's game by making it the version to be emulated.

Football

Professional Football

As MLB owners struggled to maintain their power in the 1970s, professional football rose to prominence and, some would argue, overtook baseball as the new national pastime. By and large, the popularity of football could be attributed to its marriage with television, especially for the professional leagues. Indeed, no sport benefited from television more than the National Football League (NFL) in the 1970s. A regional and working-class entity for most of its existence, the NFL under Commissioner Pete Rozelle transformed itself to appeal to a national audience through television. Game attendance steadily increased from 11 million in the late 1960s to almost 20 million by 1977. By the late 1970s, NFL broadcasts had the highest Nielsen ratings of all televised American sports programs. Furthermore, the NFL championship game, the Super Bowl, attracted more and more viewers each year. Television's first live nationally broadcast Super Bowl game took place in 1973, drawing approximately 75 million people.

In Super Bowl VII the Miami Dolphins played the Washington Redskins in Los Angeles before a sold-out crowd on January 14, 1973. Throughout the 1972 regular season and the subsequent playoffs, the Miami Dolphins had not lost a game. Commissioner Rozelle decided that the game could be broadcast live in the Los Angeles area since all the tickets had been sold very early on. The success of this broadcast led the league to modify its blackout rule in the following season, allowing games to be broadcast live in the local area if all the tickets were sold seventy-two hours before game time. Led by the "No-Name Defense," the Dolphins won the contest 14 to 7, the lowest-scoring championship game since the first Super Bowl. The 1972 perfect season still stands as a record as the 2007–8 New England Patriots failed in this pursuit by losing their one and only game to the New York Giants in Super Bowl XLII.

Televised NFL games were so popular that by 1977 Rozelle managed to negotiate with the three major television networks, NBC, American Broadcasting Company (ABC), and Columbia Broadcasting System (CBS), for a four-year television package worth $656 million. Each team received $6 million per year from this negotiation, up from $2.3 million in the last television contract.

The increasing popularity of the NFL, the accompanying prosperity, and the league's symbiotic relationship with television was nowhere more evident than in ABC's *Monday Night Football* program. First aired in 1970, the program drew large audiences as its producer, Roone Arledge, broke the conventions of sport broadcasting by introducing innovations such as multiple cameras, increased number of commentators, and slow-motion replays. Arledge hired the controversial Howard Cosell as one of the broadcast crew and Cosell's abrasive and argumentative manner elicited strong emotions among viewers. His frequent and heated exchanges with another broadcast crewmember, former Dallas Cowboys quarterback, Don Meredith, generated comments and debates among fans long after the broadcasts. Arledge also sought to appeal to audiences beyond die-hard professional football fans. In 1973, for example, Arledge invited two celebrity guests, who were unrelated to the NFL, to a broadcast as John Lennon of the Beatles and Ronald Reagan, then governor of California, appeared with the broadcast crew. This practice of including nonfootball celebrities fit nicely into Arledge's strategy of promoting football as entertainment and reaching out to audiences who might have minimal or no interest in football. Indeed, *Monday Night Football* became such a culturally important event in the 1970s that it altered people's social lives. On Monday nights, attendance in movie theatres dropped, some restaurants closed, and bowling leagues moved their games to Tuesdays.

Despite the good times, the NFL, like professional baseball, was not without its own labor troubles. Facing a more demanding labor force, NFL owners tried to break the players union, the National Football League Players Association (NFLPA). In 1971 the NFLPA hired Ed Garvey as its first executive director. Garvey, an attorney from a Minnesota law firm, had helped the NFLPA to get certified by the National Labor Relations Board in the previous year. One of his first accomplishments was to get rid of the "Rozelle Rule," which restricted free agency. In essence, the rule gave the commissioner power to compensate a team that lost a player through free agency from the team that signed him. Depending on the player, the compensation could include more than one player or future draft choices. Hence, few teams dared to sign any free agents because they did not know what the compensation would be.

Between 1963 and 1976, only four players moved to a different team after their contracts had expired. In 1972, however, John Mackey, the star tight end of the Baltimore Colts, with a group of mostly black players, filed suit against the NFL at the Minneapolis Federal District Court claiming the Rozelle Rule essentially restrained competition. In 1976, a federal court ruled in favor for the plaintiffs against the owners' appeal of a lower court's decision and urged the NFL and the NFLPA settle the issue through collective bargaining. At the same time, two other antitrust suits filed by NFL players confirmed the players' right to free agency. These developments forced the NFL to negotiate a settlement with the union in 1977. Opting for better pension and insurance coverage, the NFLPA agreed to a free-agency system whereby a player's old team had a right of first refusal by matching the offer to the free agent. Moreover, the team losing the free agent was entitled to compensation of draft choices depending on the "worth" (years of service and new salary offer) of the free agent. As a result, bidding for free agents remained scarce as the new system did not really enhance the players' bargaining power.

While judicial actions consistently favored the NFL players, the NFLPA as a labor organization fared less well. Prior to the final Mackey ruling, NFL owners were unwilling to negotiate any concessions to the union. In 1974 the NFLPA struck on July 1 after unsuccessful bargaining sessions for a collective agreement with management. The 1974 strike revealed the weakness of the union. Whereas player representatives from each team voted for and supported the strike, not all rank-and-file members agreed with the decision. In fact, nearly 20 percent of union members crossed picket lines one month after the strike began. By early August, the strike was over and the union conceded defeat. The consequence for the striking players and especially union officials were harsh and immediate. Twenty union officers and player representatives, for example, were either cut or traded by their teams.

Both the 1974 strike and the Mackey lawsuit exposed the racial tensions within the NFL. Although African Americans constituted about 45 percent of the NFL players by 1980, their earnings on average were below those of their white counterparts. As early as 1966, a federal government study revealed that black athletes lagged far behind white athletes in endorsements and other financial opportunities unrelated to their sport. While these opportunities increased somewhat in the 1970s, they still did not match proportionately to the percentage of black athletes in professional sports. Besides unequal opportunities, black players often suffered overt and covert racism, such as stacking, a practice of placing players in positions based on false racial stereotypes. African Americans were deemed to lack the intelligence and leadership required in central positions, such as quarterback or center. In 1979 the Tampa Bay Buccaneers became the first post–World War II team to use an African American, Doug Williams, in the starting quarterback position and he led the usually underachieving Bucs to the playoffs immediately. Yet Williams was an exception rather than the rule. Given the barriers they faced, African American athletes had more to gain from challenges to the existing structure of professional sport

Although player solidarity was questionable and NFL owners' control was still solid, a short-lived opportunity to improve the players' power occurred in 1974.

Gary Davidson, the sport entrepreneur who had started rival leagues in professional basketball and hockey, created the World Football League (WFL) in 1973; league play began the following year. Capitalizing on the American demographic shift from the Northeast to South and West, the desire of civic boosters in the growing cities for a professional football team, and the slow pace of NFL expansion, the WFL initially granted twelve franchises. Only four, New York, Detroit, Chicago, and Philadelphia, were in the traditional northeastern and midwestern industrial belt. (Before the first season ended, New York had moved to Charlotte, North Carolina.) By early 1974 WFL franchises began persuading NFL players to jump leagues by offering better salaries. Using the same money tactic of the AFL in signing Joe Namath in 1965, the WFL signed three Miami Dolphins, Larry Csonka, Jim Kiick, and Paul Warfield, to lucrative contracts totaling $3.884 million. In the WFL, Csonka's salary increased almost eightfold. These three players were considered to be the heart of the undefeated 1972 Miami Dolphins team and would give the WFL (and the team that signed them, the Memphis Southmen) instant credibility.

Besides the lure of higher salaries, the NFL players were facing a potential strike in 1974. For some, accepting the WFL's offers seemed to be the logical choice. Yet a majority of the WFL owners did not have adequate capital for the long-term survival of the league and their franchises. Before the first season was over, only two teams could claim financial stability. Two other teams folded and two more moved their franchises to a different city because they were in financial troubles. The league operated for another year; and when the NFL rejected the idea of a merger, the WFL went out of existence.

Although ineffective, the WFL demonstrated the public thirst for professional football franchises. Indeed, professional football's popularity could be attributed to its on-field product televised to millions of households. Pittsburgh, Oakland, and Miami with its perfect 1972–73 season were the dominant teams in the American Football Conference (AFC). Between the three teams, they appeared in the Super Bowl eight times, winning seven of them. For the National Football Conference (NFC), Dallas, Los Angeles, and Minnesota were either champions or runners-up in the conference sixteen times and Dallas won two Super Bowls (1972 and 1978). Pittsburgh, in particular, established itself as the football dynasty of the second half of the decade. Combining a strong defense, labeled the Steel Curtain, and a talented and balance offense that included quarterback Terry Bradshaw, running back Franco Harris, and wide receivers Lynn Swann and John Stallworth, head coach Chuck Noll guided the team to four Super Bowl victories (1975, 1976, 1979, and 1980), and its battles against the NFC teams, especially the Dallas Cowboys, galvanized the pride for a city that had been decimated by the demise of the steel industry.

With so many cities clamoring for an NFL franchise, owners contemplated expansion. Although demand for an NFL franchise far outstripped supply, some owners were leery about sharing the considerable television revenues with any additional clubs. After much deliberation and under pressure from politicians and civic boosters, the NFL granted two franchises, Seattle and Tampa Bay, in 1974 for $16 million each, almost twice the price tag of the previous expansion in the late 1960s.

Besides franchise fees from new admissions into the league, owners also took advantage of the favorable market conditions in another way. They played city authorities against one another by promising to move the team to the city that offered the best incentives. The New York Giants moved to East Rutherford, New Jersey, in 1972 and the Los Angeles Rams relocated across town to Anaheim in 1978. In turn, Los Angeles lured the Oakland Raiders to occupy the Rams' place in 1980, which eventually led to an antitrust law suit filed by the Oakland owner, Al Davis, against the NFL when the league blocked the move. Others, such as the Baltimore Colts' owner Robert Irsay and the Minnesota Vikings' owner Max Winter, extracted concessions and stadium improvements from their respective local authorities by merely considering moving their teams. The decade of the 1970s was good to the NFL and its franchise owners, who weathered labor challenges and court defeats with their control over professional football more or less intact.

College Football

College football had been inextricably tied to the creation and the history of the National Collegiate Athletic Association (NCAA) since the early twentieth century and this close relationship manifested itself prominently again in the sport in the 1970s. Television played an important role in changing the organizational and power structure within the NCAA and involved schools with major football program. Title IX also challenged college football's place within intercollegiate athletics (see below). Despite the defenders of college football's role in higher education, the developments in the 1970s further separated major football programs from the education mission of their parent universities and put in place a structure that had little difference between college and the early professional football leagues.

During the 1970s, college football faced a financial crisis. Part of a larger problem of university athletic departments across the country, increased expenses due to inflation, rising tuition costs, decreased enrollment (and hence reduced student activity fees), and Title IX compliance to fund women's sports put pressure on athletic department budgets. The financial pressures were especially hard for smaller schools with limited resources. While college football had been generating more revenues than other sports, it was not immune to examination and criticisms of its share of the athletic department's budget. In 1971 NCAA executive director Walter Byers called for reform in college football. He proposed changes in limiting scholarships and staff for college football, which promptly drew fire from schools with major football programs. Any attempt to restrict football scholarships could adversely impact dominance on the gridiron. In order to solve the financial crunch and placate the big-time football schools, the NCAA first revoked the freshman rule, thus allowing freshman football players to participate in scrimmages and games. In 1973 members in the NCAA came to a compromise by dividing the membership into three tiers: Division I, II, and III, hoping that the divisions would allow schools with similar resources to govern themselves.

For the top football schools, however, the restructuring of membership was wholly unsatisfactory since there would be 237 schools in Division I. As professional football reaped the financial windfall from television broadcasts, major football schools wanted to keep the college football television revenues, which had reached $16 million in 1974 and would increase to $29 million in 1978 and $$30 million in 1980, for themselves. Schools with televised games were receiving as much as $450,000 for a national broadcast and $350,000 for a regional broadcast, and they feared others in Division I would dilute their profits. For schools that did not have televised games or did not belong to a conference that shared television and bowl games revenues, however, maintaining a football program became almost an impossible proposition. When a proposal to share revenues among all Division I football programs was being circulated in 1975, commissioners of major football conferences gathered to discuss possible alternatives. In April 1976 sixty-three college football programs, with the exceptions of schools from the Pac-10 and Big Ten conferences, formed the College Football Association (CFA) as an advocacy group for major football schools. Its demand to separate itself from nonmajor football schools finally materialized in 1978 when the NCAA subdivided Division I into Division IA, with 105 schools, and Division IAA. The CFA, however, would morph from an advocacy group for major football conferences into a semiautonomous negotiating representative of its own television broadcast contracts in the next decade.

For college football, the NCAA's efforts did not necessarily produce the intended consequences. As part of the reform movement, the NCAA limited football scholarships to 105 in 1978. While this measure could potentially reduce the impact of football in the athletic budget, reducing the number of scholarships did not lessen the coaches' control over players since these scholarships were not based on a student-athlete's financial needs. With a limited number of scholarships combined with the one-year renewable term, coaches had tremendous power over their charges. Indeed, abuses of athletes by some football coaches came to surface at the beginning of the decade when Dave Meggyesy, formerly of Syracuse University, and Gary Shaw, formerly University of Texas, published critical accounts of their college football experiences (*Out of Their League* and *Meat on the Hoof* respectively). Moreover, the NCAA had lowered the admission standards for college athletes in the previous year, replacing the previous eligibility requirement that employed a combination of high school GPA, SAT scores, and type of course work with the a new standard. This opened the door for coaches to recruit talented players who were academically suspect. It also created temptations for football programs to keep these athletes eligible, by any means, since many of them were academically unprepared to enter college.

As an indicator of the success of African Americans in college football, eight of the ten Heisman Trophy winners were African Americans between 1971 and 1980 and included future football stars such as Tony Dorsett (Pittsburgh and Dallas Cowboys), Earl Campbell (Texas and Houston Oilers), and Billy Sims (Oklahoma and Detroit Lions). Yet, this success was only superficial and woefully ineffective in opening opportunities for African Americans. Since many of the African American players were ill-prepared for college, most did not benefit fully from a higher education as demands from football conflicted with demands to catch up with their studies. For some, college football served as a path toward a career in professional football and often college recruiters would promote their programs as such. In reality, only a minority of college players made it to the professional rank and even for those who did make it, a professional career was usually short and unpredictable.

Professional Hockey

In the 1970s, the marketplace also opened opportunities and created problems for the National Hockey League (NHL), the dominant professional hockey organization. Long considered a Canadian passion and a regional league in the United

States, the NHL began a phase of expansion late in the 1960s that lasted until the mid-1970s. From a mere six teams in 1967, the NHL grew to twenty-one teams by the end of the 1970s. Demographic shifts, a rival league, lure of television revenues, and threats of antitrust action drove this expansion.

By 1967 the NHL had doubled its size to twelve teams seizing on the demographic shifts to the West and pacifying untapped American markets that had a long history of hockey. The NHL added Vancouver and Buffalo franchises in 1970 after Buffalo promised to compensate Toronto for infringing on its territory. By the beginning of the 1970s, then, fourteen teams made up the NHL. In 1972 the league added two more franchises. Based on the Toronto-Buffalo market dynamic, New York argued for and received a second franchise, the Islanders. The other addition, however, departed from the cautious approach of the NHL expansion thus far. Instead of placing a team in traditional hockey markets, which were usually located near the Canadian-U.S. border or cities that had some tradition of the sport, the NHL granted the city of Atlanta a franchise as the league began to recognize the importance of the demographic movement from the Northeast to cities in the South and West. Moreover, the league also hoped the spread of hockey to nontraditional markets would make itself more appealing to major television network. Important also was the staking of major markets to pre-empt a rival organization's intrusion into the industry. Indeed, the need to fight off the rival league prompted further expansion in 1974 when the NHL added Kansas City and Washington, DC.

Sensing the conservative nature of the NHL owners who had jealously been guarding professional hockey and its profits from others since World War II, U.S. entrepreneurs Dennis Murphy and Gary Davidson founded the World Hockey Association (WHA) in 1971. They witnessed how the American Football League had forced the NFL to recognize and negotiate with its rival and believed that this business model might work in professional hockey as well. And unlike the NFL, which had thirteen teams before the creation of the AFL, the NHL had only six. A second professional hockey league looked promising indeed. Both Murphy and Davidson had no previous experience in the hockey industry, however. Hence, they recruited Canadian businessman Bill Hunter into their partnership. To take advantage of the Canadian public's displeasure with the American-focus NHL expansion scheme, the WHA announced four Canadian franchises—Calgary, Edmonton, Saskatoon, and Winnipeg—besides eight American ones. By the start of the league's first season in 1972, however, there had been changes in the franchise locations already. Of the twelve planned franchises, four had to be moved to other cities; Calgary to Cleveland, Dayton to Houston, Miami to Philadelphia, and San Francisco to Quebec City. These maneuvers speak volume about the speculative nature of the WHA and its doubtful long-term survival.

Despite the WHA's problem of finding qualified franchises, the NHL faced a competition nonetheless. Not only did the WHA place franchises in existing NHL markets such as Chicago, Los Angeles, New York, Philadelphia, and Boston, it also ignored NHL contracts, emboldened by an antitrust investigation of the NHL by the U.S. Department of Justice and a slew of lawsuits, and actively pursued NHL star players. Two of the most revered NHL stars, Gordie Howe of the Detroit Red Wings and Bobby Hull of the Chicago Blackhawks, jumped to the WHA. For the players, a rival organization meant competitive bidding and presented opportunities for a raise in salary. Although professional hockey had a players' union in the 1970s, the overall welfare of professional hockey players did not improve as much as it did in professional baseball. A major reason for this lag was the owner- and league-friendly union director, Alan Eagleson. Bobby Hull signed with the Winnipeg Jets for $1 million over ten years, an astounding figure in hockey circles. Other than star players, regular players' salaries rose as well. NHL players' salary averaged $28,500 before the WHA but jumped to $44,000 in 1972. This amount would increase to $96,000 in 1977. Moreover, the existence of the two rival leagues meant more job opportunities that extended both to the junior leagues and overseas.

As a professional league, the NHL had traditionally relied heavily on Canadian players who came out of a network of development youth leagues. Out of necessity, the WHA began recruiting European players, mostly from Scandinavian countries because the Cold War prohibited recruiting inside the Iron Curtain. The importing of European players began to erode the myth that only Canadian players who had come through the baptism of the Canadian junior programs had what it took to play in the professional ranks. By the late 1970s, some NHL coaches began adding talent from Europe and elsewhere. Indeed, several of the American gold-medal team members from the legendary 1980 Lake Placid Olympic Winter Games went on to successful NHL careers. This development did not end the preference for Canadian players. In fact, the competition for talent was so fierce that the WHA allowed its teams to sign underage players. In 1978, for example, the Indianapolis Racers signed the underage sensation, Wayne Gretzky, to a contract.

Wayne Gretzky

Born in 1961 in Brantford, Ontario, Wayne Douglas Gretzky was the dominant player in professional hockey. Even when he was a young child, Gretzky's talent as a hockey player surpassed players of his age group. In 1978 the Indianapolis Racers of the upstart WHA signed Gretzky as an underage player. Unlike other hockey contracts, Gretzky's was a personal service contract to the Racers' owner Nelson Skalbania. Skalbania ran into financial problems during the season and sold Gretzky's contract to the Edmonton Oilers, where he led the team in scoring and finished third in the league. With Gretzky, the Oilers made it to the WHA final, only losing the championship to the Winnipeg Jets four games to two. Prior to the Oilers became part of the NHL-WHA merger in 1979, Oilers' owner Peter Pocklington extended Gretzky's personal-service contract to twenty years, the longest professional contract in sport at the time.

Although Gretzky was very successful in the WHA, critics doubted whether he could compete in the established NHL especially Gretzky's physique. As an eighteen-year-old, Gretzky stood at six feet weighing only 160 pounds. In his first NHL season, however, Gretzky won the league's Most Valuable Player, an award he would win for the next seven seasons. He also tied with Marcel Dionne of the Los Angeles Kings for the scoring title although Dionne received title because he had scored more goals than Gretzky. For the 1980–81 season, Gretzky surpassed his previous season's scoring prowess and registered 164 points with 55 goals and 109 assists. In the nine seasons as an NHL Oiler, the Great One broke all kinds of records, many of which remain unbroken today, and helped to establish the Oilers' hockey dynasty in the 1980s.

Wayne Gretzky. (Courtesy of Photofest)

Despite its ability to sign young talent, the WHA remained an unstable league. In the same season that Gretzky made his WHA debut, only six teams remained and negotiations for a merger with the NHL began. In 1979 the NHL agreed to absorb four WHA teams, Edmonton, Hartford, Quebec, and Winnipeg, and paid the remaining two WHA franchises, Cincinnati and Birmingham, $1.5 million each as compensation. Although labeled as a merger, the terms were fairly one-sided favoring the NHL. All four WHA franchises had to pay a new franchise fee and NHL teams could reclaim players who had jumped their NHL contracts. Thus, the NHL ended its expansion by the end of the decade with twenty-one teams spreading across the North American continent.

The 1970s and '80s saw the last glory days of dynasties. Continuing its dominance from the 1950s and '60s, the Montreal Canadiens won the Stanley Cup in 1971 and 1973 and, beginning in the 1975–76 season, garnered four more titles consecutively. Then the New York Islanders, an expansion franchise, had its own run as Stanley Cup winners late in the 1970s and into the early 1980s. Yet, the Islanders were not the first expansion team to win the league championship. Rather, that honor went to the Philadelphia Flyers, who won in 1974 and again in 1975. Known, affectionately by their fans and distastefully by their critics, as the "Broad Street Bullies," the Flyers employed a physical style of play that intended to intimidate their opponents. This strategy often led to mass brawling between the Flyers and their opponents.

The Flyers' strategic violence contrasted sharply with the European style, which emphasized skating, puck-handling, and passing. Although NHL fans had witnessed the Europeans' capability with a sprinkling of Scandinavian players, it was the Soviets, the pre-eminent power in international hockey, who epitomized this type of play. As the NHL was not involved in any international tournaments such as the Olympic Winter Games or the World Championship, the test between the different approaches to the sport came to a head in September 1972 when the NHL and the Soviet Ice Hockey Federation agreed to play a Summit Series pitting an NHL all-star selection against the Soviet national team. In the context of the Cold War, the series occurred under intense nationalistic feelings, especially because the Soviets represented the first real test between the best in professional against the best in amateur hockey. To defeat the Soviets would be an affirmation of Western ideals and, important for Canadian hockey fans, confirmation of the superiority of NHL (translation: *Canadian*) hockey. For many followers of the sport, they expected no less than a complete annihilation of the Soviet national team by the NHL all-stars. To the surprise and dismay of Canadians and NHL fans in North America, the NHL all-stars managed only one victory, one tie, and two losses in the first four games played in Canada. Criticized and jeered by Canadians at home, the NHL all-stars traveled to the Soviet Union for the remaining four games. Frustrated by the losses, some players on the team resorted to physical intimidation. In an ugly incident in game 7, Bobby Clarke of the Philadelphia Flyers deliberately swung his hockey stick at the Soviet star Valery Kharlamov and fractured Kharlamov's ankle. People may still debate whether Kharlamov's injury affected the outcome as the NHL All-Stars managed to eke out an overall tournament victory. They won three out of the four remaining games, with a thrilling 6–5 victory in game 8 that was forever memorialized in hockey lore when Paul Henderson scored the game-winning goal with only thirty-four seconds left.

The victory by the NHL all-stars over the Soviets seemed to confirm the superiority of the NHL brand. More introspective hockey observers in Canada realized, however, that the European style of play could be just as effective. Moreover, the success of the series in terms of viewership convinced both professional hockey owners and the Soviets that this type of competition could be profitable. Indeed, the WHA, whose players were excluded in the 1972 series, held its version of the Summit Series in 1974. The NHL initiated the Canada Cup in 1976, which continued into the 1980s. Soviet club teams also toured North America, bringing their style of play to franchises located in Canada as well as the United States. While these exchanges did not help to end the Cold War, more and more NHL fans came to appreciate the European style, which aided in the acceptance of European players as well as American college hockey players.

Despite the challenge of a new league and the emergence of the Soviets and Scandinavians as hockey powers, the NHL thrived in the 1970s. Aided by a more-or-less compliant union, the league expanded its territories and helped in securing network television contracts with CBS (1968–72) and NBC (1973–75). Yet the NHL remained on the margin of a major-league status. By the middle of the decade, U.S. television networks gave up on the NHL as part of their programming because of consistently poor ratings. Whereas local television broadcasts in some of the traditional American hockey markets were profitable, the league found attracting new adherents to the NHL brand a difficult task. With rising salaries because of the bidding war between NHL and AHL, the NHL governors selected John Ziegler, a lawyer, as the new league president in 1977, replacing the retired Clarence Campbell. Ziegler became the first American to hold that post. Although Ziegler moved the NHL head office from Montreal to New York, he was no more successful in landing a network television contract than his predecessor. The difficulty in broadening the appeal of the NHL in the United States and the concomitant absence of a network television deal for a national audience would impact the NHL's growth as a major league in the United States in the next decade and beyond.

The Olympic Games

All three Summer Olympic Games in the 1970s had their share of political problems. Many groups used these sporting spectacles as opportunities to promote their political agendas, knowing that television would provide a captive international audience. For the 1972 Games in Munich, West Germany, the organizing committee and the country hoped to present a new Germany that promoted peace and renounced its racist, anti-Semitic past. Indeed, one of the highlights of the Games was American swimmer Mark Spitz winning seven gold medals. Of Jewish heritage, Spitz set a world record in every one of the seven events. His achievement was celebrated in Germany and symbolized a change in attitude in a country that systematically persecuted Jews only some thirty years earlier.

Mark Spitz holds five of the seven gold medals he won at the Olympics in Munich, Germany. In an interview on July 2, 2008, with the Associated Press, the star of the 1972 Munich Games left little doubt that he expected his thirty-six-year-old mark to be on the Olympic books for only another month or so. Michael Phelps broke Spitz's record of seven gold medals at the Olympics in Beijing. (AP / Wide World Photo)

On September 5, however, Palestinian gunmen belonging to a group called Black September entered the Olympic Village and held eleven Israeli athletes and officials hostage. They demanded the Israeli government release Palestinian prisoners in Israeli jails in exchange for the hostages. As the hosts of the Games, the Germans were horrified, as it seemed once again Jews were in peril on German soil. When the Israeli government refused to negotiate with the Palestinian hostage-takers, the German government decided to rescue the hostages who, along with five hostage-takers, died in a shootout in an airport.

The killing of the Israeli athletes and officials pointed to the reality that an international spectacle such as the Olympic Games could be used by disgruntled groups to make a political statement. In the handling of the crisis by the International Olympic Committee (IOC) or, more precisely, IOC president Avery Brundage, the ideologues of amateurism struck back. Amid calls for the cancellation of the Games, Brundage declared that "the Games must go on." Speaking in the memorial service for the slain Israelis on September 6, he lamented the encroachment of politics and commercialism into the Olympic Games. Yet he assured the world that the IOC would not surrender to these intrusions. Brundage and other like-minded proponents of amateurism were fighting against the evils and cynicisms of the world in order to preserve all that is good in sport and, as the 1972 Games massacre of the Israelis showed, they were barely holding on.

Of course, money and politics had been with the Olympic Games long before 1972. Even though the mixture of politics and sport was most visible in the hostage crisis as television cameras followed the incident, politics had also quietly ousted Rhodesia's Olympic membership before the 1972 Games began. Amidst a wave of anticolonial, anti-imperial sentiments at home, the African nations convinced the IOC and, against Brundage's wishes, barred the Rhodesians, who had already arrived in Munich, from participating in the Games. The expulsion of Rhodesia clearly attested to the utilization of sport in achieving a political aim. In 1970 the IOC had stripped South Africa of its membership because of its racist apartheid policy. Rhodesia, however, had no such policy for its sport programs and Olympic team. Yet, other African nations wanted to bring down Rhodesia's white minority government and one strategy was to isolate the country in the international sporting community. In the face of a possible boycott of the 1972 Games by twenty-one African teams, the IOC voted to exclude the Rhodesians.

The Africans were not the only ones to use the Olympic Games as a platform to advance an agenda. Especially in the highly heated atmosphere during the Cold

1972 Olympic Basketball

Since the introduction of basketball as an Olympic sport in 1936, the United States had never lost a game. Its teams dominated the tournaments. Having handily disposed most of its opponents, the American team faced the Soviets in the final game on September 10, 1972, in Munich. The Soviets led the game most of the way until three seconds were left on the clock. Doug Collins then made two free throws to give the American team a 50–49 lead. The officials, however, stopped the game with one second left after the Soviets put the ball into play after Collins's free throws. Apparently, the Soviet coach had asked for a timeout in between the free throws but the referees never acknowledged it, so the officials added two more seconds to replay the last three seconds. When the Soviets put the ball in play a second time and missed a shot from half court, the horn sounded, signaling the end of the game, and the Americans began celebrating. The Soviet coach, however, protested that the timekeeper never reset the clock to three seconds. Under the intervention of the president of basketball's international federation (FIBA), R. William Jones of Great Britain, the officials ordered the teams to back onto the court. Confusion reigned and the American coaching staff questioned the ruling. In the end, the two sides lined up for yet another in-bound play. The Soviets then threw a long pass down the court and scored just as time expired, winning the contest 51–50. Immediately the American delegation filed a protest, which was rejected by FIBA's five-member panel in a vote of 3 to 2. All three Communist-bloc members (Hungary, Poland, and Cuba) on the panel voted against the United States with Italy and Puerto Rico voting for. Feeling that they had been wronged, the Americans decided not to accept the silver medal.

War, the Soviet-led Communist bloc and the Western nations–specifically the United States—treated the Games and the achievements of their athletes as testaments to the strength of their respective nations. Indeed, failures in the Olympics, especially in events that each nation had traditionally dominated, became national disasters, which often prompted public outcry and indignation. In 1972 the U.S. basketball team lost the gold medal against the Soviet Union in a controversial final. In addition, two American sprinters, Eddie Hart and Rey Robinson, both of whom had run 100 meters in under ten seconds, missed their second-round heats because they were given an outdated schedule. Both were therefore disqualified. Worse, a Soviet sprinter won the 100-meter final the next day. Since both basketball and men's sprints in track were considered America's sure bets toward the total metal tally, Congress held hearings into the fiasco and in 1978 passed the Amateur Sports Act that restructured the United States amateur sport organization at the elite level, creating, among other initiatives, the U.S. Olympic Training Center at Colorado Springs.

Boycotts or threats of boycott of the Olympic Games based on political expediency continued throughout the 1970s. For the 1976 Games in Montreal, the Chinese and New Zealand questions dominated the IOC discussions and resulted in the absence of both the mainland Chinese and the Taiwanese Olympic teams. On the other hand, the presence of New Zealand led to a boycott by twenty-eight African nations who perceived New Zealand's sport ties, the South African rugby tour in particular, as a slight to Africans' determination to isolate South Africa from the world. While America had little involvement in the 1972 and 1976 boycotts, it was the chief instigator for the boycott in the 1980 Moscow Games.

The IOC's selection of Moscow as the site to host the 1980 Games was a controversial one. With the Cold War still raging, there had been calls in the West to boycott the Games or change the venue after the IOC awarded the Games to Moscow in 1974. By 1979 President Carter's administration had been besieged by domestic and diplomatic problems. Carter was seeking re-election, but the American public had lost faith in him as his approval rating sagged to as low as 25 percent. As a demonstration of his abilities as a leader, Carter called for a boycott of the Moscow Games, citing the Soviet Union's invasion of Afghanistan in December as a threat to America's security. About three weeks before the opening of the Winter Olympic Games at Lake Placid, New York, Carter announced that the Soviets had to withdraw their troops from Afghanistan or the United States would organize a boycott of the Moscow Games. Under an atmosphere of heightened patriotism (driven by the Cold War and the recent Afghanistan invasion) in Lake Placid, the American Olympic hockey team came from behind to defeat a highly touted Soviet Union squad in the medal round by a score of 4–3, and then defeated Finland in another come-from-behind victory two nights later to ensure the second-ever Olympic gold medal in hockey for the United States.

With a successful Winter Games in the United States over, Carter began to push for the boycott of the Moscow Games in earnest. Because the United States Olympic Committee (USOC) was (and is) a private organization, Carter had no authority over it. Hence he resorted to a combination of threats, persuasion, and appeal to patriotism. Under intense government and public pressure, the USOC voted overwhelmingly to boycott the 1980 Games, although the athletes were divided in their opinions. Carter also tried to convince other noncommunist nations to follow America's lead. Great Britain's government could not prevent its Olympic team from going to Moscow. Whether the boycott was successful or not remained in doubt as the French, Italian, and most of the non-Islamic African states also chose to participate. Sixty-five countries eventually stayed home but eighty did show up in Moscow.

Politics were not the only intrusion into the amateur foundation of the Olympic Games. As the international sporting spectacle became a more and more important event, the commercialization of the Games and the participating athletes also helped to dilute the amateur ideal. To stage a world-class event such as the Olympic Games requires financing. In the 1970s television broadcast fees, together with government support, underwrote the spectacles. For television networks in America and abroad, sport events were ready-made programming and had an identifiable target audience with which the networks could sell advertising to corporations. And the Olympics had additional appeal to American audiences. As a major international sporting occasion, the Olympic Games presented a testing ground for the Cold War and a chance for unbridled national chauvinism. Especially in head-to-head competitions against the Soviet Union, such as the Lake Placid hockey game, victories were projected as proof to the superiority of American democracy over Soviet communism. For those who were leery of the social and political turmoil since the 1960s, the amateur idealism of the Olympics reminded them of a time, though mythical, when sport represented all that was virtuous.

Roone Arledge began producing the Olympic Games for ABC at the 1968 Games and brought his innovations in televising other sport programs to the 1972 and 1976 summer Olympic broadcasts. The success of these broadcasts, in turn, drove all three major American networks into frenzied bidding for the Games' television rights. Broadcast fees had increased from $13.5 million (from ABC) for the Munich Games to $25 million (ABC) in Montreal to $85 million (NBC) in Moscow. (NBC did cancel the broadcast in compliance with President Carter's request to boycott the Games.) Increasingly, these rising television revenues became a sore point among the IOC, the various organizing committees, and the international sport federations.

Although money had driven a wedge among the different "amateur" sport governing bodies, the amateur ideal did not forbid them from benefiting financially. Only when athletes acquired financial gains from their athletic prowess did the heavy hand of amateurism come down upon them. In fact, there were few Olympic athletes who were not financially sponsored either by the government or private money. While the IOC turned its head away from government-sponsored athletes such as those in the Communist-bloc countries or the NCAA scholarships, it frowned on private money, especially commercial endorsements by athletes, even as the organization chased them itself. In the 1972 Sapporo (Japan) Winter Games, IOC president Brundage chose to make an example out of Austrian skier Karl Schranz for transgressions against amateurism. Brundage originally wanted to ban more than forty skiers. Fearing a boycott and a fiasco, Brundage came down hard on Schranz. Accusing him of receiving money from ski manufacturers in exchange for endorsement—a common practice among top caliber skiers—Brundage banished Schranz from the Games. Unable to get a hearing with Brundage, Schranz publicly chastised Brundage for embracing an ideal that would only allow the rich to participate in the Games. He also questioned why Brundage banned him from the Games, when the Communist-bloc athletes were heavily subsidized by their governments, not for their supposed positions in the armed forces or industry, but their athletic skills. Some 200,000 Austrians greeted Schranz in a hero's welcome when he returned to Austria, seeing Brundage as the villain in this drama.

Schranz's disqualification at the Sapporo Games represented a last hurrah for Brundage and his hard-line stance against professionalism, however, since his term of office as IOC president expired after the Summer Games in Munich. Although not one to promote professionalism, Brundage's successor, Lord Killanin (Ireland), did not pursue the question of amateurism as fervently as Brundage. Under Juan Antonio Samaranch (Spain), who took office in 1980, the Olympic Games would eventually distance themselves from the issue of amateurism as a condition to participate in the Games.

Although the fight for amateurism gradually faded into the background, a different battle against the violation of "pure" sport began to take shape in the 1970s. In the 1976 Games, the East German women's swim team dominated the field by winning eleven gold and five silver medals in the thirteen-event meet and, in the process, destroyed the pretournament favorite Americans. The team's star, Kornelia Ender, corralled four gold medals and set a world record in each one of them. East Germany was equally superior in women's track and field. In fact, Communist-bloc countries won all except one event in this sport. Immediately, rumors and accusations against the Soviet bloc, and especially the East German, women athletes of using anabolic steroids began to surface. While the Soviets led the medal count of the 1976 Games, many people were suspicious of East Germany's achievements. With only 16 million people, East Germany placed third in total medals won (89) behind the Soviets (124) and the Americans (94). But it had the second most gold medals (40). Only the Soviets had more with 49. Despite extensive drug testing during the Games, no one on the East German swim or track and field team failed these tests (though many were discovered after the fall of the Soviet Union in 1989). On the other hand, the IOC disqualified eight weightlifters for testing positive for anabolic steroids. These disqualifications happened to athletes in Communist and non-Communist countries alike. Of the eight, two were Americans.

Women's Sports: "I am woman, hear me roar!"

Australian singer Helen Reddy released her hit song, "I Am Woman," considered by some as the unofficial anthem of the women's rights movement, in 1972 and Congress passed the Educational Amendments Act in the same year. Included in the legislation was Title IX. Signed into law by President Richard Nixon on June 23, Title IX states, "No person in the United States shall, on the basis of sex, be excluded from participation in, be denied the benefits of, or be subjected to discrimination under any education program or activity receiving Federal financial assistance." Although Title IX did not specifically address sports, the consequences would indeed be far-reaching in intercollegiate athletics, impacting its organization and administration. Not only did college athletics feel Title IX's impact, the subsequent struggles to enforce and to undermine this legislation by defenders and opponents of Title IX provided a very salient reminder of the issue of gender beyond the sports world.

One year prior to the passage of Title IX, intercollegiate athletics for women had undergone a transformation. Deviating from the long-held ideal of de-emphasizing elite-level competition, a group of woman athletic administrators established the Association of Intercollegiate Athletics for Women (AIAW). Although AIAW instituted national championships in women's athletics, its leaders were determined to avoid the pitfalls of the men's intercollegiate athletics, namely, the corrupting influence of commercialism and the overemphasis on winning at all cost. As they saw it, one way to counter these evils was the prohibition of athletic scholarships.

Having long ignored college women athletics, the NCAA nevertheless initially tried to establish some kind of relationship with the AIAW. In a bitter struggle against the Amateur Athletic Union (AAU) for control of amateur sports in the United States, the NCAA wanted to legitimize its ambition but that meant NCAA had to offer both men's and women's programs. Since it never had any interest in women's athletics, the NCAA saw the AIAW as an answer and invited the women leaders to discuss possible affiliation in 1971. Yet the two sides could not come to an agreement because the AIAW viewed the proposed affiliation by the NCAA as a threat to its autonomy and control over women's athletics. Since the AIAW's stance on scholarship contradicted NCAA practice also, the two organizations decided to go their separate ways. After Title IX came into existence, however, the NCAA amended its regulations to make governing women's sports possible.

Although the NCAA changed its mission by including athletic championships for women in 1972, it did not entirely welcome Title IX, as its members equated gender equity to diversion of funds from the men's programs. Even before the legislation's enforcement, NCAA actively lobbied Congress and the Department of Health, Education and Welfare (HEW), the agency charged with enforcing the new law, to exempt athletic programs. Through the generally friendly media and sympathetic politicians, the NCAA argued that applying Title IX to athletic departments would destroy intercollegiate athletics. More specifically, athletic departments just did not have enough resources to fund both men's and women's programs. Women's programs had traditionally been housed in the physical education department and had little financial resources. Since the athletic department did not believe women's programs would contribute to any significant revenues, adding women's programs would only take away funding from the other men's programs. Similar cries of doom extended beyond colleges and universities and into interscholastic athletics.

In 1975, HEW issued the final Title IX regulation that included specific provisions against sex discrimination in sport programs. All institutions were given three years to comply before sanctions took effect. Efforts by the NCAA and its allies to derail and circumvent Title IX continued through the decade however. Together with Dewey Bartlett (R-Oklahoma) and Roman Hruska (R-Nebraska), Sen. John Tower, for example, again introduced a bill to exempt men's football and basketball from the law in 1977. Without exception, these efforts did not bear fruit, but the resentment toward Title IX continued into the next decade when these dissenting voices received a much warmer response in the Reagan administration.

Failing to stop Title IX in the political arena, the NCAA took a different tack. It challenged the interpretation of the legislation. Since most athletic departments did not receive federal funding directly, the NCAA argued that intercollegiate athletic programs and their administration were exempt from the law. In 1976 the NCAA filed suit against the HEW, alleging HEW had overstepped its bounds in applying Title IX to college athletics and that the HEW's interpretation of the law was faulty. In January 1978, federal District Court Judge Earl E. O'Connor dismissed the case because the NCAA could not prove Title IX actually harmed the men's athletic programs. Although NCAA had failed in the courts, its challenge on HEW's Title IX regulations revealed the ambiguity of the original statute. The spirit of the law was meant to eliminate discrimination based on sex; but how would HEW and the courts determine if the schools were complying with the law? It took another year before HEW issued a policy interpretation on Title IX and intercollegiate athletics.

In December of 1979, HEW released a set of guidelines that provided three avenues in which a school could be deemed as compliant with the legislation. Known as the Three-Prong Test, they examined if athletic opportunities for each sex were substantially proportionate to student enrollment; if the institution had demonstrated a continual expansion of opportunities for the underrepresented group; and if the interests of the underrepresented groups had been accommodated. Despite this attempt to clarify compliance, controversy over interpretation continued after the 1970s.

The continuous and unsuccessful attempts by the NCAA to stall and to reverse Title IX would significantly impact the governance of intercollegiate athletics, for both men and women. Fearing government sanctions, NCAA began to examine the feasibility of initiating women's programs. In the latter part of the decade, the

NCAA began to consider seriously instituting women's championships on its own and, in 1980, the NCAA voted to host championships in all three divisions.

For the AIAW, the intrusion of the NCAA into women's sports posed dangerous challenges. Despite the prevailing negative attitude about women in competitive sports at the time, the AIAW had seen its membership grow in this decade. Within five years of the passage of Title IX, the number of college women athletes had doubled. AIAW membership had grown from the 278 original charter members to over 900 in 1980.

AIAW forbade the granting of athletic scholarships. In 1973 Fern Kellmeyer, the director of physical education at Marymount College in Florida, and eleven female tennis players from two colleges (Marymount and Broward Community College) filed suit, naming among the defendants AIAW. In an ironic twist, they charged that the AIAW policy of prohibiting athletic scholarships amounted to discrimination and violated the equal protection provision in the Fourteenth Amendment of the Constitution as well as Title IX. Since male athletes at these schools could receive scholarships, the AIAW policy of no scholarships created a separate group with unequal treatment. Knowing that it would lose the case in court, the AIAW abandoned the policy and the court dismissed the case. Yet the Kellmeyer case was the first step toward a shift from the idealistic educational model that had its roots in the late nineteenth century to the male commercial model so abhorred by women sport leaders in educational institutions. Indeed, AIAW would begin acquiring sponsorships and contracts for televising its championships. In 1977 the AIAW formalized this change by creating a promotions committee whose goal was to seek endorsements, and Eastman Kodak became the first major corporate sponsor of AIAW.

The shift from an educational to a commercial model by AIAW presaged the eventual demise of the AIAW early in the next decade. When the NCAA announced that it would start hosting national championships, many of the top universities and colleges decided to abandon AIAW for the NCAA in 1980. With the decrease in members, the AIAW's attractiveness to sponsors and television networks also diminished, and the AIAW would cease to operate within two years. Although the AIAW no longer exists, its legacy, coupled with the empowerment of Title IX, to women athletics is significant. At a time when women sports were being belittled and ignored, a group of dedicated women decided to promote the possibilities and joy of competition. Moreover, it promoted not only women athletes but also offered opportunities to women in athletic administration, coaching, and officiating. Whether one agrees with AIAW's educational model or not, the number of girls and women participating in sports in the 1970s increased by leaps and bounds. AIAW's creation came at a time when women in general sought a greater voice in society. Both the organization's and Title IX's effectiveness were significant enough that they generated a backlash against gains by women in the next decade under the Reagan administration.

Between 1971 and 1980, the number of women athletes in intercollegiate sports increased from just under 30,000 to over 74,000. More dramatically, the participation rate in interscholastic sports jumped from about 300,000 to nearly 2 million. Yet, women's increasing assertiveness in the world of sports extended beyond the ivied walls. Little League Baseball abandoned its "boys only" policy in 1974 amid lawsuits and public condemnation for excluding girls. Between 1976 and 1980, the

International Women's Professional Softball Association had franchises located from coast to coast. In 1978 the Women's Professional Basketball Leagues began operations. Riding the wave of the women's rights movement and Title IX, women outside the confines of educational institutions also broke through age-old restrictions and perceptions on their capabilities and abilities.

SPORTS FOR INDIVIDUAL COMPETITORS

Boxing

Professional boxing also enjoyed a period of success during the 1970s. American humiliation in international politics, advances in women's causes in challenging gender roles, changing attitudes in racial issues, and American penchant for sport entertainment put the heavyweight division, in particular, in the spotlight as the title holder represented a confirmation in the relationship between hypermasculinity and individual success. Since most of the heavyweight contenders and all the title-holders were Americans, many Americans could boast American superiority in an otherwise international sport. This decade witnessed dominance of a number of boxers as well as highly-promoted rivalries. Television, of course, played a part in promoting boxing but noted promoters also played their part.

As a lightning rod of the changes in American society, Muhammad Ali perhaps represented a most visible symbol of shifting public acceptance of differences. Vilified by many for his conversion to Islam and refusal to be inducted into the armed services, Ali had drawn many more supporters in the 1970s, as the Vietnam War became more and more unpopular. In 1967, the U.S. government had taken away Ali's passport and Ali was waiting for the appeal of his five-year prison sentence for refusing to be drafted into the army. When Ali's legal team successfully challenged the New York State Athletic Commission's refusal to grant Ali a boxing license, promoters immediately arranged a championship bout dubbed "Fight of the Century" between Ali and the champion, Joe Frazier, in March 1971. The media characterized Frasier as the representative of patriotic America who took on a rebel. Long absent from the ring since he was banned from fighting, Ali lost a close decision to Frazier, but the match was a dream for the promoters who took in more than $20 million. Ali, however, would have another shot at the title.

In June 1971 the Supreme Court in an 8–0 decision accepted Ali's argument that his refusal to join the army was based on religious grounds, thus overturning his conviction and jail sentence. With his name cleared, Ali sought another opportunity to challenge for the heavyweight championship again. Ali had to wait though. After the Fight of the Century, Frazier had accepted a challenge from George Foreman, a title bout that Frazier lost. To prepare his shot for the heavyweight title, Ali also fought Ken Norton, who broke Ali's jaw in a twelve-round decision. In 1974, Ali's camp chose Don King to arrange a title match. King was a newcomer to boxing promotion and his highest-profile match until that time was a championship bout in March between George Foreman and Ken Norton.

As a black entrepreneur, King had positioned himself as a promoter of black interests. Arguing that boxing was benefiting only the white, New York–based minority who controlled the sport, King was determined to break that influence. He stunned the boxing world when he announced a $10-million title bout between

Don King

Don King (b.1931) grew up in a Cleveland ghetto and made himself into one of the most powerful figures in the boxing world. In his early years, King ran a numbers operations. He was twice convicted of killing another person. The first incident happened in 1954 but the court ruled that the killing was a justifiable homicide as King shot one of three men trying to rob his numbers operations. In 1966 the court found him guilty of beating a man who owed him money to death and sentenced him to four years in prison.

After his release from prison, King turned to promoting boxing. His first contact with Muhammad Ali was a request to the former champion to put on an exhibition to raise money for the Forest City Hospital, which faced closure because of lack of funds.

King had a knack for befriending good African American fighters, at least initially, as some, including Ali, sued him later on. One reason was that he offered fighters a much bigger purse than they usually received. He promised Ali and Foreman $5 million each, an unheard-of sum in boxing at the time, for Rumble in the Jungle in 1974.

King's detractors, however, argued that the promoter was exploiting the fighters, like most boxing promoters, and he was just as corrupt. In 1976 ABC signed with Don King Productions, Inc., an exclusive contract to broadcast a series of boxing matches to determine U.S. champions in various weight classes. Charges of manipulation of boxers' rankings resulted in a federal grand jury and Federal Communications Commission investigations as well as congressional hearings. Although investigations showed there had been false rankings and kickbacks to agents, no indictments were leveled against King.

Despite his occasional legal troubles, King remained a power in the boxing world well beyond the 1970s and indeed, his fame was such that Jimmy Carter courted King, seeking support and endorsement, during his presidential campaign in 1976.

Foreman and Ali to be held in Kinshasa, Zaire. In selecting Zaire, King took advantage of rising African nationalism and black consciousness in America. (Zaire dictator and president Joseph Desire Mobutu promised to back the purse). No doubt it was also a slight to the current boxing power in the United States, which could present possible barriers to the fight. On October 30, 1974, Ali knocked George Foreman out in the eighth round in the "Rumble in the Jungle."

Although the event lost money, the Zaire fight was significant for several reasons. Until the Supreme Court ruled in favor of Ali, his passport was held by the government and he was restricted to traveling in the United States only. As government and boxing authorities denied Ali a license to box, Ali in effect had no opportunity to make a living from boxing. The fight in Zaire symbolized Ali's freedom to travel and fight anywhere. Moreover, Ali's victory rebuked his critics who had written him off after his defeats at the hands of Frazier and Norton. Important also, the crowd and many locals in Zaire rooted for Ali, despite the fact that both fighters were Americans. This adoration affirmed Ali as a symbol and a champion for those who had been wronged and oppressed, but persisted and finally prevailed. For the Zairian government, the Rumble in the Jungle was a chance to demonstrate the capability of an African country to host a world-class event and, hopefully, an elevation of the country's status in the world stage. While it is questionable whether Zaire's reputation had improved because of the title bout, Don King certainly had increased his status as a boxing promoter, and he would follow the Rumble in the Jungle with another boxing spectacle, the "Thrilla in Manila," a third match between Ali and Frazier, on October 1, 1975. (In order to challenge Foreman for the heavyweight title, Ali had beaten Frazier in a rematch held on January 28, 1974.)

Unlike their first encounter in 1971, the "Thrilla in Manila," by and large, did not have the same political undertone as American involvement in Vietnam had ended and many Americans had changed their views on Ali. Yet the animosity that had been building between the two combatants made this match a most memorable event. Broadcast live for the first time by a television network, Home Box Office (HBO), via satellite, the match went to fourteen rounds before Frazier's trainer stopped the fight. In the last few rounds, Ali's punches to Frazier's head had disfigured his face and

Boxer George Foreman. (Courtesy of Photofest)

Frazier could hardly see with the swelling. Frazier, however, refused to go down. Instead, he kept coming after Ali. This bout so captivated the American public that in next year, the American Bicentennial, both fighters shared the honors of "Fighter of the Year."

Sportswriters, editors, and broadcasters named Ali the greatest boxer in history, over such notables as Jack Johnson, Jack Dempsey, and Joe Louis. The era of Ali and Frazier came to a close when Joe Frazier retired from the ring in 1978. Ali announced his retirement the following year but not before he lost his heavyweight title to Leon Spinks in Las Vegas on February 15, 1978. Ali then regained it in a fifteen-round match in September in the Louisiana Superdome, making him the first three-time heavyweight champion.

Aside from Ali's record, the second Ali-Spinks bout also indicated the organizational problem and corruption in professional boxing. In the 1970s two governing bodies, the World Boxing Association (WBA) and the World Boxing Council (WBC), ruled professional boxing. As an organization created in the United States, American influence dominated the WBA until the mid 1970s when Latin Americans gained control of the organization.

On the other hand, the WBC retained a significant American influence. While each crowned its own champions in different weight classes, on occasions they agreed to sanction unification bouts where the winner would be declared the undisputed world champion. The first Ali-Spinks match was such an example of cooperation between the two governing bodies.

When Spinks decided to fight Ali in the rematch, however, the WBC stripped his title because it had ordered Spinks to fight the next WBC title contender, Ken Norton. Since Spinks fought Ali instead, the WBC declared Norton heavyweight champion without Norton fighting against the current champion. At the time, there were rumors that Don King was behind the dismissal as he represented Norton, and King wanted to promote a Norton-Spinks title bout. Some even charged that the WBC had become a supporting organization for King's boxing enterprise. Still, there were two heavyweight champions, Norton and Ali, for the first time in this decade. Norton subsequently lost his title to Larry Holmes in June 1978.

In October 1980 Ali came out of retirement and challenged Holmes, who scored a technical knockout against the thirty-eight-year-old former champion. Holmes would continue as champion in the early 1980s whereas Ali would fight one more time (losing) in 1981 before he retired for good. With the dispute between rival boxing organizations and the retirement of Ali, boxing, at least in the heavyweight division, would not generate the same kind of publicity and excitement for some time to come despite Don King's knack for promotion.

Golf

On January 31, 1971, Commander Alan Shepard of Apollo 14 took a shot at a golf ball with a six-iron on the surface of the moon in the third moon landing. While the Apollo 14 mission represented the United States' growing success in the space program, Shepard's golf shots indicated the growing popularity of the sport. Arnold Palmer, the charismatic professional, had converted many middle-class sport enthusiasts to take up golf since the 1960s, despite the sport, like tennis, being traditionally associated with upper-class lifestyle and country clubs.

Like tennis, golf had its share of notable players that helped in the popularity of the sport and Jack Nicklaus was probably the most popular of them all in the 1970s. Although Nicklaus had started his golf career in the early 1960s, he really blossomed late that decade and into much of the 1970s. In 1971 Nicklaus became the first player to have won all four major championships in men's golf, the U.S. Open, the British Open, the Masters, and the Professional Golf Association (PGA) championship, twice in a career; and he bettered this feat in 1978 by being the first person to have won each majors three times. Referred by the media as the Golden Bear, Nicklaus had a powerful drive as well as an accurate short game that made him a formidable player. He accumulated nine major titles between 1971 and 1980, winning twice in the Masters (1972, 1975) and the U.S. Open (1972, 1980), once in the British Open (1978), and four times in the PGA championship (1971, 1973, 1975, 1980).

Although golfers like Nicklaus helped to popularize the sport, it was rare to see African American players in the majors. Lee Elder changed that when he became the first black golfer to compete in the Masters in 1975. Elder first became a member of the PGA when the organization abandoned its Caucasians-only policy (introduced in 1943) in 1961. In 1972 Elder accepted an invitation to play in the South African PGA tournament after its organizers agreed to have an integrated gallery and Elder and his wife enjoyed the same freedom as the South African white population while there. (At the time, the South African government had an official policy, apartheid, which legalized racial segregation and discrimination.)

Elder then won the 1974 Monsanto Open, which automatically qualified him for the Masters, held annually at the Augusta National Golf Club in Augusta, Georgia. Created for America's social elite, the Augusta National Golf Club was a private retreat for the wealthy besides being the host of the annual Masters tournament. Membership was (and still is) by invitation only.

In 1973 a group of politicians, including U.S. Ambassador to the United Nations Andrew Young, had urged the president of the Augusta National Golf Club to invite an African American to the Masters, naming Elder in the process. That request was denied. When Elder qualified, the media and other notables such as Jim Brown showed up in force. Like the treatment that Jackie Robinson received by the African Americans, the black workers at the club were in awe of Elder and catered to his every need. Elder, however, did not make the cut to the final round. While Elder played there in 1974 (and qualified again in 1977), the club had no African American members. Although the Masters was a prestigious tournament, the club hosting the tournament also represented the closed, white-only, old-boys elite clique in industry and politics. Similar to Jackie Robinson in baseball, Elder thus became the first African American to cross the racial barrier in "major-league" golf. After Elder's last appearance in Masters in 1977, no other player of African American descent would appear in Augusta for the next twenty years.

Women playing golf faced problems similar to those women faced in tennis. Between 1971 and 1980, women's professional golf purses had increased from $558,550 to $5,150,000 and the number of tournaments rose from twenty-one to forty. Yet, the number of major tournaments with large purses for women remained few. At the beginning of the decade, there were only two major tournaments, the U.S. Open and the Ladies Professional Golf Association (LPGA) championship. In 1972 Colgate sponsored the Dinah Shore Winners Circle and offered a purse of $110,000, the first six-figure prize in women's golf. In 1979 the du Maurier Classic was added as a major tournament for the women's circuit. While there is no doubt that women's golf saw advances, these paled in comparison to men's gains. Arnold Palmer had earned over $1 million in career earnings in the late 1960s. Jack Nicklaus became the first golfer to win more than $200,000 in a single season in 1971 and at the end of the decade Tom Watson established a new mark of $500,000 in one season. Watson had been the top money earner of the PGA tour between 1976 and 1980.

On the other hand, Kathy Whitworth, one of the most successful female golfers whose professional career spanned from the late 1950s to the 1980s, did not surpass the $1-million career-earning mark until 1981. Judy Rankin topped the $100,000 single-season earning in 1976 and not until 1980 did women golfers (Donna Caponi, Amy Alcott, and Nancy Lopez) reach the $200,000 mark. In 1972 Kathy Whitworth earned $65,000 from playing in twenty-nine tournaments whereas Jack Nicklaus won $320,000 from just nineteen. In 1975 LPGA hired Ray Volpe, a former vice-president of marketing of the NHL, as the commissioner for the organization, thus taking the administration of the LPGA away from the golfers themselves. Volpe's job was to market the LPGA and women golfers to the public and corporate businesses in the hopes of raising LPGA's profile and much-needed sponsorship money for the tours.

Despite the discrepancies in earning power, women did take to golf, in part due to the passage of Title IX. Golf had the first women's intercollegiate championship in 1942 and the sport became part of efforts by many colleges to comply with Title IX's mandate of equal opportunity in women athletics. As women and girls took advantage of increased collegiate and scholastic athletic programs, golf would reap the benefits in the next decade as many top professional women golfers such as Betsy King (Furman University), Pat Bradley (Florida International University), and Nancy Lopez (University of Tulsa), came from the collegiate ranks. Ironically, many in the LPGA did not take to the feminist movement that contributed to the passage of Title IX. Since professional golf for women predated Title IX and since golf was an individual sport, they did not readily identify with the movement and, in fact, some viewed feminists with suspicion.

Lopez, as a Hispanic, also illustrated the sport's Eurocentric root and lack of diversity. Similar to tennis, there were few women of color in golf. When Lopez first turned pro in 1977, she made news as she won nine tournaments and was named Player of the Year and Rookie of the Year. The media presented her to the public and golf followers as a model of a more enlightened sport in which minorities were welcomed and could succeed even though many golf clubs around the nation still would not admit minorities as members.

Tennis

For all the breakthroughs in women sports, none was as dramatic, symbolic, and visible in demystifying gender stereotypes in women tennis when Billie Jean King battled Bobby Riggs on the tennis court in 1973. Although tennis had been one of the few sports that allowed co-ed participation, the sport nevertheless had an entrenched gender divide that was crouched in upper- and middle-class Anglo gentility and gender roles. Most notably, American tennis, through its governing body, the United States Lawn Tennis Association (USLTA), advocated amateurism even though major tournaments had been paying top amateur players under the table and men had been playing professionally for a long time. In the late 1960s, the international governing body, the International Lawn Tennis Federation (ILTF), classified some of the tournaments as open, thus allowing professionals and amateurs to compete against one another. Women tennis players, on the other hand, were discouraged from turning professional because, among other reasons, women tennis was simply not attractive enough as an entertainment. Hence, there would not be a demand for women professional tennis. Behind this rationale, of course, lay the assumption that men were better athletes.

In tennis, the question of women's professional tennis had to do with the institutional control of the sport. USLTA, a conservative, male-dominated organization, had steadfastly refused to endorse professionalism openly even though many female tennis players were receiving prize money. Although the USLTA supported the ILTF's idea of open tournaments when it staged the U.S. Open in 1968, the number of tournaments offering prize money to women players remained few. Moreover, the prize money for women players was only a fraction of the men's. In 1970, for example, the Pacific Southwest Championship men's single winner took home $12,500 compared to $1,500 for the women's champion. The total prize money for women in this tournament was a meager $7,500, which was only available to those in the quarterfinals and beyond. This inequity existed in all tennis tournaments that offered prize money.

To complicate this matter more for those women who wanted to make a living playing tennis, there did not appear to be any rationale in determining one's status. Some players were able to receive prize money and participate in amateur tournaments while others could not. Frustrated with confusing eligibility rules, limited opportunities, unequal treatment, and an unresponsive USLTA, Billie Jean King and eight other players each signed a one-dollar, one-week contract as employees of Gladys Heldman, owner of *World Tennis Magazine*, in 1970 and their job was to play in a $5,000-purse tournament—a tournament that the USLTA refused to sanction. The purse was subsequently raised to $7,500 when Joe Cullman, the head of Philip Morris and a friend of Heldman, agreed to sponsor the tournament. After the tournament was over, the USLTA suspended all eight players. (One of the nine players, Patti Hogan, did not sign with Heldman but was supportive of the others). Instead of asking the USLTA for reinstatement, these eight women pros decided to band together and set prices for any tournament that wanted women professional players—$5,000 for an eight-woman event, $10,000 for sixteen players, and $18,000 for thirty-two. Their solidarity defied the USLTA's jurisdiction as the sole governing body in tennis. Since these eight players possibly represented the top eight in woman tennis, the USLTA eventually relented and lifted the suspensions. This initial relationship with Heldman by the women pros, however, led to the creation of the Virginia Slims Tour in 1971. Initially a series of eight tournaments across the country with a total purse of $75,000, the Virginia Slims circuit became the cornerstone in increasing women tennis players' earnings.

Although the USLTA momentarily avoided confrontation by welcoming the eight women pros back, tensions remained. In 1972 the USLTA signed an agreement recognizing the women professionals as an autonomous group in return for the women's promise to stay within the USLTA and abide by its rules and regulations. Later that year, conflicts between Heldman and the USLTA prompted the establishment of the Women's International Tennis Federation (WITF).

Largely backed by the Virginia Slim circuit, the WITF attracted and signed many of the top American and European female tennis players including King and Margaret Court, the world's number 1– and 2–ranked players. By 1973 the Virginia Slims circuit, as a result of good marketing and favorable public response, had grown to eighteen tournaments each with a purse of at least $25,000. To offset the breakaway group, the USLTA retaliated by setting up its own women circuit that included established players such as Virginia Wade, Evonne Goolagong, as well as a rising young talent, Chris Evert; and the ILTF, as the international governing body, sided with the USLTA and threatened to suspend all the WITF players from major championships such as the U.S. Open and Wimbledon. Similar to professional team sports, women tennis now had two competing organizations. While the USLTA had the backing of ILTF, the WITF had most of the big-name players. At the Wimbledon tournament in the summer of 1973, around fifty top international players, led by King, formed the Women's Tennis Association (WTA), replacing the WITF, and King became its first president.

Besides the creation of a separate women tennis governing body, the 1973 Wimbledon tournament also brought to light the turmoil in men's tennis. Although men's tennis enjoyed much more prosperity, different groups struggled to control the sport in the early 1970s. By the beginning of the decade, two organizations, ILTF and the World Championship Tennis (WCT), had their own circuits. Players under contract to WCT competed in WCT tournaments. For those who were not under contract, they entered in the ILTF's Grand Prix circuit as independent professionals. Caught in the struggles between the opposing organizations, the players organized the Association of Tennis Professionals (ATP). In 1973 ATP threatened a player boycott of the Wimbledon tournament because ILTF supported a ban of the Yugoslavian tennis star Nikki Pilic by his own national association. After failed negotiations between ATP and ILTF prior to the beginning of the tournament, thirteen of the top sixteen seeds withdrew. A total of seventy-nine players left the tournament, which now consisted mostly of players from the Communist-bloc countries and non-ATP players such as two young stars, the nineteen-year-old American Jimmy Connors and seventeen-year-old Swede Bjorn Borg. Despite the absence of many top male players, Wimbledon attendance did not suffer partly because the top female players were still there. It was under this context of rising power of women tennis and chaos in men's side that the King-Riggs match occurred.

Like King, Robert Larimore (Bobby) Riggs was also a world-class tennis player. But at fifty-five in 1973, his glory days had long passed. Yet he claimed that even at that age he could beat the best woman tennis had to offer because women were inherently inferior. He first challenged King, who refused. Although King declined, another top female tennis player, Margaret Court, accepted Riggs's challenge and lost to Riggs in straight sets, 6–2 and 6–1. Riggs's remarks and challenges came a year after the passage of Title IX and immediately created controversy polarizing people on both sides of the gender equity issue. With Court's defeat, King felt compelled to meet Riggs in the "Battle of the Sexes," as the media hyped the match, at the Houston Astrodome on September 20. In front of a crowd of over 30,000, the biggest audience ever to attend a tennis match at the time, and a worldwide television broadcast, King defeated Riggs in straight sets, 6–4, 6–3, 6–3.

Despite the organizational power struggles in both men's and women's tennis, the 1970s had been a glorious time for the sport. Besides the media-driven Battle of the Sexes, notable players in both men's and women's ranks helped to increase the popularity of tennis. Stars from the previous decade such as the Australian John Newcombe and American Arthur Ashe continued their successes and were now joined by other young talent like Stan Smith, Jimmy Connors, and John McEnroe. On the women's side, young stars such as Goolagong, Evert, and Martina Navratilova added to the excitement generated by King, Court, and Wade. Between 1971 and 1980 Americans did very well in major tournaments, winning the men's singles title in the U.S. Open six times, the Australian Open four times, and the Wimbledon three times. On the women's side, Americans won the women's singles title in the U.S. Open nine times, the Wimbledon seven times, and the French Open five times. This American success, however, was challenged by other nations' tennis stars, especially in the latter half of decade. Beginning with his first victory in the French Open in 1974, Swedish sensation Bjorn Borg dominated tennis from the mid-1970s into the early 1980s, winning five consecutive Wimbledon's men's singles titles (defeating three Americans in four of those matches, Jimmy Connors in 1977 and 1978, Roscoe Tanner in 1979, and John McEnroe in 1980), five French Open singles (1974, 1975, 1978, 1979, and 1980) and runner-up in the U.S. Open three times. His two 1980 Grand Slam (Wimbledon and U.S. Open) title matches against McEnroe became legendary. In July

Renee Richards, the transsexual tennis player, returns the ball, September 1, 1977, during the U.S. Open Competition at Forest Hills, NY. Richards was defeated by Britain's Virginia Wade, 6–1, 6–4. The loss marked her debut at the U.S. Open. (AP / Wide World Photo)

Borg defeated McEnroe in the Wimbledon final in a grueling five-set match. In the U.S. Open, McEnroe reversed the fortune by beating Borg, also in five sets.

On the women's side, Chris Evert was the dominant player in the latter half of the decade. Between 1974 and 1980, she won eleven Grand Slam singles titles, including four French Open (1974, 1975, 1979, 1980), two Wimbledon (1974, 1976), and five U.S. Open (1975, 1976–78, 1980) and her success continued into the mid-1980s even with the emergence of Martina Navratilova as the premier woman tennis player in that decade. In the context of the 1970s, Evert became a very popular player with many fans and media. Compared to King's prominent stance on feminism and Navratilova's Czech origin, Evert's good looks and quiet demeanor represented an updated version of American womanhood—a competitive and successful woman who also exuded femininity—a version more acceptable to many Americans than what King and Navratilova symbolized. The fact that Evert and Navratilova often faced each other in major tournaments made their tennis rivalry as fierce as the one between McEnroe and Borg. And the tennis establishment took a most public stance in promoting its definition of femininity when the U.S. Open banned Renee Richards from the 1976 tournament. Renee Richards was born Richard Raskind (b. 1935) and was a competitive tennis player before a man-to-woman sex change. In fact, Raskind had married, fathered a son, served in the navy, and was an eye surgeon before his banishment from the U.S. Open.

He had sex reassignment surgery in 1975. Richards's former identity as a man was discovered in an amateur tennis tournament and she was subsequently barred from all women's tournaments, including the U.S. Open. There was a public outcry and fear about the possibility that Richards would overwhelmed the other "women" players (even though Richards was forty years old at the time) and might even lead to other men-turned-women into the women's tennis world. When the courts ruled for Richards, she entered in the 1977 Women's Open but lost in the first round. Since Richards was never dominant in women's tennis, as some critics feared, the controversy about her presence in the tennis circle eventually died down.

To further clarify what women's tennis meant, the United States Tennis Association (USTA, formerly USLTA) created a "women-born-women" policy that was ruled illegal by the New York State Supreme Court when Richards filed suit. This tension between womanhood and athlete remained a debate for many Americans and the media throughout this decade and beyond.

Thoroughbred Horse Racing

The 1970s was the decade of the Triple Crown. The last Triple Crown winner, Affirmed, won all three races in 1978, ridden by Steve Cauthen. In each race Alydar finished second and the two horses met ten times in their careers, with Affirmed winning seven of the ten. After winning the Triple Crown, Affirmed raced in the fall in the Marlboro Cup Invitational Handicap, where the field included Seattle Slew. Slew had won the Triple Crown the previous year (1977) and few would have guessed that the next thirty years would bring no more Triple Crown winners. Seattle Slew defeated Affirmed by three lengths and then, a few weeks later, Slew won again. The two would never meet again. The next year Affirmed was named Horse of the Year as a four-year-old, then was retired to stud.

Earlier in the decade (1973) Secretariat had also won the Triple Crown, the first of the three Triple Crown winners in that decade. Coming close were Canonero II, who won the Derby and the Preakness in 1971; Riva Ridge, who won the Derby and the Belmont in 1972; Bold Forbes, who won the Derby and the Belmont in 1976; and Spectacular Bid, who won the Derby and the Preakness in 1979.

Ron Turcotte, who rode Riva Ridge and Secretariat, had the best record in the three races in the decade, while Steve Cauthen and Ron Franklin were also highly successful.

Auto Racing

What had been largely a southern phenomenon began to gain more adherents nationally in the 1970s. Formula One racing was more of a European sport, but stock-car racing, under the leadership and control of the National Association of Stock Car Auto Racing (NASCAR) grew to from its roots to a large national following. The Charlotte 600 and the Daytona 500, the two most well-known of the NASCAR races, were won most often by Richard Petty (six times) in the 1970s, but Darrell Waltrip, Buddy Baker, and Bobby Allison were also top drivers.

The Indianapolis 500 race, held every Memorial Day weekend, consists of a different class of autos, called Indy class or open-wheel race cars. Some drivers cross over from NASCAR and vice versa, while others do not. In the 1970s, the Unser brothers, Al and Bobby, were the most successful drivers with Al taking three and Bobby, one Indianapolis 500. John Rutherford won the race twice in the decade and A.J. Foyt won both an Indy race and a Daytona 500 during the decade.

A NATIONAL(?) SPORTING CULTURE

On September 7, 1979, the Entertainment and Sports Programming Network (ESPN), a twenty-four-hour, all-sports television station, began broadcasting from its Connecticut base. ESPN was unique at the time because its programs were available through subscriber-only cable television, a relatively new medium, whereas major networks aired their programs for free, recouping financially by selling advertising air time. More important, ESPN was one of the few television stations in the 1970s that employed a new business model in the television industry, narrowcasting–television that specialized on one type of programming. Seizing on the tremendous growth and popularity of sport in the United States, ESPN founders Bill and Scott Rasmussen believed that an all-sport channel could fill a desire by the American public since major networks devoted relatively little time to sport news and sport programs had to compete with other television programs for air time. While ESPN struggled initially to find enough programs to meet its needs, its eventual development into a major cable network in the next decade indicated that the Rasmussens had successfully tapped into the cravings of an existing national sporting culture.

As a mass medium, television of course contributed to the making of an American national sporting culture. Broadcasts of sport programs, especially through skilled producers such as Roone Arledge, helped to popularize certain sports by reaching beyond the sport fandom and the physical confines of the contests. People needed not be residents of Miami or Cincinnati to be fans of the 1972 Dolphins or the 1975 Reds. Besides MLB and NFL, television had contracts with the NBA and the NHL. Indeed, all four major professional team sports, the most visible manifestations of this national sporting culture, had franchises located from coast to coast by the end of the 1970s. These expansions were driven in part by the need of television to reach a national audience. The content and the target of these broadcasts, however, focused overwhelmingly on a world of white, middle-class males, although African Americans and women did have some coverage. Moreover, increased television broadcast of sport and sport news also contributed to the erosion of the amateur ideal. While sport newscasters and commentators almost always hailed amateurism as a noble idea, television networks also carried news of labor strife, politics, and commercialization.

Through mass media coverage also, modern sports such as baseball and football became normalized and standardized as what sport was supposed to be. Implicitly, the social hierarchies and relationships as well as sports' values and beliefs that existed in this male-dominated realm also became normalized and standardized. In laymen's term, they became part of the "tradition" of sport. Beginning in the 1960s and into the early 1970s, however, these traditions came under intense fire. In the 1970s, breakthroughs in race and gender in sport offered previously marginalized groups to participate in the national sporting culture even though changes in many people's preconceived notions about women and African Americans occurred in an incredibly slow and uneven pace. People often pointed toward the likes of Billie Jean King, Title IX, and Muhammad Ali as evidence of progress. Despite the high-profile coverage of these personalities and events, many African Americans and women still faced discrimination and exclusion based on long-held stereotypes in sport and in the larger society or, as in the case of women's golf, reverted back to a sexist view in hope of greater acceptance.

SUMMARY

Throughout the 1970s, the optimistic idealism of the 1960s had turned flaring activism to a simmering grind. While changes did occur, increasingly those who benefited from the status quo began to organize more effective ways to resist reforms. They realized that some changes would be hard to turn back and compromised. On other issues, they allied with and mobilized people who were sympathetic to their positions. In the main, those who lamented the erosion of traditional values, whatever they meant, felt besieged by the changing social tapestry. In the next decade, they would organize and, with a sympathetic Reagan administration in the White House, create a backlash.

RECOMMENDED RESOURCES

Print Sources

Barney, Robert K., Stephen R. Wenn, and Scott G. Martyn. 2002. *Selling the five rings: The International Olympic Committee and the rise of Olympic commercialism*. Salt Lake City: University of Utah Press.

Bodo, Peter. 1995. *The courts of Babylon: Tales of greed and glory in a harsh new world of professional tennis*. New York: Scribner's Sons.

Cruise, David, and Alison Griffiths. 1992. *Net worth: Exploding the myths of pro hockey*. Toronto: Penguin Books.

Dickey, Glenn. 1982. *The history of professional basketball since 1896*. New York: Stein and Day.

Festle, Mary Jo. 1996. *Playing nice: Politics and apologies in women's sports*. New York: Columbia University Press.

Gruneau, Richard, and David Whitson. 1993. *Hockey night in Canada: Sport, identities and cultural politics*. Toronto: Garamond Press.

Guttmann, Allen. 2002. *The Olympics: A history of the modern Games*. 2nd ed. Urbana: University of Illinois Press.

Ham, Eldon L. 2000. *The playmasters: An unauthorized history of the NBA from sellouts to lockouts*. Lincolnwood, IL: Contemporary Books.

Hamilton, Neil A. 2006. *The 1970s*. New York: Facts on File.

Harris, David. 1986. *The league: The rise and decline of the NFL*. New York: Bantam Books.

Hogshead-Makar, Nancy, and Andrew Zimbalist, eds. 2007. *Equal play: Title IX and social change*. Philadelphia: Temple University Press.

Holt, Joan S., and Marianna Trekell, eds. 1991. *A century of women's basketball: From frailty to Final Four*. Reston, VA: American Alliance for Health, Physical Education, Recreation and Dance, 1991.

Kahn, Liz. 1996. *The LPGA: The unauthorized version, the history of the Ladies Professional Golf Association*. Menlo Park, CA: Group Fore Productions.

Kirchberg, Connie. 2007. *Hoop lore: A history of the National Basketball Association*. Jefferson, NC: McFarland.

Lumpkin, Angela. 1981. *Women's tennis: A historical documentary of the players and their game*. Troy, NY: Whitston Publishing.

Miller, David. 2003. *Athens to Athens: The official history of the Olympic Games and the IOC, 1894–2004*. Edinburgh: Mainstream Publishing.

Miller, Marvin. 2004. *A whole different ball game: The sport and business of baseball*. New York: Carol Publishing.

Preston, Joseph G. 2004. *Major League Baseball in the 1970s: A modern game emerges*. Jefferson, NC: McFarland.

Rader, Benjamin G. 2002. *Baseball: A history of America's game.* Urbana: University of Illinois Press.

———. 2004. *American sports: From the age of folk games to the age of televised sports.* 5th ed. Upper Saddle River, NJ: Prentice-Hall.

Roberts, Randy, and James Olson. 1989. *Winning is the only thing: Sports in America since 1945.* Baltimore: Johns Hopkins University Press.

Sammons, Jeffrey T. 1988. Civil rights to rebellion to reaction: The era of Muhammad Ali. In *Beyond the ring: The role of boxing in American society.* Urbana: University of Illinois Press.

Schulman, Bruce J. 2001. *The seventies: The great shift in American culture, society, and Politics.* New York: Free Press.

Sperber, Murray. 1990. *College sports inc.: The athletic department vs. the university.* New York: Henry Holt.

Steen, Sandra, and Susan Steen. 2003. *Take it to the hoop: One hundred years of women's basketball.* Brookfield, CT: Twenty-First Century Books.

Stewart, Mark. 1998. *Basketball: A history of hoops.* Danbury, CT: Franklin Watts.

Voigt, David Quentin. 1983. *American baseball: From postwar expansion to the electronic age.* University Park: Pennsylvania State University Press.

Ware, Susan. 2007. *Title IX: A brief history with documents.* New York: Bedford/St. Martin's.

Watterson, John Sayle. 2000. *College football: History, spectacle, controversy.* Baltimore: Johns Hopkins University Press, 2000.

Whitson, David, and Richard Gruneau, eds. 2006. *Artificial ice: Hockey, culture, and commerce.* Peterborough, ON: Broadview Press.

Wushanley, Ying. 2004. *Playing nice and losing: The struggle for control of women's intercollegiate athletics, 1960–2000.* Syracuse, NY: Syracuse University Press.

Films

Ali. 2001. Dir. Michael Mann.

Billie Jean King: Portrait of a pioneer. 2006. HBO.

The Bronx Is Burning. 2007. Dir. Jeremiah Chechik.

The Life and Times of Secretariat, an American Racing Legend. 2005. Dir. Leonard Lusky.

Munich. 2005. Dir. Steven Spielberg.

Vintage World Series films of each year from Major League Baseball Vintage films.

Web Sites

ESPN. http://www.espn.com.

Kareem Abdul Jabbar. http://kareemabduljabbar.com.

Muhammad Ali. http://ali.com.

Wayne Gretzky. http://www.gretzky.com.

CHAPTER 12

AMERICAN SPORTS, 1980–1989

Sarah K. Fields

OVERVIEW

New political leadership marked the beginning of the 1980s, signifying a shift in cultural and social policies from the decline of the liberal movements of earlier decades to a more conservative era. The Republican governor of California, Ronald Reagan, won the 1980 presidential election against incumbent Democratic President Jimmy Carter after running a campaign that promised smaller government, free market ideals, family values, and a return to American dominance in the world. With Reagan's election, America in the 1980s changed course for the new decade. Reagan would serve two terms in office and be succeeded by his vice-president, George H. W. Bush, who won election in 1988, making the Reagan-Bush White House the political power for the entire decade of the 1980s. Immediately after Ronald Reagan took the presidential oath on January 20, 1981, Iranian militants, who had held American citizens captive in the U.S. embassy in Tehran for 444 days, released the hostages. This event, timed deliberately by the Iranian militants to further humiliate the Carter administration, seemed to signify the beginning of a new era after the turbulence of the 1970s.

President Reagan promised a return to a happier era, and the new decade was different from the 1970s in part because the 1980s was an era of excess and advancement in the United States. Under Reagan's guidance, economically the country did vastly improve over the course of the decade. A few years into the decade, inflation and unemployment rates dropped and increased military spending by the federal government helped to increase production rates. Although Reagan had run on a platform to make government smaller, the federal government and, more significantly for the economy, federal spending increased dramatically. The Reagan administration increased defense spending particularly, which had two major impacts: it escalated the Cold War and competitive military spending between the United States and the Soviet Union, and it pumped money into the American economy. Many Americans saw their economic status rise, and Reagan won re-election in 1984 in part by asking voters if they were better off than they were four years earlier (before Reagan's election). Underpinning the economic growth, however, were vast increases in the federal deficit because the Reagan administration's increased spending was not matched by an increase in revenue or taxes.

The increased money in the economy meant a growth in the stock market and disposable income of the wealthy and the middle class. The result was a rise in consumerism and the appearance of the Yuppies (Young, upwardly mobile—or Urban—Professionals). Generally mocked by the cultural pundits of the day, these youngest of the baby boomers focused on obtaining wealth and material objects as quickly as possible. Their celluloid counterpart Gordon Gekko, played by Michael Douglas in the 1987 film *Wall Street*, announced "Greed is good." The phrase would seem to sum up attitudes toward wealth in the 1980s.

The challenge of balancing change and excess in the decade was symbolized in part by the overt political alliance between the Republican party and the evangelical religious right, a group credited in large part with Reagan's election. The Moral Majority, a religious political action group, was founded in 1979 by the Reverend Jerry Falwell, but the group came to power in the 1980 presidential election and helped gain over two-thirds of the white evangelical vote for the Reagan-Bush ticket. The Moral Majority, which would disband in 1989, lobbied for more conservative social values that matched those espoused by Reagan during the election. They called for abortion to be outlawed, governmental resistance to women's and gay rights, and governmental support and promotion of "family values." The power of the group was only minimally affected by scandals involving popular televangelists of the decade. Jim Bakker, founder of the Praise the Lord television station, was indicted for bilking investors in his religious-based theme park, Heritage USA, out of $158 million. He suffered even more in the court of public opinion after confessing to paying his church secretary Jessica Hahn thousands of dollars in hush money after a sexual affair. Jimmy Swaggart, a rival televangelist whom Bakker blamed for his problems with Heritage USA, had his own problems after admitting to consorting with prostitutes. The political link between the Republican Party and the evangelicals was sharpest when Pat Robertson, founder of the Christian Broadcasting Network and host of the 700 Club, ran in the Republican primaries for the 1988 presidential nomination against eventual winner, Vice President George H. W. Bush. Swaggart's confession in 1988 came right before the southern primaries and generally hurt Robertson's campaign because the two shared the same religious calling. Robertson appeared with Swaggart as a show of support after his admission of involvement with prostitutes.

Health and social conservatism issues merged in the 1980s with the appearance in the United States of what would eventually be named Acquired Immune Deficiency Syndrome (AIDS). The disease, which appeared first in communities of gay men and intravenous drug users, initially baffled the medical community. The first official notice of the disease came in June of 1981 when the government's Centers for Disease Control and Prevention (CDC) noted an outbreak of a rare and fatal form of pneumonia striking gay men. Because the initial victims were those on the fringes of American society, early federal funding for research into the disease was limited, and a number of conservative pundits and religious leaders suggested that the disease was divine vengeance against those who violated traditional family values. Eventually research revealed that the disease was blood-borne and impossible to acquire via casual contact, but much of society in the 1980s fearfully shunned those who contracted it. One famous face of AIDS was Ryan White, a white boy from a small town in Indiana who contracted the disease from a blood transplant to treat his hemophilia. When his community learned that he had the disease, he was prohibited from attending school and social functions. Eventually he won the court battle for the right to attend school, but upon his return he was greeted with hostility, taunts, and threats. The family moved to a more welcoming community. Ryan, in the meantime, had become a national hero for his public battle for his right to live with dignity. He died in 1990, but in part because of his efforts, the country began to treat the victims of AIDS with greater compassion and respect. Sport was not immune from the specter of AIDS either. Although he would not publicly reveal that he had the human immunodeficiency virus (HIV), which can lead to AIDS, until 1991, basketball star Earvin "Magic" Johnson likely contracted the disease from a casual sexual encounter in the 1980s. Tennis legend Arthur Ashe likely contracted the disease in 1983 when he received a blood transfusion after heart bypass surgery. In the early 1980s the nation's blood banks had not been screening for the disease, so those receiving transfusions were at risk of contracting AIDS or HIV.

One of the most lasting advances of the 1980s was the rise of the computer. In 1981 IBM released the first personal computer (PC) and in 1985 Apple released the rival Macintosh computer for home use. Prior to the PC and the Mac, home computers seemed unfathomable. In 1983 Bill Gates' company, Microsoft, released the first version of Word and Windows for the PC; Gates would eventually become the world's richest man. The computer would become ubiquitous in American life.

Sports and Political and Social Changes in the 1980s

Sports, like the economy, grew in the 1980s. Socially, the 1980s saw a rise in cultural concerns with fitness and self-improvement. Self-help books were so popular that the *New York Times* gave them their own category on the best-seller lists. The federal government began campaigns against tobacco usage and the Reagan administration declared "war" on drugs. When University of Maryland basketball star Len Bias died of a cocaine overdose in 1986, just days after being the first pick in the National Basketball Association (NBA) draft, the catch phrase "just say no [to drugs]" took on new meaning for young people. The professional leagues began dealing with the effects of street drugs on their players, and several instituted drug-testing policies.

Health, however, was more than just avoiding drugs. It was also fitness. Companies like Nike recognized that the fitness craze could be profitable. In 1980 Nike became a public corporation and used that money to go international. By 1981 the company offered over 200 kinds of shoes and 200 pieces of fitness attire. By the mid-1980s Nike recognized the importance of product endorsements by superstar athletes like the NBA's Michael Jordan and Charles Barkley, both of whom would have signature shoes with the company. At the end of the 1980s, Nike introduced its marketing slogan: "Just do it." The phrase would become ubiquitous and would always be linked with the company. Nike not only sold sport and fitness to men, but they recognized a potential market in women. Fitness was linked to beauty, and women, especially, were encouraged to exercise. Aerobic exercise swept the country and those who did not join gyms and exercise groups could work out in their own homes, exercising with celebrity fitness stars like Jane Fonda via videocassette tape recordings.

The home-video revolution, beyond making the family television room an exercise room, made it easier for athletes to tape themselves for self-improvement and promotion. Capturing, editing, and viewing with film took a greater degree of money and effort than capturing, editing, and viewing with videotape. Once people had access to hand-held video cameras, they could record and edit their own material. High school and youth teams had parents record games so the coaches could go over the tape with the players and so that the players could pass the tapes along to college scouts.

Videocassettes were only part of the change in communication and mass media in the 1980s. Prior to the decade, most Americans had limited television-viewing options; they could watch three major networks (ABC, CBS, and NBC) via over-air signals. In 1986 Fox Broadcasting became the first nationwide network to join the big three as over-air competitor. The 1980s also saw the vast expansion of cable television. Before 1980, about 16 million households had cable television and the affiliated nationwide "superstations" like TBS, which broadcast Atlanta Braves baseball games. After Congress passed the 1984 Cable Act, cable became vastly more accessible and millions of dollars were spent wiring the country. By the end of the decade over 90 percent of Americans had access to cable, and about 60 percent (53 million households) subscribed to cable services. Cable networks increased from twenty-eight to seventy-nine (History of cable TV).

One of those cable networks, ESPN (Entertainment and Sports Programming Network), would have a powerful influence on sport in America. The network began broadcasting twenty-four hours a day and seven days a week in 1980, becoming the first dedicated sports programming channel in history. Early programming was challenging, given the exclusive contracts that the major networks had with professional sports leagues; therefore, early programming was often creative, showing minor sports and inventing sports like the "Strongest Man Competition." In March 1980 the network aired early rounds of the men's basketball tournament for the National Collegiate Athletic Association (NCAA) championship, giving ESPN more cachet and more power in the market. The station's centerpiece, *SportsCenter*, became the showcase for sports highlights of the day and gained a strong following among sports fans. It also allowed national sports coverage, which was vastly superior to the usual coverage on the local news because it ran for a full hour and because it provided nationwide and sometimes worldwide results that the traditional local news did not have time to cover. Over time, the programming options for ESPN increased with their viewership and financial power. In 1984 the station began broadcasting college football games. The next year, the National Hockey League (NHL) agreed to have ESPN televise games. In 1987 ESPN won the rights to broadcast National Football League (NFL) games and in 1989 ESPN began broadcasting Major League Baseball (MLB) games. ESPN continued to cover lesser-known sports, including the 1986–87 America's Cup yachting competition. By the end of the decade the network had expanded into international coverage with ESPN International and ESPN Latin America. The network was not just the first with dedicated twenty-four hours per day sports programming, it was also the largest, and it helped expand viewing opportunities for sport and helped promote sport in America by providing increased exposure. In addition, it influenced the creation of similar sports networks in Europe and other areas of the globe.

Beyond technological evolution, the 1980s was a decade of involvement for women in both political life and in sport. American attitudes toward gender equality, however, seemed mixed. Although the Reagan administration blocked reconsideration of the Equal Rights Amendment in 1982, which would have made it unconstitutional to discriminate on the basis of gender, President Reagan appointed Sandra Day O'Connor as the first female justice on the Supreme Court in 1981. He also appointed two women to his cabinet, Elizabeth Dole as secretary of transportation and Margaret Heckler as secretary of health and human services, in 1982.

Sports saw a similar paradox. The number of women coaching women's college teams decreased from 54.2 percent in 1980 to 47.7 percent in 1989. The number of women and girls participating in high school and collegiate sport, however, continued to increase. For example, NCAA colleges and universities offered an average of 6.46 teams for women in 1982; that number increased to 7.24 by 1990 (Carpenter and Costa 2005). Politics continued to entangle itself in gender equity issues in sport. In 1984 the U.S. Supreme Court ruled in *Grove City College v. Bell* that only programs that directly received federal funds were required to comply with Title IX, a law prohibiting gender discrimination in federally funded educational settings. On a practical level this meant that Title IX did not apply to athletic departments in schools and colleges. In 1988 the U.S. Congress passed, over President Reagan's veto, the Civil Rights Restoration Act of 1987. This law stated that if an institution received any federal funding, then the entire institution needed to comply with Title IX, which now meant that athletic departments were required to comply with the law and provide equitable sporting opportunities for both men and women.

Major Sports in the 1980s

The 1980s saw a growth in consumption of and participation in sport. Thanks in part to ESPN, more people watched more sports on television than ever before. The most popular sports of the decades were baseball, basketball, and football. The dominant popular institution in baseball was Major League Baseball (MLB), although minor-league baseball and college baseball also enjoyed a resurgence. For both football and basketball, many in America enjoyed both the professional leagues and the college programs. Both levels of both sports saw more time on television and enjoyed increased revenues. Other major sports of prior decades continued throughout the 1980s, and several professional leagues saw increases in popularity and revenue. Much of the success and popularity of these sports can be attributed to the greater number of sports channels, which gave sports more exposure to a broader audience. For many in the 1980s, watching sports was excellent entertainment, but participating in sports was even better. Given that few Americans could compete at the elite levels of the big three, other sports received their attention and participation.

TEAM SPORTS

Baseball

Major League Baseball faced highs and lows in the 1980s. The decade began with labor strife and ended with a World Series disrupted by an earthquake.

In between the players saw remarkable salary increases, and the owners saw increased fan attendance as well as record revenue production from the media. The decade was marred by drug usage, the banning of an icon, and the death of a commissioner.

Economics of Baseball

While free agency in MLB had first appeared in the 1970s, the labor strife in the 1980s continued to clarify how the new post–reserve clause MLB would work. In the early 1980s, the players' union and the owners could not agree on a collective bargaining agreement (CBA). Even though revenue and salaries were both increased since the 1976 court decision allowing free agency, the owners wanted to return to limited free agency as much as possible and the players vowed to fight to remain free agents. The key sticking point was compensation: if team A lost a player to team B in free agency, the owners wanted team B to give team A a different player as compensation for the loss. The players feared that a compensation plan would hinder free agency. Would teams aggressively pursue and pay the best players if they had to give up someone else in exchange? The owners feared that a complete free agency would undermine, if not destroy, a team's ability to grow and nurture young talent, suspecting that after a team devoted time and resources to developing a young player, the player would bolt to another team as soon as he reached some of his potential. Both players and owners were convinced that their fears were legitimate and that the other side's concerns were baseless.

In 1981 the negotiations over the compensation plans failed completely, and the owners decided to unilaterally implement their plan for compensating teams that lost players to free agency. If a player left one team for another as a free agent, the first team would be assigned a compensatory player from a pool of players designated at the beginning of the season. The players were opposed to the plan and on June 11, 1981, a fifty-one-day strike began. The players lost millions of dollars in salaries, although many later recouped their losses in higher salaries. The owners lost even more money in canceled games, money that they did not directly see again. Cities and stadiums lost game-day revenues. The strike ended in August when the players agreed to a lesser version of the compensation plan, and the season resumed with the All-Star game in August. Commissioner Bowie Kuhn was left to determine how to handle the divided season. He concluded that the best method would be a split season with the winners of the first half and the winners of the second half meeting in a best-of-five game miniseries to determine who would play in the regular playoffs. As a result the team with the best overall record of 1981, the Cincinnati Reds, failed to make the miniseries because they won neither the first nor second half (just the combined seasons). The Los Angeles Dodgers would ultimately win the World Series over the New York Yankees.

The labor problems in MLB would briefly reappear in 1985 when the CBA that the players and the owners had agreed upon in 1981 expired. The two-day strike was quickly resolved when the owners abandoned their compensation plans (settling instead for using draft picks) and the players agreed to a minimum salary of $60,000 instead of $48,000. In exchange, the owners were able to retain a greater percentage of media compensation. Although some twenty-five games had been canceled for the strike, all were made up.

The new bargaining agreement did not mean, however, that the owners played fair with free agency. By the early 1980s, the players' union and the courts had successfully dismantled the reserve system and introduced free agency into baseball. After the 1984 season, all of the MLB clubs signed free agents from other teams– precisely the way the system was intended. After the 1985 season, however, very few free agents were signed by different clubs, and as a result all but four free agents re-signed with their original club. The players' association suspected that the sudden stall in free agent movement was not coincidental and argued that the owners had colluded (agreed among themselves) not to sign free agents unless their original team had decided to let the player go. Collusion would violate the CBA that the owners had agreed to just that season. The owners argued that they had not colluded; the stall in free agency came from a depressed market and a lack of desire on the part of the players to move. The neutral arbitrator disagreed and concluded that the only explanation for such a universal lack of movement was collusion. Evidence that Kirk Gibson had been approached by two different teams about leaving the Detroit Tigers before the October owners' meeting, but then was told that neither team was interested in free agents after the meeting, did not help the owners' case.

After the 1986 season, the stagnant free agent market in early 1987 continued, and a new arbitrator concluded the owners were continuing to collude. The arbitrator was particularly influenced by the fact that free agent salaries actually decreased in 1987 compared to previous years. In the 1987–88 off-season, the owners tried a new tact: keeping a data bank on all free agents, which allowed owners to know the negotiation status on each player. Yet another arbitrator found this to be collusion. Thus the owners were found guilty of collusion for their behavior after all three seasons.

In 1990 the owners and the players' union agreed to a $280-million settlement for the three years of collusion. Although the settlement was huge, the impact of collusion on the players' salaries was profound. Essentially for three years, the owners artificially kept salaries low. Given how quickly salaries were rising and how quickly they skyrocketed after the collusion, it is unclear how much money the players lost. Further, after the settlement was announced, over 800 players filed claims asking for more than $1.3 billion, well over the settlement money total.

Consumption of the Game: Media and Fans

Television and media revenue increased dramatically in the 1980s. Effective in 1985, NBC and ABC agreed to pay MLB $1.1 billion for a five-year deal to alternate broadcasting the All-Star Game, the playoffs, and the World Series on the radio and television. This meant that between 1985 and 1989 each of the twenty-six MLB franchises would receive between $5.7 and $7.9 million annually, beyond what they earned from selling their own local media rights (Alexander 1991, 324).

Not only did media revenue increase, but also, despite the labor strife, attendance at major-league games generally grew throughout the decade. The growth may have been perhaps in part because no single team dominated the decade. Although the St. Louis Cardinals played in three World Series, the most of any team in the decade, they won only the 1982 Series, losing in 1985 to the Kansas City Royals and in 1987 to the Minnesota Twins. Also, the venues changed during

Cincinnati Reds batter Pete Rose waves one finger as he celebrates at first base after singling in the first inning of the game to break Ty Cobb's hits record in Cincinnati on September 11, 1985. (AP/Wide World Photo)

this time. In 1982 the Hubert H. Humphrey Metrodome, the new home for the Minnesota Twins, opened in Minneapolis. In 1987 when the Twins won the World Series with four home wins after having the league's best home record, some credited the noise in the dome, which audiologists discovered was twice that of outdoor stadiums. In 1988 venerable Wrigley Field, home of the Chicago Cubs, abandoned its fight against progress and installed lights, which allowed night games for the first time in the club's history. In 1989 the SkyDome in Toronto (home of the Blue Jays) opened with a retractable roof, the first in MLB history. Pete Rose's quest to pass Ty Cobb's record for the most hits in baseball also increased fan attendance as he got closer to the record. Amid great fanfare, he broke the record in 1985 as the player-manager of the Cincinnati Reds. Financially, MLB did quite well.

Scandals

With labor strife relatively minimal after the 1981 season, the new problem in the clubhouse was the use of cocaine. Cocaine was not a new drug, but in the 1980s it became an increasingly popular recreational drug among wealthier Americans. Keith Hernandez, the first baseman on the 1982 World Series–winning St. Louis Cardinals, estimated that as many as 40 percent of MLB players had at least experimented with cocaine. He and twenty other ballplayers testified in federal investigation after being given immunity; seven non–baseball players were later indicted in Pittsburgh on cocaine-trafficking charges. Because, however, the league had no drug-testing policy, drug usage by the players was initially dealt with inside the franchise, unless the player was arrested. Many, including Hernandez, were simply traded when their managers grew tired of the drugs. Eventually in 1986, Commissioner Peter Ueberroth persuaded the players' union to agree to sanction the thirty-one players who admitted to using drugs: those individuals were fined up to 10 percent of their 1986 salaries, performed community service, and agreed to submit to random drug testing.

Race and racism were other challenges for baseball in the 1980s. In the 1980s baseball enjoyed a resurgence: more people were watching games and the game was enjoying unprecedented success on the silver screen. Films like *The Natural* (1984), *Bull Durham* (1988), *Eight Men Out* (1988), *Major League* (1989), and *Field of Dreams* (1989) were popular with both critics and filmgoers. Some baseball scholars argued that baseball was regaining its status as "America's Game," a position it had seemed to be losing to the National Football League (NFL). Baseball, however, seemed to be becoming an increasingly white sport for both players and spectators. A 1987 survey found that a smaller percentage of fans at MLB games were African American than at NFL and National Basketball Association (NBA) games, despite the fact that MLB tickets were cheaper. Further, the percentage of African American players declined in 1980s. In 1980 20 percent of players were African American, but in 1989 only 16.6 percent of players were African American (Alexander 1991, 349-50). The racial problem was exacerbated in 1987 when Al Campanis, the director of player development for the Los Angeles Dodgers, appeared on the ABC news program *Nightline* and announced that former black players did not have the same capacity to be managers as former white players did. He was fired within twenty-four hours, but his statements highlighted the fact that, to that point, only three black men had ever been MLB managers, and none held that position in 1987. MLB responded quickly by hiring Harry Edwards, a black sociologist, as a consultant for minority affairs. A much greater number of nonwhite coaches, scouts, trainers, instructors, and front-office personnel were hired after Campanis's statement. In 1988, Bill White, an African American, was named president of the National League.

Commissioner Ueberroth stepped down at the end of his five-year contract in 1988, and he was replaced by A. Bartlett Giamatti, the president of the National League and the former president of Yale University. Giamatti's reign would be short but significant: he would be the man who banned Pete Rose from baseball. The Pete Rose affair began after the 1988 season when rumors began circulating that he was gambling heavily and betting on baseball games. The popular former player known as "Charlie Hustle" for his scrappy approach to the game was, at the time, the manager of the Cincinnati Reds. In response to the rumors, Giamatti appointed Washington attorney John M. Dowd to investigate the matter. Dowd's report, submitted in May 1989, made a compelling case against Rose. Perhaps most compelling, although they would have been inadmissible in a court of law, were the betting slips stolen from Rose's home by one of his associates. Written on the slips in handwriting that an expert testified was Rose's were the words CINCY W with dates. Further, phone records from Rose's home confirmed that he had made multiple brief phone calls to known bookmakers. Additionally two of Rose's associates, both convicted felons, testified that they had placed bets on baseball for him. Circumstantial evidence strongly suggested that Rose had bet on both baseball and on his own team, the Reds, although he seemed to have always bet that the Reds

The 1989 Earthquake Series

The 1989 World Series could have been memorable simply because it was the first time that both Bay Area teams were in the World Series. The Oakland Athletics had easily won the American League pennant with ninety-nine victories. The team was filled with All-Stars like Rickey Henderson, Jose Canseco, Mark McGwire, Dave Stewart and Dennis Eckersley. The team coasted through the playoffs beating the Toronto Blue Jays, four games to one, to go to the World Series. The Giants won the National League pennant in five games over the Chicago Cubs.

The Series began well for the Athletics. They won the first two games in Oakland in dominant fashion, winning 5-0 and 5-1. The Giants were eager to return to their home field of Candlestick Park on October 17 where they hoped to get their back on track. At five o'clock in the evening both teams took the field for pregame ceremonies and introductions in front of more than 60,000 fans.

At 5:04 P.M., the Loma Prieta earthquake struck. Registering 6.9 on the Richter scale, it was the worst earthquake in North America since the 1906 San Francisco earthquake. Al Michaels was on the air broadcasting the game nationally for ABC television when the earthquake hit. Inside the stadium, the press box swayed and the power went out, but the stadium, though shaken, stayed intact, and remarkably the fans remained reasonably calm. Eyewitness testimony reported the fans applauded after the earthquake ended. Fortunately when the earthquake occurred, it was still light and the people were evacuated before darkness fell. When ABC was able to restore its feed, Al Michaels continued reporting; he would be nominated for a news Emmy award for his work. Outside the stadium was devastation, a section of the Bay Bridge and several sections of freeway collapsed. Damage was estimated at $3 billion for San Francisco alone. Sixty-seven people were killed.

Commissioner Fay Vincent decided to postpone the Series, despite objections from some who felt the event should be canceled. Before the Series could continue, though, power needed to be restored to the area, and a structural evaluation of Candlestick Park needed to be made. Ten days later on October 27, the Series resumed in Candlestick Park, and the Athletics continued their domination of the Giants, winning 13-7 and 9-6. Out of respect for the victims of the earthquake, the Athletics did not celebrate their victory with champagne.

---

would win. Rose, though, would deny betting on baseball at all throughout the investigation.

Although the investigation was extensive, Commissioner Giamatti made mistakes during its course that did not always place him in the best light. Prior to receiving the Dowd Report, he wrote a letter to a federal court urging leniency for one of Rose's associates who was awaiting sentencing for tax fraud. In the letter Giamatti praised the man's assistance in the Dowd investigation. The judge who received the letter, however, was a Cincinnati Reds fan who thought the letter proved that Giamatti had prejudged Rose and could not be fair in Rose's cases. Had Giamatti not sent the letter or had he phrased it differently, he would have had complete control of Rose's fate in baseball as the commissioner. As soon as the allegation was made, with the letter as evidence that Giamatti was biased, the door was opened for Rose to try to have Giamatti replaced. Rose filed a series of lawsuits trying to do just that, but he had also been indicted on tax-fraud charges and the two-front legal battle was expensive. Finally, Rose agreed to settle with MLB and agreed to a lifetime ban from the game, but he offered no admission to betting on baseball. The agreement left open the possibility of a future reinstatement into baseball and a possible future election to the Hall of Fame. Rose later pled guilty to tax fraud and agreed to prison time. The scandal took its toll on the commissioner as well: Bart Giamatti died of a heart attack on September 2, 1989, just nine days after suspending Rose.

Deputy Commissioner Fay Vincent succeeded Giamatti and presided over the remainder of the season and the playoffs. The 1989 season had several bright points. Vincent "Bo" Jackson played in two professional sports leagues: baseball for the Kansas City Royals and football for the Oakland Raiders. He was the MVP of the MLB All-Star game in 1989. Ken Griffey Jr. and Ken Griffey Sr. were the first father-son combination to play in MLB simultaneously that season as well. Jim Abbott was a .500 pitcher with the California Angels in his 1989 his rookie season, but his presence was notable because he lacked a right hand. The season ended with the Oakland Athletics sweeping the San Francisco Giants in four games. The series itself was notable because it was interrupted for ten days after North America's worst earthquake since 1906.

For MLB, the 1980s were both a challenging and rewarding decade. Marred by strikes and collusion, players and owners enjoyed an uneasy co-existence. The players did profit from the first decade without the reserve clause. Despite three years of owner collusion in lowering the value of free agents, the average player's salary increased by 137 percent salary increase over the course of the decade (Fort 2003, 179). Even though the cocaine scandals and the Pete Rose affair seemed to threaten the integrity of the game, media revenue increased as did fan attendance at the games. Major League Baseball weathered the 1980s quite well.

Basketball

The 1980s were a kind of golden era for basketball in the United States. The members of the National Basketball Association (NBA), both owners and players, saw a jump in revenue and popularity. College basketball also continued to do well. The NCAA women's tournament, held for the first time in 1982, grew more than was anticipated, and the men's regular season and tournaments garnered large audiences and television fees. Much of the success of basketball in the 1980s was the confluence of increased media exposure and great players.

The NBA

The decade began with extremely high hopes. Larry Bird and Magic Johnson had captivated the nation during the NCAA championship duel at the end of the 1978–79 season and were set to enter the NBA together for the 1979-80 season. The Boston Celtics had drafted Bird, and Johnson was joining an already talented Los Angeles Lakers team. Not only were the two men outstanding basketball prospects, but they seemed to epitomize what the NBA wanted to be: they came from working-class backgrounds, believed in practicing and playing every game to their best abilities, and tried to be consummate team players. Although some saw the situation as racialized—Bird was occasionally called "The Great White Hope" in a

Lakers-Celtics Domination 1980–1990

From the 1980–81 through the 1989–90 seasons, either one or both of the Los Angeles Lakers and the Boston Celtics played in the NBA finals. The Lakers won four titles and the Celtics won three. They played each other for the finals on three occasions, with the Celtics winning one and the Lakers winning the other two. It was a two-team rivalry that the NBA could not have scripted more beautifully.

The rivalry began when Larry Bird began playing with the Celtics and Magic Johnson began playing with the Lakers in the 1979–80 season. Both rookies were re-markable players who fit in well with their teams. Bird joined a team that was made significantly better just prior to the 1980–81 season when the team traded its number 1 pick in the draft for center Robert Parrish and in the number 3 draft pick chose Kevin McHale. Johnson also had an all-star cast with him on the Lakers, in center Kareem Abdul Jabbar and forward Jamaal Wilkes. The Lakers got even better in the 1982 draft when they selected James Worthy with the number 1 pick. The Lakers' games, and sometimes the team itself, were called Showtime because of the team's fast-paced and brilliant offense.

The first of the highly anticipated Lakers-Celtics finals arrived in the 1983–84 season. Bird had won the first of three straight league MVP awards and McHale won the first of

Los Angeles Lakers center Kareem Abdul Jabbar shoots a sky hook in a game against the Utah Jazz in Las Vegas on April 6, 1984. (AP / Wide World Photo)

two straight Sixth Man awards. The Lakers had cruised under Coach Pat Riley through the playoffs to the finals, having lost only three postseason games. The finals were a hard-fought affair, culminating in a Boston victory in game 7. The next year, 1984–85, both teams easily made the playoffs and then the finals. The teams were essentially the same, except that Boston coach K.C. Jones had added Danny Ainge as a guard, and the Lakers had added Byron Scott. Although the Celtics destroyed the Lakers in game 1, the Lakers won the next four behind Abdul Jabbar's MVP performance.

The two teams would next meet in the finals in 1986–87. The Lakers had added A.C. Green to the team in the interim. The Celtics, meanwhile, were playing without their number 1 draft pick. The Celtics' dynasty was over, and they did not make the finals again. The Lakers repeated their title the next season over the Detroit Pistons, but they would fail to repeat for a third time in 1989–90, losing to the Pistons.

league that was about 80 percent African American—basketball fans and the NBA focused on their skills. The growth and popularity of the league would continue with the entrance of Hakeem Olajuwon, Michael Jordan, Charles Barkley, and John Stockton from the 1984 draft—all of whom would become All-Stars and eventually enter the Hall of Fame. Jordan and Barkley particularly profited from product endorsements that made them household names beyond their basketball skills.

Economics of NBA Basketball

The NBA, in fact, initially assumed that Bird and Johnson could carry the league. To avoid comparisons with the defunct and flamboyant American Basketball Association, the NBA prohibited players from wearing jewelry on the court and began play with a dull orange ball (in contrast to the ABA's multicolored ball). The league, under Commissioner Larry O'Brien, installed the three-point shot but in the early season it was not utilized much. Although Bird and Johnson were popular, they were but two players in a large league, and perhaps because of limited marketing or the subdued style of the league, attendance at games declined from 1980 to 1982. Fortunately for the league, television revenue was increasing. In 1982 CBS paid almost $92 million for a four-year deal and ESPN and USA Network each signed deals, which added another $11 million in television revenue (Kirchberg 2007, 174). Player salaries had increased (they would eventually increase 191 percent over the course of the decade) (Fort 2003, 180).

Declining attendance and increased salaries, however, meant that in 1982 a number of NBA franchises were in trouble. After all, Bird and Johnson could only play for two teams. San Diego, Cleveland, and Kansas City were all on the verge of collapse, and the San Diego Clippers pulled in less than half of the average attendance at NBA games. Over all, only six teams in the league were making a profit (Kirchberg 2007, 174). The CBA between the players' union and the owners was set to expire during the 1982–83 season, and rumors circulated that a strike was eminent. Commissioner O'Brien and players' union leader Bob Lanier, however, negotiated a deal that pleased both sides: the players agreed to a salary cap and the owners agreed to guarantee that the players would receive more than half of the league's gross revenues, including gate and media revenue from all games. Plus the players would get an additional $500,000 from licensing agreements.

Settling the labor concerns allowed the season to finish without a labor stoppage. The Philadelphia 76ers, led by Julius "Dr. J" Erving and Moses Malone, would go to the finals against the Los Angeles Lakers and Magic Johnson, who was trying for his third title. The 76ers swept an injury-ridden Lakers team, giving Erving his only NBA title.

In 1987 the CBA had to be reconsidered again with Commissioner David Stern representing the owners. Stern had replaced O'Brien as commissioner in 1984. As was typical of player-owner negotiations, the dealing was contentious. The players wanted a significant change (if not an end) to the salary cap and free agency sooner. The owners wanted to cut the college draft down to three rounds and wanted no changes to the salary cap or free agency. Both sides threatened the other: the owners briefly stopped signing players and the players threatened an antitrust lawsuit. In the end, however, an agreement was reached without a strike. The salary cap remained and players continued to get 53 percent of all revenues. The college draft was reduced to three rounds, and players were eligible for free agency sooner. Additionally more retired players were added to the pension program.

The financial challenges of the franchises resulted in several relocations. In 1984 the Clippers moved from San Diego to Los Angeles, and in 1985 the Kings moved from Kansas City to Sacramento. In both cases, the initial cities had lost their fan support and each finished their last season in their old city drawing very few fans to the games. No team, however, folded, which meant that the 253-player minimum that the league had guaranteed in the 1983 contract was not problematic for the league.

Players in the 1980s profited from personal and product endorsements to a degree no other basketball players in history had. Julius Erving was among the first to endorse shoes; he signed with Converse in 1981, but the company did little to publicize the relationship as they expected little profit from it. They also signed Larry Bird and Magic Johnson but again expected little profit from the relationship and did almost nothing to promote the relationship to the public. In 1984 after Michael Jordan was drafted, Nike signed him to a five-year $2.5-million shoe deal. Nike both developed the first Air Jordan shoe and introduced the "Jump Man" insignia of a silhouette of Jordan flying through the air to dunk the ball. Nike discovered the relationship was hugely profitable and netted $130 million in 1985 for all things Jordan. This success opened the door for athletes to commercial endorsements. Jordan would perhaps profit the most with endorsements from Spaulding to McDonald's and Chevrolet. He would make three times his salary in endorsements in 1986 alone, and the ratio would become even more skewed as he career progressed. Eventually he would become one of the wealthiest athletes in the 1980s and one of the world's most recognizable people.

Scandals

Basketball, like baseball, was more concerned about its players' use of street drugs than their use of steroids. Basketball was particularly plagued with story after story of talented players whose lives were destroyed by drugs, especially cocaine. Spencer Haywood, whose lawsuit had opened the NBA to players not yet finished with college, had been a huge success with the Seattle SuperSonics in the 1970s, but would end his career in the NBA, twice, because of cocaine. First he was kicked off the Los Angeles Lakers, just days before they began their 1980 championship run, because of his cocaine use (which had begun earlier while he was a New York Knick). Haywood claimed he was not the only player who used cocaine on that team but that he was the only one to ask the coach and management for help. Coach Paul Westhead said he was waived because of his performance. After spending a season in Europe, Heywood returned to play with the Washington Bullets in 1982, but his cocaine habit continued and the team released him in 1983. Rumors circulated that more than half the players used cocaine and other recreational drugs.

The league took the problem seriously. In 1981 the league and the players' union jointly offered a twenty-four-hour counseling service for players and their families for drugs and other problems, but drug testing had not yet been instituted. During the CBAs prior to 1983, the union initially opposed drug testing. The year after the agreement, however, the union agreed to the most extensive drug-testing program in U.S. professional sports at the time. A player who voluntarily admitted a drug problem was provided treatment without penalty. After a second admission, he was suspended, and after the third admission he was banned. Any player caught using drugs would be automatically suspended. An independent agency was allowed to randomly or with cause test any player up to four times during a six-week period without notifying the player. Later the program was expanded to include all league employees, including coaches and owners. Players were given an amnesty period until the end of 1983 to admit their drug problems and receive treatment without it counting toward their three strikes. In 1984 both John Drew of the Utah Jazz and John Lucas of the Houston Rockets were suspended after testing positive for cocaine in a drug test. Micheal Ray Richardson of the New Jersey Nets would become the first player banned in 1986 for his repeated use of cocaine. After two years of banishment, players could apply for reinstatement. In 1988 the league and the union agreed to test all rookies during training camp; a positive test for heroin or cocaine would result in a one-year suspension.

Unlike the NFL, steroid rumors did not haunt the NBA. The league's 1980s drug-testing policy did not include steroids, in part because Commissioner David Stern had no evidence that it was problematic. He was more worried about combating the cocaine and heroin use by his players and saving the league's image.

In addition to drugs, the NBA had to deal with the periodic race issue. Larry Bird faced additional challenges in 1987. Isiah Thomas, the African American point guard for the Detroit Pistons who won back-to-back titles in 1989 and 1990, echoed comments from his teammate Dennis Rodman, who suggested that Bird received greater attention and praise from the press because he was white. Thomas added that, although Bird was talented, he was not particularly talented compared to the black players in the league. Thomas later clarified his statements, arguing that he was not critiquing Bird himself but rather a society that credited Bird's success to his intelligence and work ethic, while simultaneously suggesting black players' success was due solely to athletic talent.

The race issue was also discussed periodically when the topic was marketing a predominantly African American league to a predominantly white audience. Commissioner Stern could point to increased attendance and television audience throughout his early tenure to prove that the color that mattered most to NBA fans in the 1980s was that of their team. Michael Jordan's enormous endorsement success suggested that race was not a barrier when it came to nonbasketball financial success.

College Basketball

The 1980s saw great growth in men's college basketball. Part of this was the result of having Michael Jordan play at the University of North Carolina. As a freshman in 1982 he hit the winning shot in the championship game against Georgetown. His sophomore and junior years he was named player of the year. He also led the United States to a gold medal at the Los Angeles Olympics in 1984. He would be drafted in that year and go third in the first round to the Chicago Bulls where he would achieve great success.

Indiana (1981, 1987) and Louisville (1980, 1986), each won two men's NCAA titles while the Big East, Big Ten and ACC were seen as the top leagues of the

---

Women's Basketball Great Cheryl Miller

In the 1980s women's basketball in the United States was just beginning to get noticed by the general public. Cheryl Miller was a major reason why the game got more attention. Born January 3, 1964, in Riverside, California, the young Miller grew up playing basketball with her family. Her younger brother Reggie would eventually grow up to be an All-Star in the NBA with the Indiana Pacers. Miller herself had remarkable talent; she combined grace and athleticism into a game that was unparalleled in the decade. Her national accolades began in high school where in four years of play at Riverside Polytechnic High, her team had a record of 132-4. She was awarded the Dial Award for the national high school scholar-athlete of the year in 1981, and she was the first athlete ever to be named a Parade High School All-American for four years. Her talent eclipsed the local competition: she once scored 105 points in a high school game.

Miller played college basketball as a forward at the University of Southern California, where her success continued both on the collegiate and the international stages. As a collegian, she was a four-time All-American and three times was named Naismith Player of the Year. As a freshman and sophomore in 1983 and 1984, she led the Lady Trojans to the NCAA national championships. She was named Most Valuable Player of each of those final four tournaments. Miller also led the U.S. women's national basketball team to unprecedented success. The team won the 1983 Pan American Games in Caracas, Venezuela, and then on an even bigger stage, the team became the first U.S. women's basketball team to win the gold medal at the Olympics. In 1986 the national team won the gold medal in the Goodwill Games and the title in the Women's World Basketball Championship.

Miller was the recipient of the YWCA Silver Achievement Award in 1986 and was voted the 1984–85 ESPN Woman Athlete of the Year. In 1986 *Sports Illustrated* named her the best college player (male or female) in the country. She graduated from USC in 1986 with a degree in broadcasting. She was the first basketball player, male or female, at USC to have her number retired. Later she would be enshrined in both the Basketball Hall of Fame and the Women's Basketball Hall of Fame. After graduating, Miller was drafted by a number of leagues, including men's leagues. A serious knee injury in 1987, however, ended her playing career, and she moved into coaching and broadcasting instead.

era. In the women's brackets, Southern California, led by Cheryl Miller, and Louisiana Tech were the top squads of the early 1980s, but by the end of the decade, Tennessee and Stanford had surpassed them both.

All three networks and ESPN and other cable stations were televising men's college basketball. Women's basketball generally was only televised nationally for the semifinals and finals of the NCAA tournament, but their share of the television audience was increasing. Unlike with football, colleges and universities seemed happy to let the NCAA negotiate television deals for the NCAA championship tournaments. In 1981 ESPN bought the right to televise some of the first-round games, and with the national audience, more of America often saw teams from outside their geographical region. The tournament was becoming so popular that the format was expanded in 1985 from forty-eight teams to sixty-four. In 1987 CBS agreed to pay about $50 million annually to televise the men's tournament, up from the $19 million they had been paying since 1981.

As television revenues increased, however, college basketball endured another point-shaving scandal. In 1985 John "Hot Rod" Williams, a star forward at Tulane University, was arrested for manipulating point spreads in at least three games in the previous season in exchange for at least $8,550 and cocaine. Two other players were also indicted and testified against Williams. He was never convicted on the charges of sports bribery or conspiracy and moved directly onto a successful career with the NBA. Tulane, however, was terribly shaken by the scandal. The entire coaching staff as well as the athletic director resigned, and the university decided to disband the basketball team just days after the scandal broke. The team was not resurrected until the 1990-91 season.

Basketball, both professional and college, grew economically in the 1980s. Although scandals ranging from cocaine use to bribery plagued the game, in general basketball held up well. Television ratings increased, which helped increase television revenue. More stars moved through the ranks from men's college level to the professional ranks, and when they arrived at the pro level, they benefited from increased salaries and endorsement opportunities. Women's basketball also gained more national attention at the college level in the 1980s after the NCAA began offering scholarships and networks televised the championship. Although women who wanted to play professionally in the 1980s had to leave the United States, the growing popularity of the game offered some hope for more successful women's pro leagues at home in the future.

Football

In the 1980s football in America saw a decade of change. In the ranks of professional football, the National Football League (NFL) was challenged by the U.S. Football League (USFL), and the NFL itself saw three teams move to new cities. Sometimes the separation was friendly and sometimes it was not. Additionally, the NFL saw the 1982 season shortened by a labor dispute, and another dispute marred the 1985 season. On the positive side, salaries for NFL players increased over the decade, the league saw huge increases in television and radio revenue with the addition of cable programming, and the financial values of the NFL teams increased. At the collegiate level, football had an explosion of popularity, thanks in large part to the increased number of games on television, but college football was also wracked by scandal as schools balanced a desire to win with the collegiate mission to educate. Despite some problems, in the 1980s football seemed poised to become America's favorite sport. The decade began, in fact, with reports that American sports fans preferred football to baseball by a margin of 48 to 31 percent (History: 1981–1990).

Economics of Professional Football

Professional football was slower to develop free agency than major-league baseball. Although the NFL's reserve clause had been struck down in the 1970s, the NFL players' association had negotiated a CBA that allowed a form of the reserve clause to remain. The compensation clause allowed teams to essentially have first right of refusal on free agents in that the original team had the option of matching any free-agent offers the player received, and if a player left through free agency, the original team was compensated with draft picks. The result was little free-agent movement; in fact, between 1977 and 1988 out of the 125 to 150 players who annually announced their free agency, only three players changed teams (Quirk and Fort 1992, 200).

The CBA was due to expire in 1982, and the players' union head proposed a minimum salary level based on position and seniority to help circumvent the compensation rules that limited free agents' salaries. The two sides were unable to reach a compromise, and the players went on strike on September 21, 1982. They remained away from the field until November 17 in the longest (fifty-seven days) strike in U.S. professional sport history. The players in this agreement accepted the compensation rules in exchange for increases in pension payments and severance pay. To deal with the eight weeks and the hundreds of games lost, the NFL decided to shorten the season to just nine games and to expand the playoffs to eight teams from each conference. This format sent two teams (the Detroit Lions and the Cleveland Browns) to the playoffs with losing records and allowed the St. Louis Cardinals a playoff appearance for the first and only time in their history. All three lost in the first round. The Washington Redskins defeated the Miami Dolphins in Super Bowl XVII.

In 1987 negotiations for the CBA were set to begin, and free agency remained the central issues for the players. The owners, who had successfully limited free agency for years, were unwilling to budge from their position, insisting on keeping a compensation plan. Given the impasse, the players went on strike again, but this time, after canceling one week of games, the owners continued the season with "scab" players—retired players, minor-league players, and unsigned former college players. A number of NFL players crossed the picket lines as well. Games were still televised and public support for the players was limited. After three weeks, the players' union gave up and ended the strike. The two games with replacement players counted toward season standings, and the Washington Redskins defeated the Denver Broncos in Super Bowl XXII.

The union refused, however, to negotiate with the owners and turned to the courts after the CBA expired in 1988. The judge at a preliminary hearing suggested that the players would likely prevail in their struggle for free agency if the case went to trial. Just before the 1989 season, the owners announced a new free agency system—Plan B—in which 65 percent of players on a roster were reserved but the

The Catch: The 49ers take on the Cowboys, 1982

In 1982 the San Francisco 49ers were facing the Dallas Cowboys in the National Football Conference (NFC) Championships. The 49ers had won thirteen of their sixteen regular-season games under Coach Bill Walsh and held home-field advantage for the playoffs. They had won the divisional playoff game fairly easily against the New York Giants in the first playoff game for Joe Montana, the 49ers young quarterback. The Dallas Cowboys were the second seed in the NFC playoffs, having won twelve of their sixteen games. They had held the Tampa Bay Buccaneers scoreless in their divisional playoff game.

On January 3, 1982, the two teams met in the much-anticipated conference championship game. The game was close, with Dallas leading by three points at the half. The second half was a back-and-forth affair with the 49ers regaining the lead in the third period only to give up ten points to Dallas in the fourth quarter. With just under five minutes to play, trailing by six points, the 49ers had the ball on their own eleven-yard line. In just ten plays, Montana shepherded his team to Dallas' thirteen-yard line. On the first play, Montana's pass missed an open receiver in the end zone, and his usually stoic head coach jumped and shouted in frustration on the sidelines. The next play netted seven yards but left the 49ers short of both a first down and a touchdown. Just under a minute remained in the game.

On third down with three yards to go on Dallas' six-yard line, Montana rolled to his right with three Cowboys chasing him. Wide receiver Dwight Clark, one of Montana's favorite targets that season, was in the back of the end zone running right as well. Montana flung the ball off his back foot and was knocked to the ground. Montana never saw anything but Clark's feet touching the ground, but he heard the home crowd roar. Replays would show Montana what the fans saw that day; Clark leapt high in the air, twisted, and caught the ball on his fingertips. The successful extra point gave San Francisco the lead with fifty-one seconds left in the game. After the catch, Dallas was unable to move the ball against the 49er defense, and when the Cowboy quarterback lost a fumble, the game was over. Joe Montana and the 49ers would go on to defeat the Cincinnati Bengals in the Super Bowl.

The catch marked a shift in NFL powerhouses. That 1981–82 season would be the first of three Super Bowl victories for Montana and the 49ers, the beginning of a dynasty. Montana was beginning a Hall of Fame career, as this first Super Bowl win was also the first of his three Super Bowl MVP awards. The game also marked the end of the Dallas Cowboys' dynasty.

---

remaining 35 percent would be true free agents. The Plan B free agents actually did switch teams, and salaries increased.

The 1980s was also a decade of movement. Three NFL teams physically moved locations during the decade. The first to go was Al Davis's team, the Raiders. Davis was not happy with the facilities at the Oakland–Alameda County Coliseum, which lacked lush, revenue-producing, luxury box seating, nor was he happy with the lease agreement. In 1978 the Los Angeles Rams had moved out of the Los Angeles Coliseum, and Davis had begun negotiations with the city of Los Angeles as well as its coliseum to move there from Oakland. At the time, NFL ownership rules required a 75 percent approval from other owners before a team could be moved, but when Davis asked for approval in 1980, he was overwhelmingly rejected. As a result, almost everyone involved filed lawsuits: the city of Oakland

and the Coliseum wanted to keep the Raiders, Los Angeles wanted the Raiders, and the Raiders themselves wanted to move. Multiple legal arguments were put forward. In the end, the city of Los Angeles and Al Davis won, and in 1984 the Raiders moved out of Oakland.

Similarly, after a long and successful history in Baltimore, Colts owner Robert Irsay announced the team would be moving to Indianapolis, where the city had promised to build a domed stadium, after negotiations with Baltimore about building a new stadium failed. The city of Baltimore responded quickly, filing lawsuits. The state got involved when the Maryland state legislature passed a law allowing the city to seize the team via eminent domain, but that new law would provoke Irsay into moving quickly. That very night, March 28, 1984, in a snowstorm, the team packed everything it owned into moving trucks and left for Indianapolis without warning and without league permission. The city of Baltimore felt betrayed and devastated, but the Colts stayed in Indianapolis.

In 1988, after a long and protracted argument over the city's failure to build the Cardinals a new football-only stadium in St. Louis, owner Bill Bidwell moved the team to Tempe, Arizona, where the community promised to build a new state-of-the-art facility. Unlike the flight of the Colts, many in St. Louis were

Washington Redskins quarterback Doug Williams is about to let go of a pass January 31, 1988, during the first quarter of Super Bowl XXII with the Denver Broncos in San Diego. (AP / Wide World Photo)

just as happy to see the team go. The St. Louis Cardinals had not been nearly as successful as the Baltimore Colts, and Bidwell was commonly seen as an owner who never spent any money on talented players and coaches. Plus, in a city with a strong economic grounding in brewing beer, Bidwell was not popular for his desire to stop selling Budweiser at Busch Stadium, which was owned by the same family that owned the Anheuser-Busch Brewery.

Although the 1980s saw labor strife, franchise movement, and the rise and fall of another professional league, in general the decade was good for football on both the professional and the collegiate level. For the NFL, television viewership and media revenue grew, especially after ESPN debuted *Sunday Night Football* in November 1987. African Americans also gained more prominence and power in the NFL throughout the decade. Breaking traditional racial stacking at certain positions, in 1983 Dwight Stephenson became the first black center named to the Pro Bowl. In 1988 Doug Williams with the Washington Redskins became the first black quarterback to win the Super Bowl when his team beat the Denver Broncos. Williams was also named the game's Most Valuable Player. African Americans also made strides in coaching, particularly after San Francisco 49ers head coach Bill Walsh made a point of hiring black coaches. In 1989 Al Davis named Art Shell the Los Angeles Raiders head coach, making Shell the first African American head coach in the NFL since Fritz Pollard in the 1920s. Such improvements, along with increased revenue and player salaries, helped the sport.

USFL: The Other Pro Football League

The NFL had long been the dominant professional football league in the United States, and although other leagues had challenged its supremacy, none had succeeded in usurping its position. In 1982 David Dixon, a New Orleans antique dealer who had helped get the NFL Saints team to the city, founded a new league, the U.S. Football League. Unlike its failed predecessors, the USFL took a different approach; the league played in the spring and not in the fall. Dixon hoped the USFL would fill a gap in the appetite of the American football fan by playing when no high school, college, or pro football teams had regularly scheduled games. The USFL lasted only three seasons (1983, 1984, and 1985) and the turnover in ownership of the teams was quick. In just three years, two of the teams were each sold five times. Originally the USFL hoped to compete in NFL cities, but during the NFL off-season, but by the third season only six teams remained in NFL cities; the rest had moved to smaller markets.

Revenue for the USFL was varied. Although some teams had strong attendance, most did not. The league had hoped each team would average 30,000 fans at each game, but only the New Jersey Generals achieved this minimum each season. The league average ranged just over 25,000 fans per game. Additionally the USFL television contracts were not nearly as lucrative as the NFL contracts. In 1983 the USFL had contracts with ESPN and ABC that brought in $1.4 million per team but the NFL television revenue averaged out to $11.12 million per team (Quirk and Fort 1992, 357–58).

The league featured some big-name players and owners. University of Georgia Heisman Trophy–winning running back Herschel Walker signed with the USFL after leaving school a year early. In signing Walker before he used up his college eligibility, the USFL broke an informal, long-standing NFL policy of not drafting college players early. Walker played for the New Jersey Generals, owned by real estate mogul Donald Trump. Quarterbacks Jim Kelly and Steve Young and defensive end Reggie White would all join the league and would all eventually become members of the Football Hall of Fame. Heisman Trophy winner Doug Flutie would also join the USFL. As a result of these high-profile signings, the quality of play in the league was quite high. The product had potential. Some of the unexpected financial struggles of the league, however, stemmed from the unexpectedly high player salaries. The talented young college players chose the USFL over the NFL because the USFL promised to be more lucrative.

The USFL decided to move to a fall schedule in 1985 but several teams disbanded and, for practical purposes, the league was finished. An unwise expansion from twelve teams to eighteen teams in the third season had not helped the league's stability. The USFL did not officially disband, however, until the conclusion of its antitrust lawsuit against the NFL. The USFL argued that the NFL had violated antitrust laws by pressuring the television networks not to broadcast USFL games. Additionally, the upstart league argued that the NFL had conspired to harm the franchises in cities with NFL teams. The USFL asked for $567 million in actual damages, but in antitrust cases damages are automatically tripled to punish the wrongdoer. This meant that if the USFL won, league owners hoped to get about $1.7 billion, which would have bought years of time to grow and expand their fan base. In fact, although the jury ruled that the NFL had monopolized professional football, it also concluded that the league did not pressure the networks to avoid the USFL and the NFL did not conspire to harm any specific teams. As a result, the USFL was awarded just one dollar. On appeal, the USFL won court costs but no changes to the original verdict. The USFL officially folded after the appeal was rejected.

Steroid Scandal

Football in the 1980s saw a new scourge. Steroids and performance-enhancing drugs, which had already become prevalent in weightlifting and bodybuilding, became prevalent in NFL locker rooms. A number of players from that decade have admitted using steroids and have estimated their use at anywhere from 20-90 percent of players, varying by position. Steve Courson, a former Pittsburgh Steeler, blamed a heart condition on steroid use in his playing days. He would testify before Congress in 2005 about steroid use and reiterate what he had written in his biography after his retirement. Courson traced the history of steroid use in the NFL to a strength coach, Alvin Roy, who had begun working with the Olympic weightlifting team. When Roy moved to the NFL, Courson claimed that steroids followed him wherever he went, and that word quickly spread of their benefits. Jim Haslett, a former NFL linebacker, and later an NFL coach, admitted to using them for at least one season as a player to gain size and strength; he estimated half the players and all the lineman took them at some point. Perennial All-Pro lineman Lyle Alzado, who would later die of brain cancer that he attributed to his steroid use, insisted that NFL coaches and administrators knew of steroid use, but liked the results so they said nothing. Confirming his story, one of Alzado's coaches admitted he knew of the drug use.

NFL commissioner Pete Rozelle did take the steroid problem seriously. Arbitrarily, and over the union's objections, the NFL began testing for steroids in 1987. In

1991 Dr. Forest Tennant, the drug advisor to the NFL in the 1980s, said that in 1986 30 percent of all players tested positive for steroid usage. Echoing Alzado, he also insisted that owners and coaches had not done enough to stop the drugs' spread. He noted that in 1986 the league, motivated by the cocaine overdose of NBA draftee Len Bias, was more concerned about the use of cocaine and tested for that. Players were not suspended for the use of steroids until 1989 after the Players' Association finally agreed to a formal drug-testing and punishment policy. Any prior positive steroid tests were forgiven. Random, year-round testing began in 1990. The drug policy in the NFL was one of the first and more stringent in American professional sports.

College Football

Much of the increase in college-football revenues and fan base came from the Supreme Court decision in 1984, which concluded that the National Collegiate Athletic Association (NCAA) could not unilaterally negotiate broadcasting rights for all its membership. The Court concluded that each individual school or, if it chose, each conference could sell its own broadcasting rights. This decision, in conjunction with the growth of ESPN and cable television, increased the number of televised games and allowed fans to see more teams on television more often. Prior to the decision, the NCAA had generally limited teams to just a few appearances nationally on television, but after the Supreme Court decision, teams and television stations had a plethora of options, which allowed the market to dictate the number of television appearances and the contract fees for those appearances.

While scandal in college football was nothing new, the increased media presence in the 1980s increased the value of a winning team and it also increased the media attention when schools did violate NCAA rules or when athletes behaved illegally. News about college sport scandals was now front-page material, and ESPN was happy to highlight the scandal on *SportsCenter* as well. Abuses at schools like the Universities of Georgia and Oklahoma were played out in the news. In 1986 Jan Kemp, a professor at the University of Georgia, won a huge lawsuit against the university. Kemp had been fired after she complained that the grades she had given football players had been changed over her objections. The players had been enrolled in a remedial English program and, despite Kemp's failing nine of them, each was promoted out of the program. Kemp sued the university for violating her right of freedom of speech, and an Athens, Georgia, jury awarded her $2.58 million. The case highlighted the attitude of many big-time sports colleges when university administrators testified that the athletes were only at the university as raw materials for the sports machine. The case may have been doomed when the university lawyer's opening statement included the assertion that "we may not make a university student out of [an athlete]. But if we can teach him to read and write, maybe he can work at the post office rather than as a garbage man after he gets done with his athletic career" (Neff and Sullivan 1986). Given that the football players at issue were African American, the racial implications did not help the university's case.

Elsewhere, stories of football players running wild scandalized the nation. At the University of Oklahoma, Coach Barry Switzer presided over teams that won football championships and also racked up impressive crimes. In 1988 star line-backer Brian Bosworth claimed that Switzer rented an off-campus apartment for players' use and also offered cars. He also claimed that some players, with Switzer's knowledge, used the team apartment to snort cocaine. Switzer denied this allega-tion, but there was not much he could do to deny the crimes of his other players. One player shot another after an argument, three players allegedly raped two women in the football dormitory, and the quarterback was arrested after selling co-caine to an undercover police officer. In 1989, after the NCAA put the university on probation, Switzer resigned.

The University of Colorado, meanwhile, also had its problems. Between 1986 and 1989 twenty-four football players were arrested for crimes ranging from burglary to assault. One player was arrested for rape and was a suspected serial rapist. Despite the criminal activities of the players, the Associated Press named the Colorado foot-ball team the 1990 National Champion (Georgia Tech University would win the championship given by the Coaches' Poll). The Buffaloes' record that season of eleven wins, one loss, and one tie, however, was marred by controversy on the field. In the middle of the season, Colorado was losing to the University of Missouri as time was running out in the game. Colorado scored to take a two-point lead as time expired, but they did so on a fifth down; the officiating crew had lost count of the number of downs. After the game, Colorado refused to forfeit the game, claiming in part they would have scored earlier if Missouri's field conditions had been better. Their coach, Bill McCartney, would later retire from coaching to promote his evan-gelical ministry, and several years into that, he apologized for accepting the victory.

From the NCAA's perspective, however, the most damaged football program in the nation was at Southern Methodist University in Houston, Texas. In the late 1970s and early 1980s, the SMU Mustang football team was a powerhouse. Between 1980 and 1986, the team's record was fifty-two wins, nineteen losses, and one tie. The team was undefeated in the 1982 football season. Winning, however, was coming perhaps because of NCAA violations. Despite multiple probation peri-ods, allegations of additional violations arose in 1986. The problem seemed to be largely that university boosters were paying players. In 1985–86, one booster seems to have paid thirteen players over $47,000. Additionally, recruits, players, and their families were given other illegal inducements; players were given cars and families were flown to games. In 1986 the NCAA gave SMU football the "death penalty"—eliminating all scholarships and prohibiting the team from playing a single game in 1987. In 1988 the team's season was canceled because of a lack of players. SMU football never reached the same levels of national success again, and the NCAA has not utilized the death penalty subsequently.

On the college level, football did well also. Increased media coverage made the game quite popular, and it allowed on-field heroics like Boston College quarterback Doug Flutie's "Hail Mary" touchdown pass to defeat the University of Miami in 1984 to be replayed repeatedly. Football fans continued their argument that foot-ball had replaced baseball as America's Game.

Hockey

Professional ice hockey saw some growth in the 1980s. The game had long been the province of Canada more than the United States, but the popularity of the sport grew a bit the United States in the 1980s. In 1980 the dominant professional league, the National Hockey League (NHL), expanded after a rival league failed. The World Hockey League (WHL) lasted throughout much of the 1970s, but like many startup leagues, lacked sufficient funding to really challenge the NHL long-term. The league did, however, increase players' salaries by providing competition, and it recruited underage and European players. The WHL had prided itself on an offense-oriented game. After the WHL failed, the Edmonton Oilers, the Winnipeg Jets, the Hartford Whalers, and the Quebec Nordiques joined the NHL in 1980. The Oilers would bring the man who could be credited with vastly raising the profile of professional hockey in the United States—Wayne Gretzky.

Gretzky had played one year in the failed WHL (where he won Rookie of the Year) and after the WHL ended in 1979, Gretzky's team, the Edmonton Oilers, joined the National Hockey League (NHL) and Gretzky was on his way to becoming a legend. With Gretzky the Oilers won the Stanley Cup championship four times (and played and lost in another final) in the 1980s. Gretzky, nicknamed "the Great One," held or would eventually hold almost every scoring record in the league. He led the league in scoring in eight of the ten years of the 1980s and came in second in the other two. He was a hockey god. In 1990 the Associated Press would name him the Male Athlete of the Decade.

In 1988 the Edmonton Oilers traded Gretzky to the Los Angeles Kings. Some speculated the owner traded him for the cash, and other speculated that Gretzky himself had asked for the trade to help advance his American wife's acting career. Regardless of why it happened, Canada as a nation was devastated. As crushed as Canada was, however, Gretzky's move jump-started hockey in Southern California. The Kings, prior to Gretzky's arrival, had not been terribly good or terribly popular. Gretzky's arrival made them competitive and resulted in a string of sold-out seasons.

The NHL in the decade saw changes in terms of their teams' locations and in terms of their television visibility. Not only did the WHL four teams join the league in 1980, but the next season an existing NHL team, the Colorado Rockies, relocated to New Jersey and became the Devils. In 1989 the Nashville Predators would be formed as an expansion team. Most credit Gretzky's star power with giving the NHL enough momentum to place a franchise in the mid-South—a place with no history of hockey and one that rarely saw ice outside of the rink.

Any increase in hockey's popularity in the United States was not likely because of television, however. No over-the-air network broadcast an NHL game between 1981 and the end of the decade. From 1980 until 1985 USA (formerly the Madison Square Garden Network) channel broadcast NHL games, and then ESPN broadcast games until 1988; at that point the NHL made the unfortunate choice of signing an exclusive contract with SportsChannel America. That contract doubled the contract money that ESPN had been paying, but SportsChannel America had only one-third the viewership that ESPN had because many cable companies across the country did not carry it. The NHL president believed that regional cable sports television was the best way to make money and to promote interest in the NHL, but some thought that the large check cost the league more than it gained in terms of national exposure. In 1990 the All-Star game would be aired on NBC, but that would be the only game of the decade available to viewers without cable. That said, the NHL generally remained stable, and the average player salary increased 33 percent over the decade (Fort 2003, 180).

The Olympics

The United States, after boycotting the Summer Olympic Games in Moscow in 1980 would attend each of the Olympic Games subsequently. In 1984 Sarajevo, Yugoslavia, hosted the Winter Games, and Los Angeles hosted the Summer Games. In 1988 Calgary, Canada, hosted the Winter Games, and Seoul, South Korea, the Summer Games. All of these were fundamentally different from previous Games in that they were part of the new "open" era. Prior to 1983 most international sport federations required that athletes who wanted to compete internationally be amateurs and receive no compensation for their victories or any but family or self-support for their training. The Soviet bloc had avoided the challenge of keeping an athlete's amateur status by using state support. For example, many Soviet and Communist athletes were part of the military system and their

---

The Record-Breaking Hurdler Edwin Moses

In the 400-meter hurdles, conventional wisdom said an athlete should take fourteen steps between hurdles. Edwin Moses was a physics major at Morehouse University who trained on public tracks, and he wondered if fourteen steps were really necessary for him. They were not. Born on August 31, 1955, in Dayton, Ohio, Moses would become one of the greatest hurdlers of all time. He appeared out of nowhere for the 1976 Olympics in Montreal and won the 400-meter hurdles, a fact even more remarkable because he had not raced that event regularly before March 1976. He set a world record in Montreal and was the only American man to win an individual track event. After the Olympics, he continued to train, essentially on his own, while he completed his double major in physics and business administration at Morehouse. He broke his own world record at a meet in 1977.

That same year, Moses competed in an event in Berlin and lost the 400-meter hurdles. That loss was significant because Edwin Moses would not lose another race for almost ten years. During that time he won 122 consecutive races and countless awards, including the Jesse Owens Award, the James E. Sullivan Award, Wide World of Sports Athlete of the Year, as well as *Sports Illustrated*'s Sportsman of the Year. Although he did not win the 1980 Olympic gold because of the U.S. boycott of the event, he broke his own world record that year in Milan. He would win his second gold medal in Los Angeles in the 1984 Olympics. In June of 1987 he would lose for the first time since that race in Berlin. He would continue to race, though, and at the 1988 Olympics in Seoul, he won the bronze medal.

Moses' success on the track, however, is not necessarily his most important impact on the sport of track and field. In the early 1980s, he lobbied for change in reforming international and Olympic eligibility rules so that athletes could train full time while earning direct stipends, payments, and commercial endorsement money. Prior to that, Olympic track athletes could not accept any payment for competition, endorsements, or victories, or they risked losing their amateur status and their eligibility to compete in international events. Moses presented the plan to the president of the International Olympic Committee and the plan was ratified in 1981. Several years later, he recognized the invasion of performance-enhancing drugs into his sport, and he lobbied again for change. He spoke out against drug usage and encouraged the international body to develop more stringent tests. In 1988 he helped develop amateur sports' first random out-of-competition drug testing program.

Olympic figure skater Brian Boitano leaps in the air, touching his skates during the free skating competition on February 20, 1988, in Calgary, Canada, during the XV Winter Olympics. (AP / Wide World Photo)

job was to train for their sport, but they were compensated and supported as a member of the military. Western Europe and North American athletes were stymied by the system; many could train and compete as scholarship holding members of their college track teams but once they ran out of eligibility, they lost their meal money and free coaching. In 1983, the International Olympic Committee acknowledged the problems of the amateur system and encouraged the international sports federations to redefine eligibility. By the end of the decade almost every federation allowed any athlete (professional or amateur) to try to qualify and compete internationally.

In Sarajevo, American athletes had one of their better Winter Olympics, winning eight medals. Brothers Phil and Steve Mahre took gold and silver in the slalom, and Scott Hamilton won the gold in men's figure skating. Hamilton had had an odd childhood illness that caused him to stop growing; eventually he grew to 5'2" and he weighed about 110 pounds during his competitive years. His gold medal at the 1984 games was not surprising, as he had won the world championships every year since 1981.

Athletes on the U.S. team were extraordinarily successful in the 1984 Games in Los Angeles, largely because the Soviet Union and the Eastern bloc of Communist countries boycotted the games in what most people perceived as retaliation for the U.S. boycott of the Moscow games four years earlier. The Soviets' official reason was their worries about the security of their athletes, given the political tensions between the two countries. Despite the absence of the Communists, a record 140 countries participated in an Olympics filled with firsts. American Joan Benoit won the inaugural women's marathon and New Zealander Neroli Fairhall became the first paraplegic athlete to compete in the Olympics. She finished thirty-fifth in the archery competition.

FloJo—Florence Griffith Joyner (1959–1998)

Florence Griffith Joyner, known as FloJo, first appeared in the American eye in 1984 at the Los Angeles Olympics. Born December 21, 1959, in Los Angeles, California, she enrolled at the University of California–Los Angeles and trained with Bob Kersee. Kersee was married to Jackie Joyner-Kersee, who herself would ultimately become queen of the heptathlon.

In the 1984 Olympics, Griffith Joyner caught the public eye not so much because of her performance (she won silver in the 200-meter sprint), but because she had flamboyant racing suits and long brightly decorated fingernails. Her self-designed racing suits were, like others of the era, racing tights, but unlike others, FloJo favored suits with one leg in tights and one leg bare. After the Games, she drifted away from training and entered a quasi-retirement.

FloJo's life would change dramatically in 1987. She married Al Joyner, who was Jackie Joyner-Kersee's brother and gold medal winner of the 1984 Olympic triple jump himself. The two would later have a daughter, and the Joyner and Kersee clans would be considered the first family in track and field. FloJo leaped back into training with Al as her new coach and changed her regime, undertaking an intensive weightlifting program and changing her starting technique for the sprints. She saw immediate improvement and became a household name because of her speed rather than her appearance.

In the 1988 Olympic trials, she set a world record in the 100-meter sprint, and beat her own personal best by more than half a second. At the Seoul Olympics, she dominated the women's sprints, winning gold medals in the 100-meter, 200-meter, and the 4×100-meter relay. She also won a silver medal in the 4×400m relay. Her winning time in the 200-meter also set a new world record. That year she won the Sullivan Award for the top amateur athlete. She would retire the next year in 1989.

Tragically, on September 21, 1998, FloJo died in her bed in her Mission Viejo, California, home. The coroner's report concluded that she had suffocated after having an epileptic seizure. The seizure had been caused by a congenital defect in her brain.

Largely because of the lack of competition, the United States won 174 medals in the games compared to the fifty-three medals won by the country with the second highest total, Romania. That said, many U.S. athletes had excellent games. American Carl Lewis won four gold medals in the two sprints, the long jump, and the 4×100-meter relay event, becoming the first man to win four gold medals in a single Olympics since Jesse Owens did it in 1936. Mary Lou Retton became the first American woman to win the All-Around gymnastics gold medal, securing her medal with perfect scores in both the floor exercise and the vault.

American athletes won six medals in the 1988 Calgary Games. Despite the low total number, the games had memorable moments. Brian Boitano won the gold medal in men's figure skating after entering the final free skate tied with Canadian Brian Orser for first place. Both men skated outstanding programs, and Boitano won the gold medal after the judges, by a score of five to four, concluded he was the better skater of the day. Debi Thomas became the first African American woman to win a medal at a Winter Olympics when she won the bronze medal in the women's figure-skating competition. Bonnie Blair, who would ultimately win more speed-skating Olympic medals than any other American woman, won a gold medal with a world record in the 500-meter sprint and then won a bronze medal in the 1000-meters. She was the only double medalist for the United States in Calgary.

In Seoul, most of the sporting world gathered at the Summer Olympics for the first time since the 1976 Montreal Games. The United States did well, earning ninety-four medals as the third-leading medal winner behind the Soviet Union and East Germany. The American teams won both the men's and women's basketball tournaments in what would be the last of the amateur basketball teams. Soon after the Seoul games, the basketball federation (Federation Internationale Basketball Amateur) opened international competition to professionals. Americans also did well in the track- and field event with Carl Lewis adding two more gold medals and a silver one to his name. Jackie Joyner-Kersee would win gold in the heptathlon, breaking the world record, and the long jump. Joyner-Kersee had won the silver medal in Los Angeles in the heptathlon and would compete in two subsequent Olympics after Seoul.

Seoul, however, would become infamous for steroid usage. Although the International Olympic Committee had tested for drugs since the 1968 Winter Games, Ben Johnson, a Canadian sprinter who had at first won the 100-meter gold medal,

USA jumper Jackie Joyner-Kersee of East St. Louis, Illinois, leaps in the early round of the women's long-jump competition in Seoul, September 29, 1988. Joyner-Kersee moved past the twenty-one-foot mark as she sought her second gold medal of the games. (AP / Wide World Photos)

Mike Tyson (Courtesy of Photofest)

tested positive for steroid use in Seoul. He was the first major track and field athlete to test positive. The Olympic community was shocked, and the IOC began investigating stiffer drug tests and more complete testing protocols; however, the shadow of drug use would linger over the Olympics of this and subsequent decades.

SPORTS FOR INDIVIDUAL COMPETITORS

Boxing

Although boxing in the 1980s did not hold the same prominence in American culture as it had in the past, the decade had a number of memorable fights and characters that kept it, for good and bad, in the public consciousness. Part of the challenge for boxing in the 1980s was replacing Muhammad Ali, the self-proclaimed "Greatest" who helped keep boxing into the public eye. The other part was a shift from televising boxing matches on over-the-air networks to televising major boxing matches on cable and pay-per-view television, taking the event away from the casual observer.

The heavyweight division lost a star when Muhammad Ali finally retired for good in 1982, and Larry Holmes held the heavyweight titles for the first part of the decade. Holmes, however, was not the same larger-than-life figure that Ali had been and many Americans lost interest in the division. That same year, long-time over-the-top sports commentator Howard Cosell, a long-time friend and admirer of Ali, retired from calling boxing matches because he was dismayed at the quality of the heavyweight fights. The heavyweight division would revive when Mike Tyson became the youngest heavyweight champion in 1986 at the age of nineteen. For a brief period Tyson seemed unbeatable; in 1988 he knocked out previously undefeated Michael Spinks in ninety-one seconds and earned himself $20 million for his effort. While it was an impressive display, its brevity did not thrill the millions who had paid extra to see the match on cable. Tyson's dominance would abruptly end in 1990 when little-known Buster Douglas knocked him out. Although Tyson would remain in the news, he was never the same fighter as he was for that brief span.

The void of personality in the heavyweight category, however, allowed some of the lighter boxers to gain recognition. More of the lighter categories were carried on network television as well, expanding their audience. Middleweights "Marvelous" Marvin Hagler, Thomas Hearnes, and Sugar Ray Leonard would dazzle the audience with their speed and footwork as they passed around the middleweight titles. Each would also win titles in different weight categories, gaining and losing weight to expand their competition.

Boxing also saw tragedy in the 1980s. In 1982 Ray Mancini retained his light-weight title with a fourteenth round knock out of Duk Koo Kim. Kim died five days later, and boxing mandated a twelve-round maximum on fights and instituted elimi-nation via the standing eight count. The fight, in Las Vegas, had been televised by CBS, which made the country much more aware of the event than it might have been. The next year another boxer died after a bantamweight title fight in Los Angeles. The victorious Alberto Davila was so distraught he stayed with the downed fighter's family at the hospital until Kiko Bejines died three days later. While tragedy did not define boxing during this decade, the lack of a dominant heavyweight, the lack of prominent boxers on over-the-air network television, and the range of sport-ing options contributed to the sport's decline in popularity.

Golf

In the 1980s, the three dominant and most lucrative professional golf tours were in the United States. The Professional Golf Association (PGA) was the home for the best male golfers in the world, the Ladies Professional Golf Association (LPGA) was the women's tour, and the Senior PGA Tour, founded in 1980, was for male golfers aged fifty or above. Golf in the United States was played predomi-nantly by white Americans from comfortable middle-class backgrounds.

In the 1980s the PGA did not see any single dominant player, but generally those who were most successful were Americans. Curtis Strange, from Virginia, won more events (sixteen) than any other golfer and won consecutive U.S. Open titles in 1988 and 1989. He also was the first on the money list for three years in the decade and in 1988 became the first man to earn a $1 million in one year on the tour. Tom Kite from Texas won thirteen titles from 1981 through 1990, and showing his con-sistency across the decade, he also led the money list in both 1981 and 1989. Calvin Peete was the only African-American on the PGA Tour. Although he never won a major, he won eleven tournaments in the decade and had the lowest average score of all golfers in 1984, earning him the Vardon Trophy.

Similarly, the LPGA did not have any single dominant player over the course of the decade, but it did have several players who dominated single years. Like the PGA, the winners on the LPGA in the 1980s were generally Americans. For exam-ple, Pat Bradley from New Hampshire had an excellent year in 1986 when she won five titles including three of the four major tournaments. She was the first member of the LPGA to earn $2 million in her career (which started in 1974) as well and would top the money list. Although Bradley did not dominate the tour again in the same way, she was consistent; in 1990 she would be the first member to reach $3 million in career earnings. Despite being diagnosed with Graves' dis-ease, a thyroid disorder, she won nineteen tournaments and five major tournaments from 1981 though 1990. Similarly, Betsy King from Pennsylvania had several good years and a solid decade. She was the leading money winner in 1984 and 1989. Over the course of the decade she won four majors and twenty-three tournaments. During this decade, Nancy Lopez, the first great Latina LPGA golfer, solidified her status as a top player by winning twenty-five tournaments, including the LPGA Open twice, and was inducted into the World Golf Hall of Fame in 1987.

The Senior PGA was designed to allow some of the more popular male golfers to continue their careers and to continue to attract fans to golf as they aged. Aside from the age restriction, the Senior Tour generally has only fifty-four holes over three days (except for the major events) instead of the PGA's usual seventy-two holes over four days. In the early 1980s some players who had been lesser stars on the PGA found their niche on the Senior Tour. Miller Barber, from Louisiana, won twenty-four Senior tournaments from 1981 through 1990 versus the eleven tournaments he had won in his entire career on the PGA Tour. Similarly, Don January from Texas only won ten times in his years on the PGA Tour but he won twenty-three times in the 1980s on the Senior Tour. Other popular players from the PGA Tour continued their careers on the Senior Tour. Chi-Chi Rodriquez from Puerto Rico won sixteen events from 1986 through 1990. Rodriguez had long been a fan-favorite because of his flamboyant approach to the game; after scoring a birdie or eagle he would wave his putter like a matador stabbing a bull. Foreign golfers were quite successful on the Senior Tour as well. For example, New Zealander Bob Charles won fifteen Senior tournaments from 1987 through 1990 and was twice the leading money winner.

Tennis

Larger-than-life characters, fierce rivalries, and youth characterized professional tennis in the 1980s. Although the sport at the professional level was truly international with players from and events located over all parts of the globe, several American players were dominant throughout the decade on both the men's and the women's side of the sport.

John McEnroe and Jimmy Connors were among the top ten players of the year according to the Association of Tennis Professionals (ATP) computer rankings for seven of the ten years. McEnroe was one of the bad boys of tennis; his nickname was Superbrat. At conservative Wimbledon in 1981, he appeared for the finals match on July 4, Independence Day for the United States but just another day for the United Kingdom, dressed in blue and white tennis clothes with a red headband. Despite his victory, the All England Club, not at all amused by his antics, declined to offer him the traditional honorary membership into the club. McEnroe was also infamous for complaining loudly about official calls during the match and for abusing officials and his equipment. In 1990 he was ejected from the Australian Open because of his abuse toward the officials. Regardless of his manners, McEnroe was a talented player who had a superb year in 1984, winning thirteen of the fifteen tournaments he entered, including Wimbledon and the U.S. Open. Connors, who had begun his dominance in the 1970s, continued to be successful in the 1980s. He won consecutive U.S. Open titles in 1982 and 1983 and remained a consistent enough player to rank in the ATP Top 10 until 1988. He too had a bit of a "bad boy" reputation, but his was not as extreme as McEnroe's. He had a history of flashing the occasional obscene gestures to officials when he disagreed with their calls, but, as he aged in the 1980s (and compared to McEnroe), Connors's on-court behavior calmed down. McEnroe and Connors faced each other repeatedly, and the younger player, McEnroe, would have the edge, beating Connors twenty times in thirty-three meetings.

Similarly, Chris Evert and Martina Navratilova were two powerful forces in women's professional tennis in the 1980s. Evert, who was married to John Lloyd until 1987 and competed as Evert-Lloyd during that time, was a consistently strong player. According to the Women's Tennis Association (WTA) year-end rankings, she ranked among the top three players every year of the decade until her retirement in 1989. She won each of four major tournaments (Wimbledon, the U.S. Open, the French Open, and the Australian Open) at least once in the 1980s. Perhaps more than any other American tennis player of the era, she enjoyed consistent popular support, in part because of her reputation as a sweet girl from California. She also became the first major rival for Navratilova, who had defected from Czechoslovakia and became a U.S. citizen in 1981. Navratilova was arguably one of the best women's player in history, and in the 1980s, she was at her most dominant. From 1981 through 1990, she won three Australian Opens, three consecutive French Opens, six consecutive Wimbledon titles, and two pairs of back-to-back U.S. Open titles. She was also a remarkably successful doubles player, winning twenty-six major doubles titles in the decade and eight mixed-double major titles. She would finish in the top three of the ATP annual rankings each year from 1981 to 1990. Evert and Navratilova faced each other in eleven major finals in the decade before Evert's retirement; Navratilova won eight of those contests.

American youth also made their mark on professional tennis in the 1980s. In 1981, at the age of eighteen, Tracy Austin, who had already been a two-time semifinalist at Wimbledon, won her second U.S. Open title, defeating Navratilova. Austin, however, would drop out of the Top 10 rankings in 1983 before she turned twenty-one and would never recapture the success she had as a youngster. Along with Austin, Andrea Jaeger also had success at a young age. She reached the finals or semifinals of each of the four major tournaments in 1982 and 1983; she was seventeen and eighteen years old during the run. Her career in tennis ended abruptly in 1983 with a major shoulder injury. On the men's side, in 1988 eighteen-year-old Andre Agassi won six singles titles; in 1989 he reached the finals of both the U.S. and French Opens. He chose not to play at the Australian Open or at Wimbledon those years. Off-court, Agassi sported long blond hair and boasted of his rebel image, enhanced by his endorsement deal with Canon for the "Rebel" camera. Michael Chang made history when he won the French Open in 1989 at the age of seventeen, and he was the first American man to win since 1955. It would be his only major title.

American tennis in the 1980s was predominantly white and the men made more money. Only two African American women had much success in the decade: Zina Garrison and Lori McNeil. Garrison had a solid career; although she did not win a major singles title, she competed in the five finals. She also won three mixed-double major titles in the decade. McNeil was not quite as successful, appearing in only two major-event singles finals and winning only one mixed-double major title. No African American men had much success, but Michael Chang was of Chinese descent and was the only successful Asian on the tour at the end of the 1980s. Continuing the history of gender segregation in tennis, the men continued to earn more than women at many tournaments. Although men and women competed for equal purses at the Australian and U.S. Opens, Wimbledon and the French Open continued to pay the men more. Part of the justification was that the men played the best of five sets while the women only played the best of three. Just as occurred with other professional sports, tennis in the United States benefited from the increased sports coverage from new sports-format television.

Thoroughbred Horse Racing

The 1980s were eminently forgettable regarding all-time great horses or races. After the excitement of three Triple Crown winners in the 1970s, the 1980s began the long stretch of having none in a decade. Only two horses won the first two legs of the crown, Pleasant Colony in 1981 and Sunday Silence in 1989. Pleasant Colony won two close races with Jorge Velasquez aboard, before finishing third in the Belmont. Sunday Silence defeated Easy Goer in the first two races, the second by a nose, but Easy Goer won the Belmont by eight lengths to end any hopes of a Triple Crown. Still, Sunday Silence was the Horse of the Year for 1989.

Two other horses won two legs of the Triple Crown, Swale and Alysheba. In 1984 Swale, a son of Seattle Slew, won the Derby, but finished seventh in the Preakness. He came back to win the Belmont, but eight days later died of a massive heart attack, during a bath. Alysheba won the Derby and the Preakness, before finishing fourth in the Belmont Stakes.

Like the horses, there were no real standouts among the jockeys of the decade. Ed Delahoussoye and Laffit Pincay won the most Triple Crown races with four each. Delahoussoye won two Derby victories and one victory in the Preakness and one in the Belmont. Pincay had wins in the Belmont and one victory in the Kentucky Derby.

OTHER SIGNIFICANT SPORTS

Sport in the 1980s grew in many ways. Participation at the youth and college levels increased, especially among girls and women. College sport grew as well and continued to become a defined product. Professional leagues, however, saw some variation in their levels of success in the 1980s.

Soccer

Soccer in the United States saw huge growth in young people's participation rates. Youth soccer, which gained popularity throughout the 1970s, continued to grow in the 1980s, and as more young people who had played soccer as small children entered high school and college, their schools began adding soccer teams. Women's soccer in college exploded in the 1980s. In 1981 only 12.5 percent of NCAA schools offered women's soccer teams, but in 1990 41.3 percent offered the sport. Soccer was one of the fastest growing sports in terms of participation in the 1980s.

Although soccer was growing in popularity, the men's U.S. national team did not have much success in international play. In 1984 the Olympics allowed men's teams from outside of Europe and South America to utilize any player they wanted, including professionals. The United States replaced most of its players with professionals but was still unable to advance out of the first round. The team failed to qualify for the 1986 World Cup. Although the team did qualify for the 1990 World Cup, they failed to win a single game and were eliminated in pool play.

In 1985 the U.S. women's national soccer team played their first international match, and in the next decade, when the women could compete in World Cup and Olympic tournaments, the women's team would attain much greater international success than the men's team ever did.

On the professional level, soccer did not fare well in the United States. The North American Soccer League (NASL), which had enjoyed some success in the 1970s with older international stars like Pelé and Franz Beckenbauer, folded in 1984, largely because of overexpansion and escalating player salaries. Part of the salary escalation came because of the rise of a competitor league: Major Indoor Soccer League (MISL). The indoor soccer game was very different than the outdoor game, with quicker, higher-scoring games that appealed to the American audience for a while. The MISL had begun in the late 1970s and would last until 1992. Although American children and young people played the game in great numbers, professional leagues failed to draw a lasting audience.

Wrestling

Wrestling faced a period of change in the 1980s. Youth wrestling and high school wrestling saw the first girls asking for the opportunity to compete in the sport, and schools addressed the sudden coeducational wrestling issue in one of three ways. Either they let the girls wrestle against the boys or they encouraged girls to wrestle against each other. Both of these approaches were acceptable under the law and sometimes resulted in enough of an increase in girls' participation to have gender segregated wrestling programs be viable. Occasionally schools and state athletic associations banned girls from participating in the sport, arguing that the sport involved touching that would be inappropriate for coed matches. In 1988, however, a federal district court in Kansas ruled that girls could not be excluded from the sport simply on the basis of their gender. A coach could cut a girl from a team because of her performance or attitude, but she had to be allowed to try out for the team. The court endorsed either coed teams or gender-segregated teams, but noted that if wrestling was offered as a school activity for boys, then it had to be available for girls.

On the collegiate level, men's wrestling saw lower participation rates and a number of college teams were cut. In 1981–82, NCAA membership offered 363 teams for 7,914 athletes, and each squad averaged 21.8 members. In 1989-90, NCAA membership offered 273 teams for 6,737 athletes, and each squad averaged 24.2 members (NCAA Year-By-Year). Many wrestling supporters blamed Title IX and its mandate that more women's sports be offered for the decline, arguing that that colleges cut men's wrestling to add women's sport. While some schools may have chosen to cut men's programs and add women's sports because of budget constrictions, these choices were administrative ones and were not forced by the law. At the time, however, wrestling periodicals blamed the sport itself for being boring and called for rule changes and an increase in media attention.

Professional wrestling, however, saw a huge resurgence. Although one could argue that professional wrestling is more entertainment than sport, Vince McMahon's purchase of existing leagues and his creation of the World Wrestling Federation (WWF) reignited the event's popularity. WWF quickly gained coverage on cable television stations and became popular pay-per-view events. McMahon created brilliant, flamboyant characters to populate his league, and these characters, like Hulk Hogan, quickly became household names, particularly in families with younger white males in the household.

College Sports

The NCAA was *the* major college sports organization in the 1980s. The "elder statesman" of men's sport, however, faced change and challenges in the decade. Having focused exclusively on men's sport, in 1981 NCAA officials were considering what role, if any, the organization should play in the growing area of women's college sport. Additionally, having faced a number of scandals in men's football and basketball, the NCAA faced a public skeptical of the true nature of amateur sport in the college ranks. To combat this public perception of athletes being separated from students, the NCAA made major rule changes.

The 1980s marked a dramatic shift for the administration of women's collegiate sport. Prior to 1981–82, the NCAA had focused exclusively on men's sport and had repeatedly refused to offer women's championships at any level. In the early 1980s the female-controlled Association for Intercollegiate Athletics for Women (AIAW) provided administration and championships for women's sport. The AIAW had been founded on the premise that women's sport could and should be different than the traditional model of male collegiate sport. The AIAW had initially opposed college sport scholarships, arguing that athletic scholarships put too much emphasis on winning and elite sport and not enough emphasis on academics and sport participation. In the early 1980s, however, the NCAA decided that because of Title IX, the federal law prohibiting gender discrimination in athletics, and the growth of amateur sport in general that the NCAA should begin offering championships for women. Both organizations offered championships in 1981–82, but after that the much larger and economically stronger NCAA replaced the AIAW. The AIAW filed a lawsuit arguing that the NCAA had violated antitrust laws in pressuring their member organizations to use the NCAA for both men's and women's sport and in pressuring television networks not to televise the AIAW events. After losing the case, the AIAW officially disbanded in 1983. The end of the AIAW meant that the mostly male NCAA now ran women's collegiate sport.

As the NCAA expanded to include women's sports in its realm, it faced the challenge of dealing with embarrassing scandals involving its student-athletes. Not only were there individual schools and players who violated NCAA rules as well as state and federal laws, but public perception was that college athletes were treated differently in general than regular students. The NCAA needed to reform that reputation. In 1983, in an effort to make sure that college athletes were prepared to be college students, the NCAA adopted Proposition 48. Prior to Prop 48, as it was called, any athlete could be awarded a college athletic scholarship provided he had a 2.0 grade point average (GPA) in high school as reported after six, seven, or eight semesters. The GPA requirement was cumulative and could be the result of a mix of academic and nonacademic courses, provided that same standard for calculating GPA was used for all students. As a result, promising athletes often avoided rigorous courses to protect their GPA. In 1982 an NCAA committee proposed an idea that would become Prop 48: the new rule would require a set of core academic courses for each student from which a GPA would be calculated. It also required a minimum test score on one of the standardized college aptitude tests. Some people, including Georgetown University men's basketball coach John Thompson, charged that the standard was problematic because they believed those standardized tests were racially biased and that African American students would be disproportionately negatively affected by the rules.

Regardless of the opposition, the rule took effect in 1986. All high school students who wanted to be considered for college athletic scholarships had to submit their high school transcript to the NCAA clearinghouse, which examined the transcript and calculated a GPA based on the core courses. Test scores were then submitted to the clearinghouse so that the athlete could be declared eligible. The NCAA argued that the rule was good because it forced student-athletes to be better prepared when they entered college, which meant more athletes could succeed academically in school and graduate with college degrees. Combating the allegations of a disparate racial impact, the NCAA noted that college graduate rates for African American student athletes increased after Proposition 48 took effect.

College sports were making more money because of the increase in media revenue and more schools were investing in more sports for men and women throughout the decade. The NCAA worked hard to keep the reputation of its student-athletes as clean as possible in order to keep the market interested in the product of college sport generally.

SUMMARY

The 1980s saw a strong growth in sports, thanks largely to a stronger economy giving Americans more disposable income, and because of the technological advances that brought cable television and sports programming to more of America. The big three sports—baseball, football, and basketball—all did well at both the professional levels and the lower levels. Player salaries increased for the professionals and each level saw an increase in television viewers. Other sports, like hockey, tennis, and golf, also did well. College sport focused on reform and on adding women's championships, which increased the number of women competing in collegiate sport.

The 1980s, however, would also serve as a kind of transition decade and act as a springboard for sports to expand in the 1990s in even more directions. In the 1980s niche sports like marathons, triathlons, motor sports, and alternative sports (like skateboarding and freestyle skiing) would slowly grow nationwide. More cities and more people would participate in long-distance running, like marathons. The growth of that sport was such that the women's marathon had enough worldwide appeal to be named an Olympic sport in 1984. The triathlon combined distance swimming, running, and cycling into a single event. The longest triathlon was the Ironman competition in Hawaii, founded in 1978, in which competitors swam 2.4 miles, biked 112 miles, and then ran a 26.2 mile marathon. The Ironman and other triathlons grew in popularity throughout the 1980s. As a new sport, it included a women's division from almost the first events.

Motor sports, particularly auto racing in the NASCAR (National Association for Stock Car Auto Racing) series and CART (Championship Auto Racing Teams—open-wheel Formula One cars), predated the 1980s but had solid growth throughout the decade. NASCAR especially did well, beginning to reach beyond its regionalism in the southern Atlantic states with personalities like Dale Earnhart and Darrell Waltrip who dominated the series in the decade.

The King of Skateboards, Tony Hawk

Born in San Diego, California, on May 12, 1968, Tony Hawk became the poster-boy of vertical skateboarding and living proof that athletes could make a profession out of competing in "alternative" sports. Skateboards predated Hawk, but when he was given his first board at the age of nine, no one knew he would reinvent the sport, particularly in vertical skateboarding on large half-pipe structures. Soon after Tony received that first skateboard, his father built a skating ramp in the backyard. A self-described overactive youth, Tony was highly competitive and physical, and skateboarding provided him an outlet for his excess energy. His parents supported his skateboarding and took him to competitions throughout his youth. At one point his father became frustrated with the skateboarding organizations, so Frank Hawk founded both the California Amateur Skateboard League and the National Skateboard Association (NSA). The NSA organized events with cash prizes and gave the sport new visibility.

Tony Hawk was the face of skateboarding in the 1980s. He got his first sponsor at the age of twelve, turned professional at the age of fourteen, and by the age of sixteen was generally considered to be the best skateboarder in the world. He was particularly famous for the tricks he invented, which helped him win the vast majority of the competitions he entered. Vertical skateboarding, done on large ramps, emphasizes aerial maneuvers and manipulations with the skateboard on the top edge of the ramp. Hawk was highly skilled at both.

With the skateboarding victories came financial rewards as well—he bought his first house when he was a senior in high school. Although vertical skateboarding waned at one point in favor of street skateboarding, when vertical skateboarding regained its popularity Tony Hawk bounced right back with it. Eventually he would have his own skateboard production company, skate tour, various video games, and a skate park–themed rollercoaster would be named after him.

Perhaps most important, Hawk was the iconic figure of skateboarding. He was one of the first skateboarders to become a household name, and he led the way in promoting what had been a marginalized sport into the mainstream of America. Inspired by Hawk, countless kids across the country built their own ramps in backyards, and communities were pressured into building skate parks.

Alternative sports would be a youth revolution. Young suburban boys, particularly white, middle-class boys, would begin building ramps and jumps in their backyards to practice skateboarding moves and BMX bicycle tricks. In the mountainous regions, some young skiers would take to snowboarding and freestyle skiing, involving tricks and jumps rather than sticking with traditional downhill ski events. Girls tended to be more involved in the winter alternative sports than they were in skateboarding and BMX competitions. Throughout the 1980s the participation rates in these sports would increase at the grassroots level so that in the next decade, the alternative sports would explode into popular culture. The 1990s would build on the sporting successes of the 1980s as technology continued to improve and expand and as the media continued to look for new programming to sate consumer cravings for sport.

RECOMMENDED RESOURCES

Alexander, Charles C. 1991. *Our game: An American baseball history.* New York: Henry Holt.

Bahreke, Michael S., and Charles Yesalis. 2002. *Performance enhancing substances in sport and exercise.* Champaign, IL: Human Kinetics.

Carpenter, Linda J., and Vivian Costa. 2005. *Title IX.* Champaign, IL: Human Kinetics.

Collins, Bud, and Zander Hollander, eds. 1994. *Bud Collins' modern encyclopedia of tennis.* Detroit: Gale Research.

Fort, Rodney D. 2003. *Sports economics.* Upper Saddle River, NJ: Prentice-Hall.

Kirchberg, Connie. 2007. *Hoop lore: A history of the National Basketball Association.* Jefferson, NC: McFarland.

MacCambridge, Michael. 2004. *America's game: The epic story of how pro football captured a nation.* New York: Random House.

Neff, C., and R. Sullivan. 1986. Scorecard: On trial in Georgia: Academic integrity. *Sports Illustrated* (January 27): 13, quoted in Quirk 1996, 64.

Prine, Carl. 2005. Courson says super Steelers were on steroids. *Pittsburgh Tribune-Review,* April 25.

Quirk, Charles E., ed. 1996. *Sports and the law: Major legal cases.* New York: Garland.

Quirk, James, and Rodney D. Fort. 1992. *Pay dirt: The business of professional sport.* Princeton, NJ: Princeton University Press.

Smith, Timothy. 1991. Football: NFL's Steroid Policy Too Lax Doctor Warns." *New York Times,* July 3.

Schaller, Michael. 2007. *Right turn: American life in the Reagan-Bush era, 1980–1992.* New York: Oxford University Press.

Thelin, John R. 1994. *Games colleges play: Scandal and reform in intercollegiate athletics.* Baltimore: Johns Hopkins University Press.

Watterson, John Sayle. 2000. *College football: History, spectacle, controversy.* Baltimore: Johns Hopkins University Press.

Whitson, David, and Richard Gruneau. 2006. *Artificial ice: Hockey, culture, and commerce.* Orchard Park, NY: Broadview Press.

FILMS

Bull Durham. 1983. Dir. Ron Shelton.
Eight Men Out. 1988. Dir. John Sayles.
Field of Dreams. 1989. Dir. Phil Alden Robinson.
Major League. 1989. Dir. David Ward.
Michael Jordan: Come Fly with Me. 1989. NBA Videos.
The Natural. 1984. Dir. Barry Levinson.

WEB SOURCES

Bray, Corey. 1982–00 Participation statistics report. NCAA Web site. http://www.ncaa.org/library/research/participation_rates/1982-2000/009-052.pdf (accessed Jan. 6, 2008).

Carpenter, Linda J., and Vivian Costa. 2006. Women in intercollegiate sport: A longitudinal, national study twenty-nine year update, 1977–2006. http://webpages.charter.net/womeninsport/AC_29YearStudy.pdf (accessed Dec. 11, 2007).

History of cable TV. http://www.k-state.edu/infotech/cable/history.html (accessed Dec. 11, 2007).

History: 1981–1990. NFL Web site. http://www.nfl.com/history/chronology/1981–1990 (accessed Dec. 11, 2007).

Iversen, Eve. 2007. An oral history of the Presidio of San Francisco during the Loma Prieta earthquake. http://www.sfmuseum.net/hist2/presidio.html (accessed Dec. 13, 2007).

Larry Bird. http://www.larrybird.com.

LPGA Players. LPGA Web site. http://www.lpga.com/players_index.aspx (accessed Dec. 27, 2007).

Olympic Games. Olympics Web site. http://www.olympic.org/uk/games/index_uk.asp (accessed Dec. 27, 2007).

PGA Players. PGA Tour Web site. http://www.pgatour.com/r/players/ (accessed Dec. 27, 2007).

Sugar Ray Leonard. http://www.sugarrayleonard.net

Teams. NBA Web site. http://www.nba.com.

Wayne Gretzky. http://www.gretzky.com.

CHAPTER 13

AMERICAN SPORTS, 1990 TO THE PRESENT

Jaime Schultz, Callie Batts, Perry Cohen,
Sarah Olson, Amie Chaudry, Jaime Ryan,
and Caitlin Shannon

OVERVIEW

As the world witnessed the simultaneous ending of a decade, a century, and a millennium, a great buzz surrounded the projected "Y2K" or the Year 2000 problem. There was widespread fear that as the date rolled over from 1999 to 2000 computer systems would break down and cripple U.S. finance, government, and electrical power. The concern, and the related media hype surrounding Y2K, quickly abated when very few problems occurred; however, the anxiety illustrated the increasing reliance on computer technology. Indeed, from 1990 to the present day, our culture has been significantly changed by the prevalence of personal computers and the time Americans spend "on line." In 1992 the World Wide Web became available for home use and millions began "surfing the 'net," sending emails to one another, conducting business transactions, and forming virtual communities. Webcasts of events, online gaming, Internet gambling, and fantasy sports leagues are some of the ways that the Web has affected sports. The instant access and dissemination of information democratized knowledge and communication, but also gave rise to a host of related problems.

Over the past nearly two decades, too, mobile telephones have moved from status symbols in the hands of few to indispensable devices glued to the ears of many. More televisions in American homes are now connected to cable and dish networks that allow viewers access to highly specialized channels, including the introduction of several devoted to sports. On the airwaves, Oprah Winfrey continues to probe the collective psyche. Shows like *Seinfeld*, *Friends*, *ER*, and *The Sopranos*, among many, have garnered high ratings. Reality programs have brought a new era in television entertainment, starting with shows like *The Real World* on MTV and growing to new game shows (*The Weakest Link*), talent shows (*American Idol*), and competitions featuring average citizens in extraordinary situations (*Survivor*). As grunge, techno, teen pop, and hip-hop styles of music took center stage, the music industry has faced the dilemma of how to handle consumers' ability to burn their own CDs and illegally download music from online file sharing. As Generation X gave way to Generation Y, Nintendo, Sega, and PlayStation engaged in console wars in attempts to corner the video game market.

Also since 1990 the stock market has taken some dramatic turns and the world's population has surpassed six billion. HIV/AIDS has reached epidemic proportions around the globe and athletes like Earvin "Magic" Johnson, Greg Louganis, and Tommy Morrison serve as powerful reminders that no one, including America's sporting heroes, is immune to the disease. Scientists began the Human Genome Project, produced genetically engineered crops, and cloned Dolly the Sheep—all of which present both significant advancements and ethical dilemmas for humanity.

Politically speaking, two Bush presidencies book-ended the era: George Herbert Walker Bush's first term came to an end in 1993. His son, George Walker Bush, left office after two terms, on January 20, 2009. The junior Bush originally increased his public profile as part owner of Major League Baseball's Texas Rangers and then as governor of Texas. His initial occupation of the White House started with a controversial election against then–Vice President Albert Gore in 2000; although Gore won the popular vote, Bush won the electoral vote by a narrow margin. In between the Bush presidencies, President William Jefferson Clinton led the country during a long period of economic prosperity and peace. The second half of Clinton's presidency was marred by allegations of sexual misconduct and his detractors attempted to remove him from office with charges of perjury and obstruction of justice. At the same time, women made great strides in politics. For instance, in 1993 the Senate confirmed Janet Reno as the first female attorney general of the United States and in 1997 Madeleine Albright became the first female U.S. Secretary of State. The Clinton administration also affected sports in a number of ways, including support for Title IX legislation and advocating the retirement of Jackie Robinson's number 42 jersey in all Major League franchises.

A number of devastating tragedies struck the country, ranging from natural disasters, to domestic catastrophes, to international terrorist threats. There were a number of horrific school shootings, the most lethal of which occurred at Columbine High School in Littleton, Colorado, when two teenaged gunmen took the lives of fourteen students and one teacher. Ted Kaczynski, dubbed the "Unabomber," was captured in 1996 after a series of bombs that killed three and injured twenty-three. The Olympic Games, held twice in the United States between 1990 and 2007 (Atlanta in 1996 and Salt Lake City in 1998), have frequently become the target of terrorist attacks, as a bombing at the Atlanta Games demonstrated. In 1993 Timothy McVeigh, Terry Nichols, and others, sympathizers with an antigovernment militia movement, killed 168 people and injured another 850 when they detonated a truck filled with explosives outside the Alfred P. Murrah Federal Building in Oklahoma City, Oklahoma. It was the single deadliest act of terror against America on U.S. soil until the horrors of September 11, 2001.

On that day, a series of attacks orchestrated by al-Qaeda, an international coalition of militant extremists working to end foreign influence in Muslim countries, forever changed the course of history in America. Terrorists hijacked four commercial jet airliners, crashing one into the Pentagon building in Arlington, Virginia, and another into a field in rural Pennsylvania as passengers heroically tried to wrest the controls from the hijackers and thwart the intended mission. Terrorists piloted the other two planes directly into the twin towers of New York's World Trade Center and the world watched in horror and disbelief as cameras captured the collision and destruction of the buildings. The unfathomable death, injury, and destruction caused by the attack continues to resonate, even as 9/11 memorials have begun to be established and opened.

In all, nearly 3,000 people died in the September 11th attacks and many remain missing. The events shook the foundation of the country. Feelings of security and safety were forever altered, and many people were affected by the loss of life and destruction of property caused by the crashes. The attacks also exacerbated racial tensions; the number of hate crimes and incidents of harassment directed toward Middle Easterners increased dramatically in the wake of the incident. The U.S. government instituted a number of efforts to reduce the likelihood of future terrorist attacks, including the Homeland Security Act, the PATRIOT Act, and increased scrutiny of foreign nationals living in the United States. Perhaps most significant, however, was that September 11th also prompted the United States to wage a global "War on Terror."

Sports, War, and Terrorism

In noting the close links between sport and war, scholar Gamal Abdel-Shehid (2002, 317) argues that "two of the most important cultural and political roles in the United States are athlete and soldier." During the period between 1990 and 2005, the roles of athlete and soldier embodied American cultural values in a complex time of war, terrorism, and fear. Sport played an integral part in mobilizing support for war, uniting the country, and creating cultural heroes who exemplified American nationalism.

The connections between sport and war were further strengthened after the terrorist attacks of September 11, 2001. Following lengthy debate on the importance of sport in the aftermath of such a tragedy, the National Football League and Major League Baseball decided to resume their full schedules after a short period of postponement. Just seven weeks after the attacks, the New York Yankees and Arizona Diamondbacks met in the World Series, providing an arena of escapism and catharsis for New York City and, arguably, for the entire nation. The fear of additional terrorist attacks, and the resulting increases in security, manifested at the 2002 Winter Olympic Games in Salt Lake City. Government and Olympic officials considered relocating or canceling the Games in response to the terrorist threat, but they decided to increase the amount and intensity of security surrounding the Games. In response, security personnel outnumbered the athletes, police snipers ringed the venues, and the flight zone immediately above Salt Lake City was restricted.

A final example of the links between sport and war is the case of Pat Tillman (November 6, 1976–April 22, 2004). A former NFL football player for the Arizona Cardinals, Tillman declined a three-year, $3.6-million contract to volunteer for the Army after the 9/11 terrorist attacks. He joined the Army Rangers in 2002 and was killed in friendly fire while serving in Afghanistan in 2004. Tillman was the first high-profile American professional athlete to die in military service since former Buffalo Bills lineman Bob Kalsu in Vietnam in 1970. Tillman's image as both an athlete and soldier was held up as the ideal American hero, the perfect representation of sacrifice, strength, and dedication. Questions later surfaced about the nature of Tillman's death and how the United States military manipulated and exploited his memory.

While human-made tragedies afflicted the country around the turn of the twenty-first century, there were also a number of natural disasters during this time: The Northridge Earthquake, with a magnitude of 6.7, hit Los Angeles in 1994, killing sixty-one and leaving thousands homeless. Wildfires blazed in California, Colorado, New York, Florida, Oregon, and Arizona. In 1992 Hurricane Andrew slammed into the Florida and Louisiana coasts. Its power and damage to both property and human life ranks second in U.S. history, placing it behind the terrible devastation caused by Hurricane Katrina. Katrina struck the north-central Gulf Coast in 2005, causing severe damage to a number of Louisiana and Mississippi cities, including Gulfport, Biloxi, Long Beach, and Pascagoula. Hardest hit was New Orleans, whose levee system proved woefully inadequate, causing flooding in over 80 percent of the city. Bridges collapsed, roads were damaged, nearly 2,000 people were killed, and looting violence, murders, assaults, and other crimes ensued in the hurricane's aftermath. The Louisiana Superdome, home to the NFL's New Orleans Saints, became "shelter of last resort" for the thousands of citizens evacuated from their homes. At the stadium, they were met with unsanitary and unsafe conditions, a lack of power, water, and medical supplies, and additional flooding as the dome's roof began to peel back. Although many sports franchises have been dubbed "America's Team," the Saints truly earned the moniker in 2005. The extensive damage to the Superdome forced the team to be itinerant throughout the season, setting up temporary residence in Texas and without the chance to play any "home" games.

The U.S. government's reaction to the storm and its aftermath was roundly criticized, particularly in connection to race, as the majority of those most affected by the catastrophe were African Americans. Always a volatile issue in U.S. history, race was brought to the fore in several other high-profile events. Following the 1992 acquittal of four white police officers for the videotaped beating of black motorist Rodney King, riots rocked Los Angeles and left fifty-eight people dead. The trial of football great O.J. Simpson, an African American accused of murdering his ex-wife and her friend, both of whom were white, highlighted the racial divide in the United States, as did the confirmation of Supreme Court judge Clarence Thomas, the 1995 Million Man March, and the celebration of the 500th anniversary of Christopher Columbus' "discovery" of America.

The Soviet Union collapsed in 1991, ending the Cold War that had existed since the end of World War II, but real conflicts continued. Throughout the 1990s, American troops were deployed to Panama, Somalia, Haiti, Bosnia, and elsewhere. Following the Iraqi invasion of oil-rich Kuwait, the United States waged the Gulf War and Operation Desert Storm and successfully forced Iraq's withdrawal. After the attacks of September 11, 2001, President George W. Bush ordered what he termed a global "War on Terror." The first step in this campaign was the invasion of Afghanistan in order to overthrow the Taliban regime, destroy Al-Qaeda, and capture their leader, Osama bin Laden. In his 2002 State of the Union address, Bush identified Iraq as part of an "axis of evil" that threatened world peace. With support from more than twenty other nations, the United States invaded Iraq, took control of the capital city of Baghdad, and ended the regime of Saddam Hussein. It has been a controversial war, dividing the nation and affecting all facets of American life.

It is against this backdrop that present-day sport developed in America, and the dialectical relationship between sport and society is evident in a number of situations. While sport has been affected by the triumphs and tragedies of history since 1990, at the same time, we must acknowledge that sport is not just a product of society, but a producer as well, influencing the course of history in a number of significant ways.

TEAM SPORTS

Baseball

The history of American baseball since 1990 is characterized by globalization, soaring salaries, record-breaking feats, innovative architecture, new opportunities for women, and doping scandals. The popularity of baseball during this time fluctuated as fans abandoned the game after the 1994 players' strike, came back to follow the 1998 home-run chase, and expressed disappointment at the alleged widespread use of steroids in the game. Faced with the rising dominance of football and basketball, Americans questioned the status of baseball as the national sport. Yet the health of baseball remains strong and the game perseveres.

Expansion and Globalization

One of the most significant developments in professional baseball during this time was the increasing globalization of the American game. Many teams opened training academies in such places as the Dominican Republic and Australia to scout talent, and Major League Baseball (MLB) created an international arm of business operations in 1989 with offices in New York, London, Sydney, and Tokyo. The expansion of baseball contributed to this development by adding more teams and tapping new fan markets. Players from such countries as Japan, Korea, and Venezuela entered the major leagues and found a strong fan base among the numerous ethnic and immigrant groups in the United States. No longer was baseball exclusively an "American" sport (if it ever was)—its global character was now directly expressed through the players, the fans, and the business strategies of MLB.

After a rigorous selection process completed in 1991, MLB decided to expand for the 1993 season, adding the Colorado Rockies and the Florida Marlins to the National League. A second round of expansion occurred in 1998, with the addition of the Arizona Diamondbacks to the National League and the Tampa Bay Devil Rays to the American League. Some critics argued that this rapid growth depleted the talent pool and caused an overall decrease in the quality of play. Proponents of expansion countered that the game was enriched with new fans, increased opportunities for players, and diverse regional representation.

In addition to expanding domestically, MLB expanded its operations abroad as well. In 1992 the World Series traveled outside of the United States for the first time when the Toronto Blue Jays hosted the Atlanta Braves. Toronto defeated Atlanta to become the first Canadian team to win the World Series, and the Blue Jays repeated as champions in 1993 after beating the Philadelphia Phillies. The 1999 season started in Monterrey, Mexico, as the Colorado Rockies and San Diego Padres traveled south to play the first regular-season games in Mexico. One year later, the 2000 season opened in Tokyo when the New York Mets and Chicago Cubs played to sold-out Japanese crowds. The traveling continued in 2004 when the Florida Marlins and Houston Astros played a series of spring training games in

Mexico City. By reaching out to international markets, MLB hoped to increase inter-est in baseball and secure additional media outlets and merchandising opportunities.

New players also reflected this globalized character. In 1994 Chan Ho Park became the first Korean-born major leaguer when he earned a spot on the Los Angeles Dodgers' roster. The Dodgers also featured Hideo Nomo, the first Japa-nese-born player to appear in a major-league game since 1965, when he pitched in an early season game in 1995. Between 1990 and 2005, a total of seventeen players born in Australia made their debut in the major leagues. Perhaps the player with the most international impact during this time was Ichiro Suzuki, an outfielder from Japan, who signed with the Seattle Mariners in 2001. Suzuki was an instant hit with the fans, both because of his playing skills and his ability to relate to the large Asian American fan base in and around the Seattle area. His games were fol-lowed widely by the Japanese media; sushi became a regular item at the stadium concession stands, and his stardom crossed international borders.

By 2005 over 45 percent of all professional baseball players (minor and major leagues) were born outside of the United States. Just over 29 percent of all major-league players were foreign born, and a total of thirty-three different countries were represented on opening day rosters of professional baseball teams in the United States. The leading countries included the Dominican Republic, Venezuela, and Puerto Rico. Perhaps Tommy Lasorda, former manager of the Los Angeles Dodgers, best captured the increasing tide of globalization by remarking with good humor: "For starting pitchers we have two Dominicans, one Italian, one Mexican, and one Japanese. In the bullpen we have a Venezuelan, a Mexican, a guy from the United States and a guy from St. Louis." Lasorda probably intended to be humorous, but his comment held truth about the growing diversity of professional baseball.

Economics and Legal Issues

With the freedom to sell their skills to the highest bidder on the free agent mar-ket, professional baseball players saw their salaries balloon after 1990. The effects of commercialization and globalization garnered increased revenues as teams capi-talized on merchandise and media rights. The wealthier teams were then able to court the best players, enticing them with promises of large contracts and perform-ance bonuses. This trend of increasing salaries is evident when comparing the highest-paid players and the teams with the biggest payrolls. For example, in 1990, Robin Yount was the highest-paid major-league player with an annual salary of $3.2 million; Cecil Fielder was tops in 1995 with a salary of $9.2 million. In 2000 Kevin Brown was paid $15.7 million for a season's worth of work; his salary was more than the entire payroll for the Minnesota Twins ($15.6 million). The salary boom reached a new height in 2001 when Alex Rodriguez (known as "A-Rod") signed the richest contract in American sports history. His ten-year deal with the Texas Rangers was worth $252 million, equating to approximately $25 million per year. Just eleven years earlier, the Kansas City Royals had the highest-overall pay-roll in MLB with a total expenditure of $23.8 million. And now Rodriguez, an individual, would be paid more than the entire Kansas City team earned in 1990. By 2005 the New York Yankees had the largest payroll at $208 million and Rodri-guez remained the highest-paid player after being traded to the Yankees when the Rangers could no longer afford to pay his salary.

One of the major reasons that player salaries and team payrolls increased so dramatically during this time was the impact of the 1994 players' strike. Beginning in the middle of August, the strike lasted for 232 days and caused the cancellation of 938 games, including the 1994 playoffs and World Series. As such, Major League Baseball became the first professional sport to lose an entire postseason due to a labor dispute.

The players decided to strike after a series of negotiations between team owners and the Major League Baseball Players' Association (MLBPA—the union representing players and their families) broke down. To cut expenditures and encourage parity, the owners demanded the imposition of a salary cap. In addition, the owners wanted to share local broadcasting revenue to secure financial equity among the teams. The enactment of a salary cap, which reduced the amount of money any one player could receive, would keep operating costs down and allow small-market teams such as the Kansas City Royals to compete more equally with large-market teams such as the New York Yankees. This plan required the approval of the Players' Association for ratification, but the athletes did not support the salary cap because they believed it hampered their right to seek full market value for their skills. The Players' Association thus rejected the owners' plan. In response, the owners voted to withhold $7.8 million from the players' pensions and benefits plans and the players decided to strike.

During the course of the strike, both the players and the owners were vilified for being greedy millionaires, and many fans resolved to abandon baseball forever. The strike resulted in a loss of $580 million in revenue for the teams and $230 million in player salaries. The Montreal Expos suffered the worst effects of the strike and could not bear the financial deficits from the lost season. The team was forced to cut its payroll for the 1995 season, its fan base all but disappeared, and the players languished in obscurity. The Expos never recovered from the strike, leading MLB to purchase the team in 2001 before facilitating its relocation to Washington, DC, in 2004.

As a result of the strike, players could seek the best deal available without the restriction of a salary cap. The free agent market has thus produced a substantial rise in salaries and the occasional mega-deal like the one signed by Alex Rodriguez. It exposed the hidden economics of baseball and revealed the desire of the players and the owners to maximize their own financial interests. The strike also alienated many fans. Yet, the game returned and the economic excess of professional baseball became an accepted fact. Aided by the incredible feats of Cal Ripken Jr., Mark McGwire, and Sammy Sosa, baseball eventually recovered from the 1994 strike to retain its place in American popular culture.

Records and Remembrances

Several significant events in American baseball history have occurred in recent history. Long-held records were broken, new personalities have emerged to shape the character of the game, and old favorites were remembered. These are the stories that become part of American cultural lore and help to form the fabric of baseball history. Rather than existing merely as factual occurrences or statistical data, these events give color to the game and contribute to the collective American sporting memory.

One of the most remarkable moments in professional baseball occurred in 1995 when Cal Ripken Jr. of the Baltimore Orioles broke Lou Gehrig's record for consecutive games played when he started his 2,131st straight game. Ripken's accomplishment helped reinvigorate interest in baseball after the 1994 players' strike and provided a powerful piece of history for fans to savor. Between 1990 and 2005 Ripken achieved iconic status in the game and cemented his place as one of the best to ever play the game.

Two other iconic figures took center stage in 1998, when Sammy Sosa and Mark McGwire enthralled the country with their chase to break the single-season home-run record set by Roger Maris in 1961. Sosa, a black outfielder from the Dominican Republic, and McGwire, a white first baseman from California, played for different teams but were united in their attempt to break the record of sixty-one home runs in one season. McGwire reached the record first and ultimately ended the season with seventy homers, setting a new single-season mark. Sosa ended with sixty-six,

The Iron Man: Cal Ripken Jr.

On September 6, 1995, Calvin Edwin "Cal" Ripken Jr. (born August 24, 1960) of the Baltimore Orioles broke Lou Gehrig's record for consecutive games played when he appeared in his 2,131st straight game. Long thought to be an impossible record to break, the streak came to define Ripken and his style of play. Known for his workmanlike approach to the game, he embodied the qualities of perseverance, loyalty, and commitment. He started his run in 1982 and officially ended it in 1998 after playing in 2,632 consecutive games. Over this sixteen-year period, Ripken never missed a start for the Orioles and became an iconic figure in Baltimore and across the country. While Gehrig had been known in the popular press as the "Iron Horse" for his physical prowess and determination, Ripken earned the nickname "Iron Man" to symbolize his similar strength and unyielding dedication.

Ripken's career was unusual in that he played for only one team. In the modern age of free agency, it is common for professional athletes to accept the most lucrative offer they receive, regardless of team allegiances or preferences. Ripken, a native of Maryland, chose to spend his entire career with the Orioles, due in large part to his affinity for the region and his family ties to the team. Ripken's father, Cal Sr., spent most of his adult life in the Orioles' organization as a minor-league player, scout, coach, and manager. Ripken's brother Billy enjoyed eleven seasons as a major-league second baseman and played with the Orioles from 1987 to 1992. During the 1987 season, Ripken Sr. became the first father to manage two sons on the same major-league team when he took the helm of the Orioles. Thus, for Ripken, playing for the Orioles was not merely his job, it was a connection to family, region, and identity.

Ripken retired from professional baseball in 2001 after twenty-one seasons in the major leagues. In addition to setting the new record for consecutive games played, he also garnered numerous awards and honors. Ripken became only the seventh player in major-league history to collect 3,000 hits and 400 home runs. He was also a nineteen-time All-Star, a two-time MVP of the American League, and a two-time Gold Glove winner for defensive excellence at shortstop. In a ceremony before the final home game of the 2001 season, the Baltimore Orioles retired Ripken's jersey number 8, a fitting tribute to a player whose career accomplishments will long be remembered. Ripken was inducted into the Baseball Hall of Fame in 2006.

also eclipsing the record set by Maris. The gracious relationship that Sosa and McGwire shared throughout the chase captured the collective imagination. Each player celebrated the success of the other, imbuing their competition with a sense of respect and admiration. The excitement, unpredictability, and genial air of the home-run chase exhilarated baseball fans and made the 1998 season truly special.

Like Ripken in 1995, Sosa and McGwire helped to reignite a national passion for baseball after the debilitating effects of the 1994 players' strike. While emotionally compelling and deeply meaningful, Ripken's impact hit at the end of the season and for only two nights. Fan interest was piqued, but not consistently sustained. In 1998 Sosa and McGwire battled for weeks, steadily building fan fervor and excitement until the explosive end. By the end of the 1998 season, MLB games had attracted a total of approximately 70.6 million fans. Just two seasons prior, in 1996, the total was 60 million. Undoubtedly, Sosa and McGwire's home-run chase had a significant impact on bringing fans back to baseball and imbuing the game with vitality.

Impressive as it was, McGwire's home-run record stood for only three years. In 2001 Barry Bonds hit seventy-three homers to set the new single-season record and later broke

Chicago Cubs Sammy Sosa connects for a two-run home run on a pitch from Colorado Rockies starting pitcher Darryl Kile in the first inning of the Cubs' 4-3 victory in Denver's Coors Field on Sunday, August 30, 1998. It was Sosa's fifty-fourth homer of the season. (AP / Wide World Photos)

Hank Aaron's all-time home run record of 755, finishing with 762. During the 2001 season Bonds also set new records for highest-slugging percentage at .863 and total number of walks at 177. In addition, at the age of thirty-seven, Bonds became the oldest player to lead the National League in home runs. In honor of his incredible season, Bonds was named the National League's Most Valuable Player, a title he retained for the next three seasons, as he won seven MVP awards. By 2003, however, Bonds faced intense scrutiny over allegations of his use of illegal performance-enhancing drugs. Sportswriters, fans, and baseball officials began to question the authenticity of Bonds's records from 2001, wondering if he achieved those feats through honest effort and hard work or through the use of illegal steroids. Former home-run kings McGwire and Sosa later confronted similar accusations, leading to a comprehensive review of Major League Baseball's drug policy and skepticism about the legitimacy of the home-run records. A December 2007 report, authored by former senator George Mitchell, done for Major League Baseball, named almost 100 players alleged to have used steroids or other drugs.

A counterpoint to the distressing steroid controversy emerged at the end of the 2004 season when the Boston Red Sox shattered one of baseball's most enduring myths upon winning the World Series. The Red Sox swept the St. Louis Cardinals

St. Louis Cardinals slugger Mark McGwire acknowledges the crowd in Busch Stadium after hitting his sixty-second home run of the season, Tuesday, September 8, 1998, in St. Louis. The homer, off Chicago Cubs pitcher Steve Trachsel, broke Roger Maris' single-season home-run record set in 1961. (AP/Wide World Photo)

in four games to win the crown, the team's first World Series title since 1918. For eight-six years, the Red Sox had suffered from the "Curse of the Bambino," the supposed bad luck that followed the team since trading Babe Ruth to the New York Yankees in 1920. The 2004 Red Sox team, an eclectic bunch of veteran players, created a jovial atmosphere within the clubhouse. As writer Dan Shaughnessy observed, "[T]hey were raggedy men who proudly called themselves 'idiots'" (Shaughnessy 2005, 4). Rather than promote an image of cool and detached professionalism, the members of the 2004 Red Sox team displayed their exuberant personalities on and off the field, captivating baseball fans all over the world. Three years later, the Red Sox returned to the World Series and won their second title in three years, defeating the Colorado Rockies (in their first appearance in the championship) in four straight games.

A number of pitchers also deserve mention during this time. Both Randy Johnson and Roger Clemens are five-time Cy Young Award winners, given annually to the best hurler in each league of professional baseball. Clemens's dominance spanned three decades and he won the award for the American League's Red Sox in 1986, 1987, and 1991. In 1997 and 1998 he earned the title with the Toronto Blue Jays and won again in 2001 with the New York Yankees. Johnson began in the American League with the Seattle Mariners, winning the Cy Young Award in 1995. He moved to the National League's Arizona Diamondbacks, claiming the prize in 1999, 2000, 2001 (when they won the World Series), and 2002. In 2008 Clemens faced questions regarding his truthfulness regarding the use of performance-enhancing drugs and other questionable issues of personal judgment.

Other pitchers of note include four-time Cy Young winner Greg Maddux (Chicago Cubs, 1992; Atlanta Braves, 1993, 1994, 1995—when the team won the championship) and Pedro Martinez (Montreal Expos, 1997; Boston Red Sox, 1999, 2000). This pitching has contributed to several World Series–championship teams, though between 1990 and 2005 the New York Yankee claimed four of fifteen titles (excluding the missed series of 1994). The Toronto Blue Jays and the Florida Marlins have each won two championships during this era as well.

Architecture

Starting in 1990, the landscape of American of baseball changed dramatically as teams constructed new stadiums at a rapid pace. Between 1990 and 2005, a total of seventeen new major-league ballparks were constructed. With the building of the new came the abandonment and destruction of the old. For example, Comiskey Park in Chicago, built in 1910, was demolished in 1991 to make way for U.S. Cellular Field. Detroit's Tiger Stadium, built in 1912, was deserted in 1999 as the team moved downtown to Comerica Park. Across the country, from Baltimore to San Francisco, new stadiums opened at the rate of more than one per year. This distinct period of new ballpark design and construction marked a return to traditional architectural styles. It also signaled a belief that the economic power of sport could facilitate urban revitalization and generate community development. As major pieces of the built environment, ballparks reflect the cultural tastes and values of society at the particular time they were constructed. Thus, they are not simply a passive stage upon which the drama of baseball unfolds. Each ballpark is an active part of its community and a piece of urban American history.

In 1990 stadium designers ushered in a new era of ballpark construction. Drawing inspiration from the past and playing upon powerful emotions of nostalgia, architects incorporated classical elements into the new parks and created a neotraditional style characterized by asymmetrical field dimensions, traditional building materials like brick and cast iron, and smaller seating capacities. These new stadiums combined the best features of classic parks such as Wrigley Field and Fenway Park with the modern amenities that fans expect and demand. Most of these new parks were sited in the urban core of the community, a deliberate planning decision to draw people into downtown and encourage economic development.

The pioneering ballpark of this phase was Oriole Park at Camden Yards in Baltimore. Completed in 1992 at a cost of $205.5 million, it was the cornerstone of urban development efforts to revitalize downtown Baltimore. By offering an alternative to the sterile, multipurpose super stadiums popular in the 1960s and 1970s, Oriole Park at Camden Yards successfully blended tradition with modernity. The fans responded with curiosity and excitement, as the average attendance rose to over 43,000 during the first decade of the park's existence. The success of Oriole Park at Camden Yards spurred a neotraditional ballpark boom. Other teams and cities followed the trend of building new urban ballparks that featured unique historical elements and the best of modern amenities.

Another aspect of ballpark architecture unique to this period of history is naming rights, which became an important strategy in financing the wave of new ballpark construction. The right to affix a particular name to a stadium is granted in exchange for financial support, primarily from large corporations. As taxpayers demanded more financial restraint from the municipalities that previously financed many professional sports teams and stadiums, teams were forced to seek alternative means of funding and turned to national and international corporations. In exchange for multimillion-dollar capital investments, companies received exclusive naming rights to the parks. In addition to the advertising that corporations receive from their naming rights deals, they are also able to leverage their investments beyond a simple name. For example, at Coors Field in Denver, Colorado, Coors is the only beer sold at the park.

Perhaps the most controversial case of naming rights occurred in 2001 when the Houston Astros struggled to name their new park. In 1999 the naming rights were sold to the locally based energy corporation Enron in a thirty-year, $100-million contract. The park was thus known as Enron Field. Two years later, Enron collapsed in one of the biggest corporate scandals in American history. The team bought back the naming rights from Enron, temporarily called the park Astros Field, and searched for a new corporate sponsor. In 2002 Minute Maid, the juice subsidiary of Coca-Cola, acquired the naming rights on a twenty-eight-year contract and the park was renamed Minute Maid Park. In the span of only two years, Houston's ballpark was known by three different names.

Women in Baseball

Beginning in the early 1990s, women's baseball experienced an increasing degree of organization, formalization, and professionalization. Women have played baseball since the introduction of the game in the nineteenth century, but have rarely had the opportunity to compete at the high school, collegiate, or professional level. In addition to playing the game, women have also occupied a place in baseball as fans, journalists, umpires, and administrators. Throughout the 1990s, women gained increasing access to baseball through these various means and made significant contributions to the game both on and off the field.

At the amateur level, after 1990 women's baseball leagues both grew and consolidated across the country. In 1992 a group of players and volunteers formed the American Women's Baseball Federation (AWBF) to organize and promote baseball as a mainstream and lifetime sport for women. The AWBF serves as an umbrella organization for more than twenty-five women's teams from Boston to Seattle, providing networking services for the teams and overseeing domestic and international tournaments. In 2001 the AWBF played an instrumental role in creating the Women's World Series, an international competition held from 2001 to 2004 that attracted elite teams from the United States, Australia, Canada, and Japan. In 2004 the newly formed Women's World Cup of Baseball eclipsed the Women's World Series as the premiere international tournament. Sanctioned by the International Baseball Federation to run on a biannual basis, the Women's World Cup was first held in Edmonton, Canada, in 2004 and featured teams from the United States, Canada, Australia, Japan, and Taiwan. Bulgaria and India were also scheduled to compete but withdrew before the tournament began. The team from the United States, chosen by officials from USA Baseball, won the gold medal. With support from the International Baseball Federation, the Women's World Cup will be held through at least 2012.

Prior to the advent of organized women's teams and leagues, girls and women interested in playing baseball had to find ways to play with boys and men. In the 1990s Julie Croteau and Ila Borders were pioneers in securing a woman's right to play baseball with men. Croteau grew up playing Little League baseball and intended to play baseball on the boy's varsity team in high school. In 1988 the high school coach cut her from the team on the grounds that baseball wasn't an appropriate sport for a girl. In response, Croteau sued the school for the right to play on the boys' team. She lost the case, but she did not lose the desire to keep playing baseball and walked on to the men's baseball team at St. Mary's College (Division III) in 1989, where she played first base for three seasons. By doing so, she became recognized as the first woman to play men's NCAA college baseball on a regular basis (in 1985, Susan Perabo had pitched in one game for Webster College). After college, Croteau continued her career in baseball by coaching the men's teams at Western New England College (Division III). In 1995 she joined the coaching staff at the University of Massachusetts–Amherst as an assistant, thereby becoming the first woman to coach men's baseball at the NCAA Division I level. Since 2004 she has worked as a coach for the U.S. women's national baseball team, helping to ensure that future generations of girls and women have the chance to play baseball at the highest levels.

Like Croteau, Ila Borders had to fight to play baseball. After being rebuffed by her local high school's baseball team, Borders enrolled in a private high school and made the boys' varsity team as a freshman. She played on the boys' team throughout high school and received the team's MVP award as a senior in 1993. Eager to continue playing baseball, Borders accepted an offer to play ball at Southern California College (National Association of Intercollegiate Athletics). Her pitching debut came in 1994, accompanied by constant media attention and opposing players unhappy at the prospect of striking out against a woman. Borders played at Southern California College for three seasons and then transferred to Whittier College (Division III) for her final collegiate season in 1997. At Whittier College, Borders pitched in seventeen games and recorded thirty-eight strikeouts. Immediately following her college graduation, Borders signed with the St. Paul Saints of the Independent Northern League, fulfilling her dream of playing professional baseball. She became the first woman to pitch in a men's professional baseball game in the summer of 1997. In 1999 *Sports Illustrated* named Borders among the 100 top female athletes of all time for her groundbreaking play and dedication to baseball. After spending three seasons in the Northern League, she moved on to the Western Baseball League in 2000. Halfway through the season, exhausted by life on the road and ready for a new direction, Borders retired from professional baseball. Her accomplishments are recognized in a display on women in baseball at the National Baseball Hall of Fame.

While Croteau and Borders negotiated the terrain of men's collegiate and professional baseball, another group of women became part of an experiment to create an all-women's pro baseball team. Formed in 1994, the Colorado Silver Bullets was the first all-women's professional team to play in the United States since the folding of the All-American Girls Professional Baseball League in 1954. It was also the first and only all-women's team to be officially recognized by the National Association of Professional Baseball Leagues, a distinction that opened up playing opportunities for the team across the country. Sponsored by the Coors Brewing Company and managed by former major league pitcher Phil Niekro, the Silver Bullets recruited players through a series of open tryouts held in eleven cities. Of the approximately 1300 women who tried out, Niekro chose twenty-four for the final roster. Starting in 1994, the team played a barnstorming schedule of games against minor-league, semipro, college, and amateur men's teams. In their first season, the Silver Bullets played forty-four games but won only six. By 1997 the team achieved a winning record and won a total of twenty-three games. After four years of sponsorship during which it invested $8 million in the team, the Coors Brewing Company withdrew its financial support after the 1997 season. Unable to find a sponsor for the 1998 season, the team disbanded after four years of play. Although the experiment was short-lived, the Colorado Silver Bullets proved that women could play baseball at the men's professional level. Perhaps more important, the members of the Silver Bullets embodied the notion that baseball is a sport accessible to all.

Doping in Baseball

Similar to other sports such as cycling, swimming, and track and field, baseball is not immune to doping scandals. The troubles and speculations began in late 1998 when Mark McGwire admitted to using the performance-enhancing drug androstenedione, or "andro." At the time, andro was not illegal in MLB so McGwire did not receive an official reprimand. His public reputation, however, was tainted. Journalists, fans, and casual observers who had been so electrified by McGwire's home-run chase during the 1998 season now questioned the authenticity and honesty of his efforts.

Responding to such speculations, MLB implemented random drug testing in its minor-league system in 2001 to determine the use performance-enhancing drugs and recreational drugs. Charging that this program did not adequately address the issue of doping in professional baseball, the U.S. Senate Commerce Committee convened a hearing in 2002 to demand the negotiation of a major-league drug-testing program. After collaborating with the MLBPA to construct an appropriate policy, MLB began survey testing in 2003 to gauge the use of steroids at the major-league level. The anonymous tests were administered to all major-league players at the beginning of the 2003 season. Ultimately, the survey reported that 5–7 percent of the players tested positive for performance-enhancing drugs, though no one was punished.

The need for an overarching drug testing program became clear in early 2003 when Steve Bechler, a pitcher for the Baltimore Orioles, collapsed and died during a spring training workout. An autopsy revealed that Bechler had died of cardiac arrest brought on by the abuse of the performance-enhancing drug Ephedra. As a result of Bechler's death, MLB (and other professional organizations and universities) placed Ephedra on its list of banned substances but did not implement a formal drug-testing program at the major-league level. In December 2003 ten major-league ballplayers testified before a grand jury in the case against the Bay Area Laboratory Co-Operative (BALCO), a private company under investigation for providing illegal performance-enhancing drugs and steroids to prominent athletes. Barry Bonds, Jason Giambi, and Gary Sheffield were among the ballplayers who testified against BALCO. None of the players were charged with using steroids, and none of them were sanctioned for their involvement with the drug company.

The BALCO scandal prompted the U.S. Senate Commerce Committee to take action again in 2004. The committee held a second hearing on MLB's drug program and concluded that the existing policy was not strong enough to deter drug and steroid use. In conjunction with the Committee and the Players' Association, MLB drafted a new Joint Drug Agreement. Under this agreement, players were guaranteed anonymity upon a positive test and the punishment for a first offense was counseling. While this agreement appeased the committee, it lacked a structure for repeated offenses and sheltered guilty players from the public. The problem of doping in baseball was further reiterated in 2004 when Ken Caminiti, a former MVP of the National League, died at the age of forty-four from the combined effects of opiates, cocaine abuse, and coronary disease. Later in the year, President Bush signed the Anabolic Steroid Control Act of 2004. In response, MLB adopted the list of banned substances recorded in the act.

Pressured to strengthen its drug policy, MLB formulated a new program of testing and penalties in early 2005. Major-league baseball players would now be subject to random testing for performance-enhancing drugs. Upon the first positive result, the player's name would be released to the public and he would be suspended for ten days with no pay. A second offense netted a thirty-day suspension, the third offense resulted in a sixty-day suspension, and a fourth offense equated to a one-year ban from the game. Speculations about rampant drug use in baseball rose after the 2003 release of former major leaguer Jose Canseco's book *Juiced*, an exposé that detailed his use of steroids and implicated several of his teammates. When MLB officials refused to investigate the allegations in Canseco's book, the U.S. Congress decided to intervene. The House Government Reform Committee then issued subpoenas to MLB executives and players in an effort to determine the extent of the drug problem in professional baseball. Players who testified at the hearing included Jose Canseco, Mark McGwire, and Sammy Sosa. Later hearings in 2008 followed the release of the Mitchell Report for Major League Baseball in December 2007. This named more than seventy-five major-leaguers who seemed to have used prformance-enhancing drugs, including two top pitchers on the New York Yankees, Andy Pettite and Roger Clemens.

Shortly after the 2004 hearing, Alex Sanchez became the first major league player to test positive for performance-enhancing drugs under the Joint Drug Program. Per the policy, his name was released to the media and he was suspended for ten days. By the end of the 2005 season, a total of eight major-leaguers tested positive and received suspensions; in the minor leagues, eighty-two players tested positive. Clearly, drug use in American professional baseball had become a matter of significant concern.

By November 2005 Major League Baseball, the Players' Association, and Congress had reached an agreement on a substantial overhaul of the existing drug program. The new policy included stringent penalties and authorized testing for amphetamine use. Upon testing positive for the first time, a player's name will be released to the public and he will be suspended for fifty games without pay. A second offense results in a 100-game suspension, and the third offense is just cause for a lifetime ban from the game. This strong policy was the next step in a continually evolving process of monitoring and preventing the use of performance-enhancing drugs in baseball. In the course of seven years, the issue of drug and steroid use went from minor concern to major problem.

Basketball

Since 1990 significant changes have occurred within U.S. basketball. At the NBA level, a generation of superstars left and younger athletes took the league to unforeseen levels of popularity and success, both at home and abroad. Along with that success, players, teams, and leagues saw unprecedented amounts of money change hands through contracts, ticket sales, media contracts, and merchandising. Women established professional leagues and the NCAA Final Four became the largest revenue-producing annual women's sporting event in the country. Nike's sales outpaced Adidas' for the first time, largely due to its contract with Michael Jordan. Across all levels the concept of the "three-peat" became a hallmark of successful competition: the NBA's Chicago Bulls, Los Angeles Lakers, and Houston Comets, and the University of Tennessee Lady Volunteers and the University of Connecticut Huskies women's basketball teams all accomplished this at least once.

Michael Jordan of the Chicago Bulls in action.
(Courtesy of Photofest)

The San Antonio Spurs and the Duke University Blue Devils men's basketball team also won at least three nonconsecutive championships of their own. Though basketball was predominantly an American game in 1990, it is now a global phenomenon. Its international significance was demonstrated by the dramatic increase of foreign players drafted into the NBA, moving selected preseason NBA games to Asia, the United States' failure to win the gold medal in the 2004 Olympics in Athens, and the possibility of five new European franchises in a new NBA European division.

The National Basketball Association

The concept of "sportainment"—the blurring of boundaries between what constitutes sport and what constitutes entertainment—is particularly apparent in professional basketball. During much of the 1990s there was a division among NBA athletes between those classified as "competitors" such as Scottie Pippen, David Robinson, Patrick Ewing, Hakeem Olujawon, and those considered "entertainers" such as Charles Barkley and Dennis Rodman. The "competitors" were perhaps best known for their achievements on the court while the "entertainers" were known almost equally for their basketball prowess as for their off-the-court words, behaviors, and personalities. As Shaquille O'Neal once said, "I'm a basketball player slash entertainer. Basketball is entertainment."

Perhaps no other team reflects this sentiment better than the Los Angeles Lakers, who revived their ascendancy in the mid- to late 1990s with the addition of O'Neal, wunderkind Kobe Bryant, and coach Phil Jackson, winning three consecutive championships in 2000, 2001, and 2002. One of the NBA's most successful franchises in terms of both performance and economic success, the Lakers have a large number of celebrity fans in attendance at their home venues (the Forum until 1999 and later the Staples Center), which underscores the elision of sport and entertainment.

Lakers coach Phil Jackson established himself as one of the greatest in the game during his tenure with the Chicago Bulls from 1989 to 1998. His six NBA titles with the Bulls, combined with his additional three with the Lakers, tied him with famed coach Red Auerbach for the record number of championships. By no means was Jackson the sole ingredient for the Bulls' success, for he was joined by some of the best players the game has ever known, including "His Airness," Michael Jordan. The Bulls began their first run in the 1990–91 season when they totaled a franchise-record sixty-one wins en route to a five-game championship over the Lakers. The Bulls' second title of this era came the next season against the

Portland Trail Blazers, and they capped their "three-peat" over the Phoenix Suns the following year. Though he did not do it alone, Jordan was awarded the Finals MVP and scoring champion in each of the three championships.

Jordan briefly retired in 1993 following the murder of his father, and then rejoined the Chicago Bulls with a succinct press release: "I'm back." The next two years belonged to the Houston Rockets. Coached by former-Rocket player Rudy Tomjanovich, players including Hakeem Olajuwon and Clyde Drexler, who had been former teammates at the University of Houston, claimed the 1994 and 1995 championships. In 1995 Jordan rejoined his Bulls teammates and, along with Scottie Pippen, Ron Harper, Luc Longley, and the always-controversial rebound specialist Dennis Rodman, the team began another streak—their second "three-peat" in 1996, 1997, and 1998 over the Seattle SuperSonics, and twice over the Utah Jazz, respectively. The Bulls also had an NBA record-setting seventy-two wins in the 1995–96 season. The end to the Bulls' dominance was punctuated by Jordan's shot over Utah's Byron Russell in the last seconds of the championship game. After the 1998 victory Chicago's roster was dismantled. The Bulls traded Pippen, Longley, and Steve Kerr and did not re-sign Rodman. Phil Jackson left the game and vowed never to return to coaching (he changed his mind after a year to coach the Lakers) and Jordan entered his second retirement, but again his hiatus was brief. He returned to the NBA to play two final seasons with the Washington Wizards, for a remarkable professional career that spanned three decades.

Jordan tested his talents in many different arenas during his two short retirements, including a short stint playing minor-league baseball. He also played himself in the lead role of the movie *Space Jam*, the message of which was consistent with Jordan's public persona: if you believe in yourself and work hard, anything is possible. During his second retirement, he joined the front-office staff of the Washington Wizards. In addition to his advertising campaigns, his own shoe and apparel line, and his front-office work, Jordan has also published several autobiographical books.

Throughout this long and successful career, Jordan established himself as not only the most talented and competitive player in the league, but also the most marketable player in NBA history. He has supplemented his lucrative, record-setting contracts with the Bulls with endorsement deals estimated at several hundred million dollars. But as much as he has profited from these deals, those who employed him have profited more. Tickets to Bulls' games, both home and away, consistently sold out when Jordan donned their red and black uniform. In addition, studies demonstrate that the products for which he serves as the spokesman have made over $1 billion because of the association with "His Airness" (Mathur, Mathur, and Rangan 1997).

The amount of money involved in professional basketball as a part of the entertainment industry has increased drastically since 1990, as reflected in the salary demands of younger players like Kevin Garnett. Taking advantage of what became known as the "Larry Bird Exception" (a rule that allowed a team to exceed the NBA's salary cap to re-sign a player) Garnett inked a six-year contract extension with the Minnesota Timberwolves for an unprecedented $126 million in 1997, following the expiration of his rookie contract. This would become a primary dispute between owners and players, resulting in a lockout during the 1998–99 season. The result of the lockout was a drastically shortened season and a new collective

Air Jordan, Michael Jordan

Although there were many amazing athletes in the NBA from 1990 to 2005, none created or epitomized the ideals of American basketball more than Michael Jordan (born February 17, 1963). Quite simply, he stands as the league's undisputed "greatest of all time." According to an ESPN survey he is North America's top athlete, in any sport, of the twentieth century ("Top North American Athletes of the Century"). Jordan's individual athletic accolades are simply too numerous to list in the space provided here; suffice it to say that they include multiple MVP and All-Star honors, scoring and steals titles, defensive awards, two Olympic gold medals, and appearance on a record forty-nine *Sports Illustrated* covers. Beyond the court, Jordan's charisma, talent, and playing style have been channeled into unprecedented, and unparalleled, marketing campaigns by the NBA, Nike, Gatorade, Coca-Cola, Ballpark Franks, McDonalds, Wheaties, Chevrolet, Hanes, and others.

As a young shooting guard poised to redefine the world of basketball, Michael Jordan was drafted by the Chicago Bulls from the University of North Carolina in 1984. His prolific scoring and unbelievable slam-dunks, in which he did not just jump, but seemed to defy gravity, earned him the nickname "Air Jordan," which he parlayed into his own brand of shoes. First released in 1984, Nike has put out a version of "Air Jordans" each subsequent year, which have been in consistent consumer demand, often selling for hundreds of dollars. By 1990, he was an international sporting celebrity, scoring a personal record sixty-nine points in a single game. In the midst of winning the first of his six championships with the Chicago Bulls in the 1990–91 season, Jordan signed a marketing deal with Gatorade, appearing in a commercial featuring a jingle on the desire to be "like Mike," a sentiment that resonated with a large segment of the population. Indeed, many people—in all sports and, indeed, all walks of life—are quick to cite Jordan as their role model, athletic or otherwise.

Although we can try to quantify the number of titles he has earned, points he has scored, endorsement deals he has landed, and impact he has had on sport and society, in truth, the influence of the Jordan factor is incalculable. It would be difficult to overstate the importance of Michael Jordan's importance to the game of basketball or to overemphasize his enormous talent. As Laker's star, Earvin "Magic" Johnson, once remarked, "There's Michael Jordan and then there is the rest of us."

---

bargaining agreement (CBA) restructuring the salary cap regulations, all but eliminating the "Larry Bird Exception." Under the new agreement, players are limited to the amount of money they can earn from their teams, based on their years of playing experience, years played for a particular team, and how valuable their talents are perceived to be to that team.

The NBA also grew in global significance during this time, influenced by the marketing success of Michael Jordan, as well as Commissioner David Stern's commitment to his "Basketball Without Borders" campaign. Though international players in the NBA were not a new phenomenon in 1990, by 2007 the percentage of NBA players, especially NBA stars whose preprofessional basketball training occurred entirely overseas, increased significantly. Following in the footsteps of players like Vlade Divac from Yugoslavia and Arvydas Sabonis from the former USSR, Toni Kukoc, a Croatian and NBA champion with Jordan's Chicago Bulls, was one of the most touted internationally trained picks of the 1993 draft. Around the turn of the twenty-first century, rising stars such as Dirk Nowitzki from Germany, Tony Parker from France, Yao Ming from China, and Manu Ginobili from Argentina were perceived to be the next generation of NBA superstars. The global popularity of Ming, the first player from an international league to be the number 1 selection in the draft, inspired the NBA to begin to play selected preseason games in China. The NBA also opened up All-Star voting to international fans via the Internet and Ming broke Jordan's record for most All-Star votes in a season.

As international talent flooded the NBA, Americans searched for the next homegrown talent to fill the void left by Jordan's exit. Though many players such as Kobe Bryant, Kevin Garnett, Allen Iverson, and Tracy McGrady took turns as the leading candidate for this title, it was a teenaged player who captured fans' attention and inspired ESPN to start national broadcasting of high school games. LeBron James, who dominated Ohio high school basketball and became the first overall selection by the Cleveland Cavaliers in 2003, was compared and contrasted to Jordan in many ways. Aside from their undeniable talents, James had been born after Jordan's rookie season and was drafted just months after Jordan's final retirement. Money was another part of the equation, including James' $100 million in endorsement contracts—the most money any first-year player had been guaranteed before securing his first NBA contract. In 2007 he led his Cleveland Cavaliers team to the NBA Finals where they lost to the San Antonio Spurs. The 2003 draft was the last time that players were allowed enter the league straight out of high school.

Despite the enormous increase in the marketing of the league and its superstars, the NBA did not escape negative publicity. Several high-profile incidents, including the rape trial of Kobe Bryant—charges that were ultimately dismissed—damaged the reputation of the sport and the individuals involved. Another blow to the NBA's profile occurred in 2004 when, during the second half of a tightly contested game between the Indiana Pacers and Detroit Pistons, members of both teams erupted in violence that spilled off the hardwood. The brawl continued, involving both players and fans, and the game was called off. The NBA gave Pacers' Ron Artest, who entered the stands and punched a spectator, a season-long suspension and served several other players with various sanctions. Both players and fans were investigated and, when deemed appropriate, were charged with assault in a Michigan court. Yet despite this and other troubles that have plagued the league in recent years, the NBA boasts some of the most successful and exciting competition in all of sport.

Women's Professional Basketball

In the late 1990s women's basketball was taken to unprecedented heights with the launch of two professional leagues. During the winter of 1996–97 the American Basketball League (ABL) played its first season, promoting the best talent and largest salaries available in women's basketball to cities where college and high school teams had already established success. Despite concerns about competing with the NBA, the NHL, the NFL, and both NCAA football and basketball, organizers decided that the women's professional league would benefit most from playing during the traditional winter basketball season. Unfortunately, this would

WNBA basketball players (*from left*) Lynette Woodard (Detroit Shock) and Sheryl Swoopes (Houston Comets), shown in 1998. (Courtesy of Photofest)

later be one of the largest factors leading to the ABL's collapse following its second season of competition.

The other issue that sank the ABL was the success of the second women's professional league, the Women's National Basketball Association (WNBA), which had the financial backing of the NBA. The WNBA began its inaugural season during the summer of 1997, competing with the ABL for talent from international leagues, the 1996 Olympic team, and the college level. Due to the higher salaries and a longer season, most of the high-profile, highly sought athletes signed with the ABL. Stars Lisa Leslie, Sheryl Swoopes, and Rebecca Lobo, however, opted to join the WNBA, citing the summer season and the financial endorsement of the NBA as significant decision-making factors. Since then, the league has grown in excitement, talent level, and sustainability; indeed, former NBA great Bill Russell once predicted that the WNBA might someday overcome the NBA in popularity due to its emphasis on fundamentals and team play that basketball purists crave.

The WNBA began with eight teams in 1997 and has consistently added teams (and lost two) to create the fourteen-team league of today. There are seven Western Conference teams and seven Eastern Conference teams that begin their season in May, hoping to meet in the October finals. The league began with the advertising slogan "We Got Next," referencing the playground call for "dibs" on the next game on the court and staking their claim on the future of the sport. Within a few years, the league's marketing catchphrase became "We Got Game," a claim that cannot be disputed once fans have the opportunity to witness the phenomenal level of play that these athletes consistently exhibit. In order to remain economically viable, however, the WNBA must develop a successful strategy to market its product and increase its fan base.

The College Game

With the opportunity to play professionally and the prevalence of athletic female role models, the popularity of the sport at the youth level has increased accordingly and collegiate women's basketball has never been more exciting. The same year that the WNBA and the ABL were launched, ESPN signed a multiyear, multimillion-dollar contract with the NCAA for the television rights to the women's Final Four. At the time, this contract was the largest in women's sports history.

Led by Pat Summitt's University of Tennessee Lady Volunteers, college women's basketball experienced extreme growth during the 1990s. The winningest coach in

NCAA history, Summit took her team to three consecutive national championships in 1996, 1997, and 1998, a streak perhaps not possible without the phenomenal talents of players like Chamique Holdsclaw. But Tennessee's dominance was challenged by the formation of a new dynasty: the University of Connecticut Huskies. After winning the first national championship in school history in 1995, the team, led by coach Geno Auriemma, repeated the accomplishment in 2000, 2002, 2003, and 2004. In fact, between 1995 and 2008, aside from UConn and Tennessee, the only other teams to win national championships were Purdue University (1999), Notre Dame (2001) Baylor (2005), and Maryland (2006), with Tennessee winning in 2007 and 2008. As such, the rivalry between the Vols and Huskies is incredibly intense, which has led to the airing of their regular-season games on network television and the public recognition of names like Diana Taurasi, Jennifer Rizzotti, Tamika Catching, Swin Cash, Candace Parker, and Sue Bird.

Not to be left out, the University of Connecticut men's basketball team also won the national championship in 2004. Led by international player and Rhodes scholar Emeka Okafor, the University of Connecticut became the first NCAA Division I institution to win both the men's and women's titles in the same season. The victory of UConn's men's team temporarily drew attention away from perennial powerhouse teams like Duke, University of Kentucky, University of North Carolina, University of Kansas, and UCLA. Duke won national championships in 1991, 1992, and 2001, and multiple ACC championships, and made several Final Four appearances under the tutelage of "Coach K" (Mike Krzyzewski), who began his reign in 1981. Duke's rivalry with the University of North Carolina Tar Heels—with just eight miles separating the two campuses—is among the most exciting in all of sport. Duke boasts the all-time consecutive appearance record at the NCAA tournament with twenty-seven straight performances between 1975 and 2001.

In addition to exciting competition, men's college basketball in the years between 1990 and 2007 was also marred by several scandals. The college game was not immune to the increasing commercialization of sport and, with role models like Jordan, James, and Garnett, many boys and young men dreamed of million-dollar paychecks. In 1992 the University of Michigan made history by starting five freshmen (nicknamed the "Fab Five") in the national tournament and the group repeated their NCAA Finals appearance in 1993. Later, it was revealed that the players, the school, and supporters of the program had been involved in illegal activities, and the investigative findings resulted in the negation of their success in the early 1990s.

Suspicions involving the Michigan basketball program first arose when players were involved in a car accident. There were immediate concerns about whether player Robert Traylor owned the expensive car that he was driving at the time of the crash and it was soon determined that players involved had taken a recruit to visit Michigan booster Ed Martin—an NCAA violation. A subsequent investigation revealed that Martin had given hundreds of thousands of dollars in cash and other gifts to members of basketball team and their families, including future NBA star Chris Webber, who profited from the corruption while still in high school. Furthermore, Martin's money came in part from his illegal gambling operation, which he then laundered by giving it to those associated with Michigan's program as well as potential high school prospects. The scandal rocked the world of collegiate athletics and it was arguably the largest, most corrupt, and most flagrant infringement of NCAA rules in the history of sport.

As a result, Michigan voluntarily forfeited 112 regular-season and tournament wins, as well as its semifinal victory in the 1992 NCAA tournament. The school took down the associated banners from its arena, removed mention of the accolades from its programs and media guides, and returned the $450,000 awarded by the NCAA for its postseason play. The NCAA handed down additional sanctions, including suspending the program from postseason play in the 2003–4 season, placing it on probation for four years, eliminating one scholarship, and requiring the school to disassociate itself from the four players named in the scandal for the next ten years.

The issue of players' age and experience level was again brought to public attention after Kevin Garnett became the first player drafted straight out of high school into the NBA and college basketball faced greater challenges in recruiting young talent. This, as well as the demand for high-caliber basketball, contributed to a series of NCAA violations. When the NBA created the age requirement for the 2004 draft, it was greeted with mixed emotion among colleges and universities. Some welcomed the opportunity to coach the nation's best high school players even if it was only for a year, others warned against the detriments of this rule and the implications that the college game would be reduced to a farm system for the NBA. In a related controversy, Division I men's college basketball reports an abysmally low college graduation rate. It is argued that the belief that college basketball can be used as a stepping-stone to the professional level—whether that dream is achieved or not—is a contributing factor to the lack of players receiving their diplomas.

Other scandals in college hoops revolve around academic dishonesty and gambling. In the 1990s Arizona State University and Northwestern University basketball players were embroiled in point-shaving and bribery controversies. The day before the University of Minnesota was scheduled to compete in the 1999 NCAA tournament, a local newspaper reported that an academic counselor at the school claimed that over the course of several years she had written hundreds of papers for at least twenty athletes on the Gopher squad. Several players were suspended and disqualified from the tournament and the university launched an investigation into the allegations. A number of prominent members of the Gophers' athletic department resigned or lost their jobs as a result, including the athletic director and others; the university bought out head coach Clem Haskins's $1.5-million contract. In 2000 Haskins admitted to paying the academic counselor $3,000 for her services. Further evidence surfaced to suggest the coach had been involved in mail fraud, had given money to his players, covered up allegations of sexual harassment against his athletes, and attempted to inflate his players' grades in order for them to remain eligible to compete. The NCAA conducted further investigations and determined that the school would forfeit all awards and titles dating back to the 1993–94 season.

Other coaches involved in controversies during this time included Jerry Tarkanian, who repeatedly clashed with the NCAA throughout his career. Tarkanian, who coached at UNLV from 1973 to 1992, brought the Running Rebels their first and only national championship in 1990. He also brought the school numerous NCAA sanctions. Leaving UNLV in 1992, he returned to his alma mater Fresno

State, where he coached the Bulldogs from 1995 to 2002. Following his retirement, the NCAA found that the school had committed a number of violations during Tarkanian's reign and placed the school on probation.

A friend and peer of Tarkanian's, Bobby Knight—"The General"—deserves mention for both the success he achieved and the controversies he caused in men's college basketball. Knight spent the majority of his career at the University of Indiana, where he coached the Hoosiers from 1971 to 2000, winning three national championships in the process. Currently, Knight has won more NCAA Division I men's basketball games than any other coach in history, but a number of high-profile, damaging events have dotted his career. These incidents came to a head in 2000, when a former player asserted that the coach had choked him during a 1997 practice, a charge later substantiated by videotaped evidence of the assault. In response, Indiana's president announced a "zero tolerance" policy for Knight's behavior.

The policy was enacted shortly thereafter, when Knight allegedly physically and verbally assaulted an IU student who the coach felt did not show him proper respect (it was reported the student addressed him by saying "Hey, Knight, what's up?"). Though Knight denied he had touched the student, he was asked to resign. He refused and IU stripped him of his post. Thousands of Indiana students converged to protest his dismissal and Knight remains a popular figure in the state. He continued his career at Texas Tech University and although his coaching techniques and dictatorial style are often critiqued, with Knight at the helm the program quickly improved. It should also be noted that despite his often less-than-praiseworthy behavior, the NCAA has never sanctioned Knight for any recruiting violations and his teams consistently boast higher-than-average graduation rates.

Professional Football

American football during the 1990s and first years of the twenty-first century was characterized by organizational changes, economic growth, phenomenal athletic achievements, and tremendous expansion. Technological advances surged and the media infiltrated every aspect of the sport. The NFL crossed continents, women's professional football leagues were established, and collegiate football endeavored to crown an undisputed national champion.

The National Football League

The post-1990 NFL experienced incredible change, and football fans witnessed some of the most legendary performances by coaches and players to date. With professional football frequently named the favorite spectator sport of the American public, the NFL took great strides to ensure its continued popularity. One of the most notable ventures occurred in 1993 with the signing of the CBA by the NFL and the NFL Players Association. The agreement marked the most extensive benefits package in professional sports and secured more than $1 billion in health, pension, and retirement assistance for active and retired players. The agreement was extended five times between 1993 and 2006.

Numerous record-breaking performances took place during this time as well. While not necessarily a boast-worthy accomplishment, the Buffalo Bills suffered four disappointing losses in the 1991–94 Super Bowls, a league record. More positively, Don Shula became the winningest coach in NFL history on November 14, 1993, when his Miami Dolphins beat the Philadelphia Eagles. The win marked Shula's 325th, putting him ahead of a record set by the legendary George Halas nearly three decades earlier. The Dallas Cowboys became the first NFL team to win three Super Bowls in four seasons with their 1993, 1994, and 1996 victories, and the New England Patriots became the second team to achieve this feat with their 2002, 2004, and 2005 Super Bowl wins. John Elway and the Denver Broncos took home back-to-back Super Bowl championships in 1998 and 1999, giving the team its first titles after four failed attempts. Quarterback Steve Young broke out in 1991 with an opportunity to fill in for the legendary San Francisco 49ers' quarterback, Joe Montana. In the years that followed, Young would throw for 3,000 or more yards in six of his eight starting seasons with the 49ers, rushing for forty-three touchdowns en route to a Super Bowl XXIX victory in 1994 and two NFL MVP titles (1992, 1994). He earned six passing titles between 1991 and 1997, tying him with Sammy Baugh for the most passing crowns in league history. Young was inducted into the Football Hall of Fame in 2005, the first left-handed quarterback to be selected.

Denver Broncos quarterback John Elway warms up before the team's 40-14 victory over the Oakland Raiders in Denver's Mile High Stadium on November 22, 1998. Elway became the second quarterback in NFL history to surpass the 50,000-mark in passing yardage during the victory, which moved the Broncos' season record to 11-0. (AP / Wide World Photo)

Any discussion of professional football would be incomplete without mentioning the Dallas Cowboys. Dubbed "America's Team" in the 1970s, the Cowboys reached a low point in franchise history in the 1980s, leading new owner Jerry Jones to fire hall-of-fame coach Tom Landry in 1989. Under the helm of the new coach, Jimmy Johnson, along with the acquisition of standout athletes like Troy Aikman and Emmitt Smith, the Cowboys quickly regained their prominence in the league. In 1992 and 1993 the team met the Buffalo Bills in the Super Bowl finals, coming out on top in both matchups. With Johnson's win in Super Bowl XXVII, he became the first football coach to win championships at the collegiate (as coach at the University of Miami) and professional level. Constantly clashing with owner Jones, Johnson surprised the country by announcing his resignation following Super Bowl XXVIII (1994) and was replaced by the University of Oklahoma's coach Barry Switzer. The team won Super Bowl XXX for their fifth title, but began a downward slump in 1997. Despite this trend, the Cowboys won more games in the 1990s than any other team in the NFL.

Professional football experienced expansion both at home and abroad. The league introduced four new franchises: the Carolina Panthers and Jacksonville Jaguars in 1993, the new Cleveland Browns in 1998 following their relocation to Baltimore and renaming to Ravens in 1996, and the Houston Texans in 1999. This growth caused a realignment of the thirty-two-team league into eight four-team divisions in 2001. In 1991 the NFL went global, forming the World League of American Football, which consisted of ten teams competing in the United Stated and Europe. The league took a two-year break in 1993 and reestablished itself for the 1995 season as the World League and became NFL Europe in 1997, NFL Europa in 2006, and terminated shortly thereafter in 2007.

Along with expansion, the NFL experienced a number of other organizational alterations. Draft eligibility was changed during the 1990 season, allowing college juniors to enter the draft but requiring them to relinquish their collegiate eligibility. This decision was hotly debated because of the rising numbers of college athletes who failed to graduate as a result of turning professional. The playoff format was also modified that year, with the addition of two wild-card teams, one for each conference, bringing the total to six wild-card spots. The use of limited instant replay was eliminated in 1992 after six consecutive seasons in the league, and a new system would not be put into place until 1999. Instant replay was once again permitted and allowed coaches the opportunity to challenge referee calls on the field and be penalized with the loss of a time-out if their challenge did not result in an overturned call.

Leading up the 1994 season were a series of rule modifications designed to increase offensive production, including the introduction of the two-point conversion, moving the kick-off point back to the thirty-yard line, and modifying roughing-the-passer rules. That same year the NFL launched one of the most comprehensive drug and alcohol policies ever seen in professional sports. League administrators strengthened this policy even more in 2005 when the NFL announced it would be adopting Olympic testing standards to combat illegal steroid use. This increased the number of random drug tests players could be subjected to during the off-season from two to six, added several substances to the list of banned products, and made it possible to test for what had been previously undetectable "designer" drugs.

Advances in media technology and aggressive advertising allowed American football to reach new markets, increasing both the commercialization and popularity of the sport. Television contracts have been at once lucrative for the league and costly for television networks as revenue generated by advertisements during the games fail to meet the astronomical costs required to secure broadcast rights of the NFL. Agreements authorized in 1990 between the NFL and ABC, NBC, CBS, TNT, and ESPN for broadcasting the 1990 to 1993 seasons totaled $3.6 billion and were the largest in television history. The satellite channel NFL Network was launched in 2003, becoming the first television programming service entirely devoted to the sport. In 1993 CBS, which had aired National Football Conference (NFC) games for thirty-eight years, lost the broadcast rights to FOX Network in a bidding war that reached $1.58 billion over a four-year period. The deal made FOX a major player in network television, while CBS felt a tremendous loss. FOX extended this contract in 1998, paying $4.4 billion over the next eight years to the NFL. CBS, still reeling from the loss of NFC programming, acquired the rights to American Football Conference (AFC) games in 1998, a move that squeezed out NBC from broadcasting NFL games.

Audience records were surpassed nearly every year between 1990 and 2007 and the Super Bowl became one of the most anticipated annual television broadcasts. Contributing to the entertainment value of the broadcast were the commercials that aired and sponsors cashed in on the interest in the ads; in 2008, a thirty-second commercial during the Super Bowl sold for $2.6 million. In addition to the game, the commercials, and the opportunity to gather with friends and family, the Super Bowl halftime show generates significant viewer interest. The Super Bowl has featured a number of popular and high profile artists through the years, including Michael Jackson, the Rolling Stones, Tom Petty and many others. It seems, however, that no halftime show generated more interest, more controversy, or will linger in American memory longer than the 2004 performance of Janet Jackson and Justine Timberlake. At the end of their sexually charged duet "Rock Your Body," Timberlake tore a piece off Jackson's costume and revealed her breast to millions of spectators. Both claimed that the nudity was unintentional, calling it a "wardrobe malfunction," and no one could have predicted the ensuing aftermath.

The Federal Communications Commission (FCC) received over 535,000 complaints from viewers regarding the incident and multiple lawsuits were launched against Timberlake and Jackson regarding the so-called indecency of their actions. Although both performers, as well as Viacom (the parent company of CBS and MTV), the NFL, and the show's sponsor, AOL, apologized, the FCC fined Viacom $550,000: $27,500 for twenty of the CBS-owned television stations that broadcasted the exposure. The NFL refunded AOL the $10 million they had paid to sponsor the event and forbade MTV from ever producing another half-time show. Viacom paid an additional $3.5-million settlement regarding the event and the U.S. House of Representatives passed a bill that raised the maximum penalty for FCC violations from $27,500 to $325,000 per violation. As a result, many networks now require time delays for live broadcasts.

Women's Professional Football

In 1999 the "No Limits" Barnstorming Tour featured some of the best women athletes across the country competing in football exhibition games. The success of the experimental season resulted in the formation of the Women's Professional

Football League (WPFL), an eleven-team, two-conference, four-division league in 2000. The year 2000 also saw the formation of two additional football leagues for women, the National Women's Football Association (NWFA) and the Independent Women's Football League (IWFL).

Created by sport entrepreneur Catherine Masters, the NWFA originated with two teams, the Alabama Renegades and the Nashville Dream, who showcased six exhibition games from October to December 2000. Another eight teams were added for the 2001 season, eleven more for 2003, and eventually as many as thirty-five teams operated under the NWFA. The IWFL was created in 2000 with the intent to foster a safe environment for women athletes and bring nationwide credibility to the emerging sport of women's tackle football. Operating on a different level than the other leagues, the IWFL works as a nonprofit organization that allows member teams and their owners to operate independently and focus on each team's strategic local marketing needs. The number of different leagues and teams have been a detriment to the women's game, with many folding as rapidly as they develop, and the lack of coherent organization, media attention, and longevity has kept the sport from developing popularity around the country.

Gender and the Football Spectacle

As legitimate women athletes fought to play legitimate football, other women took to the field in a sexualized, commercialized, and exploitative form of the game: the Lingerie Bowl. The first Bowl aired as a pay-per-view special during the Super Bowl XXXVIII halftime special and featured "Team Dream" and "Team Euphoria," made up of models clad in lingerie and protective gear (helmets, joint pads and shoulder pads), playing tackle football. From this first controversial event stemmed the Lingerie Football League and a reality television series based around which team would compete in the next Lingerie Bowl. In 2005 the league expanded from four to eight teams and elected former NBA player Dennis Rodman to serve as commissioner. Rodman played into the sexism that permeated the "sport," announcing he would conduct mandatory uniform inspections and random cosmetic surgery checks throughout the season. The Lingerie Bowl continues to air annually on pay-per-view during the Super Bowl halftime show and does little to promote women's athletics to the predominantly male audience. Rather, they perpetuate the objectification of women's bodies and detract attention away from the achievements of women in the professional football leagues, and women athletes in general.

While the Lingerie Bowl emphasized sexualized femininity, the XFL (for "Xtreme Football League") glorified violent hypermasculinity. In early 2000 World Wrestling Entertainment owner Vince McMahon announced his intentions for the league as a return to "old-time smash mouth football," with fewer rules and no penalties for roughness in order to make the game more violent and thus, arguably, more exciting. The league also standardized the salaries players would receive, citing that "real football players" played for the love of the game. There was a hierarchy of pay based on the position one played: kicking specialists earned $3,500 per week, quarterbacks earned $5,000 per week, and all other players earned $4,000 per week. Winning teams received bonuses to be divided among the players and the league championship competition was named "The Million Dollar Game," in recognition of the cash purse awarded to the winning team.

The league's opening game took place February 3, 2001, and was broadcast on NBC, a co-owner of the league. The XFL debut recorded an estimated 14 million viewers, double what NBC had guaranteed investing advertisers and significantly more than those who tuned in for the NFL Pro Bowl. Almost immediately, however, ratings dropped to embarrassing numbers. Some critics blamed the poor quality of play. Others faulted the lack of organization and the continual modification of rules throughout the season as a detriment to viewership. But the sentiment that rang loudest was the fact that the XFL was the brainchild of Vince McMahon, a personality who was constantly derided for his involvement in the "fake" world of professional wrestling. Audiences questioned whether or not a league game was scripted in the way WWE matches always were. Whatever the reasons may have been, NBC announced it would not broadcast a second season of the XFL as planned, alluding to significant monetary losses and poor judgment. McMahon publicly announced May 10, 2001, that the league would no longer continue.

College Football

Throughout the twentieth and into the twenty-first centuries, football has remained "king" on college campuses across the nation. But with money, power, and prestige often comes corruption, and in the past two decades college football has seen a number of scandals, including recruiting violations, gambling, sexual misconduct, and drug use. Several women competed on men's collegiate teams and the University of New Mexico's Katie Hnida became the first woman to score in a Division I game. Hnida's success, however, came after she transferred from the University of Colorado where she alleged she had been the target of sexual harassment and assault. Later, she, along with a group of other women, accused her former teammates of sexual molestation and rape. Ultimately, no charges were filed against the players but the allegations contributed to the already-tarnished reputation of Colorado's football program. Coach Gary Barnett's handling of the charges against his athletes was roundly criticized for being both sexist and insensitive, adding further fuel to the fire. The coach was temporarily suspended and placed on paid leave, but was reinstated before the start of the 2004 season. Barnett was fired in 2005 as a result of a string of losses during the season.

The Colorado Buffaloes, winning their first and only national championship in 1990, faced several football-related scandals over the years. The rape allegations, brought by several different women beginning in 2001, were part of a larger controversy made public in early 2004 that uncovered the team's strip-club visits, as well as the prevalence of alcohol, exotic dancers, and sexual contact at parties for recruits. There was evidence to suggest that several officials connected with the school had knowledge that these things went on and the negative attention these events brought to the school served warning on other big-time college football programs.

Another controversial incident concerning an athlete's violence and the response of a coach concerned University of Nebraska's Lawrence Phillips. After amazing performances during his freshman and sophomore years, in which he led his team to a national title, the running back was named a contender for the prestigious Heisman Trophy in 1995. In the midst of the season, however, Phillips was charged with assaulting his then-girlfriend and was temporarily suspended from the team by Coach Tom Osborne. That he was not permanently removed from

Nebraska's roster drew much criticism of Osborne, who further outraged detractors by allowing Phillips to rejoin the team and start in the 1996 Fiesta Bowl, where he produced a spectacular performance and then became the number 6 pick in that year's NFL draft. His career was continually plagued with legal transgressions and Phillips was unable to achieve success as a professional athlete.

The Quest for a National Champion

The NCAA sponsors twenty-three sports in each of the Division I, II, and III levels and, with the help of expert coaches and administrators, organizes eighty-eight total championships through end-of-the-season tournaments. However, football in the Division I–Football Bowl Subdivision (Division I-FBS, formerly called Division I-A) is the only NCAA-sponsored sport without an NCAA-organized tournament to determine a national champion. This has been the topic of heated debate, as various attempts to award an uncontested national championship have resulted in controversial rankings and matches.

Because big-time college football does not rely on a postseason playoff system to determine a national champion, there have been a number of discrepancies in declaring which team deserves the number 1 title. In 1990, for instance, the Associated Press (AP) poll declared the University of Colorado the national champion, while the United Press International (UPI) awarded the crown to Georgia Tech. The following year, the polls split again, so that different organizations claimed that the University of Washington and Florida State University each was the country's victor.

In order to stage a game that would determine a clear-cut winner, organizers established the Bowl Coalition in 1992 to match teams in postseason play for both conference finals (Atlantic Coast Conference, Southeastern Conference, the Big 8, the Southwest Conference, the Big East, and Notre Dame, which remains independent of any conference) and determining an overall national champion. A major flaw in this system was that it did not include the Pac-10 or Big Ten conferences, the winners of which were contractually committed to participate in the annual Rose Bowl. This proved especially problematic in 1994 when undefeated Big Ten team Penn State, ranked second in the nation, was obligated to play the much lower ranked Pac-10 winner Oregon in the Rose Bowl rather than the University of Nebraska in the national championship Orange Bowl. Although both Penn State and Nebraska emerged with undefeated seasons, the Bowl Coalition determined Nebraska to be number 1.

In an effort to create more equity, the Bowl Alliance replaced the Bowl Coalition in 1995. The Alliance still did not include the Pac-10 and Big Ten conferences, but it did dissolve the contractual commitments that previously prohibited highly ranked conference teams within the coalition from playing one another. This modification was intended to increase the likelihood that the top two teams would meet one another in the championship game. But the Big Ten's University of Michigan football team experienced the stinging limitations of the Bowl Alliance in 1997 when it was ranked number 1 and invited to play in the Orange Bowl championship game against eventual champion Nebraska. Due to contractual obligations, however, Michigan had to play Pac-10 champion Washington State in the Rose Bowl. Without the inclusion of the Big Ten and Pac-10 conferences, the

Bowl Alliance, much like the Bowl Coalition, failed to provide a true national champion in big-time college football.

At the conclusion of the 1997 season, the Pac-10 and Big Ten conferences agreed to integrate into the existing Bowl Alliance to structure to create what was informally referred to as the "Super Alliance," which eventually became known as the Bowl Championship Series (BCS). The Rose Bowl would now rotate hosting responsibilities of the national championship game along with the Orange, Sugar, and Fiesta bowls. Again, like the Bowl Coalition and the Bowl Alliance, the BCS was designed with the intention of pitting the top-ranked teams against one another in a national championship game.

The concept of the BCS was unique in that a mathematical formula was used to arrive at the rankings. These composite rankings were determined by analyzing team records, schedule strength, three computer-ranking systems, and the Associated Press (AP) and ESPN-USA *Today* Coaches' polls. Fairness within the new ranking system was quickly questioned, given that the six BCS conference champions (ACC, Big East, SEC, Pac-10, Big 10, and Big 12) received automatic Bowl game berths, leaving only two spots to be filled by the remaining five non-BCS Division I-A conference football teams. By 2004 the overwhelming feeling was that it would be nearly impossible for a non-BCS conference team to be given the opportunity to play in the national championship game, as four non-BCS conference teams had finished the regular season undefeated since 1998 and were never awarded the chance.

Problems arose long before the injustices felt in 2004. In the first year of BCS action, the Kansas State University Wildcats finished third in the final BCS rankings, but were denied participation in all of the bowl games; however, the fourth- and eighth-ranked teams did get to partake in bowl games that year. In response, the BCS adopted the "Kansas State Rule," which ensured an invitation to a bowl game for the third-ranked team in the final BCS standings. But the controversies continued to erupt. Despite ranking first in the final regular season AP and Coaches' polls, the University of Southern California was denied a shot at the national title game. The mathematical formula employed by the BCS had ranked two other teams, the University of Oklahoma and Louisiana State University, ahead of USC. Those teams played for the national championship title with LSU coming out on top, while USC defeated fourth-ranked University of Michigan in the Rose Bowl. In an attempt to smooth over the chaos the USC incident created, the BCS reconfigured its ranking systems to put more weight on human rather than computer polls. The Associated Press responded to the commotion by disallowing the use of its polls as part of the BCS ranking formula. Shortly thereafter ESPN removed its name from the Coaches' poll. While the BCS system is still in place as of this writing, BCS administrators continuously adapt the formulas and rules for which teams are invited to particular bowl games, but it seems nearly impossible to imagine a situation that would take into account the various results, schedules, anomalies, and outcomes, as well as the conference configurations that keep changing.

The amount of money the games generate for the teams who play in the bowls, as well as for their respective conferences, makes it likely that the system—in one form or another—will continue to exist for some time. At the same time, the BCS system has only worked out as planned twice since its 1998 inception, with two teams remaining undefeated by the end of the regular season in 2002 and 2005. There has been strong support for a college football playoff system, but this has been met with arguments that playoffs would reduce the importance of regular-season games and incite the same kind of lackluster performance by NFL teams that play their second and third string toward the end of the regular season when a loss will not hurt their chances of playoff action. Division I-FBS football remains the subject of great contestation and with the continual use of flawed ranking systems it may never be able to truly determine a national football champion.

Success in College Football

In spite of the controversies involving the BCS, a number of teams achieved success and notoriety between 1990 and 2007. The University of Southern California leads the pack in terms of the number of BCS appearances—winning five of the six matchups in which they competed. Currently, Ohio State, Oklahoma, and Florida State have also participated in six BCS bowl games. Between 1998 and 2007, the BCS has named (in chronological order) the following champions: University of Tennessee, Florida State, University of Oklahoma, University of Miami (FL), Ohio State University, Louisiana State University, University of Southern California, Texas, Florida and LSU, making it difficult to claim that one team has been particularly dominant in Division I-FBS. Based on polls from 1990 to 2003, national co-champions were named three times: Colorado and Georgia Tech in 1990, Washington and Miami in 1991, and Michigan and Nebraska in 1997. Two other times during this era, Nebraska was named the sole consensus national champion (1994, 1995), making it the most prominent team of the time.

Much of the credit goes to Nebraska coach Tom Osborne who, at the time of his retirement in 1997, boasted the best winning percentage among active NCAA Division I-FBS coaches with 83.6 percent and a 60-3 record over his final five seasons. An online poll conducted by ESPN in 2007 named Osborne the "greatest college football coach of all time." Attesting to his popularity in his home state, in 2000 Nebraskans overwhelmingly voted him into the U.S. House of Representatives. To date only one coach has reached 200 victories in fewer games than Osborne: Penn State's Joe Paterno. Paterno began as an assistant coach in 1950, taking the head position in 1966 and by 2008 he had celebrated his forty-third anniversary in that role. During this time he appeared in more bowl games than any coach in history, boasts the record for most bowl games won, has won two national championships, and has coached the Nittany Lions to five undefeated seasons.

Eddie Robinson coached at Grambling from 1941 to 1997 and accumulated 408 victories. Grambling, however, was not an accredited institution until 1949 so Robinson is only credited with 363 wins. Also among the top coaches ranks Florida State's Bobby Bowden, currently tied with Paterno as the winningest coaches in Division I-FBS history. He has garnered two national titles (1993 and 1999) and the Seminoles were named one of the top five teams by the AP poll for fourteen straight seasons (1987–2000). The team has produced two Heisman Trophy winners: Charlie Ward (1993) and Chris Weinke (2000), both of whom played quarterback. But in terms of Heisman trophies, USC leads the pack with seven (sharing the number 1 position with Ohio State and Notre Dame) and as college football transitioned into the twenty-first century, the Trojans were among the most dominant teams in the nation. Coach Pete Carroll took the helm in 2001 and, despite having the 2002 Heisman Trophy–winning quarterback Carson Palmer, the nation's top defense (led by Troy Polamalu), a tough schedule, tying for first place in the Pac-10 Conference, and an 11-2 record overall, USC finished the season with a number 5 ranking in the BCS system.

The following season again provided USC with BCS frustrations. Although the AP poll ranked the Trojans as the best in the nation, the BCS located them at third, placing the University of Oklahoma at the top spot, and setting a matchup against number 2 Louisiana State (LSU won the 2003 national championship 21-14). USC went on to beat Michigan 28-14 in the Rose Bowl and split the national title with LSU, prompting a handful of corporate sponsors to push for a competition between the Trojans and the Tigers, which the NCAA did not allow. Finally, following the 2004 season, USC was declared the undisputed national champion. With Heisman winner Matt Leinart at quarterback, along with running back Reggie Bush, who finished fifth in the Heisman voting that same year, the undefeated Trojans squared off against the also-unbeaten Oklahoma, with Jason White at quarterback—the winner of the 2003 Heisman Trophy. It marked the first time in history that two players who had already won the coveted award faced one another. USC went on to win, 55-19, and again competed for the national title in 2005, losing 41-38 to the Texas Longhorns in the Rose Bowl, despite the talents of Reggie Bush, who won that year's Heisman award.

In the end, the booming popularity and sweeping expansion of American football witnessed between 1990 and 2005 was incredible. Fantastic record-making moments characterized this era. The formation of multiple women's leagues, the brief existence of the XFL, and the overseas NFL Europe venture allowed for new groups to get a taste of what the NFL and NCAA has experienced for so long. The debate surrounding the Bowl Championship Series and its fallibilities raised questions about the best way to crown a true national champion. Within professional football, continual modifications have been made in an effort to improve the structure and function of the organization. Along with strengthening the foundation of the NFL, the advance of media technology and its symbiotic relationship with the league reinforced football as the prevailing sport in American homes. If American football experiences another fruitful time period like that of 1990 to 2005, there is no telling what new limits may be pushed in terms of leagues, expansion, and record.

Hockey

Professional Ice Hockey

Ice hockey, as one of the "big four" sports in North America that includes basketball, baseball, and football, has never enjoyed the same popularity in the United States that it has in Canada, though there are regional pockets where the game is widely celebrated, especially in New England and the Midwest. There were both highs and lows for the United States' ice hockey community. Women made great strides while the men's professional league, the National Hockey League (NHL), faced several major blows, including notable acts of violence, two major player lockouts, and a substantial decrease in television viewership and overall popularity.

But the NHL landscape was not entirely bleak; it was particularly brightened by some of the greatest athletes the sport has ever known.

There is a bit of truth to the old joke, "I went to a fight the other night and a hockey game broke out." While combat and excessive violence are penalized, it is nonetheless common for players to break into on-ice fighting. Many argue that the potential for violence spurs enjoyment of and attention to the sport, though this may detract from the amazing skill and athleticism players exhibit. In one extreme example of such violence, Boston Bruins player Marty McSorley was suspended during the 1999–2000 NHL season after a vicious stick to the head of Vancouver Canucks' player Donald Brashear, causing a loss of consciousness and severe concussion. Aside from its brutality, what made the act unique was that McSorley was then charged in federal court and convicted of assault with a weapon. Four years later another brutal act of violence made headlines. The Canucks' Todd Bertuzzi attacked Colorado Avalanche player Steve Moore, which caused serious injuries, including three fractured vertebrae and a severe concussion. Bertuzzi was suspended from the NHL indefinitely and the International Ice Hockey Federation (IIHF) extended the NHL suspension into their jurisdiction, thus barring Bertuzzi from international play. Like McSorley, Bertuzzi was charged with assault by authorities outside of hockey.

The NHL experienced additional negative press during this period because of two player lockouts, which combined to devastate the league's seasons and tarnished its image. The first occurred in the 1994–95 season as a result of the controversy over the players' salary cap. NHL owners wanted to establish a maximum amount that players could earn in a season and, not surprisingly, the athletes were opposed, arguing that they would not be paid their real worth if a ceiling was placed on their wages. Contract negotiations were at a deadlock for 104 days during what should have been the regular season, cutting the number of games from eighty-four in 1993–94 to only forty-eight in 1994–95. Owners and players eventually came to an agreement halfway through the season and the cap was not enacted. The event, however, laid the foundation for future disputes between NHL players and franchise owners.

In 2004 the NHL made history with its second lockout of the past ten years—at 310 days, it was the longest in North American major professional sports history. As it had earlier, the 2004–5 lockout occurred over a labor dispute between the players, represented by the NHL Players Association (NHLPA), and the league. Citing financial deficits caused by players' salaries, the NHL once again fought for a salary cap to combat the league's financial crisis. The opposing sides finally came to an agreement just in time for the 2005–6 season, but even with the return of the NHL's regular season, many argue that the game and its presence in U.S. society have been forever changed. In May 2005, one of the major consequences of the strife became evident when ESPN terminated its $60-million television deal with the NHL.

In response to the decrease in viewership, the NHL endeavored to make hockey more appealing. The best example of the league's efforts was in its overhaul of the sport's rules. Several major changes for the 2005–6 season made the game faster, encouraged more offensive scoring, and make the game more exciting overall. Some of the adaptations included forcing a victor in the event of a tie through a shootout, decreasing the size of the goalie's pads and gloves, and altering official

Pittsburgh Penguins' Mario Lemieux celebrates after Martin Straka scored an overtime goal to lift the Penguins to a 4-3 win over the Washington Capitals in game 6 of their first-round playoff series in Pittsburgh on April 23, 2001. (AP / Wide World Photos)

rink dimensions. Although the changes were met with general praise, to date, the league's tactics have not successfully increased ratings and game attendance continued to decline.

Despite the general decline of the NHL in the 1990s, one athlete continued to stick out: Wayne Gretzky, "the Great One." Widely regarded as the greatest player of all time, during his twenty-one-year career Gretzky racked up scoring titles and records, MVP awards, All-Star appearances, and playoff records, and set or tied sixty-one NHL records, many of which pundits deem untouchable. At the time of his 1999 NHL retirement he had a career point total of 2,857, which is over 1000 points higher than the next all time leading scorer, Gordie Howe. He earned nine Hart trophies, the NHL's version of the MVP award, which is three more than any athlete in the NHL, NBA, NFL, and MLB. He was a phenomenon in the world of ice hockey and his incredible athletic prowess paired with his clean-cut image was a winning media frenzy formula. The NHL retired his number 99 from all teams—he is the first and only player in the league to be awarded this honor.

The Canadian-born Gretzky was a long-time star for the Edmonton Oilers. In the late 1980s, however, "The Trade" as it came to be known, included his move to the Los Angeles Kings. This action greatly disturbed many Canadians, so much so that they attempted to force government intervention. South of the border, Gretzky's performance for the Kings invigorated American's interest in the sport, momentum that continued as he joined the St. Louis Blues in 1996 and concluded his stellar career with the New York Rangers, where he joined other greats, including Mark Messier and competed against the likes of the Pittsburgh Penguins' Mario Lemieux, who overcame multiple injuries, bouts with cancer, and severe pain to become one of the most dominant players in the game.

Amateur Ice Hockey

Amateur hockey experienced tremendous growth during this period, particularly with the formation of the first U.S. National Women's Ice Hockey Team. The team competed in the 1990 International Ice Hockey Federation (IIHF) World Women's Championships, which was the first IIHF-sanctioned international women's competition. The United States made a successful inaugural showing, which brought them the silver medal behind Canada's gold. Their performance also changed the international rules of women's ice hockey. Prior to the 1990 World Cup tournament, full body-checking was allowed within women's hockey. The American women were so physically dominant against many of their matchups that competitors argued the body-check gave them an unfair advantage. The IIHF recognized this disparity and eliminated the full-body check in an effort to level the playing field.

Throughout the decade the popularity of women's ice hockey's grew globally. The 1998 Nagano Japan Olympic Games marked the first time that women's ice hockey was recognized as an Olympic medal sport. The U.S. national team stepped onto the international stage and dominated the tournament, winning the gold medal. Their success put hockey into the spotlight and brought positive attention to the sport. Four years later Team USA Women and Men's Ice Hockey teams continued their international success when both teams won the silver medal at the Salt Lake City Olympic Games.

The success of women's hockey at the 1998 and 2002 Olympic Games encouraged the NCAA to recognize women's ice hockey as a sanctioned sport. In 2001 the first women's collegiate ice hockey championship, or "Frozen Four," was held with the University of Minnesota–Duluth Bulldogs skating away with the title. Since that time there has been considerable growth in the number of collegiate women's hockey programs offered at Division I, II, and III levels.

Soccer

Soccer is far more popular throughout the rest of the world than in the United States. Up until the mid-1970s' North American Soccer League (NASL), the United States did not have any premiere professional leagues. There are several arguments concerning soccer's relative lack of success and popularity at the national and professional levels. Some cite the foreign development and dominance of the sport. Others believe that Americans find it less exciting and slower paced than other popular sports because it is typically a low-scoring sport. Despite these arguments, 1990–2007 saw an explosion in U.S. soccer participation and it became the fastest growing sport at both the high school and collegiate levels. This surge was influenced by two factors: 1) the incredible success of the U.S. Women's National Soccer team and; 2) the United States hosted several international championships, including the 1996 Olympic Games, and the Women's and Men's The Fédération Internationale de Football Association (FIFA) World Cup tournaments.

The U.S. Women's soccer team experienced unprecedented success throughout this fifteen-year period, consistently dominating international competitions and demonstrating the success of Title IX legislation. Their supremacy began with the dawn of the first FIFA Women's World Cup tournament in 1991. Twelve national teams vied for the title in hosting country China and the United States trounced the competition, winning gold and encouraging interest in soccer back in the United States.

The popularity of soccer was rising nationwide in the mid- to late 1990s and its climax came in 1999 as the United States hosted the FIFA Women's World Cup tournament. The United States fielded an all-star team of veterans who had played the better part of the decade at the national level. The tournament was held in seven different areas across the United States and game attendance smashed previous records. A sold-out crowd at the Pasadena Rose Bowl, along with a substantial television audience, watched the final match between as Team USA dramatically beat China in a shootout for the title. The nation rallied around its new sport heroes and the team won accolades never before awarded to women in the world of sport.

Out of this media frenzy, several stars emerged, most notably Mia Hamm, the all-time leading scorer for Team USA with 158 international goals. Her athletic success catapulted her into the media spotlight and Hamm became a popular icon. While other players such as Michelle Akers, Julie Foudy, Tiffany Milbret and Kristine Lilly also gained fame, Brandi Chastain seemed to garner a disproportionate amount of attention. Chastain scored the winning penalty kick in the U.S.-China shootout and, in a fit of excitement, tore her shirt off and celebrated in her sports bra, an action that came under immediate scrutiny, often distracting attention from the significance of her accomplishment and that of her teammates.

As the women found international success, the U.S. men's team fought to claim respect during this period. Throughout much of the twentieth century the U.S. men's national soccer team struggled to stand out from the global pack. In an effort to turn the program around and inspire stateside "soccer madness," the United States hosted the 1994 FIFA Men's World Cup. This decision came under tremendous international scrutiny because of the perceived lack of interest from U.S. fans.

Michelle Akers, Women's Soccer Champion

When considering the history of sports, it is important to acknowledge the contributions of Michelle Anne Akers (born February 1, 1966) who, from the beginning of her career, set the tone for the U.S. women's dominance in soccer. During her time at the University of Central Florida she was a four-time National Soccer Coaches Association of America All-American and the first woman to win the prestigious Hermann Trophy in 1988, awarded to the top soccer player in the United States. Without the benefit of a U.S. league, she traveled to Sweden to become the first American woman to play professional soccer, competing for Tyresco Club for three years. She began playing for the U.S. National team in 1985 and scored her first international goal, which was also the first time any U.S. player had scored against Denmark. Through the late 1980s, Akers continued to lead the United States in international play, but her talent came to the fore in 1991 when she amazed the world at the first FIFA Women's World Cup tournament, scoring ten goals in six matches and leading the U.S. women to victory.

Akers played in two more FIFA Women's World Cups in 1995 and 1999. Team USA finished with a disappointing bronze medal in the 1995 tournament, in part because Akers was injured. However, many believe it was this loss that motivated Akers and the team to come back at the 1996 Atlanta Olympic Games to win gold. Akers's final international tournament was the 1999 FIFA Women's World Cup where she once again helped the Team USA win gold in the tournament by scoring on a crucial penalty in the semifinal match. Akers retired after the 1999 FIFA win with 153 international appearances, 105 career goals, 37 assists, and 247 total points. She was named FIFA Women's Player of the Century in 1999 and in 2004 she and Mia Hamm were the only two women, and the only two Americans, included in the FIFA 100, a list of the top living soccer players in the world. She was inducted into the National Soccer Hall of Fame in 2004. Akers's incredible fifteen-year career is a testament to how opportunities to participate in sport can empower girls and women.

The world questioned whether a country that did not have a premiere professional soccer league could or should host a major international competition. In order to prove their competency, the United States founded Major League Soccer (MLS) in 1993 and play began in 1996. The men's national team also stepped up their play and began to see moderate international success.

Beginning with ten teams in 1996, MLS created three expansion clubs by 2005 and with a possible two additional teams slated for the 2009 season. Although the league faced dwindling attendance numbers after its first few seasons, the unexpected FIFA World Cup success of the U.S. men's team in 2002 reestablished interest in the American premier league. The creation of the MLS was highly publicized and strategically planned. From its onset MLS teams were purposely placed in cities with high immigrant populations in order to plug into an already established soccer fan base. Soccer-specific stadiums were built for many of the MLS clubs, which has encouraged greater profitability. In addition, young superstars such as Brian McBride, DaMarcus Beasley, and Landon Donovan were highly marketed to both general sport audiences to generate interest in the league.

Mia Hamm, forward on the U.S. National Women's Soccer Team, gets ready to unleash a shot on net against the Russia National during first half action in the Nike U.S. Women's Cup '98 at Frontier Field in Rochester, NY, on September 18, 1998. Hamm scored 100th and 101st career international goals as the United States toppled Russia 4-0. (AP / Wide World Photo)

The women also tried their hand at a professional league with the Women's United Soccer Association, or WUSA. Play began between eight teams across the country in April 2001. With the incredible popularity and the sellout crowds of the 1999 FIFA World Cup, promoters and players alike anticipated successful attendance and support. However, this was not the case and due to the general lack of fan and financial support, the league was forced to suspend play after its third season in 2003, though it is expected that play will resume in the spring of 2009.

Overall this time period featured rapid growth for the sport of soccer in the United States for both men and women. Soccer's popularity continues to grow with increased interest in FIFA World Cup and premiere professional soccer leagues such as MLS. The sport's momentum is supported by strong youth, high school, and collegiate organizations.

Title IX Comes of Age

By the mid- to late 1990s, girls and women began to reap the athletic benefits of Title IX, the law passed in 1972 banning sex discrimination in education. In 1996, there were 2.4 million girls participating in high school athletics, representing 39 percent of all athletes at that level, an eightfold increase since 1971. At the

college level, more than 100,000 women played sports by the time Title IX celebrated its twenty-fifth anniversary. The increasingly dynamic rivalry between the
University of Tennessee and the University of Connecticut women's basketball
teams brought unprecedented media coverage and, therefore, public attention to
the sport. The University of North Carolina soccer team earned the title of
"dynasty" by winning eight national championships in the 1990s (overall, the team
has a total of nineteen national titles). Indeed, women's soccer in the 1990s was
the fastest-growing sport at both the high school and collegiate level for girls and
women during this decade.

But perhaps nowhere was the success of Title IX legislation more apparent than
on the international stage. The public could not help but take notice of the excitement generated by women's sport in 1996, dubbed "The Year of the Female
Athlete" and that year's Olympic Summer Games in Atlanta became "The Wom-
en's Games." It was the first time that soccer was an Olympic sport for women and
the United States secured the gold medal in front of a crowd of more than 76,000
spectators. Softball debuted as well, and the American team kicked off a string of
three consecutive first-place performances.

At the inaugural hockey tournament of the 1998 Winter Games in Nagano, Japan, Team USA turned in a perfect 6-0 record to secure the championship, an
accomplishment replicated by the U.S. women's basketball team. In the end,
American women won a record number of medals in swimming, synchronized
swimming, gymnastics, and track and field, but it was the gold-medal winning performances in the team sports of soccer, softball, hockey and basketball in 1996 and
1998 Games that particularly owed their success to "Title IX babies"—the first generation of women to fully benefit from the legislation during their elementary
school, high school, and college years.

The successful performances sowed the seeds for professional women's leagues.
In 1996 the American Basketball League tipped off its inaugural season, employing
many Olympic athletes. This was followed in 1997 by the WNBA (Women's
National Basketball Association). In 2000, the Women's United Soccer Association (WUSA) announced it would begin play the following year. Sadly, the ABL
folded in 1999 and the WUSA suspended operations in 2003. Only the WNBA
remains as the opportunity for women to play professional team sports in the
United States.

Despite the progress of women in sport, things are far from equal. At the high
school and college levels, boys and men continue to enjoy the majority of athletic
opportunities. Reports from the NCAA demonstrate that the money invested in
men's sports, particularly football and basketball, eclipses that devoted to women's
sports. The percentage of female coaches and administrators continues to decline
and there are vast discrepancies in the salaries that they earn in comparison with
their male counterparts. Evidence suggests that women of color have not benefited
from Title IX to the extent that white women have. There must also be considerations made for girls and women who are differently abled or disabled and continue
to lack athletic opportunities. Furthermore, Title IX legislation is under constant
threat from lawsuits and politicians. In 2005 the Bush administration allowed colleges to comply with Title IX by showing they were meeting the interests of their
students through email surveys. This is a highly problematic method, not the least
of which is because a lack of student response is interpreted as a response of

noninterest, which severely skews the results of the survey and excuses schools from providing more opportunities for women.

As we celebrate the great strides female athletes have made since 1972, we must be constantly vigilant about the future. As former Olympic and professional basketball player Cheryl Miller stated, "Without Title IX, I'd be nowhere." The country cannot afford to leave over half the population stranded in the middle of "nowhere."

THE OLYMPIC GAMES

Between 1990 and 2005, Olympic Games were held twice on U.S. soil (Atlanta, Georgia, in 1996 and Salt Lake City, Utah, in 2002). Throughout the majority of the Games' history, the Summer and Winter Olympic Games were held during the same calendar year on a four-year cycle. In 1992, however, the rules changed and the events now alternate every two years. By the 2002 Summer Games, 44 percent of Olympic athletes were women and had made further strides at the organizational level of Olympic committees. Anita DeFrantz, an attorney who had been a bronze-medal winning member of the 1976 Olympic rowing team, was the first African American and the first American woman to serve on the International Olympic Committee (IOC). In 1997 DeFrantz became the first female vice president of the IOC and Sandra Baldwin became the president of the U.S. Olympic Committee in 2000, making her the first woman to hold that position in the 106-year history of the organization. Despite these milestones, the IOC remains a predominantly male enclave and the total number of Olympic sports for men still outnumber those for women: In 1992 men competed in 171 compared to 98 events for women; in 1996, men could enter 174 events, while women could enter 108. By the turn of the twenty-first century that gap closed a bit more, with 180 events for men and 132 for women.

Summer Games

The year 1996 marked the 100-year anniversary of the modern Olympics. Boxing great Muhammad Ali lit the cauldron in the host city of Atlanta to kick off the event. At the time, it was the largest Games in history and security was tight. Officials had ratcheted up their safety measures following the explosion of TWA Flight 800, just two days before the opening ceremonies began, yet tragedy still struck the Games when a pipe bomb exploded in Centennial Olympic Park, where people had gathered to listen to a concert. The blast killed one person and injured 111 more. Officials decided that the Games should continue, though flags were flown at half-mast in observance of what President Clinton called an "evil act of terror."

The number of events at the Summer Games continued to increase for male and female participants between 1990 and 2007. Women's softball, soccer, hockey, beach volleyball, triathlon, and epee (a type of fencing) were added to the program during this time period. Women ran the 5000-meter races for the first time in Olympic history in 1996. In 1992 baseball became an Olympic sport (but will be removed, as will softball, after the 2012 Games in London); two years later, mountain biking premiered at the Games. Tennis was reintroduced in 1988, marking the end of a sixty-four-year hiatus. Andre Agassi won gold in 1996 on the men's side. On the women's side, Americans won three straight Olympics' singles titles:

Jennifer Capriati (1992), Lindsay Davenport (1996) and Venus Williams who in 2000, along with her sister Serena, took home a second gold in the doubles event. But in 2004, Americans won only one tennis medal at the Athens Games.

Track and Field

In 2000 the International Amateur Athletic Foundation (IAAF) added women's hammer throw and pole vault (America's Stacy Dragila took home the gold) to the track and field lineup and for the first time men and women competed in the same number of Olympic field events. The year 2000 also marked the first time that there were the same number of team events for women as there were for men. The breakout star of the 2000 Summer Games in Sydney, Australia, was Marion Jones. Before the Olympics, Jones predicted she would win five gold medals, but finished with three gold (100- and 200-meter sprints, 1600-meter relay) and two bronze medals (long jump, 400-meter relay), becoming the first female track and field athlete to win five medals in a single Olympics. Jones translated her popularity and charisma into lucrative endorsement deals and was a favorite of fans and the media alike. She did not compete in the next Olympics and turned in disappointing finishes in 2004. Her vow to return in 2008 would not materialize; plagued by doping allegations throughout her career, Jones tested positive for banned performance-enhancing substances at the 2006 USA Track and Field Championships. She confessed to steroid use in 2007 and was stripped of all the medals she won in 2000. Her name no longer appears in the record book. To single out Jones for the use of banned performance-enhancing drugs, however, is unfair. Incidents of doping have cropped up in numerous sports—in many different countries—and track and field has been especially marred by such scandals.

It would also be unfair to focus on just the scandalous side of track and field, for a good number of American athletes performed well at the Games between 1990 and 2007. Evelyn Ashford, who won her first gold medal at the 1984 in 100-meter event and the 400-meter relay, finished her illustrious career in 1992 with another victorious result. At age thirty-five, Ashford became the oldest woman to win a gold medal for her performance in the 400-meter relay. She joined such noteworthy teammates as Gail Devers, Gwen Torrance, and Jackie Joyner Kersee in producing amazing performances as members of the U.S. track and field team.

There were impressive performances by male athletes as well. In addition to winning nine world championships, Michael Johnson racked up five Olympic gold meals, beginning his streak in 1992. Four years later he became the first male sprinter to win both the 200- and 400-meter races at the same Olympics, surging to victory in a custom-designed pair of Nike racing spikes that earned him the nickname "The Man with the Golden Shoes." He defended his title in the 400-meter event in 2000, adding another gold to his collection in the 1600-meter relay race before retiring from the sport.

Perhaps the greatest male track and field athlete competing during this era was Carl Lewis, whose lengthy international career began in 1979 and continued until 1997. His sprinting and long-jumping career ascended in the 1980s and his two gold medals in 1992 brought his total to eight. With his gold-medal long jump in 1996, his fourth Olympics, he became one of only three athletes to win the same individual event four times. His total of nine Olympic medals left him just one shy

Doping in Sports

Lamentably, it is impossible to discuss American sports in the late twentieth century and early twenty-first without mentioning the rising prevalence of steroids, blood doping, and other illegal, performance-enhancing tactics. The ingestion of substances to give one athlete an edge over others is certainly not a new phenomenon; however, with constant advancements in science and technology, the stakes have increased dramatically. New drugs came to the fore around the end of the twentieth century, forcing the World Anti-Doping Agency (WADA) to continually update their list of banned substances. In particular, the use of human growth hormones (HGH) and anabolic steroids like tetrahydrogestrinone (THG or "The Clear"), designed to increase muscle building, regeneration, and enhance physical strength, have led to the disqualification and additional castigation of several high-profile U.S. athletes in such sports as baseball, running, and cycling.

Established in 1984 by Victor Conte, the Bay Area Laboratory Cooperative (BALCO) is arguably the most well-known American source of performance-enhancing drugs. Between 1986 and 2000 BALCO distributed a supplement called ZMA that, while not banned at the time, was an important precursor to the development of subsequent substances. Later, BALCO began manufacturing and selling "The Clear," so called because it was initially undetectable. In 2003 a series of investigative reports by Lance Williams and Mark Fainaru-Wada, journalists for the *San Francisco Chronicle*, including allegations against athletes like Barry Bonds, Marion Jones, and Jason Giambi, led to an investigation of the laboratory. Since then, a staggering number of athletes have been alleged to have used The Clear, many of whom have tested positive and faced severe retributions.

The information brought to light by the BALCO scandal additionally contributed to the initiation of the 2005 U.S. Senate hearings on steroids in baseball. The hearings were an embarrassment for the major leagues, with many of its top stars admitting to using performance-enhancing drugs. Although the BALCO case primarily involved track athletes and professional baseball players, its ramifications reverberated throughout the sporting community and have traveled into cycling, tennis, and golf. One significant revelation from the BALCO case was that athletes had used performance-enhancing drugs without registering positive test results, primarily because the technology to produce the drugs outpaced the technology to detect them.

Not just professional and Olympic athletes have become pharmacological guinea pigs, with increasing evidence of performance-enhancing drug use at the collegiate level and, according to a survey by the Center for Disease Control and Prevention, steroid use among high school students more than doubled between 1991 and 2003. Such practices have been linked to physical and psychological damage to athletes, as well as to premature death.

---

of the all-time record set by Ray Ewry, who won ten in the early twentieth century. Carl Lewis set numerous world records and held sixty-five consecutive victories in the long jump. In addition to his many awards and achievements, the International Olympic Committee voted him "Sportsman of the Century," the International Association of Athletics Federation (IAAF), track and field's international governing body, declared him "World Athlete of the Century," and Carl Lewis was declared "Olympian of the Century" by *Sports Illustrated*.

Swimming and Diving

With successful performances from Misty Hyman, Megan Quann, Brooke Bennett, and Laura Wilkinson, the U.S. swimming and diving fared well in international competition, and Amy Van Dyken and Jenny Thompson developed particularly noteworthy careers. Van Dyken swam her way to four gold medals in 1996. Thompson represented the United States in the 1992, 1996, 2000, and 2004 Olympic Games, winning a total of twelve medals during her illustrious career and becoming the most decorated U.S. Olympian in history. Male swimmers contributed additional victories to the U.S. medal count. Swimmers like Tom Dolan, Ian Crocker, and Lenny Krayzelburg thrilled fans with amazing races, as did Michael Phelps who, at age fifteen, failed to medal in the 2000 Games. He more than made up for it the next time around. At the 2004 Olympics in Athens, Phelps won a record-number eight medals, including six gold medals (100-meter butterfly, 200-meter butterfly, 200-meter individual medley, 400-meter individual medley, 4×200-meter freestyle relay, 4×100-meter medley relay). Phelps's 400-meter freestyle relay team finished in third place and he added a bronze-medal performance in the 200-meter freestyle. In the 2008 Games in Beijing, Phelps set a new record with eight gold medals in one Olympiad.

Gymnastics

Shannon Miller, the most successful U.S. gymnast in history, won five medals in the 1992 Games—three bronze (team, uneven bars, floor exercise) and two silver (all-around, balance beam) medals. In 1996 she joined Amy Chow, Amanda Borden, Dominique Dawes, Dominique Moceanu, Jaycie Phelps, and Kerri Strug to make up the "Magnificent Seven"—the only American gymnastic team to finish first in the Team Competition. Miller added another gold to her collection in 1996 in the balance beam, making her the only American to win the event at the Olympics. She remains the most decorated gymnast, male or female, in U.S. history. Despite Miller's brilliance, many will remember the 1996 women's gymnastic competition for the dramatic style in which Kerri Strug completed her vault, despite having injured her ankle in her first attempt.

Softball and Baseball

Both softball and baseball are recent additions to the Olympic program and, unfortunately, their appearance was short-lived. Softball was introduced in 1996, and the American women won the event in 1996, 2000, and 2004. Baseball, a long-time Olympic exhibition sport, was granted medal status for the 1992 Games. The American men finished first in 2000, though Cuba has been the dominant team in the event, winning in 1992, 1996, and 2004. In 2005, the IOC determined that both sports would be discontinued following the 2008 Olympic competition.

Basketball

Throughout the history of the Olympics, the men's team from the United States has dominated basketball competition. In 1989 the International Basketball Federation declared that professional NBA athletes would be eligible to compete in the Games. This announcement paved the way for the "Dream Team" of the 1992

Barcelona Games, an incredible assemblage of the top players in the sport including Charles Barkley, Larry Bird, Magic Johnson, Michael Jordan, Karl Malone, Scottie Pippen, Chris Mullen, Clyde Drexler, David Robinson, John Stockton, and Christian Laettner, the only collegiate player of the bunch. To report that the team won a gold medal does not do its performance justice. Quite frankly, the Dream Team dominated their opponents. The United States won their games by an average of forty-four points; their thirty-two-point victory over Croatia for the gold medal was their closest competition of the tournament. Five members of the original team (Barkley, Malone, Pippen, Robinson, and Stockton), along with several talented additions, repeated their supremacy in the 1996 and 2000 Games. In the 2004 Summer Games, however, the United States took home a disappointing bronze medal.

The U.S. women's basketball team has also been impressive and between 1994 and 2006, they did not lose a match in international competition. They won a bronze medal in 1992, followed by three consecutive gold-medal performances in 1996, 2000, and 2004.

Winter Games

Between 1990 and 2007, four Winter Olympics took place and the Games continued to evolve in many ways. Skeleton was reintroduced in 2002 after a fifty-four-year absence from the program and curling came back in 1998, appearing as a competitive sport for the first time since 1924. The moguls became an event in 1992, as did women's ice hockey in 1998. Events like snowboarding have been added, demonstrating the increasing popularity of "alternative" sports. In 2002 the Games were held in Salt Lake City, Utah. It was the first Olympics following the terrorist attacks of September 11, 2001, and, as a result, the competition required extra security measures and took on extra significance. The opening ceremony included a flag that had been at Ground Zero in New York, though some felt this ran antithetical to the ideals of the Olympics that, ostensibly, are to be separate from politics.

Women's bobsledding also debuted at the Salt Lake Games, a competition won by American teammates Jill Bakken and Vonetta Flowers. Flowers, a talented track and field athlete in college, became the first black person to win a gold medal in the Winter Olympics. This is at once an important milestone and a reminder of the lack of racial and ethnic diversity in the Games. Contributing to the racialization of the event, representatives from many countries are disadvantaged by their geography and climate when it comes to training for and competing in the Winter Games.

In addition, there was the 2002 Olympic Games bid scandal, in which it was determined that Salt Lake organizers had bribed members of the IOC to be the host city. As a result, ten members of the IOC were expelled, another ten were sanctioned, and the organization adopted stricter rules to govern the bidding process. There were also doping scandals and controversial judging in the pair figure-skating event resulted in an unprecedented awarding of two gold medals.

Hockey

The American men came in second at the 2002 Games, edged out by Canada. NHL players enjoyed much success at the Olympics beginning in 1998, when the league temporarily suspended operations in order to permit its players to compete. The women's event was added in 1998 and Team USA took home the inaugural gold, followed by a silver in 2002.

Downhill Skiing

Three-time Olympian Picabo Street has been called the greatest downhill skier in U.S. history, with nine World Cup wins and a gold medal in the 1996 world championships. She placed second in the Olympic downhill event in 1994 and won gold in 1998 in the Super Giant Slalom or "Super G," an event that incorporates downhill and giant slalom racing. Street suffered a series of potentially career-ending injuries prior to the 1998 Games, but persevered. Shortly after the Games, she experienced the worst crash of her career—one that left her left femur broken in nine places and tearing the anterior cruciate ligament (ACL) in her right knee. Miraculously, after two years of rehabilitation, Street came back to the sport and proved just how talented and tough she really is, striving to be the first U.S. skier to win a medal in three straight Olympics. Street announced her retirement from competitive skiing after a disappointing sixteenth-place finish in the 2002 downhill event

Skating

Bonnie Blair began her Olympic career in 1984, the first of four consecutive games in which she would compete. In the 1992 Olympics in Albertville, France, Blair won her second and third gold medals in the 500- and 1000-meter events. Her latest victory in the 500-meter race made her the first U.S. athlete to win the same event in three straight Olympics. Blair added two more gold medals to her collection, making her final count six—five gold and one bronze. Winning countless awards and setting several world records during her illustrious career, Blair set an American record in her final race before retiring in 1995. In her absence, speedskater Chris Witty medaled in the 1998 Olympics and won a gold medal in the 1000-meter event in 2002, setting a world record. A multifaceted athlete, Witty also competed in the 2000 Summer Games in Sydney, placing fifth in the 500-meter cycling time trials.

At the 2002 Games in Salt Lake City, Apollo Anton Ohno emerged as the silver- and gold-medal winner in the 1000-meter and 1500-meter races, respectively, though both events were fraught with controversy. In the 1000-meter competition, Ohno had taken the lead, but a fall by South Korea's Ahn Hyun Soo as the skaters rounded the final corner took out Ohno and two other athletes, allowing Australia's Steven Bradbury to become the first person from the southern hemisphere to win a gold medal at the Winter Olympics. Scrambling to his feet, Ohno won the silver. He would improve his standing in the 1500-meter, but only after South Korea's Kim Dong-Sung had been disqualified for blocking Ohno, sparking a massive debate.

Figure Skating

Women's figure skating celebrated a number of great champions between 1990 and 2007, beginning in 1992 with Kristi Yamaguchi's gold medal. Michelle Kwan, the most decorated figure skater in U.S. history, won nine U.S. Championships and five world championships, placing second at the 1998 Games and third in 2002. Kwan's silver in 1998 put her just behind Tara Lapinski, who became the youngest gold medalist in the history of the Winter Olympics. Sarah Hughes added to America's medal count with her 2002 first-place finish. Figure skating typically draws the largest television audience of the Winter Olympics

In addition to the many American triumphs, women's figure skating also gave audiences one of the biggest scandals in the history of sport. In 1994 Tonya Harding and Nancy Kerrigan were among the best U.S. skaters, providing sports fans with fantastic competition. Harding, although known for her amazing triple axels and powerful skating, is perhaps best remembered for her role in the attack on Kerrigan before the 1994 Olympic trials, when an assailant clubbed Kerrigan in the knee with a metal baton. It was soon discovered that the attacker had been hired by Harding's then-husband. Kerrigan was forced to drop out of the event because of her injury and Harding went on to win. Kerrigan recovered to take a silver medal

Nancy Kerrigan performing in "Disney on Ice," 1994. (Courtesy of Photofest)

in the Olympics, while Harding failed to place. Later that year, Tonya Harding pled guilty to helping cover up the assault. The U.S. Figure Skating Association stripped her of her title and issued a lifetime ban, barring her from competing or coaching at sanctioned events. It is unfortunate that the Harding-Kerrigan debacle received the lion's share of attention during the 1994 Games, because it meant that fantastic stories of athletic accomplishment during that time went relatively unnoticed and reduced women's sport into a titillating soap opera.

Paralympics

As American Olympic athletes experienced success, failure, and redemption between 1990 and 2007, so too did American Paralympic athletes. Existing *parallel* to the Olympic movement, the Paralympic movement seeks to provide a space for international competition for elite athletes with physical disabilities. The Paralympic Games occur immediately following the Olympic Games, hosted by the same city and using the same facilities and venues. While not as large or well known as the Olympics, the Paralympics have gained increasing prominence since their inception in 1960.

The scale of the Paralympics grew steadily between 1990 and 2007, both in terms of participation and the number of events. For example, the 1992 Summer Paralympics in Barcelona, Spain, attracted a total of 3,020 athletes from eighty-two countries competing in fifteen sports. Eight years later, the 2000 Games in

Sydney, Australia, featured 3,824 athletes representing 122 countries. These Games included a total of eighteen sports, including the debut of wheelchair rugby as a medal event. The Winter Paralympics experienced similar growth, but on a much more modest scale. During the 1992 Winter Games in Albertville, France, approximately 365 athletes from twenty-four countries competed in only two sports, alpine and Nordic skiing. By the 2002 Games in Salt Lake City, sledge hockey had been added to the program and 416 athletes from thirty-six countries participated. The 2002 Games also marked the international debut of delegations from Andorra, Chile, Croatia, Greece, Hungary, and People's Republic of China, making it the most diverse Winter Games yet.

Throughout this time period, the dominance of the American Paralympic teams wavered. Long accustomed to sitting atop the medal tables, the American teams faced increasingly strong competition in both the Summer and Winter Games. In 1992 the United States topped the Summer and Winter medal tallies, garnering 45 medals in the Winter events and 175 medals in the Summer. With more athletes participating and the level of competition improving, the United States lost its dominant grip and slipped to fourth place in the total medal tally in the 1998 Winter Games, behind Norway, Germany, and Japan. In the 2000 Summer Games the United States finished third with 109 medals, following host country Australia and Great Britain. China displayed its rising success as a sporting nation during the 2004 Summer Games, amassing a total of 141 medals, 63 of which were gold. The United States finished fourth in the 2004 medal table, behind China, Australia, and Great Britain. While these medal tallies do not provide a comprehensive account of a nation's sporting achievement, they do indicate a pattern of growth and diversity in the international Paralympic movement. The preeminence of the United States was no longer a guarantee; the previous dominance of the American teams became increasingly challenged as more countries developed Paralympic training programs and entered the Games.

The Paralympic movement within the United States received a boost of financial and organizational support upon its integration into the governance structure of the USOC. Spurred by the passage of the Ted Stevens Olympic and Amateur Sports Act of 1998, this restructuring allowed the Paralympic movement to weave into the wider framework of the USOC. Prior to this act, the USOC was not directly involved in any aspects of Paralympic competition. The various sport-governing bodies and disabled-sport organizations held responsibility for running events, selecting competition sites, and choosing the national team athletes.

SPORTS FOR INDIVIDUAL COMPETITORS

Boxing

In both record and title, the 1990s belonged to Roy Jones Jr., named by *Boxing Magazine* as the "Fighter of the Decade." The organizations that sanction fights and crown champions become a veritable alphabet soup of acronyms and Jones's success is illustrative of the different boxing associations: he has been the middleweight, super middleweight, and light heavyweight International Boxing Federation (IBF) champion. In the light-heavyweight division, he has also been the titleholder in the World Boxing Council (WBC), the World Boxing Association (WBA), the

IBF, the World Boxing Foundation (WBF), the International Boxing Organization (IBO), and the International Boxing Association (IBA). Jones was also named the WBA heavyweight champion, showing his dominance over four different weight classes.

Jones began his professional career in 1989 and knocked out several opponents en route to a unanimous decision over Bernard Hopkins for the IBF middleweight title in 1993. The following year, Jones beat James Toney for a unanimous decision and the IBF super-middleweight title, which he defended in 1994. Jones suffered his first professional loss in 1997 when he was disqualified for twice punching opponent Montel Griffin while he was down on the canvas. The disqualification stripped Jones of his title, but he quickly regained it in a rematch with Griffin. There was also a series three highly acclaimed fights with Antonio Tarver, with Jones taking a majority decision in 2003, Tarver knocking out Jones in 2004, and Tarver winning a majority decision in 2005.

Throughout his career, Jones has been plagued with allegations that he has not always faced the toughest challengers and, as a result, the number of viewers who have shelled out money to watch his fights on pay-per-view television has declined. Despite these charges, as well as speculations that he devotes too much time to extra-boxing activities such as his rap career and short-lived stint as an HBO boxing commentator, he is among the elite to be referred to as the "pound-for-pound" best fighter in the world, joining the ranks of Hopkins, Floyd Mayweather Jr., and Oscar De La Hoya, so named by *Ring* magazine in 1997.

Ring had previously crowned De La Hoya the 1995 "Fighter of the Year," adding to his list of accolades. De La Hoya first captured American attention with his performance in the 1992 Olympic Games, when he took home the gold medal in the lightweight division. As a professional fighter later that year, he won the WBO junior-lightweight title. He moved up in weight class again to challenge WBC junior-welterweight champion Julio Cesar Chavez, a fight stopped in the fourth round because of a cut to Chavez's eye, which gave De La Hoya the victory. He then went on to take the welterweight title from Pernell Whitaker in 1997, a title that he defended several times.

In 1999 De La Hoya faced the undefeated IBF welterweight champion Felix "Tito" Trinidad for what was billed as the "Fight of the Millennium." In the end, Trinidad won a controversial majority decision in contest that grossed the most of any nonheavyweight fight in the history of the sport. De La Hoya regained the WBC welterweight trophy before moving up to the junior-welterweight division, where he knocked out rival "Ferocious" Fernando Vargas in a contest both admired and celebrated in the boxing world. Once again, De La Hoya changed weight classes and won a unanimous decision over WBC middleweight champion Felix Sturm. He then knocked out by IBF, WBA, and WBC middleweight champion Bernard Hopkins in 2004, and his career has continued in the years that followed.

The career of heavyweight champ Mike Tyson was at its apex in the 1980s, but the tenth decade of the twentieth century began a downward spiral for the one-time "Baddest Man on the Planet." In 1990 Tyson lost his title to James "Buster" Douglas and 1992 an Indiana jury convicted Tyson of sexual assault, sentencing him to six years in prison. Tyson served half of that sentence before his release, at which point he endeavored a comeback. Heavily favored against Evander Holyfield in 1996, Tyson lost on a technical knockout (TKO). The next year, the two fighters met for a rematch in what was, at the time, the largest purse in boxing: Holyfield earned $35 million; Tyson was to take home $30 million, and the fight grossed $100 million. The match, however, was stopped in the third round when Tyson was disqualified for biting both of Holyfield's ears, ripping off a substantial piece of one. As a result, the Nevada State Athletic Commission temporarily revoked Tyson's boxing license and fined him $3 million plus court costs.

Tyson again faced incarceration in 1999 after assaulting two motorists following a traffic accident. He served nine months of a one-year sentence and, upon his release, faced Lennox Lewis, who held the WBC, IBF, and IBO heavyweight titles. Tyson was thirty-five years old at the time and lost that fight. His last victory in the ring took place in 2003. In 2005 he surprised the boxing world by announcing his retirement just before the start of the seventh round against Kevin McBride, stating he no longer possessed "the fighting guts or heart anymore."

Women boxers have faced an uphill battle, not just for the sporting world and the general public to recognize their accomplishments, but to simply have the right to fight. In 1992 Gail Grandchamp was finally granted the opportunity to box, but only as the result of an eight-year Massachusetts court battle. Sadly, by the time the Superior Court judge ruled that it was illegal to deny an athlete the right to box based on gender, Grandchamp had turned thirty-six years old, which meant she was ineligible for amateur competition. The following year, sixteen-year-old Dallas Malloy took her case to court and overturned USA Boxing's bylaw that forbade women from competing. The *New York Daily News* Golden Gloves tournament first allowed women to fight in 1995 and many consider the Christy Martin–Deirdre Gogarty match of 1996 to be the birth of modern professional women's boxing.

Christy Martin, billed as "The Coal Miner's Daughter" (a nickname that accurately describes her West Virginian background), is a former collegiate basketball player and "Tough Woman" champion who began her professional boxing career in 1989. Starting with a three-round knockout of Beverly Szymansky in 1993, Martin became the WBC junior-welterweight champion, a title she successfully defended several times. Throughout her career, she has had many marquis matchups with other high-profile athletes. In 2002 she won a ten-round decision over Mia St. John. Because St. John had appeared in *Playboy* (1999) and Martin had previously graced the coveted cover of *Sports Illustrated* (1996), the fight was billed as the "Battle of the Covergirls." Martin also fought Lucia Rijker, nicknamed the "Million Dollar Lady," one of the most successful female boxers in history. Martin defended her title against prominent female boxers including Deirdre Gogarty, Laura Serrano, Melinda Robinson, and Sue Chase before losing to Sumya Anani in 1993. Anani would go on to win the IBA lightweight title as well as Women's International Boxing Association (WIBA), International Female Boxing Association (IFBA), IBA, and Global Boxing Union (GBU) welterweight titles and in 2003, *Ring* magazine listed her as the best female pound-for-pound boxer. Martin also faced Laila Ali, the daughter of the legendary Muhammad Ali, in 2003. Ali, who began her professional career in 1999 by knocking out April Fowler in the first round, knocked out Martin in four rounds. Prior to that victory, Ali had won a majority decision against Jackie Frazier-Lyde, the daughter of the great Joe Frazier and one-time rival of Muhammad Ali, in 2001. Over the years, Laila Ali has been named the Super Middleweight Champion by the IBA, WIBA, and the IWBF, though she has been criticized for avoiding the top contenders.

Between 1990 and 2007, there were a number of scandals in boxing involving drug use and steroids. Promoter Don King was sued by several boxers that he represented and faced criminal charges based on his alleged association with organized crime. These issues have contributed to the sport's decline in U.S. popularity, but the biggest criticism of boxing comes from medical concerns regarding the brutality of the sport. Several countries have made boxing illegal and it seems the majority of the world's medical community supports those decisions. For instance, the *Journal of the American Medical Association*, the most widely circulated medical journal in the world, has urged the banning of boxing for decades and the British Medical Association, which represents 84 percent of the doctors in the United Kingdom, also opposes the sport. Certainly boxers, as in other sports that involve some type of impact or collision between athletes, risk cuts, broken bones, and internal bleeding; however, it is the brain damage that results from boxing to which there is the greatest attention. Doctors have labeled such damage as chronic, severe, catastrophic, and permanent. Boxers periodically die as a direct result of a match, but it is the sustained injuries to their brains that accounts for diminished capacity and, arguably, fatalities in later life.

Horse Racing

The coveted Triple Crown of thoroughbred racing (the Kentucky Derby, the Preakness Stakes, and the Belmont Stakes) is among the most illusive in all of sport. Indeed, only eleven horses have ever won all three events in a single year and 1978 marked the last of the Triple Crown champions. Twenty-one horses have won two of the three events, coming achingly close to the esteemed triumvirate. Of those twenty-one, five horses ran away with two-thirds of the Triple Crown between 1990 and 2005. Interestingly, each of those five has failed to win the Belmont Stakes, the longest of the three races at 1.5 miles, held annually at Elmont, New York's Belmont Park.

In 1997 Silver Charm took home the Kentucky Derby title at Churchill Downs in Louisville, Kentucky. The Derby, called "the most exciting two minutes in sport," is held the first Saturday of every May and is steeped in pageantry and tradition. Two weeks later, organizers stage the Preakness Stakes at Pimlico racetrack in Baltimore, Maryland. In 1997 Silver Charm won that race as well. Three weeks after the Preakness, the third American Grade I stakes race for three-year-old thoroughbreds is held at Belmont (called "The Test of the Champions") where Silver Charm, like many others, fell short of the Triple Crown.

Two years later, a horse named Charismatic followed nearly the same pattern, but the outcome at Belmont would prove a bit more tragic. Beating the odds to win both the Derby and the Preakness, Charismatic was favored to take the last event and, in the final furlong, it looked as if he just might do it, but he began to fade and finished a disappointing third. At the end, jockey Chris Antley sensed something had gone wrong. He quickly dismounted and discovered that Charismatic's leg had been broken in two places. Antley's discovery may have saved the horse's life, but following surgery, he would never race again.

In 2002, after victories in the first two legs of the Triple Crown, War Emblem stumbled at the beginning of the Belmont and was unable to win the third. The next year, Funny Cide became the first New York horse to win the Derby, and followed with a triumphant performance at Preakness, only to come up short at Belmont. In 2004 Smarty Jones, whose pedigree includes several former Triple Crown winners, seemed to generate tremendous excitement in horse racing and even graced the cover of *Sports Illustrated* after his Derby win. When he followed up with another victory at Preakness, many thought that the Triple Crown drought would finally end. Alas, Smarty Jones would finish second at Belmont.

The 2004 Belmont race brought up charges of unethical behavior when a review of the film suggested that two jockeys "rode not to win" but to deny Smarty Jones the victory. Although such tactics are not illegal, this type of behavior in "the sport of kings" is considered unscrupulous, particularly when Triple Crown winners are so rare. Other controversies in horse racing are indicative of the more general changes in sport. Jockeys have sued to be allowed to wear advertising patches during races, a practice that began in 2004. The horse racing community has been rocked with scandals involving gambling and the doping of the animals. Recently, the Kentucky Derby introduced prerace testing for the presence of performance-enhancing drugs in the horses.

A new issue arose in 2007 and 2008 and it was whether horses were being treated cruelly in the way they were prepared and trained for racing. The concerns were magnified when Eight Belles, a filly, finished second in the Kentucky Derby, but broke both her legs directly after the race and had to be destroyed while still on the track. Earlier, in 2006, Barbaro won the Derby, but broke three bones in his right hind leg at the start of the Preakness. The efforts to save his life extended for eight months and captured the hearts of millions. Unfortunately, he was unable to fully recover and was euthanized in January of 2007.

Finally, it is not just the horse that deserves credit for a successful performance, but rather a strong relationship between the animal, its trainer, its owner, and the jockey. Between 1990 and 2007, several jockeys rode with amazing distinction, including Kent Desormeaux, Gary Stevens, Julie Krone, Jerry Bailey, Chris Antley, and Pat Day, who has won nine races in the Triple Crown series. Among trainers, Bob Baffert has conditioned an astonishing number of champion horses while D. Wayne Lukas is one of the most successful in the business, winning the year's top money fourteen times. Lukas was also the first trainer to be inducted in both the Thoroughbred and the Quarter Horse Halls of Fame.

Golf

As Michael Jordan is to basketball, Eldrick "Tiger" Woods is to golf, and the amazing talents and commercial success of these athletes are impossible to ignore. A golfing prodigy who began playing at age two, Woods was a six-time Junior World champion. At just fifteen years old, he became the youngest U.S. Junior Amateur Champion and proceeded to win the event for the next two years. In 1995 Woods attended Stanford University and amassed titles such as Pac-10 Player of the Year and NCAA First Team All-American. The following year he won the NCAA individual championship and declared his professional status, which included $40-million and $20-million endorsement deals with Nike and Titleist, respectively. With the addition of other sponsorships that include Buick and TAG Heuer, Woods has become the highest paid professional athlete. He is also involved in a number of philanthropic endeavors: with his father and mentor, Earl

Woods, he established The Tiger Woods Foundation, which aims to help disadvantaged children through programs including "In the City" golf clinics, the "Start Something" character development program, and the "Tiger Woods Learning Center" among other initiatives.

In 1997 Woods won his first major, the Masters, by twelve strokes and became number 1 in Official World Golf Rankings. In 2000 he won the U.S. Open by fifteen strokes, breaking a record that had been held since 1862, and 2001 marked his Grand Slam, or "Tiger Slam" achievement. Between his professional debut and 2005, Woods accumulated a staggering number of titles: four-time winner of the Masters (1997, 2001, 2002, 2005), three-time winner of the U.S. Open (2000, 2002, 2008), the British Open (2000, 2005, 2006), and four times at the PGA Championship (1999, 2000, 2006, 2007). He has literally changed the game of golf. In an effort to hamper Woods's success, courses began to "Tiger-Proof" their tees and fairways by adding yardage in attempts to make the game more difficult for him to win. His victory at the U.S. Open in 2008 in sudden death after an eighteen-hole playoff, while playing with a broken leg, is already the stuff of legends.

In addition to Woods, many other notable golfers excelled during this era. Phil Mickelson is one of the best golfers of this time period, winning three majors and over thirty tournaments on the PGA Tour. Davis Love III has won nineteen events since turning professional in 1985, including the 1997 PGA Championship and the Players Championship in 1992. Jim Furyk, known for his consistent play and interesting swing, reached number 2 in 2006 after winning his first major in 2003. Mark O'Meara, who credits Woods as an inspiration for his career, has also reached the second position. David Duval, hit the links and joined the PGA Tour in 1995, achieving seven second-place finishes in two years. Rounding out the ranks of these impressive golfers was William Payne Stewart, whose prolific career was cut short on October 25, 1999, when he was tragically killed in a plane crash. The knickerbockers-tam-o'shanter-kneesock-wearing tour favorite, Stewart was a two-time men's U.S. Open and PGA champion and, at the time of his death, was ranked in the top ten of the Official World Rankings.

The Ladies Professional Golf Association (LPGA) organizes the major women's tournaments, most of which are held in the United States. With the increasing presence of international players like Lorena Ochoa, Annika Sorenstam, and Karrie Webb, American women have struggled to gain prominence in the sport since the mid-1990s. Between 1990 and 1995, however, Betsy King, Beth Daniel, Dottie Mochrie, and Pat Bradley racked up titles and honors. Alison Nicholas's win in the 1998 U.S. Open, with a score of 274, marked the lowest score in the fifty-two-year history of the tournament. Juli Inkster, who won thirty-one tournaments on the LPGA tour, became the first woman emerge victorious in a professional golf tournament in which men and women competed against one and other. Nine years later she became only the second woman to complete a career Grand Slam. The same year, golfer Beth Daniel shot a 66 to win the LPGA Championship and a $150,000 purse, the largest to date, helping her to amass $5 million dollars in career earnings by 1996.

In 2002, golfer Michelle Wie qualified for her first LPGA tournament. Two years later, during her ninth-grade year in school, she became the youngest female ever to play in a PGA Tour event. In 2005 Wie turned professional, signing sponsorship contracts with Nike and Sony worth about $10 million per year. Rules and regulations prohibit her from becoming an official member of the LPGA Tour until she turns eighteen years old, thus limiting her to six LPGA events annually.

Wie's youth, talent, and Korean ancestry have brought comparisons with Tiger Woods as both athletes challenge the white hegemony of American golf and exemplify the increasingly multiracial character of American society. Woods is careful and proud to articulate his multiracial heritage, explaining that he invented his own term to describe himself: *Cablinasian*, which refers to his Caucasian, black, Indian, and Asian heritage. In his 1996 "Hello World" campaign for Nike, Woods reminded viewers that "There are still courses in the US I am not allowed to play because of the color of my skin." Despite his Chinese, Thai, African American, Native American, and Dutch background, Woods is often ignorantly and problematically coded as a "black golfer." Perhaps no other incident highlighted this better than golfer Frank "Fuzzy" Zoeller's comments following Woods's 1997 Masters' victory, in which he referred to him as "that little boy" and urged Woods not to order fried chicken or collard greens for the next year's Champions Dinner. Zoeller was roundly criticized for the comment and lost his sponsorship from Kmart as a result, but his careless remark emphasized the undeniable persistence of racialized ideologies in sport and U.S. society.

As another example, the Shoal Creek golf club near Birmingham, Alabama, had no African American members until 1990. This was hastily rectified, but only because the club was to host the Professional Golfers' Association championship and television sponsors threatened to pull their support unless a black member was admitted. Subsequent polls have demonstrated that Shoal Creek is not alone in regards its racial makeup, and country club sports remain, primarily, the domain of white, upper-class men.

Women's exclusion from membership at the most prestigious golf clubs received nationwide attention in 2002 when Martha Burk, chairperson of the National Council of Women's Organizations (NCWO) challenged the "good old boys" legacy at Augusta National Golf Club in Atlanta, host of the renowned Masters tournament. While women could play at Augusta as guests, they could not become members (like Shoal Creek, Augusta had admitted its first black member in 1990). Club chairman William "Hootie" Johnson stood firm in his opposition, arguing that it was a private club with the right to extend membership to whomever it liked. Burk did not disagree with this stance, but countered that by hosting the Masters, which was broadcast on network television, Augusta opened itself up to the public. The NCWO urged corporate sponsors, including Coca-Cola, IBM, and MasterCard, to support its cause. In response, the Masters aired on CBS without advertisements, shielding sponsors from having to come down on one side or the other, and the event went on as scheduled. To date, Augusta has not changed its membership policies.

Tennis

The racial makeup of the top competitors in tennis is markedly similar to that of golf. A sport with a legacy of social elitism and exclusion, there are very few successful, professional tennis players of color or from working-class backgrounds. Sisters Venus and Serena Williams, however, turn that logic on its ear. Coached by their father on the public tennis courts in Compton, a suburb of Los Angeles, until

Casey Martin Playing Winning Golf with a Disability

In 1997 professional golfer Casey Martin (born June 2, 1972) engaged in a legal showdown with the Professional Golf Association (PGA). Martin, because of a rare congenital circulatory disease called Klippel Trenaunay Weber syndrome, has difficulty walking the golf course. After a successful collegiate career at Stanford, during which the NCAA allowed him to ride in a cart to accommodate his disability, Martin went on to the three-stage PGA qualifying tournament called the Q-School. During this time, Martin requested that the PGA permit him to make use of to a golf cart for professional matches.

Unlike the NCAA, the PGA was unwilling to acquiesce to Martin's request, arguing that the cart would grant him an unfair advantage. The PGA contended that Martin would be better rested than the other golfers forced to walk the course and, therefore, his level of play would be higher. Citing the Americans with Disabilities Act (ADA) of 1990, Martin brought a formal lawsuit against the PGA accusing the organization of discrimination. The case went through several years of appeals until it reached the U.S. Supreme Court in 2001, at which time the Court ruled in favor of Martin, stating that the PGA is subject to the regulations of the ADA despite its status as a private club.

This win was important, not just for Martin and his professional golf career, but for the larger community of athletes with (dis)abilities. Martin's case brought considerable media attention to the struggles of the ADA. It also raised important debates about how we define disability and what types of accommodations are to be made under the purview of the ADA. It is not a matter to be taken lightly, as organizations ranging from the NCAA to Little League baseball struggle with the best ways to treat athletes equitably.

moving to Florida to train with top coaches like Rick Macci and Nick Bolletieri, the women are among the most decorated athletes, most decorated women, and most decorated African Americans in sport.

The elder, Venus Williams, turned professional in 1994 at age fourteen and began appearing regularly at tournaments in 1997, where she made it to the final round of the French Open. By the end of 1998, Venus had reached the quarterfinals of the French Open, Wimbledon, and the U.S. Open and was ranked in the top ten of women's tennis, but it was her younger sister, Serena, who claimed the first Women's Tennis Association (WTA) title in the Williams family. With her 1999 U.S. Open victory, she became the first African American since Althea Gibson to win a Grand Slam singles title. Between 1990 and 2005, the women racked up championships and titles including Wimbledon (Venus, 2000, 2001, 2005; Serena, 2002, 2003), the U.S. Open (Venus, 2000, 2001; Serena, 1999, 2002) French Open (Serena, 2002), and the Australian Open (Serena, 2003, 2005). Always supportive of one another, the Williams sisters have frequently found each other on the other side of the net in championship matches and have teamed up to practically dominate doubles competitions.

Their talents are not limited to the tennis court. Both attended the Art Institute of Florida to study fashion design, one of their passionate pursuits. Indeed, the women have received quite a bit of press for their style of dress and adornment

Venus Williams, 1998. U.S. Open, New York. (Courtesy of Photofest)

throughout their careers. In addition, Serena has launched her own designer clothing label (Aneres) as well as lines for Puma and Nike. Venus has also become a fashion entrepreneur, with her EleVen line, in addition to being the CEO of a design firm called "V Starr Interiors"

Another U.S. woman who enjoyed success and acclaim was Jennifer Capriati, who made her mark in 1990 when she became the youngest woman to win a match at Wimbledon and the youngest Grand Slam semifinalist. She followed up by winning a gold medal at the Barcelona Olympics. Shortly after this, her career began to crumble, which some suggested was due to such intense pressure to succeed at such a young age. Capriati began her comeback in the late 1990s and won the Australia Open in 2001 and 2002 and the French Open in 2001. Lindsay Davenport is another athlete who warrants discussion, for her illustrious career spans 1990 to 2005. Davenport made her professional debut in 1991 and in 1998 captured her first Grand Slam title, becoming the first American woman to win the U.S. Open since Chris Evert's 1982 victory. In 2004 Davenport became the tenth woman to win forty individual titles and in 2007 she remained only the tenth woman to win fifty career singles titles.

Named *Tennis* magazine's greatest player from 1965 to 2005, Petros "Pete" Sampras, was the sport's superstar in the 1990s. During his fifteen-year career, he won fourteen Grand Slam titles, Wimbledon seven times, and the U.S. Open five times. Sampras turned professional in the late 1980s and won his first career title in 1990. In 1993 he was ranked as the number 1 player in the world and, with Andre Agassi, dominated men's tennis during this time. The Sampras-Agassi rivalry is one of the most intense and exciting in all of sports and brought a number of new fans and special interest to the game. Agassi, who boasts eight Grand Slam singles tournaments as well as an Olympic gold medal, is one of an elite group that won all four Grand Slam singles titles. Though his career was plagued by a number of injuries and setbacks, his longevity in the sport is a testament to his skill and dedication.

Sampras and Agassi, who had once played each another in a junior tournament in 1979, met again in 1990 as their professional careers were on the rise. Their competition peaked in 1995, as one continually ousted the other from the number 1–ranked position. During that year, they faced off in the finals of the Australian Open, the U.S. Open, the Canadian Open, and Indian Wells. The matchups between the two men brought in the highest television ratings the sport had seen and the pair continued to meet up in major competition through 2002 until Sampras retired in 2003. Agassi continued his career until bowing out in 2006.

Both athletes were successful in commercial endorsements as well, but Agassi's are perhaps the most memorable, particularly his "Image Is Everything" campaign for Canon cameras. Agassi came on the scene with what was considered a "rebel" image in tennis: he sported long hair, an earring, and colorful clothing among the prevalence of tennis whites, bringing a new sensibility and fan base the sport as a result. This placed him in further contrast to Sampras, who boasted a more clean-cut image. The sporting and commercial world capitalized on the differences between the men, as well as the phenomenal athleticism they displayed on the court, and Sampras and Agassi appeared together in a number of Nike commercials.

Most recently, men's tennis has been dominated by Roger Federer, a Swiss national who had won thirteen Grand Slam titles, matching Sampras, as well as five Wimbledon championships in a row. In 2008, after a nearly five-hour match, Federer lost at Wimbledon to Spain's Rafael Nadal. On the women's side, the surge of top young players from Eastern Europe has been most pronounced from 2004 to 2007, though Venus Williams won her fifth women's singles championship at Wimbledon in 2008, beating her sister Serena in the match.

Cycling

Although cycling is not often considered one of the major sports in the United States, between 1990 and 2005 American cyclists experienced great success on the international circuit. Cycling can be subdivided into road biking, mountain biking, BMX, track racing, and cyclocross racing; however, this section focuses on road and mountain biking because from 1990 to 2005, these were the most influential forms of cycling in the United States. Although there are many great American success stories in cycling, most notably Greg LeMond and Lance Armstrong, perhaps cycling is equally known in the United States for its many doping scandals and accusations.

Although the bulk of his success occurred in the 1980s, it is important to note that prior to the worldwide celebrity of Armstrong, Greg LeMond was the most decorated and revered American road-bike racer. In 1990 he capped his career by winning his third Tour de France, arguably the most prestigious bicycle race in the world. After winning his third Tour, *Sports Illustrated* named LeMond one of the forty most influential people in sports in the past forty years. In 1990 ABC's *Wide World of Sports* named LeMond "Athlete of the Year" and in 1999 Fox Sports Network included him in their list of "50 Greatest Athletes of the Century."

The year after LeMond's monumental third Tour win, Lance Armstrong, the reigning U.S. National Amateur Champion, turned professional and began one of the most storied careers not just in cycling, but in all of sport. Although Armstrong was successful on the professional road-biking circuit and as a triathlete, it was not until his return to sport from his battle with cancer that he reached celebrity athlete status and won his seven Tour de France Yellow Jerseys. In October 1997 Armstrong was diagnosed with testicular cancer that had metastasized to his lungs and brain and although doctors gave him less than a 50 percent chance of recovery, an aggressive treatment of chemotherapy proved successful in forcing Armstrong's cancer into remission. Despite his extended absence from the professional cycling tour, many of Armstrong's major sponsors, such as Nike and Oakley, honored their contracts and continued their endorsement partnerships with Armstrong during his illness. In 1997 the U.S. Postal Service team signed Armstrong and laid the foundation for what would prove to be one of the most dominant cycling teams in all of professional cycling—Team Discovery. Upon his return to racing, Armstrong had two goals. The first was to was to win the Tour de France which, from 1999 to 2005 he did, winning a record seven consecutive Maillot Jaune (Yellow Jerseys).

Armstrong's second goal was to raise awareness about cancer through the creation of the Lance Armstrong Foundation. The LIVESTRONG "Wear Yellow Live Strong" campaign began as a joint venture between Nike and the Lance Armstrong Foundation in 2004. In 2005 the foundation sold over 55 million wristbands at a cost of one dollar each, with the majority of proceeds going toward cancer survivor programs. At the close of 2005 the foundation had a value of just under $65 million. The Lance Armstrong Foundation and the LIVESTRONG yellow bracelet campaign not only created a clear connection between sport and philanthropy, it paved the way for many other causes to adopt fundraising bracelets such as the green Save Darfur, the pink Breast Cancer, and red HIV/AIDS awareness bracelet campaigns. Although the LIVESTRONG campaign was successful in its attempt to increase funding for cancer research, several organizations have criticized it for being but another tool in Nike's lifestyle brand marketing philosophy. Still others have suggested that the Lance Armstrong Foundation and the LIVESTRONG campaign are ways of deflecting doping accusations frequently levied against him in favor of more positive publicity.

Despite his amazing success as a cyclist, his storybook tale of overcoming cancer to win arguably the world's most difficult sporting event, and his dedication to the fight against cancer, Lance Armstrong has not escaped the suspicions and accusations of other cyclists and media outlets. In September 2005 French journalist Damien Ressiot published a controversial story in *L'Equipe*, a well-respected Paris-based sports daily, alleging that he had proof that Armstrong had used performance-enhancing drugs to fuel his 1999 Tour de France victory. He argued that his proof came from a leak at France's top antidoping lab, the Laboratiore National de Depistage du Dopage (LNDD). Although the tests and samples were anonymous and labeled only with numbers, Ressiot claimed that he had the doping control records, which linked sample numbers to rider names. In response to the accusations, Armstrong and his supporters argued that he had never used any performance-enhancing drugs. Along with the implications this testing had for Armstrong, it raised larger issues about athletes' rights to privacy and the fair and consistent application of antidoping rules.

Several of Armstrong's U.S. Postal Service (later to become Team Discovery) teammates, such as George Hincapie and Levi Leipheimer, went on to have their own successes at the Tour de France, the Giro d'Italia, and the Tour of Georgia, among others; but none of Armstrong's former teammates experienced the successes or the perils like Tyler Hamilton and Floyd Landis. Hamilton was slated to be cycling's next Lance Armstrong after he won the individual time trial at the 2004 Athens Olympics while racing for the United States. Although initial tests determined that Hamilton had evidence of blood doping in his sample, the case was dropped when the backup sample contained too few red blood cells to analyze. In September of 2004 Hamilton again tested positive for an illegal blood transfusion and was banned from cycling for two years. Hamilton was, however, allowed to keep his Olympic gold medal because the positive Olympic test was never corroborated with a second positive sample. Perhaps the biggest hit to Hamilton's reputation and career as a professional cyclist came in 2006 when he was linked to Operation Puerto, the Spanish bust of a major cycling doping ring. Although Hamilton maintains his innocence, it is unlikely he will ever race professionally again.

No American cyclist has faced greater humiliation than Floyd Landis, who is the only cyclist to have his Tour de France win and Yellow Jersey revoked. Landis had a storybook win in the 2006 Tour de France. Despite being more than eight minutes behind the leader, Landis rode a miraculous Stage 17 to earn the leader's Yellow Jersey for the remainder of the 2006 Tour. As with all stage winners, Landis was tested for doping after his victory and the test subsequently revealed the presence of synthetic testosterone, which he hotly disputed. Despite his many attempts to salvage his win and clear his name, in 2007 Landis lost his appeal to the World Anti-Doping Agency (WADA) arbitration committee and was stripped of his 2006 Tour win.

While men's cycling remains a prominent international sport, women lack the same level of opportunity and competition. There are few major events for women road cyclists and even fewer professional teams for women to compete on. As a result, the Olympics are the major cycling events for women and U.S. riders have historically fared poorly. American women have, on the other hand, experienced great success in mountain biking. Perhaps the most famous U.S. mountain biker is Missy Giove, who won a record fourteen NORBA (National Off Road Biking Association) downhill races and remains second on the World Cup list with eleven race wins. Known as "The Missile," she embodies the rebellious antiestablishment mountain-bike culture through her dress, style of speech and her habit of wearing the skeleton of her deceased pet piranha, Gonzo, on a chain around her neck.

Giove was one of the best-paid mountain bikers, male or female, with endorsement contracts in the $1 million range and actual prize winnings well over $100,000. Giove was as important a figure in women's mountain biking as she was to the lesbian community. She was one of the first openly gay athletes to not only compete and win international events, but to do so with the support of major corporate sponsors such as Volvo, Cannondale, and Reebok. Not long after Giove's sponsorship agreements were made public, Subaru began a marketing campaign directed toward the gay and lesbian community that prominently featured openly gay tennis stars Martina Navratilova and Amelie Mauresmo.

Ned Overend is considered the grandfather of professional mountain biking and the first to make a professional career of the sport. Overend was the Union Cycliste Internationale (UCI) World Mountain Bike Champion in 1991 and after his retirement in 1996 Overend became a coach for Team Specialized and transitioned to race triathlons and extreme adventure races where he has also proven to be a top competitor.

Despite the proliferation of doping scandals and accusations in professional road biking and the contradictory nature of the antiestablishment ethos spouted by both mountain and BMX bikers while simultaneously competing in the corporately sponsored ESPN X Games and starring in Mountain Dew advertisements, cycling in the United States is experiencing a tremendous increase in popularity both as a participant and spectator sport. *Bicycling* magazine is consistently listed within the top ten magazines for U.S. circulation in the *Wall Street Journal* and bike sales have increased dramatically in the past five years. The potential reasons for the increase in cycling's popularity could be attributed to America's fitness obsession, to Lance Armstrong's celebrity status, to the X Games' "cool" factor, and myriad other reasons. Regardless, a once uniquely European sport is taking hold in the United States and cult heroes such as Greg LeMond, Missy Giove, and Ned Overend are getting their due celebrity while cycling and other companies are beginning to experience the economic benefits of a sport with increasing social and cultural capital.

Xtreme Sports

Prior to the inaugural staging of the Xtreme Games, sports like snowboarding, skateboarding, bungee jumping, and the like were considered "alternative" sports. They achieved this classification not only because they were not traditional team-based sports such as football, basketball, and baseball, but also because they were athlete-centered activities in which participation was based on the pure love of the sport. Individuals cited the rush of adrenaline that came along with the performance and camaraderie that was forged out of eschewing traditional sports in favor of newer renegade forms of bodily activity as their main reasons for engaging in these activities. The lure of snowboarding was, in part, its decidedly antiestablishment ethos. The Xtreme Games (later renamed the X Games) were one of the first steps in the transition of these so-called alternative sports from subcultural underground to mainstream commodity, replete with television contracts and seven-figure endorsement deals.

The Extreme Games were held for the first time in 1995 and took place in Newport and Middleton, Rhode Island, and Mount Snow, Vermont. Competitions were held in nine sporting categories including aggressive in-line skating, bicycle stunt riding, bungee jumping, extreme adventure racing, skateboarding, skysurfing, snowboarding, sport climbing, street luge racing, and wakeboarding.

The Extreme Games were judged to be a tremendous success by their parent company, ESPN, as 198,000 spectators attended the first event and major companies provided financial backing (including Advil, Mountain Dew, Taco Bell, Chevy Trucks, AT&T, Nike and Miller Lite Ice). In an effort to promote branding opportunities and better market the Games to an international broadcast audience, in 1996 the Extreme Games were officially renamed the X Games. In 1997 the X Games proved so successful in terms of popularity, network contracts, and branded commodity sales that ESPN created the Winter X Games, featuring events such as free skiing, snowmobile, snocross, skiboarding, ice climbing, snow mountain bike racing, and shovel racing. The inaugural Winter Games were televised to 198 countries and territories in twenty-one different languages. This was the first year that ABC Sports broadcast an X Games event and as they grew in popularity, more corporations recognized the marketing and branding opportunity of the games. Toyota was the major corporate sponsor for the Asian X Games Qualifier and the Asian X Tour and as such, every time the event was advertised viewers saw it as The Asian X Games Qualifier Presented by Toyota.

In 2002 ESPN successfully executed the inaugural X Games Global Championship. The first-of-its-kind team event featured six world regions competing against each other in summer and winter action sports at two simultaneous venues: San Antonio, Texas, and Whistler Blackcomb, British Columbia. Combining both venues, Team USA registered a cumulative total of 196 points, edging out Team Europe, which finished second with 167 points. In total 69,260 spectators came to cheer on their favorite teams at X Games Global Championship and the event continues to grow in popularity.

Automobile Racing

Since the advent of the automobile, individuals have desired to race. Automobile racing occurs on dirt roads, oval tracks, road courses, straight-line courses, superspeedways, and anywhere one might conceive of driving a vehicle. In the United States, drivers engage in contests that include drag racing, sports car racing, rallying, off-road racing, dirt-track racing, midget-car racing, and the like. Although Formula One (F1) racing is immensely popular in most parts of the world, in the United States it is the series for Indianapolis (Indy) cars and stock cars that receive the most attention.

Stock-Car Racing

Stock-car racing in the United States is nearly synonymous with NASCAR— the National Association for Stock Car Auto Racing. NASCAR, with its historic and mythological roots in moonshining (the running of homemade, illegal alcohol) of the rural South, was formalized and standardized by William "Big Bill" France in the late 1940s. The popularity of the sport exploded in the 1980s and 1990s, primarily due to television's broadcasting of the Winston Cup, the sport's premiere competition series. Before that time, many races were only seen on tape delay. Now events are televised live and appear on CBS, Fox, TNT, NBC, and ESPN stations. Such broadcasting has taken NASCAR from its regional roots and turned it into a sport of national—even global—popularity.

Without question, NASCAR is the fastest-growing spectator sport in America and it currently ranks number 1 in terms of the number of fans who attend its events. Between 1990 and 2002, those in attendance of NASCAR races rose an incredible 91 percent. In comparison, attendance figures for the NBA have increased by only 20.7 percent during that same time period. By 2005 NASCAR races constituted seventeen of the twenty biggest spectator events in sports in the country, where an average of 125,000 fans attend each race, paying an average ticket price of $88. It ranks second in terms of televised sports viewership, placing it just behind the number of people who tune into watch the National Football League.

NASCAR consists of three major national series (NASCAR NEXTEL Cup Series, NASCAR Busch Series and the NASCAR Craftsman Truck Series) as well as eight regional series and one local grassroots series. NASCAR Sanctions 1500 races at over 100 tracks in thirty-five U.S. states, Canada, and Mexico. Of the more than thirty races that constitute the Winston Cup, the Dayton 500 (called the "Great American Race") is the most prestigious. Held in Daytona Beach, Florida, the Daytona 500 kick starts the annual series in February. Throughout the season, which ends in November, drivers earn points for where they finish each race and the number of laps they were in the lead for each race, accumulating their total score throughout the season to determine the final winner.

A number of drivers have achieved both significant acclaim in the sport and celebrity status with the public, and Jeff Gordon, NASCAR's 1993 Rookie of the Year certainly ranks among them. In 1995 Gordon became the youngest driver to win the Winston Cup championship and between that year and 1998, he dominated the sport, winning forty races (including an astounding streak of thirteen in a row in 1998). Another racer who claimed both success in racing and popularity with the fans was Dale Earnhardt. Nicknamed "The Intimidator," Earnhardt won his first Winston Cup championship in 1980 and repeated his dominance of the series six more times by 1994. His six titles tied Richard Petty's record. In one of NASCAR's biggest tragedies, Earnhardt hit the wall at a speed of about 180 miles per hour on the final lap of the 2001 Daytona 500.

The death of Earnhardt and the frequency with which drivers crash makes technology and safety a central concern for racing teams. The term "stock" in stock-car racing refers to the idea that, in theory, the automobiles are production-based (or "stock") models that anyone can walk into a dealership and purchase. But while the machines may look similar to those on the showroom floor, in reality, they are hand built, using the highest performance parts available and state-of-the-art technology and engineering. In addition, NASCAR officials keep close control of the technological improvements racing teams make to their cars, which helps keep races competitive.

The organizational structure of NASCAR has been called a "benevolent dictatorship" because the control of the sport is consolidated in the hands of the France family. NASCAR sets "inspection fees" for the cars, drivers only receive a small share of the revenue produced by the sport, and NASCAR controls the International Speedway Corporation, a company that has a stake in over one-half of the twenty-three tracks on which races are held, which considerable contributes to the organization's income as well as presents something of a conflict of interest. The organization does not provide a pension for the drivers who risk their lives for the sport and there are no players' unions. It is the individual racing teams, with the backing of corporate sponsors, who provide health insurance and retirement accounts to their members.

It is the ubiquity of corporate sponsorship that contributes to the uniqueness of NASCAR within the world of sports, for it provides the necessary money to finance each team. Racing events and speedways are frequently named for their corporate sponsors. Moreover, the entire racing team, including the driver, owner, pit crew, and car, are branded with the sponsor's name and/or logo, ranging from Tide laundry detergent, to STP fuel and oil additives, to Coca-Cola, to Tyson Foods, to Miller Brewing Company, to Gillette razors. In effect, the racing teams become moving billboards for the array of products associated with NASCAR, though it is an exceedingly and complex and dialectical relationship between the teams, their sponsors, and the fans that make the sport run.

To be successful, a racing team needs money. Corporations want their brands associated with successful racing teams. The association of a particular brand with a popular driver has the ability to draw in an increased number of customers, which in turn increases the profits of the corporation. This, by extension, allows the corporation to increase the amount of sponsorship for its racing team. In this cycle, drivers are celebrity endorsers and fans are the consumers of products ranging from NASCAR, to media, to material products. In addition, fans become participants in the sport when their dollars are used to buy products from corporations who fund their favorite driving teams. Research has demonstrated that NASCAR fans are overwhelmingly brand loyal, meaning that they purposefully and consistently choose NASCAR sponsors' products over other brands not associated with the sport.

One product that has had an interesting relationship with NASCAR is tobacco. Since 1971, tobacco ads have been banned on U.S. television and radio, yet automobile racing has been able to skirt the issue through sponsorship deals. Winston cigarettes, a product of the R. J. Reynolds corporation, could no longer air commercials during racing coverage, but the sport became riddled with the name "Winston." Individual races included the Winston 500, the Winston Western 500, and the Winston All-Star Race. There was also the Winston Million, a prize awarded to the driver who won the sport's four Grand Slam events in a single year, though the company is not permitted to distinguish the particular product it produces. R. J. Reynolds and Skoal are among the other tobacco-related companies associated with the sport.

The drivers that populate stock-car racing constitute a relatively homogenous population and competitors tend to be both white and male. There have been efforts to address the raced and gendered issues of the sport. A few women, including Shawna Robinson and Louise Smith have enjoyed moderate success and NASCAR's official Web site (nascar.com) now includes a list of "Women of NASCAR."

Indy Car Racing

Indy cars are also referred to as open-wheel racers, because no fenders cover their wheels. The drivers sit in an uncovered cockpit, the engines of the cars are located in the rear, and they are designed to sit low to the ground. The year 1993 saw the retirement of one of the sport's greatest drivers, A. J. Foyt, who had competed since 1957. Another racing great, Rick Mears, retired during this time as well. Family legacies like the Unsers and the Andrettis have also achieved great success in Indy Car racing.

Once the premier form of racing in the United States, Indy Car racing has been eclipsed by the success and popularity of NASCAR in the past few decades. Contributing to Indy racing's downslide was the controversial split between the Championship Auto Racing Teams (CART) and the Indy Racing League (IRL). Since 1978, the CART organization governed the sport but in 1995 Tony George, owner of the Indianapolis Motor Speedway, formed a rival IRL. George mandated that twenty-five of the thirty-three spots in the Indy 500 would be filled by drivers on the IRL circuit. This meant that only eight spots would be available for drivers in the CART series and led to deep feelings of animosity between the competing leagues, doing great damage to the sport as a whole.

The Indianapolis 500, held every year on Memorial Day weekend, has been called the "Greatest Spectacle in Racing." More than 500,000 fans fill the stands to watch drivers complete their 200 laps around a two-and-a-half-mile track at speeds that reach over 200 miles per hour. While the race traditionally begins with the announcement, "Gentleman, start your engines," a number of women have revved up at the start of the event. Sarah Fisher raced in 2001, preceded by Janet Guthrie in the 1970s. In 1992 Lyn St. James became the first woman to be named the Indianapolis 500 "Rookie of the Year" and subsequently racked up seven Indy 500 starts in nine years. St. James's sixth place qualifying position for the Indy 500 in 1994 was the highest for a woman until the appearance of Danica Patrick in 2005, who finished fourth.

Electronic Sports

As technology, computers, and the Internet developed during this time period, so too did "simulated sport," a term that refers to animated participatory sports experiences, video games, sporting technologies, online fantasy leagues, and online gambling. This industry grew tremendously in the late 1990s, in tandem with the rise of the personal computer and high-speed Internet connections. With the introduction of Sony Playstation in 1994 and Microsoft XBOX in 2001, equipment has increased at a rapid pace. Today, competitors can square off against opponents across the globe through online gaming and leagues (such as the Cyberathlete Professional League) and tournaments (like the World Cyber Games), often with monetary rewards, which accommodate the millions who engage in these virtual contests. The year 2000 witnessed the advent of the World Cyber Games and in 2003 the first Electronic Sports World Cup was organized to accommodate nearly 400 competitors. The Major League Gaming (MLG) became the first North American professional video game league in 2002. With Nintendo's release of Wii in 2005 and continual advancements in virtual reality technology, it is difficult to predict what the future holds for simulated sports and cyberathletes.

Electronic sports or "eSports" include the simulation of nearly every athletic competition imaginable and leagues such as MLB, NBA, NHL, and NBA sponsor games related to their respective organizations. Perhaps no other sports-related video game has achieved greater popularity than the multiple incarnations of *Madden Football*. Redesigned in 1988 by EA (Electronic Arts) Sports and named for former NFL coach and sports commentator John Madden, the series is among the best-selling video games in history, spurring the proliferation of a specified genre. Like *Madden Football*, many games allow users to take on the virtual identities of their favorite players. For instance, one might become Tiger Woods for a simulated PGA event, quarterback the Indianapolis Colts in the role of Peyton Manning, or assume the role of real fighters like Muhammad Ali in games like *Knockout Kings*. Voice commentaries, often provided by real-life media personalities, realistic graphics, and sounds, often give the sense that game is actually unfolding on a television screen. In other games, one might choose to play the role of coach or manager, rather than athlete, and attempt to strategize and coordinate an entire sporting system.

In addition to gaming, the Internet has revolutionized American sports other ways. Today, it takes only a click of the mouse or the touch of a screen to learn about players, sports teams, scores, and events from anywhere an individual can conceive. The online sports gambling industry is a economic juggernaut, allowing people to place bets at any time of the day as they refresh their Web browsers and check the score of multiple and simultaneous sporting events.

The Internet revolution has also produced "fantasy sports" leagues, such as football, baseball, and basketball, and has become a popular pastime for many Americans, where participants are "owners" and compete against "owners" of other teams. Sophisticated, hierarchical organizational systems govern the leagues, the winners of which are determined by complicated scoring systems based on real-life performances of athletes and teams. This virtual phenomenon, and many others, has changed how many people consume sports, encouraging greater personal investment in the performance of teams and athletes for multiple reasons.

SUMMARY

As U.S. history continues to unfurl and spread into the twenty-first century it is almost impossible to predict the directions that sport might take. Certainly, advancements in training and nutrition will build better athletes. Records will be shattered and reset, only to be shattered and reset again. New sports will develop and, if history is any indication of the changes that will take place in the future, today's "minor" or "alternative" sports will become more mainstream. In this respect, the twenty-first century is not unlike the times that preceded it.

But the future holds a vast galaxy of possibilities that one cannot predict by studying the past. As computer technology advances, the ways in which Americans play, participate in, and consume sports will certainly change. The proliferation of sport-specific television channels, radio stations, and particularly Internet sites will contribute to additional changes in the coming years. The speed at which communication and the sharing of information runs is simply mind-boggling. Technology might also influence the nature and structure of sports. Recently, the country has seen the introduction of instant replay in sports like football and perhaps the ubiquity of cameras in present-day society will be put to sporting use to reduce the likelihood of errors in officiating, cheating by coaches, and players' dirty tactics. It also seems as if the real physicality required for sporting participation could be replaced with increasingly virtual experiences, allowing individuals to experience a host of sporting activities within the confines of a single room. As such, it may be possible to one day replace humans—officials, coaches, even athletes—with computer technologies. It may sound like the stuff of science fiction, but these possibilities are not so far-fetched.

Technological advancements, scientific understandings, and medical knowledge are likely to lead to further developments in performance-enhancing substances. How might sporting organizations stay ahead of the curve? The U.S. government has begun to intervene, holding a series of congressional hearings over the use of steroids in sport. Many have begun to consider the issue of "cyborgization" or the presence of drug use, training techniques, nutritional supplements, the development and use of prosthetics, and body and genetic modification in sports. In effect, athletes become "cyborgs"—amalgamations of natural and artificial elements—and blur the boundaries between what is human and what is technology in complex ways. And what will the intensification of globalization mean for sports? Will national borders become obsolete or will sport be used to reify those boundaries as economic, population, transportation, and communication flows make them more flexible and permeable?

Throughout the twentieth century and into the twenty-first, various groups have struggled to achieve equality in and through sport. At the same time, however, inequalities persist. Positional stacking—the relegation of athletes of color to peripheral positions in team sports—continues. Despite the overrepresentation of African American athletes in basketball, football, and track and field, they remain underrepresented in key functionary positions like coaching, owners, athletic directors, and general managers. But race is more than a black-white issue, and we must take into account the changes in U.S. population, most recently calculated at 305,000,000 people. As the country continues to grow, the United States will become an increasingly multiracial society and, considering the dialectical relationship between sport and society, athletics will change as well. The division between rich and poor seems ever widening, thus affecting the access to and success in sport. Women and girls have made considerable inroads into mainstream athletics, consistently chipping away at the myth of female frailty yet their opportunities to compete and to hold positions of power still lag behind those of men and boys. It remains to be seen what effects science and technology will have on the perseverance of inequalities based on race, social class, and gender. What is certain, though, is that sports will continue to grow, to capture our imaginations, to provide us with outlets for joy and frustration, and to hold a prominent place in both the history and the future of the United States.

RECOMMENDED RESOURCES

Print Sources

Abdel-Shehid, Gamal. 2000. Muhammad Ali: America's b-side. *Journal of Sport and Social Issues* 26:317–25

Ardell, J. H. 2005. *Breaking into baseball: Women and the national pastime.* Carbondale: Southern Illinois University Press.

Armstrong, L. 2000. *It's not about the bike: My journey back to life.* New York: Berkeley Press.

Booth, D., and H. Thorpe. 2007. *Berkshire encyclopedia of extreme sports.* Great Barrington, MA: Berkshire Publishing.

Carpenter, L.J., and V.R. Acosta. 2005. *Title IX.* Champaign, IL: Human Kinetics.

Coakley, J. 2005. *Sports in contemporary society: An anthology.* 7th ed. Boulder, CO: Paradigm Publishers.

Coakley, J., and E. Dunning, eds. 2000. *Handbook of sports studies.* London: Sage.

DePauw, K. P., and S. J. Gavron. 2005. *Disability sport.* Champaign, IL: Human Kinetics.

Eitzen, D. S., ed. 2005. *Sport in contemporary society: An anthology.* 7th ed. Boulder, CO: Paradigm Publishers.

Fainaru-Wada, M., and L. Williams. 2006. *Game of shadows: Barry Bonds, BALCO, and the steroids scandal that rocked professional sports.* New York: Gotham.

Griffin P. 1998. *Strong women, deep closets: Lesbians and homophobia in sports.* Champaign, IL: Human Kinetics.

Lafeber, W. 1999. *Michael Jordan and the new global capitalism.* New York: W. W. Norton.

Longman, J. 2000. *The girls of summer: The U.S. women's soccer team and how it changed the world.* New York: Perennial.

Markovits, A. S., and S. L. Hellerman. 2001. *Offside: Soccer and American exceptionalism.* Princeton, NJ: Princeton University Press.

Messner, M. 2002. *Taking the field: Women, men, and sports.* Minneapolis: University of Minnesota Press.

Nylund, D. 2003. Taking a slice at sexism: The controversy over the exclusionary membership practices at Augusta National Golf Club. *Journal of Sport and Social Issues* 27:195–202.

Sage, G. H. 1998. *Power and ideology in American sport: A critical perspective.* 2nd ed. Champaign, IL: Human Kinetics.

Schaffer, K., and S. Smith, eds. 2000. *Olympics at the millennium: Power, politics, and the games.* New Brunswick, NJ: Rutgers University Press.

Shaughnessy, Dan. 2005. *Reversing the Curse: Inside the 2004 Boston Red Sox*. New York: Houghton Mifflin.
Summitt, P. 1999. *Raise the roof: The inspiring inside story of the Tennessee Lady Vols' groundbreaking season in women's college basketball*. New York: Broadway Books.

Web Sites

Top North American athletes of the century. 1999. ESPN Web site. http://espn.go.com/sportscentury/athletes.html.
U.S. Paralympics. U.S. Olympic Committee Web site. http://www.usoc.org/paralympics/.
Women's Sports Foundation. http://www.womenssportsfoundation.org.

Films

Hoop dreams. 1994. Dir. Steve James. Fine Line Features.
Murderball. 2005. Dir. Henry Alex Rubin and Dana Adam Shapiro. Paramount Pictures.
Nine Innings from Ground Zero. 2004. HBO Home Video.
Shadow Boxers. 1999. Dir. Katya Bankowsky. Image Entertainment.
The Year of the Yao. 2004. Dir. Adam Del Deo and James D. Stern. Endgame Entertainment.

RESOURCE GUIDE

Print Sources

Abrams, Roger I. 2005. *The first World Series and baseball fanatics of 1903*. Boston: Northeastern University Press.

Alexander, Charles. 2002. *Breaking the slump: Baseball in the Depression era*. New York: Columbia University Press.

Anderson, David. 2000. *More than Merkle*. Lincoln: University of Nebraska Press.

Baker, William J. 1986. *Jesse Owens: An American life*. New York: Free Press.

———. 1988. *Sports in the western world*. Urbana: University of Illinois Press.

Barnett. C. Robert. 2004. St. Louis 1904. In *Encyclopedia of the modern Olympic movement*, ed. John E. Findling and Kimberly D. Pelle. Westport, CT: Greenwood Press.

Berlage, Gia Ingham. 1994. *Women in baseball: The forgotten history*. Westport, CT: Praeger.

Betts, John Richard. 1974. *America's sporting heritage: 1850–1950*. Reading, MA: Addison-Wesley.

Bjarkman, Peter C. 2000. *The biographical history of basketball*. Chicago: Masters Press.

Bullock, Steven R. 2004. *Playing for their nation: Baseball and the American military during World War II*. Lincoln: University of Nebraska Press.

Cahn, Susan K. 1994. *Coming on Strong: Gender and Sexuality in Twentieth-Century Women's Sport*. New York: Free Press, 1994.

Carroll, John M. 1992. *Fritz Pollard: Pioneer in racial advancement*. Urbana: University of Illinois Press.

———. 1999. *Red Grange and the rise of modern football*. Urbana: University of Illinois Press.

Cayleff, Susan. 1995. *Babe: The life and legend of Babe Didrikson Zaharias*. Urbana: University of Illinois Press.

Chapman, David L. 2006. *Sandow the Magnificent: Eugen Sandow and the beginnings of bodybuilding*. Urbana: University of Illinois Press.

Cohen, Stan. 1985. *A pictorial history of downhill skiing*. Missoula, MT: Pictorial Histories Publishing.

Creamer, Robert. 1974. *Babe: The legend comes to life*. New York: Simon and Schuster.

Crepeau, Richard C. 1980. *Baseball: America's diamond mind: 1919–1941*. Orlando: University Presses of Florida.

Davies, Richard O. 1994. *America's obsession: Sports and society since 1945*. Fort Worth, TX: Harcourt Brace College.

———. 2007. *Sports in American life: A History*. New York: Blackwell.

Deford, Frank. 1975. *Big Bill Tilden: The triumphs and the tragedy*. New York: Simon and Schuster.

Dickey, Glenn. 1982. *The history of professional basketball since 1896.* New York: Stein and Day.

Dyreson, Mark. 1998. *Making the American team: Sport, culture, and the Olympic experience.* Urbana: University of Illinois Press.

———. 2003. Icons of liberty or objects of desire? American women Olympians and the politics of consumption. *Journal of Contemporary History* 38 (July): 435–60.

———. 2008. Mapping an empire of baseball: American visions of national pastimes and global influence, 1919–1941. In *Baseball in America*, ed. Donald Kyle, Robert R. Fairbanks, and Benjamin G. Rader, 143–88. College Station: Texas A&M University Press.

Englemann, Larry. 1988. *The goddess and the American girl.* New York: Oxford University Press.

Fox, Stephen R. 1994. *Big leagues: Professional baseball, football, and basketball in national memory.* New York: William Morrow.

Fry, John, ed. 1972. *America's ski book.* New York: Charles Scribner's Sons.

Gallico, Paul. 1938. *A farewell to sport.* New York: Knopf.

Gorn, Elliott J. 1986. *The manly art: Bare-knuckle prize fighting in America.* Ithaca, NY: Cornell University Press.

Gorn, Elliott J., and Warren Goldstein. 2004. *A brief history of American sports.* Urbana: University of Illinois Press.

Guttmann, Allen. 1984. *The Games must go on: Avery Brundage and the Olympic movement.* New York: Columbia University Press.

———. 1991. *Women's sports: A history.* New York: Columbia University Press.

———. 1996. *Games and empires: Modern sports and cultural imperialism.* New York: Columbia University Press.

———. 2002. *The Olympics: A history of the modern Games.* Urbana: University of Illinois Press.

———. 2004. *Sports: The first five millennia.* Amherst: University of Massachusetts Press.

Heaphy, Leslie A. 2003. *The Negro Leagues: 1869–1960.* Jefferson, NC: MacFarland.

Henry, Bill. 1976. *An approved history of the Olympic Games.* New York: G. P. Putnam's Sons.

Herlihy, David V. 2004. *Bicycle.* New Haven, CT: Yale University Press.

Hietala, Thomas R. 2002. *The fight of the century: Jack Johnson, Joe Louis, and the Struggle for Racial Equality.* Armonk, NY: Sharpe.

Hillebrand, Laura. 2001. *Seabiscuit: An American legend.* New York: Random House.

Hubbard, Kevin, and Stan Fischler. 1997. *Hockey America.* Indianapolis: Masters Press.

Ikard, Robert W. 2005. *Just for fun: The story of AAU Women's Basketball.* Fayetteville: University of Arkansas Press.

Isaacs, Neil D. 1984. *A history of college basketball.* New York: Harper and Row.

Isenberg, Michael T. 1994. *John L. Sullivan and his America.* Urbana: University of Illinois Press.

Keys, Barbara J. 2006. *Globalizing sport: National rivalry and international community in the 1930s.* Cambridge: Harvard University Press.

Kirsch, George B., Othello Harris, and Claire E. Nolte. 2000. *Encyclopedia of Ethnicity and Sports in the United States.* Westport, CT: Greenwood Press.

Koppett, Leonard. 1969. Flood backed by players, plans suit to challenge baseball reserve clause. *New York Times*, December 30, 42.

———. 2003. *Koppett's concise history of Major League Baseball.* Philadelphia: Temple University Press.

Lanctot, Neil. 2004. *Negro League baseball: The rise and ruin of a black institution.* Philadelphia: Temple University Press.

Lester, Robin. 1995. *Stagg's university: The rise, decline, and fall of big-time football at Chicago.* Urbana: University of Illinois Press.

Levine, Peter. 1992. *Ellis Island to Ebbets Field: Sport and the American Jewish experience.* New York: Oxford University Press.

Lomax, Michael. 2004. Black entrepreneurship in the national pastime: The rise of semiprofessional baseball in black Chicago, 1890–1915. In *Sport and the color line: Black athletes and race relations in twentieth-century America,* ed. Patrick B. Miller and David K. Wiggins, 25–43. New York: Routledge.

Lowenfish, Lee. 2007. *Branch Rickey: Baseball's ferocious gentleman.* Lincoln: University of Nebraska Press.

Margolick, David. 2005. *Beyond glory: Joe Louis vs. Max Schmeling, and a world on the brink.* New York: Knopf.

McCallum, John D., and Charles H. Pearson. 1973. *College football U.S.A., 1869–1973.* New York: Hall of Fame Publishing.

McGurn, James. 1987. *On your bicycle: An illustrated history of cycling.* New York: Facts on File.

Margolick, David. 2005. *Beyond glory: Joe Louis vs. Max Schmeling, and a world on the brink.* New York: Knopf.

Mead, Chris. 1985. *Champion—Joe Louis: Black hero in white America.* New York: Scribner's Sons.

Menke, Frank G. 1969. *The encyclopedia of sports.* 4th ed. South Brunswick, NJ: A. S. Barnes and Co.

Mrozek, Donald J. 1983. *Sport and American mentality, 1880–1910.* Knoxville: University of Tennessee Press.

Nelson, Murry. 1999. *The originals: The New York Celtics invent modern basketball.* Bowling Green, OH: Bowling Green University Press.

———. 2005. *Bill Russell, a biography.* Westport, CT: Greenwood.

———. 2005. Insular America: The NBA began in Akron? The Midwest Conference in the 1930s. *International Journal of the History of Sport* 22 (November): 990–1010.

Oriard, Michael. 1993. *Reading football: How the popular press created an American spectacle.* Chapel Hill: University of North Carolina Press.

———. 2001. *King football: Sport and spectacle in the golden age of radio and newsreels, movies and magazines, the weekly and the daily press.* Chapel Hill: University of North Carolina Press, 2001.

Peterson, Robert W. 1970. *Only the ball was white.* Englewood Cliffs, NJ: Prentice-Hall.

———. 1990. *Cages to jump shots: Pro basketball's early years.* New York: Oxford University Press.

———. 1997. *Pigskin: The early years of pro football.* New York Oxford University Press.

Quirk, James P., and Rodney D. Fort. 1992. *Pay dirt: The business of professional team sports.* Princeton, NJ: Princeton University Press.

Rader, Benjamin G. 1983. *American sports: From the age of folk games to the age of spectators.* Englewood Cliffs, NJ: Prentice-Hall.

———. 2002. *Baseball: A history of America's game.* 2nd ed. Urbana: University of Illinois Press.

Ribowsky, Mark. 1995. *A complete history of the Negro Leagues, 1884–1955.* Secaucus, NJ: Carol Pub. Group.

Riess, Steven A. 1991. *City games: The evolution of American urban society and the rise of sports.* Urbana: University of Illinois Press.

———. 1995. *Sport in industrial America, 1850–1920.* Wheeling, IL: Harlan Davidson.

———. ed. 1998. *Sports and the American Jew.* Syracuse: NY: Syracuse University Press.

Ritchie, Andrew. 1996. *Major Taylor: The extraordinary career of a champion bicycle racer.* Baltimore: John Hopkins University Press.

Roberts, James B., and Alexander G. Skutt. 2006. *The Boxing Register: International Boxing Hall of Fame official record book.* New York: McBooks Press.

Roberts, Randy. 1983. *Papa Jack: Jack Johnson and the era of white hopes.* New York: Free Press.

Roberts, Randy, and James Olson. 1989. *Winning is the only thing: Sports in America since 1945.* Baltimore: Johns Hopkins University Press.

Ruck, Rob. 1987. *Sandlot seasons: Sport in black Pittsburgh.* Urbana: University of Illinois Press.

Sammons, Jeffrey T. 1988. *Beyond the ring: The role of boxing in American society.* Urbana: University of Illinois Press.

Smith, Robert A. 1972. *A social history of the bicycle: Its early life and times in America.* New York: American Heritage Press.

Smith, Ronald. 1981. Harvard and Columbia and a reconsideration of the 1905–06 football crisis. *Journal of Sport History* 8 (Winter): 5–19.

———. 1988. *Sports and freedom: The rise of big-time college athletics.* Oxford: Oxford University Press.

———. 2001. *Play-by-play: Radio, television, and big-time college sport.* Baltimore: Johns Hopkins University Press.

Sperber, Murray. 1993. *Shake down the thunder: The creation of Notre Dame football.* New York: Henry Holt and Co.

———. 1998. *Onward to victory: The crises that shaped college sports.* New York: Henry Holt.

Tygiel, Jules. 1983. *Baseball's great experiment: Jackie Robinson and his legacy.* New York: Oxford University Press.

Voigt, David Q. 1983. *From gentleman's sport to the commissioner system.* Vol. 2 of *American baseball.* University Park: Pennsylvania State University Press.

Watterson, John Sayle. 2002. *College football: History, spectacle, controversy.* Baltimore: Johns Hopkins University Press.

Wiggins, David K., and Patrick B. Miller, eds. 2001. *The unlevel playing field: A documentary history of the African-American experience in sport.* Urbana: University of Illinois Press.

Wong, John. 1998. FDR and the New Deal on sport and recreation. *Sport History Review* 29 (November): 173–91.

Films

Baseball: Fourth inning, a national heirloom. 1994. Dir. Ken Burns. PBS Video.

Baseball: Fifth inning, shadow ball. 1994. Dir. Ken Burns. PBS Video.

Baseball: Inning six, the national pastime, 1940–1950. 1994. Dir. Ken Burns. PBS Video.

The Great Depression: "To be somebody." 1993. Dir. Stephen Stept, Joe Morton, Steve Thayer. PBS Video.

The Jackie Robinson Story. 1950. Dir. Alfred E. Green. Legend Films.

Joe Louis: America's hero … betrayed. 2008. HBO Films.

Knute Rockne and his Fighting Irish. 1993. Dir. Lawrence R Hott. WGBH.

A league of their own. 1992. Dir. Penny Marshall. Columbia Pictures.

People's century: 1930, sporting fever. 1998. Dir. David Espar. PBS Video.

Rites of autumn: Seasons of change. 2001. Dir. Don Sperling. Lions Gate Home Entertainment.

Seabiscuit. 2003. Dir. Stephen Ives. Warner Home Video.

75 seasons: The story of the National Football League. 1994. NFL Films.

Time Capsule: The Los Angeles Olympic Games of 1932. 1984. Dir. Bud Greenspan. Family Home Entertainment.

Web Sources

Arnold Palmer … a biography. Sandhills Online. http://www.sandhills.org/plantation/golf/palmer.htm.

Baseball Almanac. http://www.baseball-almanac.com.

Baseball Hall of Fame. http://web.baseballhalloffame.org.

Basketball Hall of Fame. http://www.hoophall.com.

Carter, Bob. Wilkinson created Sooner dynasty. ESPN Classic Web site. http://espn.go.com/classic/biography/s/Wilkinson_Bud.html.

History. National Invitation Tournament Web site. http://www.nit.org/history/nit-postseason-results-1950s.html.

Hockey Hall of Fame Web site. http://www.hhof.com.

International Olympic Committee (IOC) Web site. http://www.olympic.org/uk.

LA84 Foundation. http://www.la84foundation.org.

Ladies Professional Golfers Association Web site. http://www.lpga.com.

Naismith Memorial Basketball Hall of Fame Web site. http://www.hoophall.com.

National Baseball Hall of Fame and Museum Web site. http://www.baseballhall.org.

National Football Foundation's College Football Hall of Fame Web site. http://www.collegefootballhall.org.

National Football League Web site. http://www.NFL.com/history.

Pro Football Hall of Fame Web site. http://www.profootballhof.com.

Sports Century. ESPN Web site. http://espn.go.com/sportscentury.

Sugar Ray Robinson. The Official Site of Sugar Ray Robinson. http://www.cmgww.com/sports/robinson/bioography.html.

INDEX

ABOUT THE EDITOR AND CONTRIBUTORS

MURRY R. NELSON is Professor Emeritus of Education and American Studies at the Pennsylvania State University, where he taught for thirty-three years. He has held Fulbright Senior Lectureships at the University of Iceland and the Norwegian Ministry of Education, and was the 2007–8 Laszlo Orzsag Distinguished Chair of American Studies at the University of Debrecen in Hungary. He is the author or editor of twelve books, including *The Originals: The New York Celtics Invent Modern Basketball* (University of Wisconsin Press, 1999), *Bill Russell, a Biography* (Greenwood Press, 2006), *Shaquille O'Neal, a Biography* (Greenwood Press, 2007), and *Home Town League: A History of the National Basketball League, 1935–1949* (McFarland, 2009).

SARAH BAIR is assistant professor of education at Dickinson College. Her research and teaching focus on educational history and social studies education with emphasis on women educators and women's history in curriculum. Her work has appeared in *Theory and Research in Social Education, Social Studies Research and Practice*, and *The Social Studies*.

CALLIE BATTS is a PhD student in the Physical Cultural Studies program at the University of Maryland. She received a MA in international sport policy from the University of Brighton and is particularly interested in the globalization of sport, the complex relationships between sport and national identity, and the politicization of sporting bodies.

RONALD BRILEY is a history teacher and assistant headmaster at Sandia Preparatory School in Albuquerque, New Mexico, where he has taught for thirty years. In addition to numerous scholarly pieces and reviews on film and sport, he is the author of *Class at Bat, Gender on Deck, and Race in the Hole* (McFarland, 2003) and coeditor of James T. Farrell's *Dreaming Baseball* (Kent State University Press, 2007) and *All-Stars and Movie Stars* (University Press of Kentucky, 2008). He is also an adjunct professor of history at the University of New Mexico–Valencia Campus.

CHAD CARLSON earned a BA (2003) from Hope College and an M.A. (2005) from Western Michigan University. He is currently a doctoral student in the History and Philosophy of Sport Program in the Department of Kinesiology at the Pennsylvania State University.

AMIE CHAUDRY is a master's student in kinesiology at the University of Maryland–College Park. Her area of specialization is physical cultural studies, focusing on body modification subcultures.

PERRY COHEN is a PhD student in the Physical Cultural Studies Program at the University of Maryland. Her research interests involve transsexual athletes, the use of assisted reproductive technologies for lesbians, and the physical culture of warehouse labor.

MARK DYRESON is an associate professor of kinesiology and an affiliate professor of history at Pennsylvania State University and a former president of the North American Society for the History of Sport. He earned an PhD (1989) in history from the University of Arizona and has published extensively on the history of sport including *Making the American Team: Sport, Culture and the Olympic Experience* (Urbana: University of Illinois Press, 1998) and *Crafting Patriotism for Global Dominance: America at the Olympics* (London: Routledge, 2008), and the editor, with J. A. Mangan, of *Sport and American Society: Insularity, Exceptionalism and "Imperialism"* (London: Routledge, 2007).

SARAH K. FIELDS is an assistant professor in sport humanities at the Ohio State University. She is the author of *Female Gladiators: Gender, Law, and Contact Sport in America*, several book chapters, and numerous articles in a wide range of journals including the *Journal of Sport History*, the *Journal of College and University Law*, and the *American Journal of Sports Medicine*.

GERALD R. GEMS has a PhD from the University of Maryland. He is a full professor in the Health and Physical Education Department at North Central College in Naperville, Illinois, and a past president of the North American Society for Sport History. He is the author/editor of eight books, including *The Athletic Crusade: Sport and American Cultural Imperialism* (University of Nebraska Press, 2006) and *Pride, Profit and Patriarchy: Football and the Incorporation of American Cultural Values* (Scarecrow Press, 2000).

JOHN GLEAVES earned a BA (2006) from Carroll College. He is currently a doctoral student in the History and Philosophy of Sport Program in the Department of Kinesiology at the Pennsylvania State University.

MATTHEW LLEWELLYN earned a BS (2004) from Cardiff Institute at the University of Wales and an MA from California State University at Long Beach (2006). He won the 2007 North American Society for Sport History graduate student essay contest. He is currently a doctoral student in the History and Philosophy of Sport Program in the Department of Kinesiology at the Pennsylvania State University. His research focus on both the modern Olympic movement and British and American sport has appeared or is forthcoming in the *International Journal of the History of Sport* and the *Journal of Sport History*.

JIM NENDEL is an independent researcher who has taught as an assistant professor at Eastern Washington University and Penn State University. His research focuses on Olympic sport, Hawaiian sport and culture, and American football in England. His work has appeared in the *Journal of Sport History* and the *International Journal of the History of Sport*. He also has upcoming books on Olympic swimmer Duke Kahanamoku and on service-learning in physical education and sport.

SARAH OLSON received her MA in physical cultural studies from the University of Maryland, College Park.

JAIME RYAN is a doctoral student in physical cultural studies at the University of Maryland and holds a MA from the University of Connecticut in sport management and sociology of sport. Her current area of study focuses on the intersection of sport, family, and social class in the swimming community.

JAIME SCHULTZ is an assistant professor of physical cultural studies at the University of Maryland. She received her PhD in cultural studies of sport from the University of Iowa and has published articles and chapters on issues of gender, race, and cultural memory in sport history.

CAITLIN SHANNON is a master's student in the Department of Kinesiology at the University of Maryland.

MAUREEN SMITH is a professor of kinesiology at California State University, Sacramento. She teaches courses in sport history and sport sociology. She received her BS and MS from Ithaca College and her MA and PhD from the Ohio State University. She is the author of *Wilma Rudolph: A Biography* (Greenwood Publishing, 2006).

NANCY L. STRUNA is professor and chair of the Department of American Studies at the University of Maryland and the author of *People of Prowess: Sport, Leisure, and Labor in Early Anglo-America*. Her current research and teaching focus on the body, dimensions of identity, and cultural production, and she is currently working on a book titled "Transforming the Ordinary. Taverns and the Construction of Citizenship in Maryland, 1750–1820."

JOHN WONG is assistant professor at Washington State University where he teaches classes in sport management. He is the author of *Lords of the Rinks: The Emergence of the National Hockey League, 1875–1936* and is the editor of a forthcoming book, *Coast to Coast: Hockey in Canada Before the Second World War*. His research interests focus on the history of the business of sport, especially hockey and sport culture in the Pacific Northwest.